LAKṢMĪ TANTRA

A Pāñcarātra Text

LAKṢMĪ TANTRA

A Pāñcarātra Text

SANJUKTA GUPTA

MOTILAL BANARSIDASS PUBLISHERS
PRIVATE LIMITED • DELHI

4th Reprint : Delhi, 2017
First Indian Edition : Delhi, 2000
First Edition : Netherlands, 1972

ISBN: 978-81-208-1734-0 (Cloth)
ISBN: 978-81-208-1735-7 (Paper)

Also Available at

MOTILAL BANARSIDASS
41 U.A. Bungalow Road, Jawahar Nagar, Delhi 110 007
8 Mahalaxmi Chamber, 22 Bhulabhai Desai Road, Mumbai 400 026
203 Royapettah High Road, Mylapore, Chennai 600 004
236, 9th Main III Block, Jayanagar, Bengaluru 560 011
8 Camac Street, Kolkata 700 017
Ashok Rajpath, Patna 800 004
Chowk, Varanasi 221 001

MLBD Cataloging-in-Publication Data
Lakṣmī Tantra : *A Pāñcarātra Text*
by Sanjukta Gupta
Includes Index of names and technical terms and mantras
ISBN: 978-81-208-1734-0 (Cloth)
ISBN: 978-81-208-1735-7 (Paper)
I. Hinduism II. Tantra III. Lakṣmī
IV. Pāñcarātra V. Gupta, Sanjukta

Printed in India
by RP Jain at NAB Printing Unit,
A-44, Naraina Industrial Area, Phase I, New Delhi–110028
and published by JP Jain for Motilal Banarsidass Publishers (P) Ltd,
41 U.A. Bungalow Road, Jawahar Nagar, Delhi-110007

CONTENTS

LIST OF ABBREVIATIONS *

Ag. P.	Agni Purāṇa.
Ahi. S.	Ahirbudhnya Saṃhitā, ed. V. Krishnamacharya; Adyar Library series Vol. 4, 2nd ed. Madras 1966.
Āp. Ś. S.	Āpastamba Śrauta Sūtra.
Bh. G.	Bhagavadgītā.
Bhā. P.	Bhāgavata Purāṇa.
Bhāradvāja S.	Bhāradvāja Saṃhitā, ed. by Khemarāja Śrīkṛṣṇadāsa Śreṣṭhī; Bombay, Śaka 1827.
Bṛ. Ā. U.	Bṛhadāraṇyaka Upaniṣad.
Br. P.	Brahmāṇḍa Purāṇa.
Ch. U.	Chāndogya Upaniṣad.
Ga. P.	Garuḍa Purāṇa.
I. P.	Introduction to the Pāñcarātra, by F. O. Schrader, Adyar, Madras 1916.
J. S.	Jayākhya Saṃhitā, ed. E. Krishnamacharya, Gaekwad's Oriental Series No. 54. Baroda 1931.
K. K. C.	Kriya Kairava Candrika, Sri Varāhaguru, ed. Swami Ramnarayana Acarya, Ayodhya, Saṃvat 2017.
Ka. U.	Kaṭha Upaniṣad
L. T.	Lakṣmī Tantra, ed. V. Krishnamacharya, Adyar Library Series Vol. 87, Madras 1959.
M. Bh.	Mahābhārata.
M. P.	Matsya Purāṇa.
M. U.	Muṇḍaka Upaniṣad.
Mai. U.	Maitrī Upaniṣad.
Mā. P.	Mārkaṇḍeya Purāṇa.
Mā. U.	Māṇḍukya Upaniṣad.
Nā. S.	Nārada Saṃhitā.
Nṛ. P. U.	Nṛsiṃha-pūrvatāpanī Upaniṣad.
Nṛ. U. U.	Nṛsiṃha-uttaratāpanī Upaniṣad.
P. S.	Pārameśvara Saṃhitā, ed. Śrī Govindācārya, Srirangam 1953.
Pa. S.	Parama Saṃhitā, ed. and tr. Dr. S. Krishnaswami Aiyangar, Gaekwad's Oriental Series No. 86, Baroda 1940.
Pād. T.	Pādma Tantra, Sadvidya Press, Mysore 1888.
Pau. S.	Pauṣkara Saṃhitā, ed. Sree Yatiraja Sampathkumara Ramanuja Muni, Melkote, 1934.
R. U. U.	Rāma-uttaratāpanī Upaniṣad.
Rām.	Rāmāyaṇa.
Ṛg V.	Ṛgveda.
Ṛg. V. K.	Ṛgveda Khila, Dr. J. Scheftelowitz, Die Apokryphen des Ṛgveda, Breslau, 1906.
Sa. S.	Sanatkumāra Saṃhitā, ed. V. Krishnamacharya, Adyar Library Series Vol. 95, Madras 1969.

* Only the Pāñcarātra texts, secondary texts and rare texts are mentioned here with a full bibliography.

Sā. S.	Sāttvata Saṃhitā, ed. P. B. Ananthachariar, Conjeeveram 1902.
Sar. U.	Sarva Upaniṣad.
Śvet. U.	Śvetāśvatara Upaniṣad.
Tai. Ā.	Taittirīya Āraṇyaka.
Tai. Br.	Taittirīya Brāhmaṇa.
Tai. S.	Taittirīya Saṃhitā.
T. U.	Taittirīya Upaniṣad.
V. S.	Vedānta Sūtra.
Vā. P.	Vāyu Purāṇa.
Viṣ. P.	Viṣṇu Purāṇa.
Vi. S.	Viṣṇu Saṃhitā, ed. T. Gaṇapati Sāstrī, Trivandrum Sanskrit Series, No. 85, Trivandrum 1925.
Viś. S.	Viśvāmitra Saṃhitā, ed. Undemane Shankara Bhatta, Kendriya Sanskrit Vidyapeetha Series No. 13, Tirupati 1970.
Yog. P.	Yoga Pradīpikā, Kashi Sanskrit Series No. 85, Benares 1931.
Yog. S.	Yoga Sūtra.

LIST OF NAMES OF THE LETTERS

a apprameya, prathama, vyāpaka.
ā ādideva, ānanda, gopana.
i Rāma, iddha, iṣṭa.
ī pañcabindu, Viṣṇu, māyā.
u bhuvana, uddāma, udaya.
ū ūrja, lokeśa, prajñādhāra.
ṛ satya, ṛtadhāman, aṅkuśa.
ṝ viṣṭara, jvālā, prasāraṇam.
ḷ liṅgātman, Bhagavān, tāraka.
ḹ dīrghaghoṇa, Devadatta, virāṭ.
e tryasra, jagadyoni, avigraha.
ai aiśvarya, yogadhātā, airāvaṇa.
o otadeva, odana, vikramī.
au aurva, bhūdhara, auṣadha.
ṃ trailokyaiśvaryada, vyāpī, vyomeśa.
ḥ visarga, sṛṣṭikṛt, parameśvara.
ka kamala, karāla, prakṛti.
kha kharvadeha, vedātman, viśvabhāvana.
ga gadadhvaṃśī, Govinda, Gadādhara.
gha gharmāṃśu, tejasvin, dīptimān.
ṅ ekadaṃṣṭrā, bhūtātman, bhūtabhāvana.
ca cañcala, cakrī, candrāṃśu.
cha chandaḥpati, chaladhvaṃśī, chandas.
ja janmahantṛ, ajita, śāśvata.
jha jhaṣa, sāmaga, sāmapāṭhaka.
ñ īśvara, uttama, tattvadhāraka.
ṭa candrī, āhlāda, viśvāpyāyakara.
ṭha dhārādhara, nemi, kaustubha.
ḍa daṇḍadhāra, mausala, akhaṇḍavikrama.
ḍha viśvarūpa, vṛṣakarman, pratardana.
ṇa abhayada, śāstā, vaikuṇṭha.
ta tālalakṣman, vairāja, sragdhara.
tha dhanvin, bhuvanapāla, sarvarodhaka.
da dattāvakāśa, damana, śāntida.
dha śārṅgadhṛt, dhartā, Mādhava.
na nara, Nārāyaṇa, panthā.
pa Padmanābha, pavitra, paścimānana.
pha phullanayana, lāṃgalī, śveta.
ba vāmana, hrasva, pūrṇāṅga.
bha bhallātaka, siddhiprada, dhruva.
ma mardana, kāla, pradhāna.
ya caturgati, suṣukṣma, śaṅkha.
ra aśeṣabhuvanādhāra, anala, kālapāvaka.
la vibudha, dhareśa, puruṣeśvara.
va Varāha, amṛtādhāra, Varuṇa.
śa Śaṃkara, śānta, puṇḍarīka.

ṣa	Nṛsiṃha, agnirūpa, bhāskara.
sa	amṛta, tṛpti, soma.
ha	sūrya, prāṇa, paramātman.
kṣa	ananteśa, vargānta, Garuḍa.

INTRODUCTION TO FIRST EDITION

Viṣṇuism is one of the chief religions of the Hindus and the Pāñcarātra is the oldest surviving Viṣṇuite sect. The influence of its tenets on later Viṣṇuism has undoubtedly been great, but has never been thoroughly explored. Despite change and corruption the ritual worship described in the old Pāñcarātra texts is still performed today in many of the famous temples in southern India and in some in the north. A deeper insight into the historical development of the Viṣṇuite sects, into their ritual, occultism and building of temples and images can only be obtained from the scientific study of these ancient Pāñcarātra texts which formulate the relevant basic concepts.

The theological and ritualistic aspects of the Pāñcarātra system have attracted scholars for some time past [1] and a number of texts have been edited [2]. Some of these publications are of a high standard and include illuminating introductions. Amongst these, Professor F. O. Schrader's Introduction to the Pāñcarātra still ranks as the most comprehensive. So far only one Pāñcarātra text has been translated into English,[3] but the omission of explanatory notes on the meaning of special terms detracts from its usefulness to the layman. In recent years valuable work in this field is being done by H. Daniel Smith.[4]

The reason why I have chosen to translate the text of the Lakṣmī Tantra is because its philosophical pronouncements incorporate many of the sect's earlier traditions. I shall elaborate on this point later on. A second reason is because of its occultism, which throws light on an aspect of the Pāñcarātra system that is not dealt with

---

[1] H. Govindacary, The Pāñcarātras or Bhāgavatas, J. R. A. S. Oct. 1911; R. G. Bhandarkar, Vaisnavism, Saivism and minor religious systems, Varanasi 1965; H. Ray Chowdury, Materials for the study of the early history of the Vaiṣṇava sect; Mrinal Das Gupta, Early Vaiṣṇavism and Nārāyaṇīya Works, Ind. Hist. Q. 1931; Dr. S. R. Bhatt, The Philosophy of Pāñcarātra, Madras 1968; K. Rangachari, The Shri vaishnava Brahmans, Bulletin of the Madras Gov. Museum, N. Ser., Gen. Section, II, 2, Madras 1931.

[2] For a detailed bibliography see K. K. A. Venkatachari, Pāñcarātra Nūl Viḷakkam, Madras 1967.

[3] Parama Saṃhitā, Gaekwad's Oriental Series LXXXVI.

[4] See his Pāñcarātra prāsāda prasādhanam; Vaisnava Iconography.

in any other known text. Since however the size of this book has grown to be quite alarming, I have here been obliged to refrain from discussing the interesting topic of ritualistic esoterism.[1]

Before starting on my apologetics, certain preliminary explanations about my method of work are briefly called for. My translation is based entirely on the Sanskrit text edited by Pandit V. Krishnamacharya and published in the Adyar Library Series, no. 87. I have not used any manuscript of the Lakṣmī Tantra. Therefore, whenever I mention the text or the editor's commentary on it, I refer to Krishnamacharya's edition. Although I have studied the only other publication of this text, printed in Telugu and published at Mysore in 1888, I have not based my translation upon it since Krishnamacharya has utilized it in his edition.

I have aimed at accuracy in my translation—often unfortunately at the expense of style—and when explanation is needed, it is supplied in a footnote or inserted in parenthesis in the text of my translation. I have used parenthesis also to distinguish English words I have used in my translation to make a sentence complete. However the reader must not expect to find that every Sanskrit word has been translated consistently by the same English term. As words are affected by the context in which they are used, I have used alternative meanings when and as the sense required. Despite care, some irregularities may still persist in transcriptions of Sanskrit words. These are unintentional.

From chapter XXXIII onwards I have not translated the clues given for constructing the mantras, but have confined myself to supply the constructed mantras only. My translation of the first ten verses of chapter XXXIII should, I think, suffice to demonstrate how the mantras are construed.

Amongst the vast number of Pāñcarātra Āgamas,[2] the Lakṣmī Tantra stands out because of its almost exclusive treatment of the Viṣṇuite mother-goddess Lakṣmī, the Śakti of Viṣṇu-Nārāyaṇa. The text not only glorifies Lakṣmī, but also women in general as beings created in the cherished form of Lakṣmī, and it advocates their worship. Moreover it alludes to the particular sādhanā of the

---

[1] That topic is discussed in my paper on the Mantras and Special Forms of Worship described in the Lakṣmī Tantra, which is awaiting publication.

[2] See F. O. Schrader, Introduction to the Pāñcarātra, Madras 1916, pp, 6-12; and K. K. A. Venkatachari.

left-handed Tantras that requires a female partner.[1] Our text is somewhat reticent about the details of that practice, perhaps because it was apprehensive about how the majority of Pāñcarātra followers would react. It even launches into a lengthy discourse upon its ethics and the cautionary measures to be taken. Nevertheless at the end of this discussion it asserts that, though not free from the moral danger involved in disregarding strict convention, the practice is not sinful since the participants are lifted to a supra-mundane level.[2] Undoubtedly this reveals the text's sympathy with left-handed Tantric practices, which is not at all surprising considering how prevalent the worship of Śakti was in India. Later scholars of Śaktism, such as Bhāṣkararāya, the commentator of the Lalitāsahasranāmam, Nāgeśa Bhaṭṭa, the commentator of the Durgāsaptaśatī and Appaya Dīkṣita, the commentator of the Candrakalāstuti, not only mention the Lakṣmī Tantra but cite it.[3] Obviously by that time, i.e. the sixteenth century, the text had gained firm recognition as a standard Śākta Āgama. Inspite of its predominantly Pāñcarātra character, its undivided concentration on the worship of Śakti and its assertion that Durgā, Bhadrakālī and Yogamāyā are merely other names for Mahālakṣmī, who is Viṣṇu's dynamic power,[4] enabled our text to overcome sectarian boundaries.

The Lakṣmī Tantra deals mainly with Pāñcarātra philosophy and cosmogony (which are inseparable in texts of this kind), and with the mantra-śāstra ('linguistic occultism'). A minimum is said about the ritualistic side of worship, and iconography is discussed only in the form of the dhyānas of the most important deities, such as Lakṣmī-Nārāyaṇa, the Vyūhas, the main emanations of Lakṣmī, her retinue etc. Temple architecture and temple worship are totally omitted. The text also ignores public festivals, *śrāddha-dharma* (death rites) and expiatory rites. This silence about rites connected with society and its conventions indicates that the Lakṣmī Tantra concerns itself with the individual adept, who desires to be released from the miseries of worldly existence. This can be achieved by

[1] L. T. XXVII, 44-47 and XLII, 30-31; see P. C. Bagchi, Evolution of the Tantras, The Cultural Heritage of India, vol. IV, Calcutta, 1956, pp. 217-218.

[2] L. T. XLIII, 75-90.

[3] See V. Krishnamacharya, The Sanskrit preface to the Lakṣmī Tantra, Adyar Library series, Vol. 87, Madras 1949, pp. 39-40.

[4] L. T. IV, 40 and 47.

practising yogic *sādhanā* (worship of God and meditation visualizing Him as the personification of a mantra accompanied by the repetition of that mantra), which enables the initiate to receive divine grace, without which salvation is not possible.

In form, the Lakṣmī Tantra follows the tradition of both the Sāttvata and Jayākhya Saṃhitās. It deals exhaustively with the Vyūha theory. In that connection, it not only mentions the Sāttvata Saṃhitā but proceeds to elaborate on its philosophy. Thus the concept of Viśākhayūpa—only briefly referred to in the Sāttvata—is explained in detail in the Lakṣmī Tantra. The metaphysical implications of the Vyūha theory and their bearing on the mantra-śāstra are put very clearly.[1] The basic need supplied by these concepts of divine manifestations is to provide the devotee with an object he can worship in accordance with his spiritual capacity and meditate upon whilst repeating the relevant mantra. This is the most important topic in the Sāttvata Saṃhitā, which is classified amongst the texts known as Āgama-siddhānta.[2] But in regard to the ritualistic aspect of worship, the Lakṣmī Tantra follows the tradition of the Jayākhya Saṃhitā, which accords a central position to the worship of Viṣṇu and His consort Lakṣmī. Texts of this nature, advocating the worship of a single deity, are called Tantra-siddhānta. Indeed the Lakṣmī Tantra depends so largely on the Jayākhya Saṃhitā that it frequently quotes lengthy passages of it. And moreover one is often obliged to consult the Jayākhya Saṃhitā in order to clarify many of the actual procedures of worship described

---

[1] L.T, IV, 24 (dhyānaviśrāmabhūmayaḥ).

[2] The Pāñcarātra Āgamas are classed under four headings:—Āgama-siddhānta, Mantra-siddhānta, Tantra-siddhānta and Tantrāntara-siddhānta. The term siddhānta is apparently a synonym for Āgama. The classification is made according to the deity on whom the text focusses attention. When attention centres on the four Vyūhas, the text falls within the category of Āgama-siddhānta. When nine or twelve forms of Viṣṇu are worshipped, the text is classified as a Mantra-siddhānta. When a single form of Viṣṇu is the chief object of worship, the text is classified as a Tantra-siddhānta, and when worship centres on a non-anthropomorphic form of Viṣṇu (e.g. the Man-lion incarnation), the text is classified as a Tantrāntara-siddhānta. The Sāttvata Saṃhitā, the Pauṣkara Saṃhitā, the Jayākhya Saṃhitā and the Hayagrīva Saṃhitā are respective examples of these four types of Āgamas. It is very important that the initiate should be careful not to confuse the different modes of worship prescribed in the various types of texts. Cf. Vedānta Deśika, Śrī Pāñcarātra Rakṣā, Adyar Library 2nd ed., Madras 1967, pp 3-13.

in the Lakṣmī Tantra. For example, the description of the mystic diagram called 'nava-padma-maṇḍala'[1] is so terse and obscure that, without recourse to the Jayākhya Saṃhitā, it is incomprehensible. But the Lakṣmī Tantra's point of departure from the Jayākhya Saṃhitā is the emphasis it lays on the worship of Lakṣmī, rather than on that of Viṣṇu. It is her retinue that is described and only the Tārā-mantra is prescribed for almost all the various rites included in the full programme of worship. The text admits no ambiguity on this point. For instance, in chapter XVI it is said that the way to obtain liberation from the bondage of the material world is to worship Lakṣmī, the Viṣṇu-śakti. One should abandon all other activity and concentrate solely on propitiating the goddess either directly, or indirectly through Viṣṇu, in order to obtain spiritual release. Out of compassion she then comes to the devotee and liberates him by removing all his impurities ('*ahaṃ hi tatra viśvātmā viṣṇuśaktiḥ parāvarā, sākṣād eva samārādhyā, devo vā puruṣottamaḥ; iti te kathitāḥ samyag upāyās traya ūrjitāḥ, śṛṇūpāyaṃ caturthaṃ me sarvatyāgasamāhvayam. Tatra* (*sarva?*) *dharmān parityajya . . . mām ekām śaraṇaṃ vrajet, ahaṃ hi śaraṇaṃ prāptā nareṇānanyacetasā prāpayāmy ātmanātmānaṃ nirdhūtākhilakalmaśam*')[2].

The most striking feature of the Lakṣmī Tantra is its treatment of Pāñcarātra philosophy. Like most texts of this nature, ours is also basically eclectic. This point is accentuated by its preoccupation with establishing Śakti as the supreme metaphysical principle. At the same time, it attempts to make a synthesis out of all the various concepts current in the Pāñcarātra and Tāntric milieu. It does not always succeed in blending all these notions smoothly. Sometimes contradictory ideas, such as Sāṃkhya realism and radical monism (Advaitavedānta), are presented side by side.[3] Nevertheless at least some degree of harmonization has been achieved, particularly in the delineation of the cosmogony. This has given the Lakṣmī Tantra a revered position amongst the Pāñcarātra Āgamas.

Date

The next important question is when and where did this text originate. The Lakṣmī Tantra mentions the Sāttvata Saṃhitā by

[1] L. T. XXXVII, 3-19; J. S. XIII, 16-40.
[2] L. T. XVI, 43-44.
[3] Ibid. XII passim and XIII, 24-25.

name and quotes extensively from the Jayākhya Saṃhitā.[1] It also bears a close resemblance to the Ahirbudhnya Saṃhitā. But none of these Saṃhitās has been precisely dated. Seeking information from sources other than the Āgamas, we find in the Lakṣmī Tantra one list of divine incarnations which are joint manifestations of Lakṣmī and Nārāyaṇa. In that list the Buddha and Tārā (otherwise called Dhārā) are mentioned as one of these joint incarnations. It is generally conceded that the inclusion of the Buddha's name in a list of Viṣṇu's incarnations appeared fairly late in history. The other interesting point is that the text records the worship of Tārā as the Buddha's Śakti and, at the same time, identifies her with Dhārā or Vasudhārā, another Buddhist female deity representing the earth. It is true that in the usual list of Vyūha, Vibhava etc. of the pure creation, the Buddha is not mentioned. But when no loyalty to Pāñcarātra tradition is involved and purely Tāntric notions are discussed, the Buddha appears together with his Śakti Tārā. This point is significant for purposes of assessing the date of our text. In its present form the Lakṣmī Tantra cannot claim to be a very early text. In fact according to E. Conze,[2] the Buddhistic Tārā worship was not openly practised before 500 or 600 A.D. The acceptance of the Buddha as an incarnation of Viṣṇu is prominent in the Bhāgavata Purāṇa. If the ninth century A.D. is accepted as the date of this last mentioned text,[3] then the date of the Lakṣmī Tantra cannot be much earlier.

The first author to quote the Lakṣmī Tantra was Vedānta Deśika. This celebrated Śri-vaiṣṇava preceptor lived in the latter half of the thirteenth century.[4] It seems that although he attributed some importance to our text, in his view it had not yet attained the status of a fully recognized Āgama. However, by the time of Bhāṣkararāya and other commentators previously mentioned it had acquired that

---

[1] L. T. IV, 2 and 59 and XI, 28. Our text quotes the Jayākhya Saṃhitā so extensively that it is useless attempting to specify references.

[2] E. Conze, Buddhism, Oxford 3rd ed. 1957, p. 176. See also Kees W. Bolle, The Persistence of Religion, Leiden 1965, pp. 2-3.

[3] See Adalbert Gail, Bhakti im Bhāgavatapurāṇa, Wiesbaden 1969, pp. 14-16.

[4] Dr. Satyavrata Singh, Vedanta Deśika (A Study), Varanasi 1958, p. 4. Also see G. Srinivasa Murti, Introduction to the Śrī Pāñcarātra Rakṣā, Adyar Library Series, Vol. 36[2], Madras 1967, p. XXII.

status, and we find it mentioned alongside the Mārkaṇḍeya Purāṇa.[1] Hence, at latest it probably dates from the twelfth century. Since it is impossible to fix more than an approximate date for texts of this nature, we may assume that the Lakṣmī Tantra was compiled at some time between the ninth and twelfth centuries.

Place of Origin

The geographical problem of locating the origin of the Lakṣmī Tantra presents still greater difficulty. Although the text recommends that the bark of the Himalayan birch tree (bhūrja-patra) should be used for scribbling mantras on in order to endow amulets with magical properties, we have no evidence that the compiler ever actually saw that tree. Mention of bhūrja-patra as a material which can be written on, crops up so frequently in Sanskrit literature [2] that he may have only read about it. It is quite possible that this quaint bark was popularly thought to be suitable for magical purposes. Hence we cannot be sure that the text originated in the tree's natural region of growth. Since however Vedānta Deśika mentions the Lakṣmī Tantra by name, it is plausible to presume that in his day the text was available to devotees in his homeland, which was South India. The text also mentions the Malaya range situated in the South, which may be a later addition. (cf. ch. I, 19.) But whether or not it was actually compiled there still remains an open question.

General division of topics

In structure the Lakṣmī Tantra attempts to follow the classical pattern of four divisions, jñāna, kriyā, yoga and caryā. In fact however, the kriyā section has been omitted altogether and the caryā section has been reduced to a minimum. A curious sidelight explaining this omission can possibly be traced to the Appendix (ch. LIII), where the word kriyā pāda is used in the unusual sense of the ritualistic performance of upāsanā and ārādhanā, as met with in Buddhistic Tantras.[3] The jñāna pāda, or theological section,

---

[1] Lalitā-sahasranāmam with Bhāskararāya's Commentary translated into English. Adyar Library edition 4th reprint, Madras 1970, p. 116.

[2] Cf. Kālidāsa's Kumārasambhavam, I, 7, 55; VII, 11, 2; VII, 17, 10; VII, 18, 1, 4, and 19; VII, 19, 1 and 3 and Raghuvaṃśam, IV, 73. L.T. mentions it in XLIV, 38.

[3] Cf. Lalmani Joshi, The Buddhistic Culture of India, Delhi 1967, p. 337.

occupies almost one third of the entire treatise, which opens with the traditional introductory chapter and then passes on to discuss the jñāna pāda until well into the eighteenth chapter. But within these chapters other topics often creep in, and likewise theology crops up rather persistently in chapters dealing with other subjects.

After theology, the mantra-śāstra (the science of 'linguistic occultism') figures next in importance. Third in importance come upāsanā or the yoga pāda, and a short description of ārādhanā (the ritual worship of God) or the caryā pada. The only part of the kriyā pāda that is mentioned is the rite of installing the image to be worshipped privately by the initiate.[1] Pāñcarātra ritual requires the devotee to worship the deity in four places, viz. in the image, in the water pitcher, on the mystic diagram and in the sacrificial fire-pit. The text briefly touches on these points and describes the daily religious duties of an initiate. These observations help to explain the nature of Lakṣmī Tantra as predominantly a Śākta Tantra. It has two objectives in view: Firstly, to establish the supremacy of Lakṣmī as a philosophical principle ranking, if not higher than Viṣṇu, then at least as equal to Him. This is achieved by emphasizing the mystic tenet of unity in duality, the two-in-one accepted by the Śākta sects.[2] Lakṣmī as an integral part of Nārāyaṇa, the supreme Being, is the embodiment of His sovereign will and the instrumental cause of all creation. The Lakṣmī Tantra presents a systematic exposition of Pāñcarātra theology, which is firmly embedded in its description of the cosmogony with Lakṣmī at the head of it.

The second objective is to set down a full record of exclusive Śakti-upāsanā within the frame-work of the Pāñcarātra religion. On these grounds it has to be admitted that the Lakṣmī Tantra can scarcely claim to be a full-fledged Pāñcarātra Āgama in the usual sense of the term, because all four categories of the Pāñcarātra Āgamas (viz. Āgama-siddhānta etc.) share the common characteristic of worshipping Nārāyaṇa in a single or multiple form. This may explain why the text is sometimes classified in the list of

[1] L. T. XXXVII, and XLI, passim.

[2] See Lalmani Joshi, o.c. pp. 353-354. D. L. Snellgrove, Introduction to The Hevajra Tantra, part I. London 1959, pp. 22-25. Also E. Conze, pp. 192-193: "In this way a feminine principle was placed side by side with the Buddha and to some extent even above him" The same tendency can be found in the Lakṣmī Tantra.

secondary books, as in the Adyar Library catalogue and in Dr. Satyavrata Singh's list.[1] Nevertheless its exclusive nature did not diminish its value to the Pāñcarātrins, who always showed a leaning towards Tantrism. Their rivals, the Vaikhānasas, directed Pāñcarātra worshippers to practise their special type of Viṣṇu worship in some solitary and secluded place.[2]

General philosophical postulates

As pointed out, the main contribution of the Lakṣmī Tantra to Pāñcaratra theology and cosmogony lies in its systematic treatment of these subjects. There are thirty-five Sāttvata realities.[3] (Brahman of course transcends all these realities). Starting from the highest these are Bhagavān (God), the absolute void, Puruṣa (the Person), śakti, niyati, kāla, sattva, rajas and tamas, māyā, prasūti, prakṛti, the three component parts of the inner organ (buddhi, manas and ahaṃkāra), the ten cognitive and conative organs, the five subtle and the five gross elements. These represent the basic stages of the creation generally accepted by Āgama tradition. Among these, the term Bhagavān includes all divine emanations. The absolute void is the paramaṃ dhāman, where God lives and with which He is identical.[4] This is also a transcendental category not influenced by the limitation of time. Puruṣa is the collective Man (i.e. living being)[5] and his śakti is Mahālakṣmī, the kriyāśakti or the active aspect of God.[6] Niyati is Mahāvidyā, who represents the cosmic wisdom recorded in the Vedas and who controls law and order in the universe.[7] Kāla is Mahākāli, who is in fact primordial nature or the material source of creation. The further realities are variations of the Sāṃkhya categories. The subtle distinctions in the stages of primordial nature from kāla to prakṛti enable the Pāñcarātra system to achieve some degree of consistency in incorporating the Purāṇic concept of creation.

The cosmogony of the Lakṣmī Tantra coordinates various streams of ideas which were prevalent in the diverse religious traditions.

[1] O. c. p. 112.
[2] T. Goudriaan, Kāśyapa's Book of Wisdom, Thesis Utrecht 1965, p. 307.
[3] L. T. VI, 42-44.
[4] Ibid. VII, 9-10. See J. Gonda, Dhāman, Amsterdam 1967, passim.
[5] L.T. VII, 11.
[6] Ibid. VI, and VII passim.
[7] Ibid. VII, 13 and IV, 66-67. For the doctrine of niyati, see Gopinath Kaviraj, Aspects of Indian Thought, Burdwan 1966, pp. 54-60.

Some of these are: the Vedic concept of the anthropomorphic creator God Puruṣa of the Puruṣa-sūkta; the mythological concept of Prajāpati Brahmā, who creates the cosmic embryo or egg and is then reborn in it as Hiraṇyagarbha; the Upaniṣadic concept of the undifferentiated, unlimited, immutable, transcendental, supreme Being, Brahman, which is absolute consciousness and bliss and which, through Its own will, became qualified and started manifesting Itself as the variegated creation; the Sāṃkhya concept of the ultimate duality of inert consciousness and evolving unconscious primordial matter (prakṛti); and finally the Āgamic concept of creation, coming into existence in three gradual stages, the pure, the mixed and the impure.

There were also many other ideas and factors that contributed towards the making of this synthesis. Thus, the creation of Brahmā and the pure creation (the Pāñcarātra's own contribution to the theory of creation) and the Sāṃkhya cosmogony of tattvas are all fitted into a well balanced pattern. The Upaniṣadic unqualified Brahman retains Its position as absolute transcendental Being, Consciousness and Bliss. It is one and integral, but the identification of this Brahman with Puruṣa of the Puruṣa-sūkta is quite obvious.[1] Moreover, the qualified Brahman, styled Lakṣmī-Nārāyaṇa (Becoming and Being) is by no means lower in existential status, as It is in the Upaniṣads or rather in Śaṅkarācārya's philosophy. The eternal unchangeable reality has two aspects. In one It is devoid of polarity (*nirālambanabhāvanam*), yet all God's qualities are present there in total suspension like a 'waveless ocean'. In the other aspect, all these divine qualities are manifest. Thus Brahman is Absolute Being, whereas Lakṣmī-Nārāyaṇa is both Being and Becoming, or in other words manifested Being. No reason for Brahman's manifestation or Becoming is proferred and none may be asked for. It is just a will, a pleasure or sport (līlā) of the supreme Being that It undergoes change and limitation.

The nature of Śakti

This will, this pleasure and the qualities that are manifested in the second aspect of the supreme Being are combined into one concept, which is that of Lakṣmī, God's Śakti who is knowledge, bliss and

[1] L.T. II, passim. Also consult J. Gonda, The Concept of a Personal God in Ancient Indian Religion, Studia Missionalia, vol. XVII, Roma, p. 124.

activity. Thus in the second aspect Brahman is polarized into the divine power (Śakti), and the possessor of the divine power (Śaktimat). Śakti is inherent in God just as light is inherent in the moon. She is inseparable from God, yet not absolutely identical with Him.[1] Two phrases are frequently used in the text to denote this relationship existing between Śakti (Lakṣmī) and God: *bhavat-bhāvātmaka* (Being and Becoming) and *ahamartha ahaṃtā* (I-entity and I-hood). These terms exactly describe the relationship. Lakṣmī is the Becoming, or the subsistence of the absolutely existing God. She is also the self-hood of the supreme self (paramātman), i.e. of God. In other words Lakṣmī, God's Śakti, is His essential nature. She is the divine presence. She forms the so-called body of Nārāyaṇa consisting of the six divine, or ideal, qualities (guṇas). Knowledge, the first of these, forms her essence, which is also the essence of Brahman. Her other qualities emerge from her first and do not constitute Śakti's essence, but are her attributes. These six guṇas are absolute knowledge (jñāna), sovereignty (aiśvarya), potency (śakti), strength (bala), virility (vīrya) and splendour or might (tejas). The precise implications of these terms are explained in the text together with the cosmic and moral concepts attached to them.[2] It is clear that these guṇas contain all the Pāñcarātra concepts of a supreme God. Hence Śakti, embodying these gūṇas, actually replaces God by performing all His divine functions yet, being inseparable from Him, never supersedes His. This is a unity in duality, or two-in-one, the advaya tattva.

Once this is acknowledged, it becomes clear that every manifestation of God is Śakti's manifestation, be it transcendental as in the case of the Vyūhas, Vibhavas, incarnations, etc., or be it the material creation. Our text contains a striking statement about the nature of Śakti. She is not inert, she is not active, she does not even follow the middle course (i.e. of being periodically active). This declaration makes it clear that no specific characteristic can be pinned on to her. She is as unqualified and transcendental as Brahman. She is God's supreme will and she acts under His direction.

---

[1] L. T. II. passim.

[2] Ibid. IV, passim. For a detailed description of the Vyūha theory see Schrader, pp. 35-41 and also S. Gupta, The Caturvyūha and the Viśākhayūpa of the Pāñcarātra Religion, Brahmavidya, Bulletin of the Adyar Library 1971, vol. 35, parts 3-4, pp. 189-204.

Or this may simply mean that she has no separate existence from God and yet possesses an identity of her own.[1]

Śakti's five functions

The universe is a manifestation of this Śakti, and she is absolutely independent in translating her will into action. She possesses five functions. These are tirodhāna or delusion, sṛṣṭi or creation, sthiti or sustenance, laya or dissolution and anugraha or grace. These are also called her five śaktis as they sum up the different ways in which she excercises her power of action (kriyāśakti). The first is also known as māyā[2] or avidyā and, through its influence, part of her citśakti (consciousness) undergoes limitation (saṅkoca) and is called jīva (an animate being). These jīvas are numberless. They are affected by three limitations, namely that of space, of knowledge and of action. The reason for this degeneration of the jīvas is their karma-vāsanā, the beginningless accumulated potential effects of their deeds stored within themselves. Although Śakti's will is totally free, she has to create according to the requirements of these karma-vāsanās and the absolute citśakti becomes limited as bhoktās (i.e. those who experience the accumulated results of their deeds either in the form of pleasure or of pain). In order to ensure that jīvas experience the results of their actions, Śakti creates inanimate objects which are the medium through which jīvas obtain their experience of pleasure or pain. Thus basically transcendental and unlimited, citśakti becomes entangled in the process of creation and consequently in the recurrent cycle of life and death.

The second, third and fourth functions of Śakti are naturally connected with her first function. We shall revert to these when discussing the cosmogony. Like her first, Śakti's fifth function is an Āgamic innovation introduced to establish God's (here Śakti's) absolute control over living beings. It is Śakti who, by deluding them, subjects them to the ever-flowing stream of life and death. Again it is Śakti who has sole power to release them from that bondage, which she does out of compassion for the suffering jīvas. She performs this in two ways. On the one hand, she creates ways and means for the jīvas to bring about their own liberation and, on the other hand, she instils in them the inclination to seek her favour in order to obtain emancipation.

---

[1] L. T. XV, 9-10.

[2] Rāmānujācārya's concept of māyā as God's inscrutable power is inspired by this theory.

The first account of the cosmogony

There are three types of creation: the pure, the mixed and the impure. The first is the purely transcendental creation. It consists of all the emanations and incarnations etc. of God's Śakti. The sole purpose of this type of creation is to facilitate the release of living beings from the shackles of life, death and other miseries of this world by providing them with objects to worship and meditate upon. The mixed type of creation is purely mythological (the Jayākhya Saṃhitā refers to it as Brahmā's creation). Here the traditional divine triad Brahmā, Viṣṇu and Rudra are created simultaneously with their consorts. Brahmā creates the cosmic embryo, Rudra breaks it, and Viṣṇu then sustains pradhāna (primordial nature transformed into the primordial waters) within this embryo. Within this cosmic embryo, Viṣṇu floats on these waters with Lakṣmī, and remains asleep. Brahmā is then reborn in the lotus stemming out of the reposing Viṣṇu's navel. Brahmā is now identified with Hiraṇyagarbha and Virāṭ (the cosmic Person or the collective jīva, who contains all the jīvas of the world whilst still retaining his own divine nature). The position of Rudra within the cosmic embryo is not stated by the text.

The third type of creation starts from this collective jīva stage. This is the evolution of the Sāṃkhya categories. The lotus bearing Hiraṇyagarbha with his consort Trayī is Time, which evolves out of the three divine guṇas, viz. bala, vīrya and tejas. This is the primeval evolving nature whose vibration results in material creation. Time is the primary limitation of the material world. Hiraṇyagarbha, who is the conscious principle, stirs primeval nature into activity. He excercises his own power of discretion or wisdom to regulate the activities of the evolving primordial nature. The wisdom of Hiraṇyagarbha (here his śakti) is called Trayī since, according to mythology, Brahmā first created the three Vedas (collectively called Trayī), and then the world on the pattern recorded in the Vedas. These three (viz. the lotus, Hiraṇyagarbha and his wife Trayī) [1] were the first to be transformed into the category called mahat (the great). Mahat consists of the cosmic life-

[1] The Ahirbudhnya Saṃhitā 3, 29 gives a different account of these three. In that text Śakti's bhūtiśakti (material aspect) consists of three principles, viz. avyakta (i.e. prakṛti), puṃ (i.e. the collective animate being) and kāla (time).

principle, the cosmic intelligence and the cosmic Person. Vibration is the attribute of the cosmic life-principle, discretion is that of the cosmic intelligence, and the cosmic Person possesses two sets of attributes. Morality, knowledge, detachment and majesty constitute his first set. The four opposite qualities form his second set. Mahat evolves into ahaṃkāra and from its three components (the three gunas sattva, rajas and tamas) are created the sense organs, the motor organs, the mind with its three components, and the subtle and gross elements. From ahaṃkāra onwards, the process differs slightly from both the Sāṃkhya and the Vedānta concepts of creation. In the Lakṣmī Tantra, each subtle element is transformed into its own gross form and the succeeding subtle element. There are five subtle elements: sound-potential, touch-potential, form-potential, liquid-potential and smell-potential. The corresponding gross elements are ether, air, fire, water and earth respectively. Now the sound-potential transforms itself into ether as well as into the touch-potential, and so on. At every stage of evolution Śakti enters the category and activates it into the next transformation.[1] Direction (dik), lightning, the sun, the moon and the earth are the respective presiding deities of the five elements, ether etc.; Agni, Indra, Viṣṇu, Prajāpati and Mitra are the five presiding deities of the motor organs.

The second account of the cosmology

Besides dividing creation into the above-mentioned three types, the Pāñcarātra also divides it into six stages called kośas or sheaths. This term implies that in each stage Śakti projects herself into various manifestations while yet remaining the transcendental inner principle. These stages are the śaktikośa, māyākośa, prasūtikośa, prakṛtikośa, brahmāṇḍakośa and jīvakośa. The first sheath consists of Śakti herself in her transcendental form. This contains everything that belongs to the pure creation. Vāsudeva is the primary figure at this stage of creation. He has all his divine attributes and is on the verge of creating the diverse universe. He is manifest but not polarized. Saṃkarṣaṇa springs from him and represents the stage where creation still lies dormant, yet is dimly apprehensible. Pradyumna appears from Saṃkarṣaṇa and represents the mind of Saṃkarṣaṇa, while Aniruddha emanates from Pradyumna and

[1] L. T. V, 35, 37 and 39.

represents Saṃkarṣaṇa's ahaṃkāra or sense of individuality.[1] After the Vyūhas, appear the manifestations called Vyūhāntaras, Vibhavas and other incarnations both divine and human. Pervading these diverse manifestations of God's Śakti, His essence remains immutable and impervious to diversity. This is then called the Viśākhayūpa. Even though the Vyūhas show a tendency to represent a progressive manifestation from indeterminate existence to more determinate modes of being, the śaktikośa as a whole transcends material existence. Hence it is called the śaktikośa when Śakti, i.e. God's essential nature, remains basically unchanged.

Māyā, the second sheath, represents the starting point of the material creation based on the three material guṇas (sattva, rajas and tamas). It should be noted that here Śakti combines both the Agni and Soma aspects of God. The former represents God's kriyāśakti or dynamic power, and the latter His bhūti-śakti or power to sustain. Śakti is here called Mahālakṣmī and possesses both female and male characteristics.[2] Amongst other names, she is also called Durgā, Bhadrakālī and Yogamāyā. Possessing all three guṇas, she is the material source of the universe. When the perfect equilibrium of these three guṇas is disturbed, each guṇa manifests itself as a separate śakti, springing from Mahālakṣmī, the first transformation of a part of God's Śakti into matter. These three śaktis are named Mahāśrī, Mahākālī and Mahāvidyā and respectively represent the rajas, tamas and sattva guṇas. These three deities are the components of the third sheath called prasūti, or the mother. Each of these three mothers gave birth, as it were, to twins. With a part of Pradyumna, Mahāśrī created the twin deities Brahmā and Lakṣmī. With a part of Saṃkarṣaṇa, Mahāmāyā (or Mahākālī) created the twin deities Rudra and Trayī. With a part of Aniruddha, Mahāvidyā created the twin divinities Viṣṇu (Kṛṣṇa) and Gaurī. Thus whereas in the śaktikośa, the three Vyūhas Saṃkarṣaṇa, Pradyumna and Aniruddha have Śrī, Sarasvatī and Rati as their respective śaktis, in the prasūtikośa the same male deities are consorted with three other female divinities and become

[1] L.T. VI, 6-12.

[2] Contrary to the prevailing religious notion that the source of creation is nearly always a male-female unit, Mahālakṣmī remains single. But she combines in herself both male and female in the form of Soma and Agni: L. T. IV, 37.

parents of the three Purāṇic primary gods Brahmā, Viṣṇu and Rudra and their respective śakti consorts. At Śakti's bidding, Brahmā married Trayī, Viṣṇu married Lakṣmī and Rudra married Gaurī. This traditional divine triad and their consorts together with primordial nature form the components of the prakṛtikośa. Brahmāṇḍakośa consists of the Sāṃkhya categories, while all the bodies of animate beings belong to the jīvakośa.

The third account of the cosmogony

Creation is in fact a gradual condensation (styānatā) of Śakti. From absolute transcendence, she finally transforms herself into determinate beings. Side by side with this material creation there is the sonic creation in which, from indeterminate absolute sound, Śakti becomes the determinate speech of everyday use. This aspect of creation is also divided into six stages called the six courses (ṣaḍ adhvānaḥ). These are varṇa,kalā, tattva, mantra, pada and bhuvana. Resembling the absolute Being (Brahman), absolute sound is called Śabdabrahman. The next stage of sound is known as paśyantī. Here sound stands on the brink of polarization. The third stage is called madhyamā, when sound is polarized into word and its meaning, without however the polarization being fully manifest. The fourth stage is called vaikharī, which is the polarized state of sound. These four stages of sound-polarization form the varṇa course. Kalā consists of the six divine attributes. The tattva course contains the Vyūhas. The mantras, starting from the letters called mātṛkās, form the mantra course, and this is the topic that is of second special importance in the Lakṣmī Tantra. This is Tāntric 'linguistic occultism'. The pada course contains the four levels of consciousness viz. jāgrat or the waking state, svapna or the dream state, suṣupti or the state of deep sleep, and turīya or the transcendental state. The bhuvana course consists of the material creation. Strictly speaking, out of the six courses, only the varṇa and mantra courses deal directly with Śakti's sonic creation. The others are only variations of the general cosmogony.

Jīva

Jīva, or the animate being, is the self-imposed limited state of the absolute consciousness which is God's essence. All conscious beings belonging to the five kośas starting with māyākośa and ending with jīvakośa are called jīva. The three primary divine pairs (Brahmā-Trayī, Viṣṇu-Lakṣmī, Rudra-Gaurī) and all God's incarnations manifested within the cosmic embryo possess transcendental bodies. Apart from these all other conscious beings, from the celestial gods to plants, have material bodies resulting from the fruition of their deeds. Fundamentally speaking, jīva is not different from Śakti. Just as Śakti creates the universe based on herself as its support, so also does jīva manifest the universe reflected on him in the same way as a mirror reflects a mountain.[1] Like Śakti, jīva too has five functions. His cognition of objects is his creative function. His attachment to material objects is his function of sustenance. His satiation by those objects is his destructive function. His desire for material objects is his function of delusion, and his detachment from that desire is his function of divine grace. There are three types of jīvas: those who are fettered to worldly existence; those who are liberated from that bondage, and those who are ever free. Jīva's liberation always depends on Śakti's compassion which persuades her to bestow her divine grace on the initiate. This occurrence is called 'śaktipāta'.

Liberation

Liberation from worldly bondage means that the jīva has been freed from his three limitations of space (aṇu), of knowledge (asarvajña) and of power to act (anaiśvarya). There are four ways whereby a jīva may seek to attain liberation. These are karma, sāṃkhya, yoga and śaraṇāgati—the first three are the traditional paths. In describing the first, our text follows the teachings of the Bhagavadgītā where it is called the karma yoga. The second path is the jñāna mārga, or the path of knowledge, which involves exact knowledge of truth about everything, i.e. knowledge of the categories, of the system of evolution, and of the nature of God, the supreme and essential consciousness. The third path is the way of

---

[1] L.T. XIII, 24. At first glance the comparison seems incongruous. But one should remember that our text is strongly influenced by the theory of reflection (pratibimbavāda) advocated by Śaṅkarācārya, e.g. his commentary on the Chāndogya Upaniṣad VI, 2. I refrain from jumping to the conclusion that Śaṅkarācārya preceded the Lakṣmī Tantra, simply because I do not know whether or not Śaṅkarācārya himself was not voicing an already prevalent notion. This also brings to mind theistic concepts, such as seeing the universe in one's body, or the ocean in a drop of water.

meditation. This is of two kinds, samādhi and saṃyama. Samādhi means merging into the existence of the absolute Brahman and entails direct realization of Brahman, the absolute Being.[1] This is achieved by practising introspective meditation (yoga). Saṃyama, the second type of yoga, is in fact the Pāñcarātra's ritual worship of God and His Śakti. This involves visualizing the rituals as well as actually performing them. This is the path that is most pleasing to Śakti.[2]

The fourth path to liberation is called the middle way because it steers clear of both conventionally good and bad deeds. It is the complete dedication of oneself to God's will, which leads one to His presence. This is the path of self-surrender (śaraṇāgati) to God in six different forms. Resolution to perform only those acts that please God; total abstention from any deed displeasing to God; unwavering faith that ultimately God will always come to one's rescue; throwing oneself on the mercy of God alone; unconditional surrender of oneself to God and absolute humility—these are the six components of the fourth path to liberation.

The nature of liberation is proper enlightenment about the essence of the supreme Being (Paravāsudeva), which is absolute consciousness. Upon receiving enlightenment one enters Śakti, the divine presence. She alone grants this enlightenment through her grace. The first path (karma), when scrupulously followed by a person pleases Śakti who, satisfied with his steadfastness, then bestows enlightenment on him. He who pursues the second path (sāṃkhya) obtains indirect knowledge of ultimate truth. His proximity to that truth which is none other than herself, pleases Śakti and she blesses him with enlightenment. The first variety of the third way is only for persons of great spiritual capacity, which indicates that they are already favoured by God. The second variety is obviously meant for the propitiation of Śakti. The fourth way is the best one because here the initiate sheds the last trace of his ego. He depends on divine grace with such complete faith that Śakti has no option but to reveal herself to him, and then the initiate becomes united with her. This shows, however, that the

---

[1] L. T. XVI, 32.

[2] Ibid. XVI, 40. Although the text praises the fourth path to liberation (viz. śaraṇāgati) as being the best, it here betrays its preference for ritual worship.

ultimate goal of each of the four paths is to win Śakti's favour. She then excercises her fifth function, viz. that of bestowing grace and, consequently, enlightenment on the initiate.

The word knowledge (jñāna) has various connotations in Pāñcarātra philosophy as, for that matter, it has in every system of Hindu philosophy. As the essential nature of conscious being, it means consciousness; in the context of liberation, it means realization or enlightenment; whereas in ordinary usage it simply means both understanding and cognition. The Lakṣmī Tantra describes the process of cognition as follows: knowledge is of two types, indeterminate and determinate. The first is the preliminary contact a person makes with an object through one of his senses.[1] In the case of determinate knowledge, the mind acts in the following manner. Its manas part cognizes the object along with its attributes; its ahaṃkāra (ego) part connects the experience with the personality of the cognizer who has the experience: this object appears before me and I am experiencing it. Finally buddhi (the discriminating faculty of the mind) takes a decision about the experience. The Lakṣmī Tantra recognizes three means of acquiring valid knowledge (pramāṇa): pratyakṣa or direct experience, anumāna or inference and śruti or verbal authority.[2]

Sthiti and Laya

Although sustenance is primarily Śakti's function, yet she herself carries this out directly only up to the creation of the cosmic egg. Then the traditional pattern is faithfully followed, and Viṣṇu, the great cosmic god, takes over the responsibility. On the worldly level the responsibility is vested in Manus, the primary rulers of kalpas, and then in Manu-putras.[3] The burden of day-to-day responsibility falls on ordinary mortal kings.

The dissolution of creation is of seven types: nityā, the natural destruction of every being; naimittikī, the dissolution of the three worlds i.e. of the visible universe; prākṛtī, the dissolution of all cosmic categories in the category of mahat; prāsūtī, where avyakta prakṛti dissolves in the prasūtikośa; māyī, where everything

---

[1] L. T. VIII, 5-67.

[2] Ibid. XII, 50-52.

[3] Cf. the Bhāgavata Purāṇa, VIII.1. 1,5 and 7; 5.2-5; 13. 11-17; 22. 31; 1. 19-20; 13. 18-20 and 13. 27-29.

belonging to this prasūtikośa is dissolved in the māyākośa; śākti, where all that belongs to the māyākośa is dissolved in the śaktikośa; and finally ātyantikī, the emancipation of the yogin who merges in Śakti. But this is not a total annihilation of the yogin's existence. He continues to exist in a transcendental form. This is the true nature of Vaiṣṇava emancipation. The emancipated being is not absolutely extinguished in the existence of the Absolute Being, but is lifted up to the level of transcendental existence. This existence is identical with that of Śakti. The concept of emancipation basically depends firstly, on the concept of Śakti and her relation to God in the sense of two-in-one; and secondly, on the concept of jīva and jīva's relation to God as being parts of a whole. These concepts have been further elaborated by the later Vaiṣṇavas and, more especially, by the followers of Caitanya of Bengal.[1]

Conclusion

Summing up, it is not possible to claim that the Lakṣmī Tantra has followed any particular philosophical system. As in the case of most Āgamas, here too concepts have been borrowed freely from various sources with the intention of working them into a synthesis, which has not entirely succeeded in producing a well-knit system. Besides combining the two important philosophical systems, Sāṃkhya and Vedānta, which are generally accepted by the Pāñcarātra religion, the text reveals traces of Mahāyāna Buddhism.[2] The influence of the Bhagavadgītā is also clearly apparent and passages from it have sometimes been quoted literally.[3] But advocacy of Śakti's supremacy is the Lakṣmī Tantra's primary objective, and hence it has freely borrowed various concepts prevalent amongst all schools of Śakti worshippers. The text quotes extensively from the Devī-māhātmya section of the Mārkaṇḍeya Purāṇa, gives a detailed and repetitious exposition of Śakti's identity with Nārāyaṇa, introduces the Tārā-mantra whenever possible in the performance of rituals, and discourses at length on

[1] See S. K. De, Early History of the Vaiṣṇava Faith and Movement in Bengal, 2nd. edition, Calcutta 1961, pp. 269, 277-285. Also cf. terms such as '*sāmarasya*' in L. T. XXIV, 41 and Edward C. Dimock jr, The Place of the Hidden Moon, Chicago 1966. pp. 165-156.

[2] L.T. XIV, 7-16.

[3] Ibid. XVI, 43 and XVII, 85.

the Śrī-sūkta.[1] All this is done for the sole purpose of underlining the major significance of Śakti worship in the Pāñcarātra system. The main discourse closes by stating that it is an abridgement of the original Lakṣmī Tantra: 'this is a summary of the Lakṣmī Tantra which contains hundreds of millions of verses (?) . . .',[2] and then from chapter LI to the end it goes on to provide a still more compact summary of the whole. Whether or not these last chapters were added at a later date is uncertain, but the advantage of being provided with a ready-made synopsis condensing arguments scattered all over the text cannot be denied. These chapters also confirm my assertion that the main burden of the text is to establish the supremacy of Lakṣmī as the basic philosophical principle and to centre ritual worship upon her.

This completes my attempt to outline the philosophy found in the Lakṣmī Tantra. As the scope of this introduction is necessarily limited, I have not dealt with the different stages in its development. Certain points of importance have been relegated to footnotes. The main purpose of this introduction is to offer the reader a rough tracing of the philosophical system upon which the religious beliefs of the Pāñcarātra sect are based. Some guidance seemed called for before tackling the text itself.

In conclusion, I wish to express my profound gratitude to Professor J. Gonda, who has been my unfailing source of inspiration. Without his valuable assistance and encouragement it would have been quite impossible for me to have undertaken the present work. He has carefully checked my translation and suggested innumerable improvements. I also wish to thank Professor Th. P. Galestin most warmly for his kind support in promoting the publication of this book. I am indebted to Professor V. Raghavan, Sri V. Krishnamacharya, Sri Parthasarathy Bhattacharya, Sri K. K. A. Venkatachari, Sri R. Raghava Bhattar and Sri Periyathiruvadi Bhattar for the useful advice they have given me; to Mrs. C. R. Strooker-Dantra for improving my English; and to my colleagues Dr. (Miss) J. L. de Bruyne and Dr. E. te Nijenhuis for typing the MS and correcting

---

[1] A detailed description of the mantras as treated in the Lakṣmī Tantra and also dhyānas relevant to various mantras will, I hope, shortly appear in an article of mine that is awaiting publication.

[2] L. T. XLIV, 52. The text does not specify whether it is referring to hundreds of millions of verses or books.

proofs. I am deeply obliged to the Netherlands Organization for the Advancement of Pure Research for contributing towards the costs of publication. My thanks are also due to Mrs. C. Hoekstra-Vos and Miss M. Kruk for kindly giving the final forms to the coloured diagrams. Last but not least, I affectionately recall all the help so readily given me by my colleagues at the Instituut voor Oosterse Talen and at the University Library of Utrecht.

INTRODUCTION TO INDIAN EDITION

The publication in 1990 of Vāmananadatta's *Saṃvitprakāśa*, edited with English introduction by Mark Dyczkowski, has thrown considerable light on the date of the *Lakṣmī Tantra*. The *Saṃvitprakāśa* is freely quoted by Utpalācārya in his Spandapradīpikā and by many authors both in the Kashmir Śaiva tradition and in the tradition of the *Śakti sādhanā*. It is of particular interest for the study of the *Lakṣmī Tantra* because the latter quotes quite a few verses from its first chapter. Vāmanadatta is respectfully quoted by Abhinavagupta. Vāmanadatta follows Śaṃkara's theory of idealistic monism up to a point, and then, in the true Pāñcarātra tradition, refutes the distinction between the Sāṃkhya theory of evolution (*pariṇāma*) and Śaṃkara's theory of illusory manifestation (*vivarta*) to account for causality: "In you (O Lord) there exists no difference between vivarta and *pariṇāma*" (Saṃvitprakāśa I, 106). This could be equated with the ancient *bhedābheda* doctrine. This means that Vāmanadatta flourished after Śaṃkara and in the early period of the development of Kashmir Śaivism. The *Lakṣmī Tantra* also reflects some ideas found in Kṣemarāja's *Pratyabhijñāhṛdaya* and some found in Rāmānuja. Therefore the *Lakṣmī Tantra* is later than these authors; we can assign its final redaction to the late twelfth or early thirteenth century C.E.

The Lakṣmī Tantra's attempt to emphasize Śakti's position in the scheme of the Pāñcarātra theology explains why it borrowed from the Saṃvitprakaśa. In order to establish Śakti's supremacy it also heavily borrowed from the Śākta *pratyabhijña* tradition. Its general indifference to the temple cult makes me think that possibly the *Lakṣmī Tantra* belonged to the renouncer's tradition. An important feature of the *Lakṣmī Tantra* is its elaborate handling of the fourfold emanation of the supreme Deity. According to the commentator on the *Sāttvata Saṃhitā*, Alaśiṃgabhaṭṭa, this links the two texts. The *Saṃvitprakāśa's* author, a practising Pāñcarātrin, bows down at the end of the first chapter to the divine form called the Śaktīśa who has four faces. Both the *Sāttvata Saṃhitā* and the *Lakṣmī Tantra* (VIII, 19) assert that this is the form of the deity which displays total divine majesty and is a direct manifestation of divine awareness and omniscience, *saṃvit* and *jñāna* (SS IX. 50 and XII.175-6; LT XI). The same idea is found in the *Saṃvitprakāśa's* description of this form. The *Lakṣmī Tantra* quotes the *Saṃvitprakāśa* extensively in chapter IV, where the text explains the Pāñcarātra cosmogony and Śakti's nature as the quintessence of the supreme divinity, Nārāyaṇa, which is pure consciousness (*saṃvit*); and again in chapter XIV, where the text elaborates on the true nature of Śakti as pure consciousness and as the source of all creation, Vāc. Vāc is speech; Vāmanadatta calls her Sarasvatī (I, 76). The *Lakṣmī Tantra's* account of Vāc closely follows the *pratyabhijñā* tradition, including the main *bīja mantra, hrīṃ*. (See the *Yoginīhṛdaya Tantra*). For the same reason, the *Lakṣmī Tantra* enumerates the five Śaiva *kalā*, viz. Nivṛtti, Pratiṣṭhā, Vidyā, Śānti and Śāntyātītā, but adds five more, viz. Abhimānā, prāṇa, Guṇavatī, Guṇasūkṣmā and Nirguṇā and calls them just *śakti* of the ten cosmic principles, i.e. the five elements and the five *tanmātra*. (LT ch. XXXV, 14-16). On the other hand the *Lakṣmī Tantra* certainly remains in the tradition of the Pāñcarātra in describing *kalā* as the six divine attributes (chapters II and XXXV) when it describes the theory of the six courses.

Following the three important *Saṃhitās: Sāttvata, Pauṣkara* and *Jayākhya*, the *Lakṣmī Tantra* (chs. XIV and XXII) says that the active aspect of *Śabdabrahman* is Vāc and she is identified with awareness, both contentless and with content. In the theory of six courses of the divine pervasion of the creation viz. *varṇa, kalā, tattva, mantra, pada* and *bhuvana*, Vāc constitutes the primary one, *varṇa;* she is the pervasive, as yet undifferentiated, reality while the others are all pervaded by her and are differentiated as reference and referent. Śakti as Vāc is completely identified with the transcendent divine, pure awareness, but the difference is that as Vāc she represents the divine will to create, which refers to the divine act of thinking.

In fact the concept of Śakti is essential to Pāñcarātra monotheism, because the creation is not unreal, but as a projection of the Divine is in essence identical with the Divine. The Divine is, nevertheless, unchanging and unconditioned, ineffable reality. The act of creation cannot be predicated of Him; therefore Śakti, divine inscrutable Power and Majesty, embodies the paradox that God is both transcendent and immanent in all phenomena, being both pure consciousness and the evolving source of all. This is emphasized by Bhāskara in his commentary on the *Vedānta sūtra*. Vāmanadatta's monistic ideas come close to Bhāskara's *bhedābheda-vāda* and can be traced back to the *Pauṣkara Saṃhitā* XXXIII and XXXVIII. Bhāskara was a Vaiṣṇava and most probably a renouncer (*yati*). It is possible that Vāmanadatta too was a renouncer. Old Āgamas like the *Pauṣkara* and *Sāttvata* prescribe that the *yoga upāsanā* of the fourfold *Vyūha* deities are only for renouncers who have risen to the spiritual state in which they are capable of practising *nirvikalpa samādhi*. They have understood the unreal nature of all dual perceptions. All that remains for them is to directly realize in *samādhi* the essential identity between referent and reference, *vedya* and *vedaka*, both being the same *śakti.* The theory of the six ways explains that clearly. As the divine resolve, *saṃkalpa*, to make creation manifest precedes the actual act of ceation, Śakti's first discernible appearance is as divine knowledge, Śabdabrahman or Vāc. In the Pāñcarātra idiom this is called the Vāsudeva-śakti whose fourfold *vyūha* manifestation neatly corresponds to the four-fold development of Vāc, viz. parā, paśyantī, madhyamā and vaikharī. This is again expressed as the development of pure being into phenomena (*bhavat* and *bhāva*) which then diversify into ideas, the content (*artha*) of ideal speech, and finally appear as conditioned, empirical cognition (LT. IV. 25). As Vāmanadatta says (I.87.), this is how the practitioner in his *nirvikalpa samādhi* gradually removes all conditioned awareness, which finally leaves him with pure awareness (*saṃvit mātra*).

I am grateful to many people who have helped me to prepare this edition. First and foremost is Mr. Narendra Jain, a friend for many years. Without his support this edition would never have appeared. I am very thankful to Dr. Julia Hegewald for directing me to the painting on the cover, a Vaiṣṇava version of *Ardhanārīśvara* known as Vāsudeva-kamalajā mūrti. I am very thankful to Mr. Anthony Aris for supplying me with a transparency of the picture from *Kathmandu Valley Painting*, by Hugo E Kreijger (Serindia Publications, 1999). I also thank the Jucker Collection, to which this painting belongs. I thank my husband Richard Gombrich for all his critical remarks.

14, December 1999 Sanjukta Gupta

CHAPTER ONE

INTRODUCING THE ŚĀSTRA

1. My obeisance to the eternally pure, the ultimate cause of the world,[1] knowledge (absolute) [2], the being without agitation,[3] who is the soul of (both) Lakṣmī and Nārāyaṇa.[4]

2. I worship the form of Lakṣmī seated on the bird,[5] embodiment of compassion, shaped like ī,[6] and adorned with Soma,[7] the unblemished combination of Sūrya, Indu and Agni.[8]

3-6. (Addressing the sage Atri):—Discoverer of the essential purport of the Vedas and Upaniṣads, unchallenged master of all sciences, possessor of knowledge peculiar to all systems and source of all scriptures containing the tenets of all sects and creeds; who is in full mastery of his senses, has conquered the ādhāra,[9] on whom neither attraction nor hostility (towards things of the world) has any hold, who is indefatigable in practising all fourteen branches of yoga [10] and unflagging in the pursuit of true knowledge; who assumed the nature of tapana when in olden times the sun was pierced by the celestial bhānu; to whom penance is primarily addressed and who is a concentration of pure energy; (called) Atri,

---

[1] In definitions generally first the incidental, and then the essential, characteristic is mentioned. Here the immutable, non-dual, supreme God is mentioned first as the source of creation.

[2] Next the essential characteristic is mentioned as absolute knowledge, elaborated in Chapter II.

[3] The primary state of the Absolute is complete passivity. Creation entailing activity is merely an incidental aspect.

[4] The Absolute is higher, or more abstract, than the Lakṣmī-Nārāyaṇa state in which God and His attributes are less impalpable and have assumed personification. Later on however this view was modified and both were equally regarded as being two aspects of truth.

[5] Apparently Garuḍa.

[6] 'Ī' represents māyā or Mahāmāya and as such is the all-pervading Śakti.

[7] Either nectar or the moon. Nectar symbolizes Lakṣmī's immortality. The moon (seen partly in some images of the Śakti) personifies her as Time, the destroyer of all. It also means ँ on ī.

[8] The Śakti's *varṇādhvan* manifestation, elaborated on later in ch. XXII.

[9] Mastery of the *ādhāra cakra*, a special yogic achievement. See ch. XLIII.

[10] Cf. chapters XVI and XVII.

who is unaffected by the three phenomenal attributes,[1] has surpassed the first three aims of living beings,[2] is immortal, never fails to meditate at morning and at dusk and is the sage ever engaged in performing fire sacrifices.

7-9. (Anasūyā), unrivalled amongst all devoted wives, the illustrious lawful consort (of Atri), who for a certain reason became the mother of Brahmā, Viṣṇu and Maheśa[3], whom even the gods praise unceasingly, whose tranquility is never ruffled, who practises penance, is learned, familiar with all religions and ever faithful to her husband, having been instructed by her husband in many and diverse religious saṃhitās,[4] bowed down and uttered these words:

10. Anasūyā:—Sir, my master, conversant with all religions, lord of the world, from thee have I learned about various religions

11-12. as well as about their divergent systems, structures and aims. In my view the Bhagavaddharma[5] is superior to all of these. Whenever a text of the Bhagavaddharmasaṃhitās[6] is expounded by thee, it never fails to indicate the supreme power of Lakṣmī.

13. Since its lore is secret and I have not as yet enquired about it,[7] thou hast not disclosed it to me. Now I am eager to hear about Lakṣmī's power.

14. The nature of this goddess, her form, her origin, what human faculty enables one to recognize her, what is her substratum, by what means is (identification with her) achieved, and what results from knowing her?

15. All this I desire to learn from thee who art the most enlightened of all scholars of the Vedas. Through contact with thy knowledge I shall have accomplished all the aims of my life.

---

[1] *Sattva, rajas* and *tamas.*

[2] *Artha, kāma* and *dharma.*

[3] Reference to the legend that, to test Anasūyā's devotion, these three deities implored her to tend them as sons. She turned them into two-year-olds and fulfilled their wish. They were so delighted that they promised to descend to earth as her real sons: Rāmāyaṇa, Araṇya Kāṇḍa.

[4] Here denoting the book of laws.

[5] Generic term for the devotional system known as the Pāñcarātra.

[6] The Pāñcarātra saṃhitās as distinguished from the other Dharmasaṃhitās.

[7] In order to be initiated in the sacred lore, it was customary for the aspirant to present a request for initiation to his preceptor.

16. Please show me the way,[1] teach me now that I have approached thee.[2] Having heard her words,[3] the worthy Atri said:—

17. Atri:—O thou who art familiar with religion and duly practisest religious rites, it is good that thou hast today reminded me of that which I did not previously reveal since I intended to do so only when requested.

18. O virtuous one, thou art worthy to hear about the supreme power of Lakṣmī which stands on the pinnacle of the Śrutis (i.e. that which is the very gist of the most important Śrutis) and which endures for ever.

19-20. Formerly when the sages of the Malaya range,[4] devout in performing religious rites, had been instructed in the sacred lore of Sāttvata by Nārada of godly countenance, they put the same question to the noble and immortal Nārada, who resembles Brahman and is steeped in knowledge of the Bhagavaddharma.

21. The sages:—Noble sir, from thee have we heard the Bhāgavata dharma, known as Sāttvata,[5] which comprises the elements of sattva (purity) and has but one aim viz. liberation.

22. When expounding the realities Lakṣmī's supreme power was frequently alluded to but, as no pertinent question was asked, it was not revealed (to us).

23. We are eager to hear about the divine attributes of Padminī (i.e. Lakṣmī) which afford protection against the (miseries) of life. Please enlighten us.

24. We bow our heads down to thy feet that save (devotees) from the grip of transient existence. As we repeatedly appeal to thee (i.e. to thy mercy), O sage we implore thee to instruct us.

25. Nārada:—It gives me satisfaction that you sages, who have observed vows,[6] come with your request to me today. I am pleased and shall this very day relate (to you) the Tantra of the immortal Lakṣmī.

---

[1] Here there are minor variations in some Mss.

[2] *Asmy ahaṃ vibho* replaces *asmy adhīhi bho* in some Mss.

[3] Some Mss. omit this line.

[4] Reference to this South Indian range suggests that the Pāñcarātra system was influential in S. India, cf. Bhāradvāja S. ch. 1.

[5] Sāttvata is used here as a synonym for the Bhāgavata dharma; but in all later Pāñcarātra saṃhitās the term is generally used in its derivative sense.

[6] Religious disciplines.

26. in which she, the goddess Padminī, the divine consort of Padmanābha,[1] manifests herself on a lotus and appears with all her essential attributes and powers.

27. Formerly owing to Durvāsas's curse,[2] Indra lost strength and, deprived of the daily study of the Vedas and of the observance of sacrifices, the three worlds lost sight of Lakṣmī.

28-29. The gods languished and religion became almost extinct, split up (in sects) and nearly died. Then Brahmā along with (other) gods approached the Kṣīroda ocean and after doing terrible penance for many divine years awakened Janārdana, the lord of all and the god of gods (from his cosmic sleep).

30. And Brahmā informed him of the plight the gods were in. Next they (the gods) started churning up the Kṣīroda according to a plan devised by Viṣṇu.

31-32. (One by one then arose out of the ocean) Pārijāta,[3] the best horse,[4] the king of elephants,[5] the host of celestial nymphs,[6] the poison Kālakūṭa,[7] Vāruṇī,[8] and nectar; after which the goddess (Lakṣmī) emerged from the ocean accompanied by the moon, and Padminī immediately nestled on Padmanābha's breast.

33. As soon as she cast her eyes on the gods, they recovered their lost splendour but, since she did not cast her eyes on the Daityas, they were defeated.[9]

34. While Puraṃdara was rejoicing over the recovery of his entire kingdom, Bṛhaspati approached him and told him this in secret.

35-37. Bṛhaspati:—I give thee timely warning. Now listen to me, O Puraṃdara. By way of implication I have already told thee that the might of the great[10] is subject, O lord, to her control. Lest thou forfeit thy supreme sovereignty, thou shouldst endeavour, O king

---

[1] Padmanābha is here another name for Nārāyaṇa, though later on he is stated also to be Nārāyaṇa's emanation (*Vyūhāntara*).

[2] Vide, Ag. P. 3, 1-11.

[3] Cf. M.P. ch. 250, and Ag. P. ch. 3

[4] Uccaiḥśravas, M.P. ch. 250.

[5] Airāvata, ibid. ch. 250.

[6] Headed by Ghṛtachī and so forth.

[7] The deadly poison held in the throat by Śiva: M.P. ch. 250.

[8] An alcoholic drink: ibid. ch. 250.

[9] Vide Viṣ. P. ch. I; J. Gonda, Eye and gaze, Amsterdam Acad. 1969, passim.

[10] Some Mss. substitute *tasyāmāyāti te* for *tasyāmāyatate*.

of gods, to surrender thyself to the protection of Padminī. She is the source of all that is noblest in life and she is our ultimate refuge.

38. She, the eternal goddess, is the object of all the Vedas; she is the life-principle of the universe and the potent force behind all creation.

39. She is the will (volition) behind the worlds and recognition of this must be absolute. It is she who creates and, when occasion arises, it is she who protects the three worlds.[1]

40. And at the very end, as identified with the respective (material) causes, she will dissolve (within herself) what has been created. Unless she, the mother of the universe, is worshipped, how can any significant achievement be envisaged?

41. She is the state ultimately attained by the (Vaiṣṇava) yogin from which he never returns (to the world of suffering). That is the final goal of the Sāṃkhya philosophers [2] who know the Self.

42. It is the aim of all yogins to reach the state where suffering no longer exists, and that is also the goal of the Pāśupatas [3] and of those conversant with the Veda.

43-45. She is the ever-sought goal of the entire Pāñcarātra system. This is the goddess Nārāyaṇī, the abiding quintessence of Nārāyaṇa, identical and at the same time not identical (with him) like the rays of the moon. All the various philosophical systems and all the diverse Āgamas worship [4] the same supreme goddess in different ways. Therefore seek the protection of that highly exalted being who appears on a lotus.

46. By worshipping Viṣṇu's queen, by observing various forms of penance and by performing the appropriate rites for self-restraint see to it that thou ensurest thy destiny.

47. This goddess whose countenance radiates grace, fulfils every desire, satisfies the yearnings of the passionate and leads (the adept) to the state of self(-realization).[5]

48. Nārada:—Śakra, thus reminded by the preceptor who is

---

[1] Bhūḥ, Bhuvaḥ and Svaḥ, or possibly *svarga* (heaven), *marttya* (earth) and *pātāla* (the nether region).

[2] Evidence of the tendency towards reconciliation.

[3] Out of all the Śaiva systems only the Pāśupata is mentioned; possibly because it was influential in the same regions as the Pāñcarātra was.

[4] In two of the texts *samupāsyate* is replaced by *tad upāsyate*.

[5] Echoing both the Upaniṣadic and the Yogic concept. Cf. Ka. U. 2, 16 *Yo yad icchati tasya tat* etc.

none other than Bṛhaspati himself, and with his mind set on worshipping her, proceeded to the shore of the ocean Kṣīroda.[1]

49. There making his abode under a bilva tree,[2] he did divine penance by standing motionless as a piece of wood on only one foot, observing silence, and subsisting on air (alone).

50. With hands, gaze and face turned upwards to the sky he practised self-discipline. In this way he did severe penance for two thousand divine years.[3]

51. When it was time for his final bath (indicating the end of the penance), that goddess who manifests herself on a lotus and is Viṣṇu's queen appeared before him smiling.

52. Śakra was overwhelmed with amazement on seeing her, the goddess and supreme mother of the universe, standing before him.

53. In confusion Indra (lit. the slayer of the demon Bala)[4] made his obeisance and folded his palms together. Whereafter with songs of praise the avenger of Pāka delighted Śrī, who first revealed herself on a lotus.

54. The mother of the universe, gazing at him who had entrusted himself to the One (God)[5] and habitually performed sincere (i.e. spontaneous) acts of devotion, spoke as follows:

55. Śrī:—My child Śakra, you have completed such exacting penance that it has moved me. Make any request, O great one! what favour may I bestow on you?

56. Śakra:—This very day all the penance I have done, all the self-denial and self-control I have practised, fulfilled their purpose at precisely the moment that thou of supreme power becamest visible to me.

57. But if thou grantest me a boon, O great goddess, then reveal to me the nature of truth which thou, O ruler of the gods, representest.

---

[1] Bṛhaspati is the preceptor of the celestial gods; Kṣīroda the legendary celestial ocean. Vide Ag. P. ch. 3.

[2] The auspicious wood-apple tree which often figures in images of Lakṣmī. Vide J. N. Banerjea, The Development of Hindu Iconography, Calcutta 1956, pp. 370-372.

[3] Vide Viṣ. P. 3, 8-10.

[4] Reference to the famous legend of Indra's valour when he freed the world by slaying demons such as Vala, Saṃvara etc. Vide John Dowson, A Classical Dictionary of Hindu Mythology, London 1961, p. 124.

[5] The Ekāntinas are renowned for their religious devotion, Vide S. N. Dasgupta, A History of Indian Philosophy, Cambridge 1940, IV, p. 421.

58. By what means canst thou be fathomed? What is thy substratum? How art thou to be attained, O eternal one? To whom dost thou belong and what is the nature of thy relationship to him?

59. Furthermore I beg thee, O mistress (queen), to reveal to me whatsoever else concerning thee can be gleaned from various religious treatises.

60. Delighting in him as a milch-cow delights in her calf, Padmā filled with affection answered Pākaśāsana:

61. Śrī:—O Śakra, noble slayer of Vṛtra, hear who I am, what my nature is, to whom I belong and my relationship to him.

CHAPTER TWO

THE PURE CREATION

1. Śrī: The supreme state of Paramātman,[1] realized by Sūris alone, is described as devoid of misery and devoid of limitation, its essence being the experience of bliss.

2-3. One soul (*ātman*) controls others; yet another soul is master over the first, and so forth, until when this chain ends the (final soul) is called Paramātman, the end of the way of ways.[2] That which the word 'I' (*aham*) denotes is known as ātman.

4. Ātman when free from all restriction is known as Paramātman and embraces all things sentient as well as insentient.

5. The eternal 'I' denotes the Being, (called) God, Vāsudeva, the great Kṣetrajña.[3]

6. He is also named Viṣṇu, Viśva, Nārāyaṇa and Viśvarūpa. His I-hood pervades the whole universe.

7. No single material or immaterial object exists that is not infused with this I-hood. I-hood is inherent in whatever is stamped as 'this' (*idam*, i.e. phenomena).

8. He (Viṣṇu) is perfectly tranquil (without activity, *śānta*),[4] changeless and eternal. He is without end and free from all limitations of time, place etc.

9. The source of that wide diffusion which is called the vast expansion of divine power (*vibhūti*) is Brahman, the ultimate location of that power where consciousness is absolute (lit. where knowledge is free from reference to any object).[5]

10. It (Brahman) is like a waveless ocean of nectar with the six (divine) attributes fully manifested. It is unique, in the form of

---

[1] Repeating the famous Vedic mantra: *tad viṣṇoḥ paramam padam sadā paśyanti sūrayaḥ divīva cakṣur ātatam* (Ṛg V. 1, 22, 20).

[2] The concept dates back to the Upaniṣads, e.g. Ka. U. (3, 9).

[3] Echoing the Bh.G. 13, 1-2; 18, 26, 33-34; *kṣetrakṣetrajñabhāva*.

[4] Read either as *sarvataḥ śānta* or as *sarvaḥ śāntaḥ sa*.

[5] Some manuscripts mention *nirālambanabhāvanam* instead of *nirālambam abhāvanam*. As later repetition confirms, the former is the correct reading. Cf. Bh.G. 2, 25; 12, 3.

concentrated consciousness, quiescent and not subject to expansion or contraction (*udaya* and *asta*).

11-12. Since (in this state) Brahman is not differentiated from Śakti, It is said to be non-dual (*advaita*). Its supreme power, like the rays of the moon, is myself, the goddess, the immortal one, who identifies all states of being with her own self,[1] Brahman's I-hood.

13. He, Hari being 'I' (the Self), is regarded as the self in all beings. I am the eternal I-hood of all living beings.

14. I am considered to be the eternal Vāsudeva state of existence.

15. Brahman embraces both the principle of existence and its state of existence, hence It (Brahman) is the eternal state (*padam*). (When differentiated) the existing principle is God Nārāyaṇa and its state of existence is the supreme Lakṣmī, i.e. myself.

16. Therefore Brahman,[2] the eternal, is called Lakṣmī-Nārāyaṇa because the I-entity is always inherent in I-hood.

17. The I-entity is always recognized as the source of I-hood; for the one cannot exist without the other and each is invariably linked to the other.

18. Realize that the relationship between me and the Lord is that of identity because without I-hood (i.e. the essential quality of I) the I-entity would for want of association be meaningless.

19-23. (In the same way) I-hood without the I-entity would, for want of a basis, lack meaning. In this world all objects of direct or indirect knowledge are regarded as the principle of existence and its state of existence, viewed collectively or separately. That I-hood, the great goddess, remains unmanifested during the time of (Brahman's) non-manifestation and, enfolding the universe within herself, exists in Brahman.[3] The first evidence of Brahman's

---

[1] This implies that in all manifestations of God, Śakti, being His quintessence, follows Him in personal form, e.g. as Sītā when He is Rāma.

[2] Brahman, as presented in the Upaniṣads, is the one and absolute truth. In later Vaiṣṇava treatises this is the state of the Absolute when all Its powers are latent and unmanifested. In the Lakṣmī-Nārāyaṇa state the divinities manifest themselves in their fullest glory as persons (cf. F. O. Schrader, Introduction to the Pāñcarātra, Madras, 1916, pp. 29-31).

[3] Dr. Schrader, o.c., p. 31, points out that 'the transcendent aspect of Viṣṇu (*param Brahma*) remains so completely in the background in the Pāñcarātra that we are practically only concerned with the one force (Lakṣmī)'. This is due to Upaniṣadic influence where Brahman is absolutely devoid of activity (*niṣkriyaṃ śāntaṃ niravadyam nirañjanam*). N.B. In one manuscript *sarvam* is replaced by *viśvam*.

expansion, like the moon rising out of the ocean, is my own self, Nārāyaṇa's Śakti characterized by Brahman's will to create. The closing of the eyes (*nimeṣa*) of (Brahman), the supreme Self, at the time of destruction (lit. contraction) is (also) myself, Nārāyaṇa's Śakti characterized by the will to sleep.[1] My insuperable and unlimited divine power issues from my potential state, the will of God Nārāyaṇa to create.

24. (Absolute) Knowledge is the essence of Brahman Itself, which is omniscient and untainted.

25. The essence of I-hood is also knowledge, which is all-knowing and all-seeing. The absolute state (lit. form) of both myself and Brahman is identical with knowledge.

26. The other attributes of (divine power) such as aiśvarya, vīrya, etc. are the ever-present attributes of knowledge; whereas knowledge is reputed to be the primary expression of 'I'.[2]

27. Luminosity (and transparency) are its (knowledge's) features just as they are the characteristics of crystal and the like; hence it is that knowledge is the manifestation of both myself and Nārāyaṇa.

28. In referring to my primal state of creativity,[3] all scholars in all books of knowledge call my sovereignty aiśvarya as the will (*icchā*).

29. My aspect as the source of the universe is known as śakti.[4] The effortlessness (i.e. ease) with which I create is known as bala.

30. The term bala also denotes my capacity to sustain creation. Scholars regard this sustaining aspect of mine as part of my śakti.[5]

---

[1] A simile for God's waking and sleeping states. The former corresponds to creation and sustenance of the universe, while the latter refers to its dissolution. Unmeṣa denotes opening of the eyes whereas nimeṣa denotes their closing. Vide Schrader, p. 29.

[2] Knowledge is the basis of God's essential nature. The other attributes of His divinity, namely aiśvarya, śakti, bala, vīrya and tejas, are components of that essence and are related to God in the same way as the physical body and its functions are related to the soul.

[3] Here the term *udyatī* refers to the immediately preceding phase of creation.

[4] Śakti in its narrow sense means icchāśakti or kriyāśakti. In other saṃhitās this śakti is referred to as Śrī to distinguish it from Bhū and both are consorts of Viṣṇu. They should not be confused with the main Śakti representing the aggregate of all six divine attributes. Vide Ahi. S., ch. 3 and J.S. 6, 77-80.

[5] Bala in this sense denotes the Śakti's aspect as the cause of creative activity and is essential to both acts of creating and sustaining.

31-32. Although I am the material cause (of the universe), vīrya, —(i.e.) changelessness—is my permanent (attribute). When milk turns into curd it immediately changes its nature,[1] but although I evolve into worldly phenomena (as milk does into curd), these changes of mine have no permanence. Hence discerners of truth hold that vīrya is immutability.

33-34. Vīrya is (also) said to be valour, which is a component of aiśvarya. My capacity to accomplish all things without aid [2] is called by the enlightened my sixth attribute tejas. Some define tejas as the power to subjugate.

35. Yet other scholars of truth regard this (attribute) as a component of aiśvarya. These then are the five attributes directly flowing out (further developments) of knowledge.[3]

36. All six of these attributes, knowledge etc., together constitute my manifestation of the six attributes. This is how a millionth particle of myself as the will to create initiates creation (evolves into creation).

37. It (this particle) embraces both groups (of creation), pure and impure. Here, O king of gods, the course of pure creation will be explained by me.

38. That glorious manifestation (of the six attributes) of the absolute God [4] assumes four forms in which the six attributes gradually manifest themselves or else (remain) unmanifested.

39. These (four forms of manifestation) take place in three extraordinary stages —(i.e.) when the presence of the attributes is

---

[1] It should be noted that, in essence, Lakṣmī is unchanging; only in her prakṛti aspect is she changeable. Thus she is both changeable and changeless. Since her prakṛti aspect is merely a phase, her changeability is not constant. Owing to the inscrutability of her transformations she is often referred to as Māyā, magical power. Cf. J.S. 6, 82.

[2] Stressing that in all her activities of creation, etc. she is free and independent. Both almighty God and His Śakti possess this attribute reflecting their absolute sovereignty.

[3] Cf. Schrader, p. 32.

[4] The distinction between pure and impure creation is that the three phenomenal attributes, i.e. sattva, rajas and tamas are absent in pure creation which is sometimes referred to as *nityavibhūti;* whereas impure creation is termed *līlāvibhūti*. The former consists of four manifestations (*caturmūrti* or *caturvyūha*). In the first (i.e. Vāsudeva) of these four manifestations (*Vyūha*), the attributes are dormant and hence only very dimly manifested. As the process of manifestation develops they become brighter and brighter and more pronounced. Vide Schrader, p. 37.

assumed (when the divine guṇas are not as yet discernable); when the attributes are in course of becoming discernable; and finally when the divine guṇas are fully manifested.[1]

40. Through permutation and combination the three pairs of the six (attributes) referred to as knowledge etc. can be seen to constitute the group of the four manifestations (*caturvyūha*).

41. When those three pairs of attributes are simultaneously present in combination as well as separately, that state of mine, the inert one, is known as my fourfold state.

42. Even without referring to my visible manifestations and by merely basing their deduction on the attributes, philosophers identify my fourfold form with my inert state.

43-44. Through the combination of the three pairs (of attributes) this manifestation (evolution) of my supremely inert state gradually becomes discernible. The first of my (manifestations) in the fourfold state is undisturbed, undefined, enduringly pure existence lacking the concept of particularization, and is known as transcendental existence and knowledge. That is my first manifestation, my first deviation from complete inertia.

45. My (second) manifestation Saṃkarṣaṇa,[2] embodying the two attributes knowledge and bala, enfolds the entire creation (faintly discernible) like dark spots (on a human body).

46. In my Saṃkarṣaṇa aspect the wise discern (a combination of) knowledge and bala. Thereafter, in course of the process of manifestation I gradually become more and more active.

47. During that stage I am called the manifester of all created objects, i.e. Pradyumna,[3] in which form I manifest the pair of attributes known as aiśvarya and virya.

48. And when through the impetus gained from activity (*kriyāśakti*) I am swayed by the will to act, the learned call me Aniruddha.[4]

---

[1] This is the process of Vyūha-creation. Vide Ahi. S. 5, 17-48.

[2] Saṃkarṣaṇa literally means that which contracts. In this state the universe remains contracted or merged in Saṃkarṣaṇa form, faintly showing signs of its existence resembling scarcely visible spots on the human body.

[3] Pradyumna derivatively means he who is endowed with illustrious force or power. This is the starting point of the actual creation of the manifest worlds.

[4] Aniruddha, or the irresistible, is conceived as the sustainer of the created universe. Thus the śānta or inactive state is Vāsudeva, when no evolved form is manifest. Saṃkarṣaṇa is distinctly marked by jñāna and bala, and enfolds the entire creation within himself. From Pradyumna,

49-51. These consecutive and gradual states of mine are (described) as deep sleep, dream and waking (respectively). In the course of manifestation the three (attributes) vijñāna, aiśvarya and śakti, known as my innate attributes, are generally referred to as my three differentiations. On the other hand the other three attributes, namely bala, vīrya and tejas, are divine guṇas auxiliary to knowledge etc., and are defined as the eradication of imperfections such as fatigue [1] and the like. Hence my states are of two types, i.e. the inert and the active.[2]

52-56. My manifestation in creation is only another facet of my existence which involves no duality, in the same way as waves surging up in the ocean (remain the same water).[3] Generally speaking the form of my manifestation is determined by the particular pair of attributes required for fulfilment of my function (purpose). Hence jñāna in combination with bala [4] is named the god Saṃkarṣaṇa; aiśvarya with vīrya constitutes Pradyumna; and Aniruddha represents śakti in conjunction with tejas; whereas in my initial state, the undifferentiated complex of the six attributes is identified with the absolute entity Brahman. Just as the same actor may appear in several roles displaying differences in dress, plot etc., revealing various traits of character such as persuasiveness, magnanimity, cruelty, valour, etc.,[5] so because of my urge to benefit worlds and by virtue of the attributes knowledge (*jñāna*), power (*śakti*), etc. I assume the forms of Saṃkarṣaṇa etc. yet retain my single entity.

57. My motive is to aid living beings involved in the cycle of destruction, creation and maintenance by helping them to become acquainted with, by deepening their study of, and by assisting them

---

endowed with aiśvarya and vīrya, the universe emanates; and Aniruddha, manifesting kriyā and tejas, sustains it.

[1] Some manuscripts read *avidyā* instead of *avadya*. But avidyā seems to be a mistake, since śrama etc. are effects of avidyā and are accordingly regarded as avadyas or doṣas, defects.

[2] The inert state is that of Para Vāsudeva, and the active state is the Vyūha. There again the first state, i.e. Vāsudeva, is śāntodita or that of spasmodic activity; whereas the three subsequent manifestations, namely Saṃkarṣaṇa etc., corresponding to the dissolution, creation and sustenance of the universe, are characterized by constant activity (nityodita).

[3] A clear assertion of the tenet of non-duality.

[4] Vide Schrader, p. 34.

[5] A favourite analogy in Vedānta philosophy. Cf. Vidyāraṇya's Pañcadaśī ch. X (in extenso) and also Maitrī U. 4, 2; *naṭa iva kṣaṇaveṣam*.

to harvest the fruits of religious instruction [1] (through Saṃkarṣaṇa, Pradyumna and Aniruddha).

58. My Vyūha states include my four turya, suṣupti etc. states of existence. The divine manifestation (*Vibhava*) of the omniscient (God) originating with Padmanābha has innumerable forms.

59. The various manifestations of Aniruddha are revealed in the Sāttvata.[2] The arcā incarnations (cult of temple-icons) of those whose minds have been purified by God Himself (are also described there).

60. Through the influence of mantras and their presiding deities (related to the performance of *nyāsa*) [3] such images also embody the six divine attributes. They are all included in my four Vyūha states—starting with my parā state and ending with my arcā incarnation—and should be regarded as included in my (supreme) fourth (*turyā*) state and other (subsequent) states. The difference between Vyūha and Vibhavas is very slight. Now, Śakra, listen whilst I describe the impure course of creation.

---

[1] This explains the motive for creation and the Vyūha manifestation. The traditional view is that creation has meaning in fulfilment of the supreme moral law and order, the way of ṛta. This Tantra adds that God creates to help mortal beings to return to Him in love and gratitude, and thereby stresses God's compassionate nature.

[2] Sāttvata here most probably means the Sāttvata Saṃhitā, one of the oldest saṃhitās of the Pāñcarātra system.

[3] See ch. XXXV, 55-81.

CHAPTER THREE

THE THREE (PHENOMENAL) GUṆAS

1. Śrī said:—I am Nārāyaṇī, possessed of eternal, flawless, infinite and beneficial attributes, verily Viṣṇu's supreme being.

2. I am regarded as exempt from limitations of space, time or form.[1] Consciousness (*saṃvid*) alone is the essence of my being (lit. form); whereas aiśvarya etc. are (my) attributes (*guṇas*).

3. This distinction is effected by my will alone (without aid or directive) [2] and this polarized state is said to consist of knowledge, aiśvarya and śakti.

4-6. Now (I will describe) my limited manifestation comprising vijñāna, aiśvarya and śakti. In accordance with my sovereign (lit. incapable of being subordinated) will, when I, the inscrutable, become manifest (active), my form voluntarily undergoes a mutation (evolution) within the (essential) triad of knowledge etc. Just as the transparent juice of the sugarcane assumes the form of molasses (*guḍa*), so does transparent knowledge evolve into sattva (the primordial attribute). (Similarly) my aiśvarya develops into rajas and my śakti develops into tamas.

7. O Śakra, these three (primordial or phenomenal) attributes are called the complex of the three guṇas (*traiguṇya*). During the creation this traiguṇya changes into a state where rajas predominates.

8-9. During sustenance (of creation) it is dominated by sattva and at the time of destruction by tamas. Though I am essentially consciousness, primordial and all-pervasive, O Purandara, I adopt as my basis (i.e. focus my creative urge upon) the (phenomenal) attributes (guṇas) in order to undertake creation, maintenance and destruction (of the universe). Although I am attribute-less, I alone voluntarily preside over these guṇas and turn the wheel of creation, maintenance and destruction.

---

[1] Śaṅkarācārya mostly refers to objects as *nāmarūpa*. The three empirical limitations are generally time, place and object. Hence it can be deduced that here rūpa refers to objects in general.

[2] Lakṣmī's absolute supremacy is here emphasized by asserting her total independence in all phases of creative activity.

10-12. Śakra:—Why dost thou manifest thyself in these two distinct courses of pure and impure (creation) involving the three pairs (of attributes, namely) knowledge etc. I salute thee, lotus-born (goddess); as I ask this question please answer me.

12. Śrī:—My divine power [1] is sovereign, (so) my will is the sole cause (i.e. instigation for creation).

13. This point even the wise fail to grasp. Yet learn from me (who will explain) this truth (i.e. relationship). I am ever evolving both as lord and subordinate.[2]

14. Nārāyaṇa is the supreme Lord of all and I am His lord-hood. O Puraṃdara, that which is subordinate is known as (a combination of) consciousness and unconsciousness.[3]

15-20. Absolute consciousness determines the state of the enjoyer; the non-conscious state covers the things enjoyed (*upakaraṇa*). That conscious element (*citśakti*), influenced by beginningless nescience (*avidyā*) which is introduced by me, becomes the enjoyer and, on account of its own ego-hood, identifies itself with non-conscious objects in terms of the relationship I and mine. When through the influence of knowledge that avidyā is eliminated, consciousness having dropped its ego-concept recaptures my essential nature. That (absolute) knowledge present in the pure course (of creation) is introduced by me as the supreme Vyūha,[4] when out of compassion I reveal knowledge (to the adept). The relationship between the two courses is that of protector and protected. The one course (of creation), i.e. the pure, protects; whereas the other (i.e. the impure) is protected. This concludes my explanation. What else do you want to hear?

21. Śakra:—Why dost thou function in two states, i.e. as Lord

---

[1] Here aiśvarya cannot denote the second of the divine attributes, since the word is used for Lakṣmī's essential nature. Hence in this context *aiśvarya* refers to the aggregate of the six attributes constituting her essence.

[2] Lakṣmī as God's essence, the supreme truth, is primarily identical with the undifferentiated Brahman. In the next stage God and His essence are differentiated as embodied attributes, i.e. the divine presence and the supreme soul represented by Lakṣmī and Nārāyaṇa. The next stage is when God is immanent in creation yet transcends it. As transcendent He is Īśa (the Lord), while as immanent He is the governed (universe) or īśitavya.

[3] Thus the same principle evolves into the subjective as well as into the objective world. As subjective creation the supreme conscious principle retains its conscious nature; but as objective creation it changes into matter.

[4] The sentence is confused and appears to be irrelevant, but is put here in order to remind the pupil of the absolute nature of God and His Śakti.

and as subordinate? Deign to tell me how many varieties of subordinates there are and describe their traits.

22. Śrī:—This (i.e. distinction *Īśa* and *īśitavya*) cannot be related to my own or Nārāyaṇa's essential nature. The eternal God and myself do not (really possess the aspects of) Īśa or īśitavya.

23. Subordinates are of two types distinguished as conscious and non-conscious. Consciousness is here the enjoyer and assumes the forms of conscious beings.

24. Non-consciousness becomes objects of enjoyment and is of three types. The learned call that (non-conscious) aspect my third state of expansion.

25. I voluntarily divide myself into these two śaktis, i.e. conscious and non-conscious, to represent my two everlasting aspects.[1]

26. The conscious śakti is flawless and pure, consisting of consciousness and bliss. Influenced by beginningless nescience it travels unendingly (through the bondage of many lives and deaths).

27. Although the non-conscious śakti is insentient, impure, evolving and the embodiment of the three (phenomenal) guṇas, yet I voluntarily manifest myself as such.

28. Just as a blazing fire of its own accord produces smoke, so do I—though in essence pure consciousness—assume non-consciousness as a mode of existence.[2]

29. Although beyond being affected by misconception or even distortion through word, I voluntarily manifest [3] myself in the non-conscious state.

30. Although indivisible, through various limiting factors consciousness is divided into the external (non-conscious) and the internal (conscious) creation.

31. Such limitations are imposed by my own (divine) sovereign

---

[1] These śaktis are apparently accepted as different, but basically they represent the one and same Śakti. Cf. ch. IV (in extenso).

[2] The apparent paradox of the essentially conscious principle assuming unconscious form is explained by stressing the Śakti's miraculous will. The idea of God's miraculous power is derived from the Upaniṣads. (Cf. Śvet. U. 1, 10; 4, 9 and 10; Bṛ.Ā.U. 2, 5, 19; Nṛ.P.U. 3, 1; 5, 1). In the Pāñcarātra system Māyā, i.e. the miraculous power, becomes personified as a manifestation of Śakti. Vide J.S. 6, 82.

[3] The editor gives two explanations for the word *ādhyānopādhi*: i) my will as the limitation; ii) the limitation needed to visualize me. The first seems more plausible.

(will) and I am subordinate to none. Recognizing my sovereignty you become enlightened.

32. Śakra:—How is it that thou createst worlds in which both pleasure and pain exist? Would it not be better to abstain from creation altogether or to allow only happiness to exist?

33. Śrī:—I create a mixed creation (consisting of both), because I take into account the cumulative results of acts (both good and evil) committed by the living who are under the influence of beginningless nescience.

34. Śakra:—O goddess born out of the milky ocean, if thou art obliged to create both pleasure and pain on account of karman, where then is thy freedom of will?

35. Śrī:—This karman is regarded as my instrument in fulfilling my (creative) function. The dependence of a creator on use of an instrument does not impair his freedom of will.

36. Pure and independent as I am, I am subordinate to none. I divide myself variously as the performer of a deed, the object of performance and the deed itself.

37. You should not search for a reason (for my doing this). My playfulness (*līlā*) is the reason. Therefore be calm.

Śakra:—Be that as it may, O goddess! If thou hast such a free hand (in creation), then deign to explain the process of creation. O lotus-born, I salute thee.

CHAPTER FOUR

VYŪHAS AND THEIR ŚAKTIS

1. Śrī:—In essence I consist of consciousness and matchless bliss like pure space. I am Nārāyaṇī, Hari's state of existence and my nature resembles His.

2. My essence being consciousness, I am neither inert nor active, nor an intermediary state between the two. I represent the nature peculiar to Hari, the all-pervasive (Viṣṇu), who is the soul of all and has the same character as myself.[1]

3. His form is undifferentiated, homogeneous and inscrutable; and I, also undifferentiated, am of His form and possess perfect tranquility.

4. From time to time a billion-billionth particle of ourselves, composed of consciousness, stirs into activity.

5. (That particle) which is known as the urge to create (*sisṛkṣā*) is in the form 'I will create according to my liking', whereupon I, with that particle of myself, instantaneously evolve into pure creation (*viśuddhādhvā*).

6. As the brilliance of a diamond shines forth in all directions, so does my pure course (of creative activity) diffuse its rays in every direction.

7. Pure creation issues from my form of concentrated (absolute) knowledge, whose (tranquility) resembles a cloudless sky or a still ocean.

8. Devoid of all activity, ever blissful, pure, all-embracing and supreme, the primeval jñāna (knowledge) [2] becomes manifest and is called Saṃkarṣaṇa.

---

[1] This is the natural state of the truth principle (Viṣṇu), and is a completely tranquil state of pure knowledge and bliss. Lakṣmī represents the same state and remains identical with Him, as in that state the principle and its quintessence cannot be differentiated. This is the ultimate, absolute truth which has been variously denoted in the tantras by terms such as *sāmarasya*, *yāmala*, *advaya-tattva* and the like.

[2] This is the state when the first of the divine attributes is in full display. See ch. II, 9-10.

9. Aiśvarya [1] (the divine attribute) is my sovereign power to create the universe without dependence on any factor outside myself. That is my (form) Pradyumna, the excellent Person.

10. My śakti that is immanent, irresistible and which pervades the whole of this variegated universe is known as my Aniruddha [2] form.

11. These resplendent, blue lotus-eyed Puruṣas (Pradyumna, Aniruddha and Saṃkarṣaṇa) are my forms manifesting (the divine attributes) vijñāna, aiśvarya and śakti (*kriyā*). Pradyumna, Aniruddha and Saṃkarṣaṇa are respectively [3] responsible for the creation, maintenance and dissolution of creation.

12. My primordial form when the urge to create (the universe) first stirs in me is Vāsudeva,[4] who may be compared to an absolutely waveless ocean or to a cloudless sky.

13. The manifestation of (all six of my divine attributes) jñāna, śakti, bala, aiśvarya, vīrya and tejas in equal proportion is called Vāsudeva.

14. When of these (attributes) only jñāna and bala are manifested, I am Saṃkarṣaṇa who supports the entire creation without aid. He manifests himself dimly like black marks (faintly discerned on human bodies).

15. Hence in Vedānta [5] literature he is named Bala (Saṃkarṣaṇa). My manifestation [6] of vīrya and aiśvarya is named Pradyumna.

---

[1] Aiśvarya is the supreme Lordhood investing the deity with absolute authority over creation.

[2] Aniruddha denotes that God is omnipotent, as can be inferred from the name itself.

[3] In the sequence of the creation of the Vyūhas, according to tradition Saṃkarṣaṇa comes first, next comes Pradyumna and finally Aniruddha; and that is the order in which every object is created (vide Śaṃkara's commentaries on the Brahma Sūtra 2, 2, 42-45 and 1, 1, 2 and on T.U. 3, 1, 1). This order differs however from that stated here in the Pāñcarātra, which mentions that the Supreme God has two states, viz. sleeping and waking (i.e. the state of creation), Saṃkarṣaṇa representing the first, Pradyumna and Aniruddha the last (vide Schrader p. 38).

[4] Vāsudeva represents the first stage of creation when the Supreme God passes from His state of rest to activity in which the impulse to create is well defined.

[5] Here the term Vedānta is used generically to cover Vaiṣṇava literature, in which Bala, or Balarāma, is an incarnation of Saṃkarṣaṇa (vide Schrader, p. 44). Sometimes he is identified with Ananta, the serpent incarnation of Viṣṇu.

[6] Two Mss. read *samunmeṣo* for *samunmeṣe*.

16. Since vīrya signifies immutability, he (Pradyumna) is changeless. My manifestation of śakti and tejas is known as Aniruddha.

17. Tejas means absolute sovereignty and irresistibility. The sacred literature, like a clap of thunder, issues from Saṃkarṣaṇa.

18. All activities originate from god Pradyumna.[1] All fruits of such activities are said to issue from Aniruddha.

19. Here (in the creation of this universe) Aniruddha [2] is verily the creator; Pradyumna sustains what the former has created, and the creation thus protected by him is devoured by lord Saṃkarṣaṇa.

20. These gods function [3] with spontaneous benevolence through acts of creation, maintenance and dissolution in accordance with sacred texts, religious duties (*dharma*) and the fruits thereof.

21. Though each god manifests only one particular attribute (or aspect), yet all the six (divine) attributes are vested in all three of them, (so that in fact) they stand on the same footing as (lit. neither less nor more than) the eternal Vāsudeva.

22. Their major and minor limbs and intelligence etc. are not phenomenal; their bodies containing the (divine) sixfold attributes are divine and eternal.

23. O Lord of heaven, it is erroneous to think that there is any essential difference between these (manifestations). In order to stress the particular activity associated with each, (such differentiations) are envisaged (by scripture).

24. Aiśvarya is not different from knowledge; and again śakti is

---

[1] Most Mss. read *yataḥ* instead of *uta*; but the latter reading is more suitable here.

[2] Contradicting the statement in Chapter II that Pradyumna is the creator. But as Schrader (pp. 37 f,) has pointed out, "Through Pradyumna the duality of Puruṣa and Prakṛti makes its first appearance: he is said to perform, by means of his Guṇa aiśvarya, both the *mānava sarga* and the *vaidya sarga*, that is, the creation of the Group Soul and of Primordial Matter plus Subtle Time. Aniruddha finally "gives opportunity for growth to body and soul" (Ahi. S. 52, 51-52) by taking over the creation of Pradyumna and by evolving out of it Manifest Matter with Gross Time, and, on the other hand, the so-called Mixed creation (*misra-sṛṣṭi*) of souls; that is to say: he becomes, through his Guṇa 'śakti', ruler of the Cosmic Eggs and their contents".

[3] The Vyūhas have a twofold function, one creative, the other ethical; cf. Schrader, o.c., p. 36.

not different from aiśvarya. These, O Śakra, are my (forms) envisaged to focus meditation.[1]

25. First there is only the substance (of reality); then comes the state of being; next there is the object created and, last of all, there is activity.[2] All created beings pass through these four consecutive states.

26. I (voluntarily) divide myself into four as Vāsudeva etc., but continue to infuse all four forms with my consciousness (*saṃvid*).

27. In each form the gods Vāsudeva and the others (in turn again) divide themselves into three forms, i.e. into Keśava etc.[3]

28. These are the Vyūhāntaras, so called by the Pāñcarātra,[4] and these twelve gods are engaged in conducting the activities (involved in creation).

29. These projections (manifestations) as Padmanābha etc. are the Vibhava (evolution) of Hari as Aniruddha who, though omnipresent, yet assumes these manifold forms for the benefit of the worlds.[5]

30. From time to time to benefit the world the Lord of the world appears in the form of a man or god.[6] Such manifestations constitute a different type of Vibhava.

31. God's image conceived by Himself or by various deities, sages, manes, or demigods for favouring the worlds are His arcā forms[7] consisting of pure knowledge.

32. Thus I have briefly explained the pure course (of creation). Now listen as I describe the other course (of creation) containing the three guṇas (components of phenomenal existence).

33. The (pure) knowledge described to you earlier evolves into

---

[1] In some Mss. the reading is *dhyeyāḥ viśrāmabhūmayaḥ* and elsewhere it is *dhyānaviśrāmabhūmayaḥ*; I have accepted the latter.

[2] Being is the underlying trait of every object existing alongside its quintessence; then comes the object with its distinctive activity (or function).

[3] A full list is given by Schrader p. 41.

[4] This is a definite indication that the term Vyūhāntara belongs only to this system.

[5] Vide Schrader, p. 48.

[6] This alludes to descents such as Kapila, Vyāsa, Dattātreya, Matsya, Varāha, Kūrma etc. A detailed description is given in the Sāttvata Saṃhitā, ch. 12 (in extenso).

[7] Schrader explains these as the descents where the Lord, "Owing to His omnipotence is capable of descending into such images with a portion of His śakti, that is, with a subtle body". Apparently that subtle body is here described as Śuddhasattvamayī (pp. 48, 49).

sattva(guṇa), aiśvarya evolves into rajo(guṇa) and śakti into tamo(guṇa).[1]

34. In the process of evolution, rajo(guṇa) plays the leading role, whilst sattva and tamo(guṇas) stand by (as auxiliaries).

35. As I have already stated a millionth of a millionth part of myself is (again divided, and) using a millionth of a millionth particle of that fraction, I create the universe.

36. At the very beginning of all (of saguṇa creation) I, Mahālakṣmī,[2] the great goddess vested with the three guṇas, focussing my (creative) urge upon the rajo(guṇa) start creating (emanating).

37. In order to promote the welfare of the worlds, Mahālakṣmī who is beautifully formed, manifests, with herself as the substratum, the two divine states of being Agni and Soma,[3] characterized as man and woman.

38. She has four arms, large eyes, a complexion like refined gold, and she holds a mātulaṅga (a citron),[4] a club, a shield and a vessel containing amṛta.

39. That is myself famed as the exquisitely limbed Mahālakṣmī, also known as Mahāśrī, Caṇḍā, Caṇḍī and Caṇḍikā.

40. (I am also called) Bhadrakālī, Bhadrā, Kālī, Durgā, Maheśvarī and Triguṇā; and since I am the wife of Bhagavat (the Holy One), I am also known as Bhagavatī (the Holy One).

41. These and many more are considered to be my names caused by the various modifications of my original state and I shall describe them in full.

42. I am called Mahālakṣmī because I am characterized all over the universe as merit and demerit, as completed and yet to be completed, and also because I am respected as the highest (*mahat*).

43. In my aspect as the ultimate resort of the noble (*mahat*), I am

---

[1] See ch. III, 6.

[2] Due to the preponderance of rajas, Mahālakṣmī is the form in which the creative śakti is most pronounced, since rajas is a condensation of aiśvarya and so represents irresistable creative power. This is the saguṇa śakti corresponding to Aniruddha Vyūha.

[3] Mahālakṣmī is the all-embracing creative form of Śakti, representing both Puruṣa and Prakṛti in the phenomenal creation, and Agni and Soma in mystic formulae.

[4] Vide J. N. Banerjee, The Development of Hindu Iconography, Calcutta 1956, p. 373.

called [1] Mahāśrī. As the wife of Caṇḍa,[2] I am Caṇḍī; and being of a fierce nature, I am Caṇḍikā.

44. In my aspect of being beneficial, I am Bhadrā; when I encourage goodness, I am Kālī, which is also my name when I destroy the hostile.

45. As I simultaneously (regulate) the conduct of both friends and enemies by good or bad means respectively, I am renowned as Bhadrakālī; furthermore (I am called) Māyā [3] of inscrutable qualities.

46. As I am great (all-pervading), I am called Mahāmāyā; since I bewitch all, I am called Mohinī. I am called Durgā, as I am difficult to reach, and also because I save my devotees.

47. As I connect (link), so I am known as Yogā or Yogamāyā; as I confer knowledge on men, so I am known as Māyāyogā.[4]

48. By virtue of my existence in the form of all six (divine) attributes, I am known as Bhagavatī. Because I participate with Bhagavān in performing the sacrifice called 'bhagavat', I am regarded as His wife.[5]

49. Owing to my vastness, I am regarded as Vyoman; because of my characteristic of abundance, I am known [6] as Purī. As I represent the Absolute (*parāvara*), I am called Parāvarā.[7]

50. On account of my power to render all things possible, I am called Śakti; because of my invariable power to delight, I am Rājñī. As I am always in the condition of inertia, so I am described as Śantā.

51. The universe is produced [8] from me (as a 'mode' of myself),

---

[1] *Gīyate* is sometimes found instead of *gadyate*.

[2] Mā.P. 83, 28. See also ibidem, ch. 73-85 for Durgā's exploits.

[3] Apparently the word Māyā here refers to the inscrutable power of performing miracles.

[4] *Māyā* here denotes supernormal knowledge. Cf. Bh.G. 4, 6 *sambhavāmy ātmamāyayā*. Interestingly enough māyā actually is the capacity to work miracles and in course of time came to mean omnipotence.

[5] A woman becomes a wife by performing sacrifices with her husband. Here the sacrifice is *bhagavadyajña*, i.e. God's protection of those who have taken refuge in Him. It is to be noted that Ahi.S. 3, 11 holds a different view.

[6] In some Mss. *smṛtā* is *sthitā*.

[7] This name is analogous to the Upaniṣadic description of Brahman as *parāvara* in *tasmin dṛṣṭe parāvare* (M.U. 2, 2, 9).

[8] Prakṛti means the source of all material existence. Thus the creation originates from the goddess. In this aspect She is the primordial matter that evolves into creation.

hence I am called Prakṛti. I am the (only) shelter to be resorted to and I destroy the misfortunes of the pious.

52-54. I listen to the lamentations (of devotees) and gladden the world with my virtues.[1] I inhere in all beings (*śaye*) and take delight in (*rame*) the virtuous. I am ever worshipped by the gods and am the embodiment of Viṣṇu. Beholding these attributes of mine, the learned in the Vedas and Vedāntas, who know how to relate attributes to their possessor, extol me as Śrī. The same Myself am eternal, manifested as all and ever existent.

55. As the tutelar deity of the complex of the three (phenomenal) guṇas, I am named Triguṇā. Through my urge to create, I cause a disturbance in the (perfect equilibrium of the) three guṇas.[2]

56. With a complexion like pure gold and adorned with golden ornaments, I fill the (otherwise) dark world with my own brilliance.[3]

57. In the beginning, in order to fill the empty universe with myself, I assumed another form (mainly) consisting of only tamoguṇa.

58. She (the goddess) is dark like a mass[4] of collyrium, her worthy face has ferocious teeth and large eyes, and she is a lady with a slender waist.

59. She has mighty arms adorned with sword, pot, (severed) head and shield. She wears a garland composed of severed heads and has a diadem of snakes.

60. Emanating from me, she, Tāmasī choicest of maidens, said to me, 'O my mother, I salute thee again and again. Deign to give me a name and function'.

61. Śrī:—I said to the fair Tāmasī, choicest of maidens, 'I shall give you names and functions.

---

[1] Here the name Śrī is derived in different ways according to its three sources: *śa* and *śra* stand for the verb-root *śri-* (sheltering), or for *śṝ-* (destroying), or for *śru-* (listening), or for *śṝ-* (pleasing), or for *śī-* (sleeping). *ra* represents the verb-root *ram-* (playing) and *ī* stands for the verb-root *īḍ-* (praising).

[2] This explanation of the original act of creating stresses the Śakti's independence.

[3] As essentially consisting of consciousness, Śakti is the illuminating principle of the creation. Her golden complexion suggests this luminosity.

[4] Since *bhinnāñjana* makes no sense, I have made one word of *sābhinnāñjana* and broken it down into *sa-abhinnāñjana*, *abhinna* denoting 'a mass'.

62. Mahākālī, Mahāmāyā, Mahāmārī, Kṣudhā, Tṛṣā,[1] Nidrā, Kṛṣṇā,[2] Ekavīrā, Kālarātrī and Duratyayā —

63. these are your names and your functions are to be inferred from those names; and he who learns them with understanding attains happiness'.

64. Considering the creation to be incomplete, I fill it up with my first form which resembles the (beauty of the) moon and is pervaded by the manifestation of sattva.

65. She (that form) became a noble lady holding (in her hands) a rosary (made of akṣas), a goad, a vīṇā and a book, and I conferred upon her the following names and functions:

66. Mahāvidyā, Mahāvāṇī, Bhāratī, Vāk, Sarasvatī, Āryā, Brāhmī, Mahādhenu, Vedagarbhā, Dhī and Gīḥ.

67. Her functions are related to these names and represent the various aspects of the miraculous activity generated by sattva(guṇa). These three of us are said to be the support of the universe and the mothers (of all).[3]

---

[1] *Tṛṣā* is replaced by *Kriyā* in some Mss.

[2] *Kṛṣṇā* is replaced by *Tṛṣṇā* in the same Mss.

[3] A detailed description of the various aspects of śakti is to be found in Ahi.S., ch. 3. Schrader has discussed these in the I.P., pp. 62-65.

CHAPTER FIVE

EVOLUTION OF THE MATERIAL WORLD FROM PRAKṚTI

1-6. That primary I-hood of Hari, which has evolved into all forms, which is eternal, which incorporates pure bliss and consciousness, and which is absolutely inert (is myself). I, the same one, stimulated by my urge to create, have evolved the pure creation with an infinitesimally small particle of myself, embodying (the creation which is) pure and consists of a form containing all six of the divine attributes. Without changing my own (transcendental) form, a small part of my self, called Mahālakṣmī, evolves into the complex of the three guṇas.[1] There, (in the process of evolution) when I am dominated by rajas (I am called) Mahāśrī, the supreme Goddess. My form dominated by tamas is regarded as Mahāmāyā. My form dominated by sattva is regarded as Mahāvidyā. I myself (Mahāśrī) and those two ladies (Mahāmāyā and Mahāvidyā) are (all) three stimulated (to create) and have created the three pairs according to our (three) forms.[2] The pair created to tally with my [3] (form) is envisaged as beautifully formed.

7. You should know that this (pair), pregnant with the golden (cosmic egg), has lotus(-shaped) eyes, is handsome and seated on lotuses, and is a mental creation based on my form and is created from a part of Pradyumna.[4]

8-15. The male (of the pair) is known as Dhātā, Vidhi, Viriñci and Brahmā; while the female (of the pair) is called Śrī, Padmā, Kamalā and Lakṣmī. The pair that is created mentally in Mahāmāyā from

---

[1] This is the same particle of Śakti which is referred to in the previous verse.

[2] Mahālakṣmī, the transcendental particle of Śakti, evolves into primordial nature incorporating the three guṇas in equal proportion. Mahāśrī, Mahāmāyā and Mahāvidyā represent Mahālakṣmī, but each emphasizes only one special aspect or guṇa and hence, as they evolve further, the guṇas manifest themselves in unequal proportion. A male and female pair endowed with all the characteristics of its respective parental source emanated out of Mahāśrī, Mahāmāyā and Mahāvidyā, one from each.

[3] Mahāśrī's.

[4] Mahāśrī and Pradyumna are the parents of this pair called Hiraṇyagarbha, which possesses the traits of its parents.

the part of Saṃkarṣaṇa, possesses three eyes and is beautiful in all parts of the body.[1] There the male is (called) Rudra, Śaṃkara, Sthānu, Kapardī and Trilocana. Trayī, Īśvarā, Bhāṣā, Vidyā and Akṣarā, also Kāmadhenu, Go and Sarasvatī are the names by which the female of that (pair) is known. Born from Mahāvidyā from a part of Aniruddha is the pair whose male is (called) Keśava, Viṣṇu, Hṛṣikeśa, Vāsudeva and Janārdana. The female there, known as Umā, Gaurī, Satī and Caṇḍā, is full of virtue and loyalty. By my order, Trayī became Brahmā's wife; Gaurī became Rudra's wife and Ambujā (Padmā) became Vāsudeva's wife. With these evolutions of rajas, tamas and sattva, the three pairs, the description of the first phase (of creation) is concluded. Now listen, I shall describe the middle phase of (that evolution) of the guṇas.[2]

16. Viriñci along with Bhāṣā produced the (cosmic) egg. At my command Śaṃkara with Gaurī broke it (open).

17. Brahmā created Pradhāna in that egg and Keśava along with Padmā preserved it.

18. Thus is described the middle phase (of evolution) of the guṇas. Now listen with attention to me while I describe the third phase.

19. Pradhāna that exists in the (cosmic) egg consists of both reality and non-reality. It has the complex of the three guṇas as its source, it is of the nature of the void (*vyoma*), it is the source (of all) and is itself undecaying.

20-21. Then having turned this principle (*pradhāna*) that is called avyakta (unmanifested) into water,[3] god Hṛṣikeśa along with Padmā accompanied by Vidyā[4] lay on that water as He took

---

[1] The three-eyed pair has Mahāmāyā and Saṃkarṣaṇa as parents.

[2] Saguṇa, or the impure creation, has three phases of development: i) manifestation of Mahāśrī, Mahāmāyā and Mahāvidyā and the creation of the cosmic twin-deities, whose marriages produce the mythological divine couples with definite duties; ii) creation of the cosmic egg with pradhāna therein and the preservation of both; iii) step by step, the creation of the gross world.

[3] This primordial nature embodying the three guṇas is Śakti herself as disclosed later in the text.

[4] An echo of the mythological concept of Viṣṇu's two wives Lakṣmī and Sarasvatī, named Śrī and Bhū in other Pāñcarātra texts; but possibly also implying that Śakti in saguṇa condition has three manifestations, of which each emphasizes one of the three guṇas and actively participates in directing the third phase of creation: Padmā with rajas, Vidyā with sattva, and Māyā with tamas, transformed later into Viṣṇu's sleep.

to meditative sleep; and she who is called Mahākālī became (His) sleep consisting of tamas.

22. Then O Puraṃdara, when He was lying (there asleep) a lotus stemmed out of His navel. This (lotus) Paṅkaja, which did not grow from mud (*paṅka*), is called Kālamaya (that which consists of time).

23. It is also called Jalādhikaraṇa, Padma, Ādhāra (the substratum), Puṣkara, Cakra (the wheel of time) and Puṇḍarīka.

24. Śakra:—Both the realities, the conscious and the non-conscious, have been described; the sentient is said to consist of consciousness; the insentient of the complex of the three guṇas. How is finite time to be conceived? [1]

25-26. Śrī:—Finite time is a component of the non-conscious and is regarded as comprising the finite three guṇas. During cosmic evolution the triad of bala etc. (i.e. *bala*, *aiśvarya* and *vīrya*), previously described amongst the six (divine) attributes, evolves into time. That (triad) itself is changeless, whereas only its (aspect) of three guṇas evolves.

27-29. The pair of time and its effect (*kāla* and *kālya*) is said to be non-conscious. That time, consisting of me, acts as an instrument used by my goddess (*śakti*) Mahāśrī to create the diversity of objects. Emerging from that lotus, which consists of Time (eternal) and sprouts from Viṣṇu's navel, holding the Vedas and accompanied by Trayī, the same mighty Brahmā appeared who formerly emanated from Lakṣmī and is called Hiraṇyagarbha.[2]

30. Trayī is the woman who emanated from Mahākālī. Thus this pair (Brahmā and Trayī) was born out of the lotus from Viṣṇu's navel.

31-32. These three composed of this lotus and the pair arising from it, compose, as ancient savants describe, the evolving principle called mahān, consisting of tamas (and) characterized by mahathood. These three aspects are the lotus representing the life-principle (*prāṇa*): the male representing Hiraṇyagarbha and the female representing intelligence (*buddhi*).

---

[1] Infinite time, or Time eternal, is the lotus stemming from Viṣṇu's navel.

[2] Brahmā's second appearance is inside the cosmic egg, whereas His first was outside it and He was its creator.

33. The quality of the life-principle is spanda [1] (vibration); that of buddhi is adhyavasāya (process of decisive thinking). The quality of puṃs (the male) is twofold, dharma and adharma (merit and demerit).

34. The qualities dharma etc. are dharma (merit), jñāna (knowledge), vairāgya (renunciation), and aiśvarya (sovereignty). The (qualities) opposed to these are called adharma etc. (i.e. demerit, ignorance, attachment and limitation).

35. To benefit my own creation, I stimulated mahat by penetrating it. When so stimulated, ahaṃkāra (the ego principle) evolved out of it (*mahat*).

36. The wife of the aforesaid Śaṃkara, Gaurī, who emanated from Mahāmāyā,[2] evolved into egohood (*abhimati*).

37. Penetrating ahaṃkāra, I caused it to evolve (further). Under influence of the three guṇas it (*ahaṃkāra*) then became threefold.

38. The tamas aspect is then (called) bhūtādi.[3] Now listen to its description. The potential element (*tanmātra*) of sound (*śabda*) was evolved out of bhūtādi; and sound emerged from that tanmātra.

39-40. The touch potential (*sparśa*(*tan*)*mātra*) arose out of the sound element when stimulated by me. The touch (element) evolved out of the touch potential. From that (touch) element, the form potential (*rūpa*) arose. From that when stimulated by me, appeared the (element of) the primeval form followed by the liquid potential (*rasa*).

41-42. This liquid (potential) when stimulated by me produced the element of liquid, from which emanated the smell potential (*gandha*) that, in turn, when stimulated by me, produced the element of pure smell (*gandha*). This is the classification of elements. Mātras (element potentials) are the subtle elements; the others are gross elements.[4]

43. The qualities such as sound etc., belonging to the (elements

---

[1] The life-principle is the vibrating life manifest in all living beings. The word spanda suggests close association with Śaiva theology as found in Kashmir and in Southern India amongst the Pāśupatas.

[2] See verses 9-10.

[3] Bhūtādi = Ahaṃkāra, the origin of all elements producing the microcosmos and macrocosmos.

[4] Tanmātras are the subtle elements, the immediate source of the gross elements (ether, air, fire, water, earth). Tanmātras are called sound, touch, form, liquidity and smell potentials respectively.

of) sound etc., are mere products (*visarga*) of the gross elements and have no separate existence.

44. The manifested qualities of the (*guṇas*) sattva etc., namely tranquility (*śāntatva*), movement (*ghoratva*) and ignorance (*mūḍhatva*), are absent in the subtle elements.

45. That is why the subtle (elements) are regarded as possessing the quality of tanmātra (potentials, elements of potentiality). The others are therefore (said to possess) grossness since they cause pleasure and pain.

46. The gross elements are each said to have three states, the subtle, the pitṛjas and the prabhūtas.[1]

47. The diverse objects of the material world, such as a pitcher etc., are classified as prabhūtas. The pitṛjas consist of those who are born through the conjunction of semen with blood.

48. The subtle (state) consists of the five elements [2] that form the subtle body. This concludes the gradual evolution from (*ahaṃkāra* as) bhūtādi.[3]

49-50. Of the two other components of ahaṃkāra based on sattva and rajas, the component consisting of sattva is called vaikārika; the other is called taijasa by the learned. Now hear how creation evolved from these (components). The cognitive senses, such as the auditory organ etc., emerge from vaikārika ahaṃkāra.

51. The conative senses, such as the organ of speech etc., evolve from taijasa (*ahaṃkāra*). Manas, which is a combination of the cognitive and conative senses, emanates from both (*vaikārika* and *taijasa ahaṃkāra*).

52-53. The organs of audition, of touch, of sight, of taste and of the fifth organ smell, are called the five cognitive senses and (their inherent) śakti (*buddhīndriya* or *jñāna-śakti*) is myself.[4] Speech, hands (the organ for holding), feet (the organ for movement), the organs of reproduction and of excretion, these five conative senses possess the (other) śakti (*kriyā*), which is also myself.

54. My own vijñānaśakti (śakti of intelligence) descending

[1] Explained in the next verse in reverse order showing their degree of grossness. Prabhūta denotes profusion, hence the diversity of external creation.

[2] The elements of ether, air, fire, water and earth.

[3] The tamas aspect of ahaṃkāra or bhūtādi.

[4] Each sense organ has an inherent śakti, a manifestation of the original Śakti.

through the successive stages of evolution, directs the cognitive senses towards their (relevant) objects.[1]

55. My own kriyā śakti (power of action), descending through the successive stages of evolution, directs the conative senses to their respective functions.

56. The object of the organ of audition is sound, and hearing is recorded as its function. The object of the organ of touch is touch, and touching is regarded as its function.

57. The object of the organ of sight is form, and seeing is considered to be its function. Taste is the object of the organ of taste, and tasting is regarded as its function.

58-60. Odour is the object of the organ of smell and smelling is regarded as its function. The functioning (*vṛtti*) of the auditory organs etc. in relation to their (respective) objects, viz. hearing etc., is called ālocana [2] and implies cognition of the undifferentiated object. Diś (the four points of the compass), lightning, the sun, the moon and the earth are the respective presiding deities of the five (senses) of audition etc. Their respective objects, sound etc., are called elements.

61-62. The (cognitive senses) consisting of the auditory etc. organs are called adhyātma. Since the five senses of audition etc. emanate from the sattva (component) of space etc., these five organs of audition etc. are said to belong to their respective elements. Sound is the object of the organ of speech and speech is said to be its function.

63. That which is held is the object of the organ of holding, and holding is its function. Destination is the object of the organ of movement and moving is its function.

64. Pleasant things are the objects of the reproductive organ and enjoyment is its function. What is excreted is the object of the organ of excretion and excretion is its function.

65-67. The four organs [3] of holding etc. relate to five objects.[4]

---

[1] The senses, being insentient, can only function through contact with śakti.

[2] Ālocana means nirvikalpa pratyakṣa of the Vedānta. See Sanjukta Gupta, Studies in the Philosophy of Madhusūdana Sarasvatī, Calcutta 1966, p. 150.

[3] This omits the organ of speech.

[4] The relation between five objects and their respective conative organs is not clear.

Agni (fire), Indra, Viṣṇu, the original Prajāpati, and Mitra are considered by the wise to be their respective presiding deities. Those five, namely sound etc. that are regarded as the objects of speech etc., are known as adhibhūta (related to the elements); and the (senses) of speech etc. are called adhyātma (related to a subject). Manas (the mind), on the other hand, functions as the auxiliary (sense) in both groups of the five (senses).

68. This mind assisted by the cognitive senses grasps (i.e. determines) the distinctive (object). Vikalpa denotes that which is differentiated (*vividhā kḷpti*), and that is called modification.[1]

69. This (modification) is said to be the relationship between a quality and the object qualified. Vikalpa (polarization in object and quality) is of five types classified according to its being an object, or an activity, or a quality etc.[2]

70-71. Daṇḍin as an object, whiteness as a quality, movement as an activity, man as a genus, and ḍittha as speech are (examples of) these five classifications (of *vikalpa*). Mind in combination with the conative senses contains saṃkalpa (the will).

72. The elimination of indifference is saṃkalpa, which is known as udyoga (preparation) and, with the ego, relates to both groups (of senses).

73. In the group of the cognitive senses it (*ahaṃkāra*) is identical with abhimāna. (The awareness) of the knower in relating time and place to himself is called abhimāna.

74. An object is (always) cognized as 'today (this) appears before me'. In the group of the conative senses, on the other hand, it (*ahaṃkāra*) operates as saṃrambha.

75. Saṃrambha is described as that which is antecedent to saṃkalpa. In the group of the cognitive senses, buddhi is adhyavasāya.

76. Buddhi as adhyavasāya implies the determination of objects (*avadhāraṇam*). The avadhāraṇa of objects is called niścaya (decisive knowledge).

77. In the group of the conative senses, buddhi functions as

---

[1] Viśeṣaṇa is the trait of vikalpa which is derived from *vi* + *klp*- meaning "standing in relation to diverse (natural phenomena)"; hence polarized knowledge of objects.

[2] Matter, quality, function, genus and species are the general classifications of an object (*padārtha*).

prayatna (endeavour). Scholars regard these thirteen varieties as instruments (of cognition).

78. The external instruments are ten in number, whereas the internal instruments number three. These twenty-three are called vikāras (effects).

79. The ten (external) instruments and the three subtle instruments [1] produced from the gross (effects i.e. ahaṃkāra's components of *vaikārika* and *taijasa*) constitute the (cosmic) subtle body, which is called virāja.

80. Every individual subtle body differs in each living being (*jīva*). At the time of liberation this product of the evolutionary process withdraws itself from the (liberated) being.[2]

81. These twenty-three resulting (categories), starting from mahat and ending with viśeṣa,[3] mutually assist each other in creating the egg.

82. That golden egg became as bright as the thousand-rayed (sun). In it Prajāpati, the four-faced god, was born as Virāj.[4]

83. Manu was born from Virāj, and the descendants of Manu are known as Mānavas. This world, consisting of both movables and immovables, has originated from them headed by Marīci.

84-85. So far I have disclosed only a fraction of my active state. Although the śakti of consciousness is pure in essence, through contact with beginningless avidyā (nescience) caused by misery, birth, decay etc., she (*citśakti*) manifests herself in an impure state. But when avidyā is destroyed through contact with pure knowledge accompanied by pure deeds, she regains her original blissfulness.

---

[1] The internal organ has three components, mind (*manas*), intelligence (*buddhi*) and ego (*ahaṃkāra*).

[2] In the liberated state, the liberated being is permanently relieved of this sūkṣma śarīra (subtle body) which usually accompanies the individual from one life to another. Cf. *etat kośatrayaṃ militaṃ sat sūkṣmaśarīram ity ucyate* (Sadānanda, Vedāntasāra p. 5. Ed. by M. Hiriyanna, Poona 1962).

[3] The five gross elements.

[4] Another fusion with prevalent mythology. See Viṣ. P. 4, 2-10 and 50-52.

CHAPTER SIX

THE SIX KOŚAS OF ŚAKTI

1. Śrī:—I am the primordial I-hood of Hari who possesses, though in unmanifest form, the aggregate of the six divine attributes. Hari is the great ocean of consciousness and bliss and (His tranquility and pervasiveness) resemble the waveless ocean.

2-5. Although I am so pure, sometimes I project myself. Then I —Viṣṇu's absolute essence, the Goddess (Śakti) consisting of reality and consciousness, and distinguished by my urge to create—evolve into the states of the six kośas:[1] śakti, māyā, prasūti, prakṛti consisting of the three guṇas, brahmāṇḍa (the cosmic egg) and the jīvadeha (individual living being). These six are called the six kośas. Śakti, the first kośa, follows the pure course (of creation) and is the urge to create that emanated from Hari's I-hood. Kośa is a synonym for kulāya (nest), which is another name for body.[2]

6. The supreme God Saṃkarṣaṇa, the Lord, Ego-consciousness, is manifested in this first pure kośa, which is characterized by the initial appearance of creative activity (*unmeṣa*).[3]

7. In Him all effects (created things) lie (dormant, indistinct) like faint marks on a (human) body. The goddess consisting of His I-hood is myself, called the absolute Sāṃkarṣaṇī.

8. Known as Śrī, I possess (the divine attributes of) vijñāna and bala. My (further) emanation from her is called Pradyumna.

9. Divine Pradyumna, the supreme Puruṣa (*Puruṣottama*), exists as the intelligence (*buddhi*) of divine Saṃkarṣaṇa, who is manifest in śaktikośa.

10-11. There in Him, all the enjoyers and their objects of enjoyment lie dormant. That which is said to be the I-hood of the divinity who forms the (cosmic) mind, is myself, bearing the name Sarasvatī who (out of herself) evolves vīrya and aiśvarya. My emanation from her is known as Aniruddha.

---

[1] These six kośas roughly correspond to the Upaniṣadic *kośas*: *ānandamaya, vijñānamaya, prāṇamaya, manomaya, annamaya*. See Sar.U. 2. in extenso.

[2] Kośa literally means a sheath, hence an abode (*kulāya*) or body.

[3] Śānta is the inert state of God and Śakti; unmeṣa is their active state marking the beginning of creation.

12-13. I (Aniruddha) exist as the egohood of Saṃkarṣaṇa. These three ancient divinities headed by Saṃkarṣaṇa are known as jīva, buddhi and ahaṃkāra (egohood).[1] These are indeed not phenomenal (*aprākṛta*, i.e. do not consist of the three guṇas), but consist of pure consciousness.

14. In keeping with the special functions of the first Vyūha, the resplendent God Vāsudeva, each [2] is designated by a special name.

15-16. All of them are said to possess all six divine attributes and all of them are Puruṣottamas.[3] He who appeared first out of the eternally blissful ocean of all six inert guṇas is called Vāsudeva, in whom all six guṇas simultaneously became active.

17. His I-hood is called Śānti (who is) myself, (and) is known as Śakti, who is considered to contain the three divinities existing in the śaktikośa.[4]

18. Aniruddha's I-hood is named Rati who is identified with the goddess Mahālakṣmī, and he is called the māyākośa.

19. The two, Mahākālī and Mahāvidyā, are said to be the active state of Mahālakṣmī which is known as the guṇa of māyā.[5]

20. My third great kośa is known as prasūti and consists of Mahālakṣmī, Mahāmāyā and Mahāvidyā.

21-25. (In that kośa) were the three pairs about whom I have already spoken.[6] That (famous) pradhāna, wherein Puruṣottama lay afloat after it had been transformed into water, is called prakṛti, the source (of all), in which the three guṇas exist in (perfect) equilibrium. The (cosmic) egg that was formerly created by Viriñci, and which consists of Himself and exists in Himself, is called prakṛti by some scholars of philosophy. The egg, evolving into (creation) starting with mahat and ending with pṛthivī (i.e. gross elements), is called brahmāṇḍa, in which Brahmā became Virāj.[7] The sixth kośa,

---

[1] In this scheme Saṃkarṣaṇa stands for the individual self, Pradyumna is intelligence and Aniruddha is ego-consciousness.

[2] Saṃkarṣaṇa, Pradyumna and Aniruddha.

[3] Distinguishing them from ordinary living beings.

[4] Śānti is the substratum of Saṃkarṣaṇa, Pradyumna and Aniruddha I have accepted the alternative reading in the Mss: E and I, viz. *trayas te*.

[5] Mahālakṣmī presides over māyākośa. Her further manifestations as Mahālakṣmī, Mahākālī and Mahāvidyā respectively reveal the three guṇas rajas, tamas and sattva incorporated in the prakṛtikośa.

[6] See ch. V, 6-14.

[7] cf. Nṛ.U.U., 9; Chūlikā, 13; R.U.U. 13.

comprised of bodies of living beings incorporating organs and limbs, gradually became gross.[1] These are the six descents of myself, who am called the Absolute.

26. In the first kośa God Himself exists in all three[2] types of I-hood. In the other five kośas the jīvas (manifestations of God) exist in diverse forms.

27-28. (These) suffer different fates resulting from (deeds) classified as good or bad. But the three divine goddesses and the pairs (emanating from them) and their incarnations in the egg are created to (share my) sovereignty, and are not affected by the results of their deeds.[3]

29-31. The bodies of both (gods and goddesses) are not products of prakṛti (i.e. are not influenced by the three guṇas). In the five other kośas, jīvas manifest themselves on different levels of existence, starting from the (celestial) gods and ending with the immovables (i.e. the plants), and proceed (from life to life) affected by their deeds. Having destroyed the effects of their deeds (*adhikāra*)[4] through intense righteousness, living beings gain abundant knowledge and yoga redeems their sins, whereafter they start ascending the kośas step by step and never fall downwards.

32. Once having attained the level of satyaloka, from there onwards they do not return. (They stay there) or proceed higher (up).

33. Śakra:—O Goddess, who appearest from the milky ocean, wife of the God Padmanābha, I prostrate myself before Thee, who art lotus-born. Deign to explain who a living being is.

34. Śrī:—The primordial, absolute I-hood of Hari is myself and I am the transcendental, supreme Goddess. O celestial Śakra, it is held that I, the above-mentioned, have four states.

35. One of these states is (that of) pramātā (the knower); the next is (that of) antaḥkaraṇa (inner sense); the third (state) is (that of the) external senses and the fourth (state) is the state of (the created) objects (*bhāvabhūmikā*).

---

[1] These six kośas are the stages through which Śakti gradually becomes gross or empirical.

[2] Śaktikośa consists of Vāsudeva in whom Saṃkarṣaṇa, Pradyumna and Aniruddha lie dormant and Vāsudeva's I-hood, Śānti, contains their three I-hoods.

[3] These are part of the pure creation and so are not affected by karman.

[4] Adhikāra in this sense is adopted in the V.S. 3.3.32.

36-37. Pramātā is said to consist of the sentient and is said to be a finite state of mine. Though I am not limited by place, time, etc., yet of my own free will I (voluntarily) impose limitations on myself without, however, abandoning my true nature (i.e. my eternal, transcendental nature). The first limitation that occurs in this way is called pramātā.

38. Just as this universe is enclosed within me, who am consciousness, so also is it enclosed within the knower in the same way as a hill is enclosed in a mirror.[1]

39-41. The uniqueness of the knower, or his twofold, threefold, fourfold, or thirty-fivefold aspects are explained (as follows). He is unique as identical with the revealing Self; as the knower and the objects known, he is twofold; he is threefold when the process of cognition is added (to the list),[2] and as identified with all the cosmic principles, he is thirty-seven in number.

41-42. Śakra:—O lotus-eyed Goddess, what are these principles, how many are they, what are their characteristics? I prostrate myself before Thee, who wast born in the sea. Since I ask, deign to answer me.

42-44. Śrī:—The elements classified according to their gross and subtle forms number ten; the senses also number ten when divided into their cognitive and conative groups. The inner senses are three in number. The realities propounded by the Sāttvatas are: prakṛti, prasūti and māyā; then sattva, rajas and tamas; kāla, niyati (fate), śakti, Puruṣa, absolute space (*paramaṃ nabhaḥ*) and Bhagavān (God).

45. Śakra:—I prostrate myself before Thee, O Goddess Padmā. I have heard the list of principles from thy lotus mouth. Now deign to explain them to me.

---

[1] Influence of the Vedāntic theory of reflection.

[2] The knower's fourfold aspect is not described, but obviously it is *māna*, *mātā*, *meya* and *miti*, respectively instrument of knowledge, subject of knowledge, object of knowledge and cognition.

CHAPTER SEVEN

TATTVAS AND THE JĪVA AS THE OBJECT AND SUBJECT OF KNOWLEDGE

1. Śrī:—O Śakra, I shall now describe the gradual (development of) the courses (*paddhati*) of the cosmic principles (*tattvas*). This tattva-paddhati is said to be pure, impure or mixed.

2-3. God (Bhagavān) is known to be the eternal supreme Self (soul): absolutely unlimited by form, place or time; (pure) like the cloudless sky; (tranquil) like a calm sea; pure (*svaccha*) and absolute (*svacchanda*) consciousness—the great ocean, as it were, of ever existent bliss.

4. Nārāyaṇī is His supreme I-hood, His eternal Godhood. She is absolute, subtle, undifferentiated and without taint.

5-7. When, as it were, in the great ocean of the six (divine) attributes, jñāna (knowledge), śakti (potency), bala (irresistibility), aiśvarya (majesty), vīrya (valour) and tejas (indefatigability) simultaneously enter the active state (*unmeṣa*), that primary (state) consists of both the essence of existence and the state of existence, and is depicted in two ways: the essence of existence is Vāsudeva, and His state of existence is Vāsudeva-hood (Vāsudevatā), which is called Śānti and is identified with me, the eternal Goddess. I have already explained the Vyūhas such as Saṃkarṣaṇa etc. along with their I-hood.[1]

8. These three (Vyūhas) together with that which is the aggregate of all four Vyūhas (Vāsudeva)—these four indicated by the term Bhagavat [2]—are, O Sureśvara, the sublimest reality unrelated to other principles.

9-10. The sky is the great firmament (*parama vyoma*); it is called the great space (*parama ākāśa*), where God Viṣṇu, the eternal supreme Self, divided Himself in two and sports with me, Ramā. That space, where all the six (divine) attributes become active, is called the supreme void.[3]

---

[1] Śrī, Sarasvatī and Rati. See ch. VI, 7-17.

[2] Bhagavat is the collective designation of the Vyūha manifestation of God in which all bhaga, or divine majesty is fully displayed.

[3] The Goloka.

11. Puruṣa (i.e. Samaṣṭipuruṣa otherwise known as Hiraṇyagarbha) is inherent in the aggregate of enjoyers (*bhoktā*), and is omniscient and omnipresent. All the eternal jīvas issue from a particle of Him.

12. At the time of dissolution, the beings (*jīvas*) who are identified with their deeds (*karmātmānaḥ*), become reabsorbed in this great Puruṣa. This is my state as knower (*mātṛdaśā*), which I have already described.[1]

13. Mahālakṣmī is the name the learned accord to the essence of Śakti. Niyati is Mahāvidyā and Kālī is time (*kāla*).

14. The three guṇas, sattva, rajas and tamas, have already been mentioned. Sattva is regarded as happiness (*sukha*), as being transparent, conducive to knowledge and light (*laghu*, i.e. subtle).

15. Rajas is regarded as misery,[2] full of movement, red and active. Tamas is known to be deluding, heavy (gross), black and repressive.

16. O Vāsava, I have already [3] revealed māyā, prasūti and prakṛti which are the three fundamental sources (producers) of the material world.

17. Elements (*bhūtāni*) are ten in number; and the senses (*khāni*) are thirteen. Earlier these twenty-three (*tattvas*) were clearly explained.[4]

18. The afore-said knower, who is my limited state, is pure consciousness. Illuminated by his inner consciousness, (the knower) exists like a mirror.

19. Now listen with concentration to his (the knower's) four states of existence. The first is when the cognizer exists as void [5] (*śūnyamaya*, i.e. unrelated), as when a person is unconscious etc.

20. Next, when in the state of deep sleep (*suṣupti*), the knower is said to exist in the form of prāṇa (vital air), because during the state of puruṣa's deep sleep only prāṇa is manifested.

[1] See ch. VI, 11-13 and 34-40.

[2] Rajas is conducive to action, which results in the living being's bondage to an existence entailing life and death and causing misery.

[3] See ch. VI, 43.

[4] See ch. V, 50-77.

[5] This is the turīya state when the individual self is identical with the unpolarized consciousness of the supreme Self. The explanation offered in verse 21 substantiates this. The term *śūnya* for unpolarized integral consciousness is unusual. Parallel use can be found in the Buddhist Tantras. Cf. D. L. Snellgrove, The Hevajra Tantra, part I, Oxford University Press 1959, p. 24.

21. Since in the states such as loss of consciousness, poisoning etc. even prāṇa reverts (to its source), puruṣa remains integrated with nothing but his own essence, so that in such cases he is regarded as being in the state of the void.

22-23. In the third state of dream (*svapna*), the knower is regarded as consisting of only eight cities (*aṣṭapurī*).[1] These eight are known to be: prāṇāḥ, the elements; karman, the senses; the three guṇas; the impressions left by previous experiences (*prāgvāsanā*); nescience (*avidyā*); and liṅga (śarīra, the transmigrating subtle body). These are called the eightfold city. In the dream state, the knower acts with volition aided by the inner organ.

24. When the embodied (being) [2] enters the waking state, its functions are performed through physical effort. These are the four states of Puruṣa. Now hear about my (i.e. jīva's) threefold state.

25. The three types of modifications (which limit puruṣa), finite knowledge, limited function and finite essential form, are his threefold state. Now hear a description of it.

26-27. Jīva's knowledge becomes finite through māyā's influence. His power of action undergoes limitation owing to the absence of the (divine attribute) aiśvarya. Not being Śakti, he is *aṇu* (atomic) in size. He is characterized in three ways as being *aṇu* (atomic in size), as limited in his capacity to act (*kiñcitkara*), and as possessing finite knowledge (*kiñcijjña*).[3] I have already explained (the jīva's) dual and single states.

28. Thus I have now fully described my state as knower (*mātṛdaśā*). Now Śakra, hear about my state that relates to intelligence (*āntaḥkaraṇikī*).

29. I am absolute knowledge and have voluntarily become sentient;[4] from that (first) sentient state I have continued to descend step by step (i.e. to become more and more limited).

30. Mind, which limits the sentient (*caitya*), is called the inner

---

[1] Cf. Ka.U. 2.2, 1. for the concept of a city to represent the embodied self (*jīva*).

[2] Cf. Bh.G. 2. 13, 22, 30 and 59 for the term *dehin* for the self.

[3] As opposed to God's being omnipresent (*vibhu*), omnipotent (*sarvakṛt*) and omniscient (*sarvajña*).

[4] Absolute consciousness becomes limited consciousness as the individual self. But there is an echo of the materialistic notion that the individual self has consciousness as its quality.

sense (*antaḥkaraṇa*) and that has three components, viz. mind (*manas*), intelligence (*buddhi*) and egohood (*ahaṃkāra*).

31-32. Vikalpa (polarization in subject and object), adhyavasāya (decision) and abhimāna (ego-sensation) are their respective functions. Mind receives the polarized knowledge (*vikalpayati*); ahaṃkāra makes it personal (creates the impression that it concerns one's own person, *abhimanyate*); and buddhi, always infused by the sentient (being), takes a decision about the objects (of cognition). Buddhi is said to be related to the ātman (self), whereas decision is phenomenal (*ādhibhautika*).

33-34. Sheltered in the mirror of buddhi, kṣetrajña (i.e. the jīva) is the divinity (*adhidaivata*) there (in buddhi). Ahaṃkṛti (ego-hood) is spiritual, whereas the ego-sensation is phenomenal. Rudra is the divinity there (of ego-sensation). Mind is spiritual, polarized knowledge is phenomenal and Candra is its divinity.

35. In the sphere of action, the respective qualities of these (viz. intelligence, ego-hood and mind) are prāṇa, saṃrambha and saṃkalpa.[1] Prāṇa is said to be activity (*prayatna*); and saṃrambha is called self-esteem (*garva*).

36. Self-esteem is awareness of owning the fruits of one's deeds and that is called saṃrambha (zeal). Scholars call the loss of indifference (i.e. the awakening of interest) saṃkalpa, which is a quality of the mind.

37-38. Thus I have finished describing my second state, viz. the āntaḥkaraṇikī. Passing on from my āntaḥkaraṇikī state, I gradually become grosser and am called the external senses. I have previously explained all these external senses.

39. It is indeed the mind that functions through the activities of the cognitive senses. (When) the eyes see an object, it is the mind that (actually) cognizes the object in polarized knowledge.

40. (Then) ahaṃkāra relates the object of the polarized visual knowledge to the self, whereafter buddhi, having classified it, presents it to the kṣetrajña (self).

41. The reverse course is considered to take place in the function-

---

[1] Each of the three components of the inner sense has two aspects, one representing sensation and the other volition. Thus buddhi has decision as its first aspect and prāṇa as its second; ahaṃkāra has ego-sensation and zeal; mind has polarized knowledge and saṃkalpa.

ing of the conative senses, because acts such as speech etc. take place only after the functioning of saṃkalpa etc. (decision etc.).

42. All the particulars about these, such as (the classification of) adhyātma etc. have been discussed before. This completes the description of (my) third state as inherent in the external senses.

43. Now hear me describe my fourth state as the objects of cognition. Objects are of two kinds; those that are external and those that are internal.

44. Examples of external objects are blue, yellow etc.; whereas pleasure, pain etc. are internal objects. In these four states I become gross.

45-47. Owing to the (influence) of polarization into subject and object in (the perceiver's) own mind, although I am perceived, I am not recognized. (When) guided by virtuous preceptors, in the course of keen speculation, the intelligent clearly recognize me (as manifest) in all objects, and thus the whole range of created objects is dissolved, then I manifest myself as absolute, complete consciousness, pure and purer (than anything else) and am known as the instrument.[1]

48. And becoming still more transparent, I manifest myself in the knower as consisting of pure consciousness. After having realized me in both my descending and ascending states, (the devotee), whose mind is fixed upon me and whose existence (life) is dedicated to me, attains my status.

---

[1] The recognition of Śakti and God in true perspective is emancipation and, as such, Śakti is the aim of spiritual endeavour, but she is also the instrument assisting the aspirant to that end by voluntarily revealing herself to his vision.

CHAPTER EIGHT

THE AVATĀRAS OF LAKṢMĪ IN THE SIX SHEATHS

1. Śakra:—I salute Thee, who wast born in the ocean, I salute Thee lotus-born; O Thou, who abidest in the lotus and art the wife of Nārāyaṇa, I salute (Thee).

2. O Padmā, deign to describe fully to me, who request Thee, all (the forms of) Thy descents in the five sheaths which have been mentioned.[1]

3. Deign, O eternal omniscient goddess, to tell me what objects they possess, what their characteristics are, how many they are, and what their essential nature is.

4-8. Śrī:—Brahman is Nārāyaṇa, the single, void, pure and flawless one, devoid of any disturbance (*ataraṅga*), undefinable, without vibration, matchless, unqualified, integral, undifferentiated and changeless. All (things) contained in this world that are cognized, mentioned in the scriptures, or inferred, (that is to say) all that can be apprehended (directly or indirectly) through the three instruments of knowledge, whether of a positive or a negative nature, whether movable or immovable, subtle or gross, sentient or insentient, all these consist of Brahman, of Nārāyaṇa, second to none. (Brahman) is bliss without nescience (*avidyā*), pure, absolute and concentrated consciousness consisting of both the existent (reality) and its state of existence; the divine and ultimate goal of the (spiritual) way. It (Brahman) differentiates (Itself) in two ways, both as the possessor of Śakti and as the Śakti (herself).

9. That absolute Brahman, as the possessor of Śakti, is (manifest) as Nārāyaṇa, the I-entity, i.e. the existent (principle). As Śakti, (It) is Nārāyaṇī, who is myself, the I-hood of (Nārāyaṇa) representing (His) state of existence (*bhāva*).

10. There is no place where He exists without me. There is no place that contains me without containing Him.

11. We, the source of all, are sometimes described singly and

---

[1] The sheaths from māyā to jīvadeha. Śakti, the primary sheath, is excluded because, since it is Śakti's primary state of existence it cannot be listed as her descent.

sometimes dually [1] in the scriptures that have reached, as it were, the other side of the ocean of the cosmic principles.[2]

12. Some (scriptures) describe creation (as evolving) out of (the principle representing) the state of existence (of Nārāyaṇa, i.e. *bhāva*); in others, it is described (as evolving) out of the existent (reality, i.e. *bhavat*); while in yet others (it is said to evolve) out of both the existent reality and its state of existence; (but since all refer to the same reality, i.e. Brahman) the learned are not confused by them.

13. When Nārāyaṇa descends alone to further the cause of the gods, I then manifest the active aspect of His nature.

14. When (on the other hand) I descend alone in order to help the gods, then it is He, God, the I-entity, who manifests His I-hood in me.

15. When in order to benefit the gods, each of us descends in a similar manner (i.e. as separate incarnations), we exist (inseparably in each other) as the existent reality and as its state of existence.[3]

16-17. While the realities remain thus (i.e. are absolutely integrated), the position of the incarnations is (as follows). Listen (now). Aniruddha is the eternal omnipresent divine being, the supreme deity, who emerged, O Vāsava, from Mahāvidyā.[4] I then emanated out of myself, Mahālakṣmī, and am called Kamalā.

18. This divine couple are considered to be the parents of the universe. In the incarnation as Padmanābha,[5] neither of them has been born of parents (*ayonija*).

19. The incarnation of Nārāyaṇa known as the lord of Śakti has many forms. I follow His functions (*anuvratā*) in all cases.

20. (My descents may be of) one form, two forms, four forms, six forms, eight forms, or again twelve forms. Now hear my names (in these forms).

21. Bearing the name Śrī, I, the fair one, sit on the lap of the

---

[1] This source is the śakti sheath, the monistic aspect of which is represented by Brahman, and the dualistic aspect by the Lakṣmī-Nārāyaṇa pair.

[2] Scriptures that deal exhaustively with cosmology and the realities.

[3] That is to say that in those incarnations Śakti and God exist inseparably both as the state and the essence of existence, e.g. Kṛṣṇa and Rukmiṇī.

[4] See ch. VI, 18-20.

[5] In the prasūtikośa.

two-armed God.[1] O Vāsava, I am (called) Śrī and Puṣṭi when I am manifested on either side of Him.[2]

22. Viṣṇu enjoys me in the forms of Śrī, Kīrti, Jayā and Māyā (when I am manifested) on all four sides of Him.

23-25. O Vāsava, I manifest myself around Him in a hexagonal position in six forms, and now listen to their names. (These are) Śuddhi, Nirañjanā, Nityā, Jñānaśakti, Aparājitā and the sixth, is supreme prakṛti. I assume eight forms when occupying the eight sides [3] of the same (God). (My names then are) Lakṣmī, Sarasvatī, Sarvakāmadā, Prītivardhinī, Yaśaskarī, Śāntidā, Tuṣṭidā and the eighth is Puṣṭi.

26-27. When I (surround) Him and assume twelve forms in double hexagonal position (I am called) Śrī, Kāmeśvarī, Kānti, Kriyā, Śakti, Vibhūti, Icchā, Prīti, Rati, Māyā, Dhī and Mahiman. Following the same order I surround the four-armed God in six (forms).[4]

28-29. O Vāsava, (likewise) I differentiate myself in multiple forms through various manifestations of myself as (Śakti) of the same (God) who possesses six, eight, fourteen, sixteen or eighteen arms (according to His various manifestations).

30. I surround the incarnation of Viṣṇu called Sindhuśāyī [5] in four forms.

31-36. (These) different (forms are) Lakṣmī, Nidrā, Prīti and Vidyā. When Viṣṇu incarnates as Śrīpati, I, named Śrī, occupy his left side, When Viṣṇu appears in the incarnation named Pārijātajit I am seated on Hari's left thigh, with my hand resting on His shoulder. Assuming the form of a ship, I follow in Viṣṇu's wake when He appears in the auspicious incarnation of Mīnadhara.[6] The Traivikrama [7] appearance is considered to be Viṣṇu's supreme

---

[1] Nārāyaṇa.

[2] The positions of the deities are indicated with a precision that image makers are obliged to observe.

[3] The four cardinal points of the compass and the four diagonals intersecting them.

[4] The śakti-manifestations viz. Śrī; Śrī and Puṣṭi; and Śrī, Kīrti, Jayā and Māyā belong solely to the two-armed image of Nārāyaṇa. Other afore-said groups of śakti-manifestations may accompany either the two-armed or the four-armed image of Nārāyaṇa.

[5] The Anantaśāyī incarnation, cf. Mā.P. 276, 8.

[6] Cf. Bhā.P. VIII, 24; II, 7, 12 and XI, 4, 18.

[7] Cf. Br. P. III, 3, 118 and IV, 34, 79; Mā.P. 176, 59; 53, 45 and 260, 36. Viṣ.P. V, 5, 17 and Vā.P. 108, 38.

manifestation, (and then) I flow out of His feet as (the) delightful Gaṅgā. I occupy the four sides of Hari in four forms when He is incarnated as Anantaśayana,[1] and am then called Lakṣmī, Cintā, Nidrā and Puṣṭi.

37-44. In this way I appear jointly with (each of His incarnations) in the (cosmic) egg. When the incarnations in the cosmic egg appear singly then too I appear there in the same way but separately co-operating in their (specific) functions. When Viṣṇu descends as Varāha [2] who is famous in the Vedas, I too appear separately and am called Bhū. (When He appears as) the ancient incarnation of Viṣṇu called Dharma,[3] at that time I, Śrī, become the famous Bhārgavī. (At the time of) the incarnation called Dattātreya,[4] the son of Atri, I emerge from the lake to be enjoyed by him. (At the time of) the holy incarnation of Viṣṇu called Vāmana,[5] I, Padmā, appear and am known by the name Padmā. When Viṣṇu descends as Rāma,[6] the son of Bhṛgu, I then become the earth (Dharaṇī), the unborn Śakti. At the time of God's descent as holy Rāma, the son of Daśaratha, from the field in which Janaka performs his sacrifice, I spring out of the furrow made by his plough, and am named Sītā, the illustrious destroyer of Daśānana.

45-50. When at Madhurā Viṣṇu will descend in four forms (Balarāma, Kṛṣṇa, Pradyumna, Aniruddha), I too shall manifest myself in four forms called Revatī, Rukmiṇī, Rati and Uṣā.[7] In God's other incarnation as the enchanting Buddha, (I am) Tārā, also known as Dhārā.[8] When Viṣṇu descends singly as Dhruva [9]

---

[1] Same as Sindhuśāyī.

[2] Cf. Bhā.P. III, 13, 18-45 and X, 2, 40.

[3] Cf. Bhā.P. III, 12, 25 and IV, 1, 48-50; Br.P. II, 9, 1, 49-50 and IV, 1, 40.

[4] Cf. Bhā.P. II, 7, 4; IV, 1, 15 and 33; XI, 4, 17; Br.P. III, 8, 82 and IV, 28, 80. Vā.P. 70, 76-8.

[5] Cf. Bhā.P. I, 3, 19; II, 7, 17-18; VIII, 18, 20-32; VIII, 19; VIII, 21 and X, 62, 2.

[6] Rāma bearing the axe; cf. Bhā.P. IX, 15, 13 to end.

[7] Cf. Bhā.P. I, 11, 16; X, 50, 12-32; I, 10, 29.

[8] The identification of Tārā and Dhārā is an interesting point. I have not yet found any Buddhist text confirming this identity. Dhārā could be a shortened form of Vasudhārā or Basundharā, corresponding to Bhū śakti (cf. J. Gonda, Nominal compounds in Sanskrit, in Pratidānam, The Hague 1968, p. 220). The Sādhanamālā does not describe Dhārā, but in one place a passing reference is made to this goddess as presiding over the third finger of the adept: Sādhanamālā, Vol. I, Gaekwad's Oriental Series No. 26, Baroda 1968, p. 69.

[9] Cf. Bhā.P. I, 3, 17 and VIII, 8, 41-46.

etc., then I only form their bodies and am to be enjoyed by them. But in my incarnation as the enchantress holding nectar, (God) is manifest both as the existent reality and as its state of existence (*bhavat* and *bhāva*) perceived in a single form, of which the gods saw the male form whereas the others (i.e. the demons, saw) the female form.

50. Thus I have explained my marvellous incarnations either in conjunction with (god) or singly. Now, O lord of gods, hear from me about my exclusive incarnations.[1]

---

[1] Śakti's incarnations in fulfilment of her purpose, unaccompanied by God's manifest descent on earth as her spouse or partner.

CHAPTER NINE

THE EXCLUSIVE INCARNATIONS OF ŚAKTI

1. I am Goddess Nārāyaṇī, ever co-operating in performing the functions of Nārāyaṇa, who consists of jñāna (knowledge), ānanda (bliss) and kriyā (activity); and I too consist of knowledge, bliss and activity.

2. There is not a single place nor moment when it is possible for me to exist without Him, or for Him to exist without me.

3. Serving some specific purpose, we exercise our supreme power to manifest ourselves in a form that may be regarded as normal, or even as supra-normal.[1]

4-5. (When), on account of the austerities practised by the world-destroying demons, Brahmā and the other (high gods) were obliged to grant their excellent boons, (then) in order to please the gods, we, the two eternal ones, assumed different forms to meet the particular requirements of each occasion, and roamed about to fulfil the purpose of the gods.

6. Concealing my transcendental nature through my inscrutable power (*māyā*), I, through my (divine) capacity, descend (to this earth) for the purpose of slaying these destroyers.

7. In the beginning, I, the holy Goddess, (manifested myself) as the goddess called Mahālakṣmī. Next I became two by assuming the forms of Kṛṣṇā and Brāhmī.[2]

8-11. These are my three supreme forms, as classified by the three guṇas. O Śakra, during the reign of Svāyambhuva (Manu), for the benefit of all worlds, I, Mahālakṣmī,[3] appeared as Mahiṣa-mardinī. The elements of my śakti inherent in each god combined to constitute my dazzlingly beautiful form (of Mahiṣamardinī). O king of gods, the śaktis belonging to the special weapons of each god turned into my weapons without undergoing change of form.

---

[1] As normal human beings such as Dhruva, or as supra-normal manifestations such as Nṛsiṃhāvatāra.

[2] Kṛṣṇā is the dark goddess Mahākālī and Brāhmī is Mahāvidyā. Cf. ch. IV, 57-67.

[3] See Mā.P. chs. 74-76.

Worshipped by the gods I, in that form (Mahiṣamardinī), instantaneously slew the (demon) Mahiṣa.

12. Then the laudatory hymn (addressed) to the slayer of Mahiṣa, which opens with the words *devyā yayā* etc. and fulfils every wish, was revealed to all the gods including Indra and the sages.[1]

13. O king of the gods, Brahmins skilled in the Vedas relate in detail (Mahiṣamardinī's) origin, prowess in battle and the eulogies (addressed to her).

14. He who praises, meditates on, or even bows down to so powerful a goddess, is rewarded with everlasting supremacy.

15. You should realize that the mysterious (*duratyayā*) goddess, identified with Hari's meditative slumber (*yoganidrā*), is myself, the eternal goddess in the form of Mahākālī.

16. When the two (demons) became overbearing because Viṣṇu, the God of gods, had granted their boon, it was she (Yoganidrā) who slew Madhu and Kaiṭabha.[2]

17. O Puraṃdara, in order to praise me, the Goddess Yoganidrā, for ever, the laudatory hymn, starting with the words *Viśveśvarī* etc.,[3] was revealed to Brahmā.

18. The inscrutable power of the mysterious Mahākālī, who belongs to Viṣṇu, is such that when gratified by praise she makes the praiser master of the movables and immovables in this world.

19. The brahmavādins (who expound the Vedas) hold that constant reminder of this goddess's origin and exploits accompanied by the chanting of her praises, has a beneficial effect on all living beings.

20-21. O Śakra, during the period of Tāmasa (Manu) I, the supreme Mahāvidyā, was Kauśikī, who sprang from the body of Gaurī to slay all those notorious demons, including Śumbha and Niśumbha. Thereby I rescued the worlds and helped the gods.

22-23. In order to help me (fight the demons), my powers inherent in the bodies of the greatest of gods manifested themselves in diverse forms. (By virtue of these powers), having slain the demon chieftains who deserved death, I drew back to within myself all my infinitesimal particles (lit. drops).

---

[1] Mā.P. 76, 3-35.
[2] Mā.P. 73.
[3] Mā.P. 73, 53-67.

24-25. Whereafter I killed those two (demons) Śumbha and Niśumbha. Then to all the gods led by Agni (the fire god) was revealed the very beautiful hymn praising me, which is known as the eulogy of Nārāyaṇī and opens with the words *Devi prapannārtihare prasīda* etc.[1]

26. O lord of all gods, when worshipped with devotion I, the goddess Kauśikī fulfiller of many desires, bestow omniscience (on the devotee).

27. The ancient brāhmins, who are conversant with the Vedas and auxiliary sciences, (pay homage to me) in three ways by reciting accounts of my origin and exploits in battle and by extolling (me).

28. During the period of Vaivasvata (Manu), these demons Śumbha and Niśumbha will be reborn (and), intoxicated by the granting of their boon, will torment the gods.

29. I shall then be born as Sunandā, child of Yaśodā, in the family of the cowherd Nanda and, residing on the Vindhya, I shall slay them (the demons).[2]

30. Once more descending to earth in a terrible form, I shall kill the mighty demons of the Vipracitti line.

31. And whilst devouring those terrifying demons of Vipracitti lineage, my teeth will become as red as the flowers of the pomegranate tree.

32. Then all the gods and men on earth will propitiate me by calling me Raktadantikā (the Red-toothed one) for ever.[3]

33-34. O Śakra, during that period in the fortieth era, drought and scarcity of water will prevail all over the earth for one hundred years. When the sages then remember me, I shall appear on earth as (an) unborn [4] (deity) and shall cast a glance [5] on those sages with my hundred eyes.

35-36. O Śakra, men will then extol me as the hundred-eyed (deity) and I shall nourish the whole world with wonderful life-sustaining plants issuing from my own body and filled with (my

---

[1] Mā.P. 83, 2-35.
[2] Mā.P. 83, 38-39.
[3] Mā.P. 83, 40-42.
[4] i.e. not in mortal frame, hence as a goddess.
[5] For the significance of a divinity's glance cf. J. Gonda, Eye and Gaze in the Veda, Amsterdam 1969, passim.

essence: *āviṣṭaiḥ*). Then, Vāsava, the gods will worship me as Śākambharī [1] (the embodiment of vegetation).

37. Whereupon I shall indeed slay the great demon called Durga and gain renown as the goddess Durgā.[2]

38. O Śakra, he who praises, meditates on, worships and salutes Śākambharī obtains quick and permanent satisfaction of his desires for food and drink.

39-41. During the fiftieth era containing four ages, when supplicated by the sages I shall appear on the Himālayas in a beautiful (but) at the same time ferocious form; (and) to protect the sages I shall devour the demons. Then all the sages with heads humbly bowed will eagerly praise me, the terrible, but protective deity (with the hymn that starts) with the words *Bhīme devi prasīda* etc.[3]

41-43. During the sixtieth era there will be one demon, called Aruṇa who will do much harm to men and sages. Then I shall appear in bee-form incorporating innumerable bees, and I shall slay the mighty demon and rescue the three worlds. From then on people will praise me for ever and address me as Bhrāmarī.[4]

44. Thus on each occasion that the demons disturb the earth, I shall descend on (the earth) to kill these powerful asuras.

45. O Śakra, here I have given you a brief account of my mysterious, exclusive and fearless incarnations.

46. Ranking highest among these is said to be the immutable, mighty, illustrious and supreme Goddess Mahālakṣmī, the source (*prakṛti*).

47. In praise of her the holy hymn *namo devyā* etc., which ensures the fulfilment of wishes, was revealed to all the gods, headed by Brahmā.[5]

48. Here (in this world) he who daily worships me, (who am) this Goddess, by reciting these laudatory hymns, overcomes all difficulties and attains great prosperity.

49-50. O virtuous Śakra, formerly during the period of Svārociṣa (Manu), Vasiṣṭha told the noble-souled king Suratha all about my

[1] Mā.P. 83, 45-46.
[2] Mā.P. 83, 46.
[3] Mā.P. 83, 48.
[4] Mā.P. 83, 49-50.
[5] Mā.P. 77, 7-39.

births and exploits when I manifested myself as the pure Mahālakṣmī, and (recited) the hymn describing my divine power, etc.

51-55. And ever reverent and devoted to me, Vasiṣṭha, whose mind was filled with my descents, exploits and praise of me, chanted (the laudatory hymn) to humble and dispirited Samādhi of Vaiśya descent.[1] He who has learnt about these from a brāhmin, after dispelling all illusion, obtains true knowledge, gains prosperity and succeeds in destroying all effects of evil; and assisted by me, achieves good fortune and fame. Although these are my exclusive (appearances), yet without Viṣṇu I have no separate existence; hence here (in these, my manifestations) He exists as my Self. The reason for this is that we are inseparable and are inherent in each other.

56-59. The supreme God of gods ever abides in me and I, the ever-existent, in Him. Thus, Śakra, I have briefly revealed to you my incarnations, along with their modalities, which appear within the five sheaths (other than the pure sheath). In the absolute, and its natural state manifested in the pure sheath, the (inseparable) existence of myself and Viṣṇu must also be viewed in the same light. Discerning that in my generally accepted appearance my nature consists of a combination of various natures, and worshipping me in diverse ways, (the aspirant) escapes the misery caused by his deeds and attains my own state of existence (*madbhāvam*).

---

[1] Mā.P. 73, 15-27.

CHAPTER TEN

THE THREE TYPES OF GOD'S AVATĀRAS

1. Śakra:—I salute thee, brought into being through the mighty efforts of the gods to churn the milky ocean, sister [1] of the moon of immortal origin.

2. From thy own lotus-mouth have I heard all about thy modalities characterized by bhāva (the state of absolute existence). Now I want to know about thy various incarnations, characterized by Being (*bhavat*, i.e. Nārāyaṇa).

3. O Ambujā, what are the forms of all those incarnations (avatāras) of Viṣṇu, how many are they? Asking this, I pay thee obeisance. O thou, seated on the lotus, deign to tell me.

4. Śrī:—Well Śakra, I shall enlighten you about all Viṣṇu's modifications that are characterized by bhavat, disclosing their number and their nature.

5. Brahman possesses the six (divine) attributes, is pure, flawless, undecaying, constant, all-powerful (possessed of all śaktis), undaunted and has transcendental knowledge.

6-7. It was first manifested both as the possessor of Śakti and as the Śakti herself. As the possessor of Śakti, It exists as Nārāyaṇa, the supreme God, (and) I am His, the omnipresent One's ever-existent, omnipotent Śakti. To benefit the world both of us [2] underwent various modifications (incarnations).

8. I have already told you about my different avatāras. Now listen to me describing the modifications of Viṣṇu, the unmodifiable.

9-11. In order to serve the world, the Lord of the world, who presides over and makes use of me, His own Śakti—the great mysterious source (*prakṛti*)—manifests Himself in three (types of) forms which are supra-phenomenal, matchless, and resplendent with inconceivable majesty. The first (of these three types) is the

---

[1] As both the moon and Lakṣmī rose out of the ocean they are considered to be sisters. See Viṣ.P. I, 9, 97-100.

[2] In all God's manifestations and descents Śakti becomes His 'body.' Thus Śakti, the divine presence is manifest in all God's manifestations including the Vyūhas.

absolute form; the second is when (He is manifest) in the Vyūha-form; (the third type) is when He is manifest in the Vibhava-forms. Thus, to help His devotee, the glorious and all-pervasive God appears in various forms.

12. He assumes a form which is incomparable, undefinable, supreme, refreshing to all and lovely as tens of thousands of full moons shining together.

13-14. His two hands are held in the gesture of granting boons and promising protection; he is lotus-eyed and his hands are traced with lines representing the (auspicious) disc and conch-shell; his legs are in the normal posture (i.e. in sthānaka posture); he is exquisitely beautiful, adorned with all six of his own attributes.

15-16. He is erect with perfectly proportioned limbs and has a uniformly handsome body richly adorned with splendid ornaments. His traits such as acyuta etc. invariably surround him like a halo and are as white as a surging sea of nectar. This is said to be Viṣṇu's supreme and most exalted form, representing his absolute manifestation.[1]

17. Sages, who have achieved the goal of their meditation, worship in their hearts this (form) belonging to the fourth (*turya*) state. Next I shall tell you of the second (type of) form consisting of Vyūha.

18. The deity divides his Vyūha-self into four as Vāsudeva etc. spread over (the four points of the compass), the East etc., and pervades the states of deep sleep (*suṣupti*) etc.

19-21. The primary form of all these (Vyūha-forms) is considered to be identical in posture. The first (of these four Vyūha-)forms possesses (all) six (divine) attributes, and I have mentioned how the (three) pairs of jñāna etc. are assigned to the remaining (three Vyūha-forms). O Vāsava, the first fourfold form belonging to the suṣupti state contains the seed of all activity. Characterized as a pleasurable vibration[2] with the brilliance of thousands of fires, suns and moons, it is the seat from which all forms of diversity (polarized thinking) arise.

22-25. Then in the svapna (dream) state too, the deity, the excellent Person, divides himself into (four) as Vāsudeva etc.

---

[1] In His absolute state of existence Viṣṇu is envisaged as possessing only two hands, since additional limbs indicate progressive grossness.

[2] *Ānandaspandalakṣaṇam.*

spread over east etc. and pervades that (state) in (those) four forms marvellously coloured white, red, gold and like a cloud (respectively). These (four forms) possess the (divine) attributes either in aggregate or in pairs (in the manner described before).[1] This is the second form, beautiful as a profusion of nectar, and fulfiliing the (human) aspiration of (either) liberation (or) enjoyment, and destroying the seed of worldly existence.

25-27. Next, in the state of jāgrat (waking), the omnipresent deity sportively divides himself into four Vyūha-forms called Vāsudeva etc. and respectively coloured white, red etc. These possess four arms, a serene countenance, marks of the śaṃkha (shell) and the cakra (disc) etc. and are decorated with various banners.

27-31. There (in that jāgrat state) the first form of God is as (white) as snow or the kunda (jasmine) flower or the moon. He has four arms, a handsome face, eyes resembling a lotus, wears yellow silk raiment and displays the banner of the bird (Garuḍa).[2] His main right hand is held in the gesture of protecting (*abhaya*) the timid; his main left hand holds the sacred conch-shell. His other right hand holds the disc called Sudarśana, (and) in his other left hand he holds a heavy mace resting on the ground. Vāsudeva's appearance should be so visualized in the East.

31-33. With a form like a mound of vermilion (i.e. red), a handsome face, four hands, wearing raiment as (yellow as) the atasī flower, displaying the standard of tāla (palm),[3] his two main hands are held in the same posture as God's, whereas the other two hands hold a plough instead of a disc and a club instead of a mace. Thus should Saṃkarṣaṇa be envisaged in the South.

34-36. Glowing like a host of fireflies assembled at nightfall in the rainy season, wearing a raiment of red silk, adorned with the banner of makara (fish), with a handsome face and four arms, thus appears the third (form) of God. The two main hands of this noble one are in the same position as in the previous (form); the other left hand holds a bow and the right holds five arrows. This form known as Pradyumna should be visualized in the West.

---

[1] See ch. II, 39-55.

[2] Vāsudeva's standard is stamped with the sign of Garuḍa and is therefore called the Garuḍa-standard.

[3] Besides other characteristic insignia, Saṃkarṣaṇa, being identical with Balarāma, possesses the latter's palm-tree-standard.

37-39. (Dark) like a mound of collyrium covered by a cloth of flawless yellow, possessing four arms, large eyes, adorned with the standard of the deer, (the fourth form of God) should be so visualized. His two main hands are held in the same positions as in his previous (form), while the two other hands from right to left hold sword and shield respectively. Thus should Aniruddha be visualized in the North. All these (Vyūha-forms) wear a garland of flowers of all seasons (*vanamālā*) and the mark made by śrīvatsa.[1]

40. This unsurpassed fourfold deity pervading the state of jāgrat wears the kaustubha,[2] the king of jewels, on his chest.

41. One should recognize him, the divine one, to be the controller of existence, origination and dissolution, possessing all ornaments and as controlling the continuation of the world.

42. The three manifestations of the fourfold deity in the states of suṣupti etc. are well defined; but in the state of turya the Lord of All can only be inferred from His attributes.

43. Thus I have described Viṣṇu's second (type of) form, assumed through His urge to create the worlds aided by His (attributes) jñāna, kriyā etc.

44. Now hear about the third form of Viṣṇu known as Vibhava, manifest in the temples of the world in diverse images, efficacious in performing manifold deeds.

---

[1] See Vā.P. 96, 204 and Viṣ.P. V, 34, 17.

[2] See Bhā.P. II, 2, 10; VIII, 4, 19; XI, 14-40; XI, 27, 27 and XII, 11, 10.

CHAPTER ELEVEN

VIŚĀKHAYŪPA AND THE VIBHAVA INCARNATIONS

1. Śrī:—Viṣṇu Nārāyaṇa is pure, not governed (by anything), flawless, eternal, the possessor of Śrī and of the everlasting supreme soul.

2. He embodies the six (divine) attributes, is ever existent, supreme and the most exalted ever existing Brahman. I am His eternal Śakti (potency) and I possess all the attributes possessed by Him.

3. You should know that I co-exist with God (Viṣṇu) in all His states of existence. I am pure and absolute; the omnipotent (Śakti) belonging to Viṣṇu, the immutable.

4. Expanding my own state of existence (*bhāva*) consisting of both the pure and the impure, I am continuously producing the Vyūhas of Hari as distinguished by Paravyūha etc.

5-6. Whenever required, by aid of the pure sixfold (divine) attributes I instantly manifest God's different (forms) of bhavat (the absolute existing principle) by appearing in the diverse states of Vyūha etc. in whatever manner is appropriate. Without question I am the action (*vyāpāra*) of God.

7. All that I do is regarded as done by Him. In fact I am considered to be the function of God.

8. Thus, Śakra, I have revealed to you the absolute, as well as the Vyūha-forms (of God). Now hear about (His) third (type of) forms known as Vibhavas.[1]

9. The four states I have described,[2] starting with the turya state and ending with the jāgrat (waking) state, are pervaded by (the Vyūha-forms of God) originating with Vāsudeva and ending in Aniruddha.

10. As already explained to you, in each particular state the relevant fourfold (deity) appears in his own unmanifest or manifest form (as the case may be).

11. When one Vyūha emerges from a (previous) Vyūha, like one

[1] See Schrader, pp. 35-58.

[2] See ch. VII, 19-24.

step immediately follows the one that precedes it, all the intermediate space is filled with the brilliant energy (*tejas*) of (God).

12. That revered (divine entity) consisting of amassed brilliance is unmanifested and without embodiment and consists of reality, knowledge etc. and is called Viśākhayūpa.[1]

13. O Śakra, in each particular state, the four-branched embodiment of God, viz. Vāsudeva etc., is manifested in graduated order.

14. Thus when the vyūha develops out of the transition from the dream (*svapna*) state to the waking state, the great taijasa (the deity called Viśākhayūpa) is worshipped (filling all the space) lying between the start of the dream state and the end of the waking state.[2]

15-17. He is the holy god, Viśākhayūpa, the repository of dazzling energy. Aided by the six (divine) attributes, which are distributed in varying proportions over the three groups of the four deities, vested with the divine majesty relevant to each, and extending from the turya to the dream state with divine pure consciousness ranking foremost, He Himself splits His own self up into the forms of Vāsudeva etc.

17-19. Again at the time of the Vibhava[3] incarnations, the same Viśākhayūpa, not being divided in the fourfold embodiment,

---

[1] See Sā. S. ch. 4, 1-7. This is a great brilliant column divided into four sections. Each section is allocated to one of the Vyūha deities, but also contains all four of them respectively occupying the four points of the compass. This symbolizes the uninterrupted continuity of Vyūhas through all the four states of consciousness, namely: Vāsudeva's domain turīya, where there is no polarization; Saṃkarṣaṇa's domain suṣupti, where the first signs of polarization are faintly discernable; Pradyumna's domain svapna, where consciousness is subtly polarized; and Aniruddha's domain jāgrat, where consciousness is fully polarized and limited. These four deities Vāsudeva etc. being identical with God, each incorporates all four Vyūha deities and hence in each state all four are present. In each successive state they become more and more distinct to tally with the distinctive character of the main deity of the section. The entire column thus represents the one and single deity. See S. Gupta, Caturvyūha and the Viśākha-yūpa of the Pāñcarātra religion, Adyar Library Bulletin Vol. 35, parts 3-4, pp. 189-204.

[2] Viśākhayūpa extends over the states that follow after the suṣupti state and fills up the intermediary positions between two states as well as the states themselves. Hence it is the unmanifested totality of all Vyūha forms whether manifest or unmanifest. It is called taijasa, as in Vedāntic tradition that is the designation of consciousness in the svapna state. cf. M.U. I, 2-5 and II, 1.

[3] For a detailed description consult Schrader, pp. 42-49.

develops the Vibhavas. These Vibhava deities are considered to be Padmanābha etc.

19-25. Padmanābha, Dhruva, Ananta, Śaktīśa, Madhusūdana, Vidyādhideva, Kapila, Viśvarūpa, Vihaṅgama, Kroḍātmā, Vaḍavavaktra, Dharma, Vāgīśvara, Ekārṇavāntaḥśāyin, the tortoise-shaped deity, Varāha, Narasiṃha, Amṛtaharaṇa, divinely shaped Śrīpati, Kāntātman bearing amṛta, Rāhujit, Kālanemighna, Pārijātahara, Lokanātha, Śāntātmā, the great master Dattātreya, Nyagrodhaśāyin, Ekaśṛṅgatanu (the deity) in the form of a one-horned creature (i.e. the fish), the deity possessing a Vāmana (dwarf's) form, the all-pervading Trivikrama, Nara and Nārāyaṇa, Hari, Kṛṣṇa, Rāma with the burning eye, and the other Rāma with the bow, god Kalkin, Vedavid and Pātālaśayana. These thirty-eight[1] deities, (named) Padmanābha etc., are God's manifestations known as the Vibhava deities.

26. In fulfilment of a specific objective conceived by the all-pervasive Viśākhayūpa, manifestations called Vibhavas devolve into existence and their duties are clearly defined.

27. Padmanābha is stationed in the intermediary[2] region between the pure and the impure courses (i.e. creation). The other deities, viz. Dhruva etc., are on view in (various) temples of the world.

28. Their forms, weapons and other śaktis belonging to them are well known from the Sāttvata(-saṃhitā); so here these are only referred to by name.

29. The branches, viz. Vāsudeva etc., which are generally recognized as belonging to the all-pervasive God, have been extended by Lord Viśākhayūpa.

30. The deities (belonging to the group) starting with Keśava and ending with Dāmodara[3] are manifest in groups of three arising out of these four branches (of Viśākhayūpa) and are called Vyūhāntara (secondary Vyūha).

---

[1] Ahirbudhnya enumerates thirty-nine Vibhava manifestations of God Vāsudeva. As the list of names is almost identical in both texts, I presume that Ahirbudhnya reads Nara and Nārāyaṇa as two separate Vibhavas whereas L.T. treats them as one.

[2] Padmanābha is the only Vibhava deity whose domain is defined.

[3] These four groups consist of Keśava, Nārāyaṇa and Mādhava; Govinda, Viṣṇu and Madhusūdana; Trivikrama, Vāmana and Śrīdhara; Hṛṣīkeśa, Padmanābha and Dāmodara. These groups are respectively traceable to Vāsudeva, Saṃkarṣaṇa, Pradyumna and Aniruddha.

31. Again from the same branches the śaktis, viz. Śrī etc., originated in groups of three tallying with the aforesaid groups of threefold deities.

32. O king of the Tridaśa [1] (the gods), all these divine beings, from the Absolute down to the Vibhavas, possess bodies incorporating (all) the pure sixfold (divine) attributes.

33-36. O, Sureśvara, all weapons such as shells, discs etc. associated with these deities, (their) various ornaments, diverse garments, different forms of marks, standards, special colours such as white etc., diverse vehicles, such as satya [2] etc., the śaktis of various forms, that provide objects of enjoyment, the group (category) pertaining to the internal organ with all its functions (*vṛtti*), all other adornments shared in common with other puruṣas (deities)—O slayer of Bala, regard all these as composed of (all) six attributes.

37. It is I, consisting of pure consciousness and totally infused with (the whole range of) the six attributes, who assume each particular form as and when required in order to serve the world.

38. I have no (separate) existence apart from the Supreme God, nor has God Viṣṇu any existence apart from me.

39. Thus though we form a single entity, we remain divided in two, and (jointly) participate in whatever mode of appearance circumstances dictate.

40. Śakra:—I salute Thee, O daughter of the ocean; I salute Thee, Padmā. Deign to explain to me why the Supreme God chooses to manifest Himself in the diverse forms of Paravyūha etc.

41. Śrī:—The purpose of the diverse manifestations of the Supreme God as Paravyūha etc. is to benefit human beings and show compassion towards His devotees.

42. Śakra:—I salute Thee, O lotus-born, beloved of the Supreme

---

[1] 3 × 10 = 30, i.e. 33 gods. But later this term also meant possessing only three phases (*daśā*) of life, namely childhood, adolescence and youth, and no old age.

[2] Satya cannot be the name of any vehicle belonging to a deity. The J.S. enumerates a series of supreme Vāsudeva's successive manifestations, namely Acyuta, Satya and Puruṣa, which are identical with supreme Vāsudeva and represent His gradual limitation. The similes given there—lightning for Vāsudeva, for Acyuta a cloud clinging to the sun (representing Vāsudeva), for Satya a bubble produced by the ocean (representing Acyuta)—suggest that Acyuta, Satya and Puruṣa respectively represent Saṃkarṣaṇa, Pradyumna and Aniruddha. J.S. 4, 4-7.

God. Deign to tell me why God does not manifest Himself in a single way to help the devotees.

43. Śrī:—O Śakra, the accumulated merits of souls vary in quality and quantity and in no sense mature to fruition at the same rate for all (lit. collected at the same time).

44. Very rarely does it happen that, owing to the ripening of merits at the time of birth, a particular individual is viewed (in a favourable light) by the lotus-eyed (God), the Lord of Śrī.

45. Some other individual is however (given the opportunity) at some other time. Thus good fortune (merit), varying both in character and in proportion, causes different grades amongst the worthy.

46. Then again, the intelligence (capacity) of some to apprehend the real nature of God is low; in the case of others it is of average level; whereas in the case of yet others it may be divinely (strong).

47-48. Thus owing to the various degrees of God's grace, inequalities arise. In order to meet the requirements of each particular function the supreme God manifests Himself in Paravyūha etc. forms by presiding over me, His Śakti. Those who have become enlightened through meditation and realize the truth are fit to (comprehend) the absolute self.[1]

49. Persons of average intelligence, who achieve partial enlightenment through meditation, are allowed access to the Vyūha developments.[2] Those lacking discrimination (true knowledge) are allowed access to the forms belonging to the Vibhava group.[3]

50-53. Considering differences in (the mental) qualities of devotees still afflicted by the illusion of egoism and selfishness, and so fit (to understand God in different degrees of perfection),[4] He (God) assumes states of existence (on different levels) known by the names of Paravyūha etc. Thus, O Śakra, I have explained to you in brief the manifestations consisting of both (*bhavat* and *bhāva*), and of the Vyūhas which follow (the separate existence of) bhavat

[1] Those who have undergone the discipline of yoga and mastered it are worthy for the pursuit of Absolute unqualified truth. They do not need any lower truth closer to ordinary experience and capacity of mind.

[2] This second group have achieved some depth of mind and are capable of understanding the transcendental qualities of these Vyūha manifestations.

[3] Each of the Vibhava deities symbolizes only one aspect of God and hence those deities are much easier for the ordinary person to grasp.

[4] Somewhat freely translated.

and bhāva. All these manifestations represent myself and Nārāyaṇa. In the group of sheaths (*kośa*, enclosing me), whether pure or impure, I have today related to you our (combined) existence, either separately, in combination with each other, or exclusively.[1]

53-54. Thus clearly discerning me with the approval of all, and ceaselessly worshipping me who am of manifold nature, in diverse ways, (the votary) can eliminate the effect of suffering resulting from accumulation of his deeds and can reach my state.

[1] Separately implies that both are manifest at the same time, but as two entities, e.g. Varāha and the Earth; in combination with each other implies as a couple, e.g. Rāma and Sītā; exclusively implies as only one, e.g. Prahlāda or Durgā.

CHAPTER TWELVE

THE FIVEFOLD DIVINE FUNCTIONS[1]

1. Śakra:—O Saroruhā (lotus-goddess), if the beginningless Jīva is thy power of pure consciousness, how comes it that it suffers from the effects of kleśa, karma and āśaya?

2. What are these kleśas? How many are they? What is the nature of deeds and how do they operate? What is āśaya, O goddess, and what are its consequences?

3. O, daughter of the ocean, please clarify all this to me. I bow down to thee again and again. O omniscient (Goddess), thou alone canst explain these (to me).

4. Śrī:—I am Goddess Nārāyaṇī consisting of pure and infinite consciousness; I am Viṣṇu's independent and absolute Śrī.

5-6. I have created two distinct categories: one relates to Īśa (the Lord); the other to īśitavya (that which is governed). Again, on my own initiative I have split up the īśitavya into two groups, (through my) power of consciousness (evolving) on the one hand as the enjoyer (*bhoktṛ*) and, on the other, as the object enjoyed (*bhogya*) etc. In this (latter group) I again make two classifications, viz. kāla and kālya (time, and those influenced by it).

7. Between (time and those influenced by it), the Śakti representing kālya acts as a temptress. She captivates and is at the same time the primordial source (*prakṛti*). The Śakti of consciousness (i.e. the *bhoktṛ*) is fettered by her (i.e. *prakṛti*) and by all her evolutions (*vikārāḥ*).

8-9. There are five ways in which the Śakti of consciousness as the bhoktṛ is subjected to suffering; and these five are called kleśas.[2] Now hear their names. Tamas, moha, mahāmoha, the darkness called andha, and avidyā. These are the five phases of the supreme course of darkness (illusion or *kleśa*).

10. Though the Śakti of consciousness is essentially aloof, pure

---

[1] The fifth function is in fact elaborated in ch. XIII.

[2] *Kleśa*, as propounded by the Yogasūtra, is the source of worldly suffering and is of five types: *avidyā*, *asmitā*, *rāga*, *dveṣa* and *abhiniveśa*. See Yog.P. on Yog.S. 2, 3-12.

and changeless, she manifests herself in a form that is affected by kleśas.

11. Śakra:—I find the notion of connecting the Śakti of consciousness with kleśas confusing. My mind is baffled. O Padmajā, please dispel my confusion.

12. Śrī:—I am the eternal, independent Śakti of Nārāyaṇa, the source of all achievement, the mysterious goddess, continuously engaged in creating.

13-14. O king of the gods, I have five ever existing functions, viz. tirobhāva, sṛṣṭi, sthiti, saṃhṛti and anugraha. O Śakra, hear a systematic description of these functions.

15-16. Among these, tirobhāva is said to be appearing differently (i.e. disguise of one's own nature).[1] That particular śakti of mine —through whose influence my citśakti (*śakti* of consciousness) called the enjoyer, which though pure (by nature) is affected by prakṛti—is called tirobhāva and is also known as avidyāśakti.

17. In accordance with my firm resolve I differentiated myself; the descending order of which (differentiated) forms I have already revealed to you.[2]

18. Citśakti is called by the learned jīva (the individual self). Its multiplicity is attributable to my own free will.

19-20. The supreme avidyāśakti, referred to as tirobhāva, is (the śakti) by which I identify my modification (*caitya*)—created by me in accordance with my firm resolve—with citśakti (understanding). Tirobhāva [3] has five components, now hear me describe them.

21. Tamas is indeed its first component, named avidyā. It represents the element of cognition whereby jīva identifies itself with material objects other than souls or the self inherent in the jīva.

22-27. This tamas or avidyā is regarded as (jīva's) ego (*sva*) and self-consciousness (*aham*). When a material object is identified with the self-consciousness (of *jīva*), the ego-consciousness thereby originated is the second component (of the *kleśa*) mahāmoha, also

---

[1] *Tirobhāva*, or disappearance, implies the influence of nescience covering the real nature of Self, which leads to all sorts of false notions of individuality and involvement.

[2] See Chapter V in extenso.

[3] *Tirobhāva* is a synonym for *kleśa*.

referred to[1] as asmitā. The identification of consciousness with material objects through the influence of avidyā is termed moha, asmitā and mahāmoha. An impression (*vāsanā*) combined with asmitā, which causes pleasant recollections, is called rāga, whose objects are pleasant things; and that is the third component of kleśa. An impression combined with asmitā, which causes unpleasant recollections, is called dveṣa, whose objects are repulsive; this is the fourth component of kleśa. The anxiety about (possible) obstacles experienced by aspirants while they attempt to repel misery by (various) forms (of) yoga and are eager for happiness, is the abhiniveśa called andha, which is the fifth component of kleśa.[2]

28-30. Regarding the body as soul and hence identifying the two; seeking objects of pleasure and shunning those that do not (afford pleasure); fearing obstacles to that (attainment of pleasant, and avoidance of unpleasant, objects) and attempting to remedy that situation; whatever activity the conscious (*jīva*) is engaged in to acquire what is coveted and to avoid what is repugnant, can be classified under three headings to tally with the three (*sukha* etc.).[3] Such activities are referred to as karman by sages and true masters of Sāṃkhya and Yoga.

31. In the science of the (cosmic) principles, the learned call the consequences of this (*karman*), which entail happiness or misery, or a mixture of both, the threefold vipāka.

32. Impressions produced by the vipākas of kleśa karman are known as āśaya, for they lie completely buried in the internal organ.

33-37. Vāsanās (impressions) are constantly produced by the five components of kleśas. Vāsanā is, on the other hand, the source from which appropriate action springs; (and again) the vipākas produce three types of vāsanā consisting of happiness etc. (Thus the cycle of vāsanā, karman and vipāka continues without break). In

---

[1] Apparently *moha, mahāmoha* etc. referred to in verse 9 do not correspond exactly with the five kleśas described in the Yog.S.

[2] *Avidyā* is *tamas*; *asmitā* is a combination of *moha* and *mahāmoha*; *rāga* and *dveṣa* are together termed *tāmisra*; and *abhiniveśa* is *andha*. There seems to be no rational connection between these last two, excepting that andha is the climax of total involvement of self in the mundane world, and the suffering thereby entailed finally drives the individual self to seek a way out, which is *abhiniveśa*.

[3] Happiness, sorrow and a mixture of both.

this way (the śakti) called tirobhāva, marked by the four kleśa etc. (i.e. *kleśa*, *karman*, *vipāka* and *āśaya*) imposes bondage on the jīvakośa. Through this power (*tirobhāva*) of mine arising from the fettered jīvas, my (other) śaktis such as sṛṣṭi etc. function uninterruptedly.[1] According to purity and impurity my sṛṣṭiśakti can be classified in two categories which I have already [2] described to you in detail. She (*sṛṣṭi-śakti*) in her turn can be classified in seven ways. First is the state when she creates incessantly through exercising the functions called *prājāpatya*.[3]

38. The others (the six consecutive states of *sṛṣṭi*) occur in the six (respective) kośas at their respective times.[4] In the course of cosmic creation, sṛṣṭi, evolving from prakṛti, is known to be of three types.

39-44. (These) are (called) bhāvikī, laiṅgikī and bhautikī. Just as the banyan tree exists (dormant) in the seed, so does the creation consisting of mahat etc. exist (dormant) in prakṛti, composed of the three guṇas (i.e. *sattva*, *rajas* and *tamas*). This is known as bhāva-sṛṣṭi (the dormant state of creation). The liṅga (the subtle body) which I create is classified as cosmic and as individual belonging to Virāj [5] and to the individual souls (respectively), and represents the (state) of creation (called) liṅgajā. The twenty-three (cosmic principles) starting with mahat and ending with viśeṣa,[6] are said to be incorporated by the subtle body of Virāj. The unit of the collective senses with antaḥkaraṇa existent in the three states (viz. *buddhi*, *ahaṃkāra* and *manas*), which inheres in each jīva and has been described before [7] as the subtle (bodies) of gross living beings—the eighteen individual (inner and outer senses), and kleśas, karmans, vāsanās and the prāṇas (vital airs)—goes to make up the above-mentioned liṅga (subtle body) inherent in the (gross bodies of) the jīvas.

---

[1] *Tirobhāva* is the basic impetus to create, the motive for creation. The śaktis of creativity etc. are instrumental in that they complete the process started by *tirobhāva*.

[2] See ch. V, 25-27.

[3] *prājāpatya* is the creative process indicative of her role as the creator. It is also the name of a sacrifice which refers to the creative function.

[4] In the six sheaths *māyā* etc. she extends herself as the created object during the different phases of creation. Thus *sṛṣṭiśakti* as the creator and the created has seven classifications.

[5] The macrocosmic aspect of Self immanent in every created object.

[6] The gross elements ether, air, light, water and earth.

[7] See ch. V, 23 to end.

45-47. The citśaktis existing in the subtle bodies (usually) journey through the transient world from (life to death). (Only) when in consequence of good deeds individuals acquire true knowledge of God, do these subtle bodies of the jīvas cease to exist, but not before that. Virāj's gross body, otherwise referred to as brahmāṇḍa, and the other four types of (gross) bodies of the embodied (*jīvas* viz. *yonija, aṇḍaja, svedaja* and *udbhijja*), go to make up my bhautikī creation; and this ends my consideration of creation.

48. Now listen, Śakra, whilst I explain to you the nature of the third of my śaktis (functions) already referred to as sthiti.

49-51. Through my ability to assume various forms, the function of sustaining that which exists in the period between the moment of creation and the moment my will to destroy (the creation) awakens, is called my supreme śakti of sthiti (integration). My coexistence with Viṣṇu, the supreme God, in each specific form is considered by the enlightened to be the first sthiti. My (coexistence) with the rulers of Manvantaras (i.e. Manus) is said to be the second (*sthiti*).

52. My (coexistence) with the sons of Manus (i.e. the saptarṣi etc.) is the third (*sthiti*); and (my coexistence) with the kṣudra (i.e. the ordinary creation) is the fourth (*sthiti*). My fourth śakti is saṃhṛti and now hear her different types.

53-55. That which causes the constant destruction of individuals classified as jarāyuja etc. (i.e. *yonija* etc.), is called the nityā saṃhṛti (*śakti* of destruction); while the second type of saṃhṛti, O Śakra, is called naimittikī.[1] She affects all three worlds and is the cause of Brahmā's deep sleep. The third type of saṃhṛti is known as prākṛtī (belonging to *prakṛti*) and influences mahat etc. The fourth type is called prāsūtī (belonging to *prasūti*) and influences avyakta (i.e. *prakṛti*). Māyī is the fifth type of saṃhṛti affecting prasūti.

56. Śāktī is regarded as the sixth type of saṃhṛti affecting māyā. The seventh type (śakti of destruction) is called ātyantikī and she merges the yogins in me (i.e. liberates them).

57. When that (liberation) takes place, the pious (votaries) exist only in their subtle bodies. O Śakra, I have thus dealt with the seven types of my śakti of destruction. Now hear my explanation of my fifth śakti (i.e. functional capacity) known as anugraha.

---

[1] This is the destruction of gross creation occurring at the end of each kalpa when all the three worlds with their contents are dissolved and Brahmā falls asleep. In the purāṇic tradition only three types of dissolution are listed, viz. nitya, naimittikī and ātyantikī.

CHAPTER THIRTEEN

THE TRUE FORM OF THE JĪVA

1. Śrī:—O Śakra, the anugraha śakti is traditionally known as my fifth (śakti). My son, I am now going to describe her true nature to you.

2-3. These (jīvas) are deluded by avidyā, subjected to the (illusion) of asmitā and overwhelmed by my śakti called tirodhāna. In general they fall from a higher to a lower position; (but) at the same time they also show a tendency to ascend from lower to higher positions.[1] Such jīvas are subjected to three types of bondage and move through the three states (regions).

4. Broiling in their own deeds, (they) are in the very centre of the hot coal that represents mundane life; they inveterately seek happiness but (instead), owing to ignorance, get crushed by misery.

5-8. As movable and immovable beings they continuously pass through an endless chain of births. Inextricably enmeshed in the miseries of body, senses, mind and intelligence through the results caused by certain deeds, (jīvas) are ever subjected to recurrent birth and death, and undergo affliction through systematic exertion or its absence (i.e. attempts to avoid misery or to pursue happiness, as the case may be). (These considerations) engender (in me) endless compassion for these jīvas. I obliterate their sins and I, Śrī, ensure that (such) jīvas escape beyond the clutches of misery. (This act of compassion) is called anugraha, which is also referred to as the 'descent' of the supreme Śakti.

9. Having received my grace, they are absolved from their karman (i.e. extinction of consequences). The jīvas infused with my grace possess only apaścima [2] (non-phenomenal) bodies.

10. The precise moment of the descent of this śakti (i.e. *anugraha*) is known only to me. It cannot be brought about by human effort, or by any other means.[3]

---

[1] The individual selves become progressively involved in worldly objects as they proceed through life but, as if to counteract this, the more involved they get, the keener grows their hankering to escape such involvement.

[2] A pure, or sāttvika, body transcending the material body.

[3] cf. Ka.U. 2.23.

11. Solely through the arbitrary exercise of my own discretion do I sometimes look upon a certain individual with favour. Thenceforward that individual (becomes) pure and his internal organ becomes cleansed.

12-14. And he, having reached the state of karmasāmya (pacification of karman), then confines himself to performing good deeds, to attaining knowledge of the Vedānta, to following (the course of speculation and meditation laid down in) the Sāṃkhya and Yoga and through a correct understanding of Sāttvata (philosophy), becomes imbued with pure devotion for Viṣṇu. Then (gradually) after lapse of time the yogin (the meditating adept), who has shaken off all accumulated afflictions (*kleśas*) by freeing himself from every shackle, glows brightly (liberated) from all attachments and (ultimately) becomes one with the supreme Brahman represented by Lakṣmī and Nārāyaṇa.[1]

15. This is my fifth śakti known as anugraha. The reason for my engaging in activities such as tirobhāva etc. is purely a matter of my own choice.

16. Thus, O Śakra, understand my fivefold divine functions, about which I have nothing further to add.

Śakra:—I salute thee, who livest in the lotus, I salute thee, who shelterest in Nārāyaṇa.

17-18. I salute thee, eternal and flawless Goddess, who art, as it were, the ocean of all blessings. (Though) the great darkness (of my mind) has been dispelled by the flow of thy nectar-like words, (yet), I am eager to know more about the excellent form of citśakti.

18. Śrī:—Nārāyaṇa is the unique God, the eternal supreme soul.

19. He is the everlasting embodiment of (all the attributes, viz.) jñāna, bala, aiśvarya, vīrya, śakti and ojas (i.e. *tejas*). He is beginningless and without limitation in space, time or form.

20. I, the supreme Goddess, am His Śakti, consisting of His I-hood, resplendently displaying the six (divine) attributes; omnipotent and eternal.

21. My unique essential form consists of pure and unlimited consciousness. All the successful (yogins) amongst all the jīvas exist in me.[2]

---

[1] Emancipation (*mukti*) is being identical with Brahman, the supreme Essence, which is but a return of the part to its original whole.

[2] The yogins who have become enlightened through the practice of Yoga.

22. Through my sovereign will, I manifest the whole of creation on myself as the substratum. All the worlds dart (start) into existence on me, as birds dart on water.

23. Of my own choice I descend (through limited forms) in fulfilment of my five functions. This, my descending self is called citśakti.

24. This is my limited (self) consisting of concentrated consciousness, which is pure and at the same time independent. Even in this (concentrated consciousness) the universe is manifest, similarly as the reflection of a mountain may be caught in a (small) mirror.[1]

25. This (limited manifestation of mine) is transparent and ever shining like a diamond. As pure brilliance is the quality of the sun, so is consciousness its quality.

26. Jīva is spontaneously manifested by her (*citśakti*) possessing similar traits and this jīva is also continuously occupied in performing the five daily duties.[2]

27. The contact (of citśakti) with (objects such as) blue, yellow etc. is called by the wise sṛṣṭi. Attachment to such objects (of citśakti) is called sthiti.

28. The cessation of (the jīva's) attachment to objects, caused by the desire to seize another, is referred to by the learned in the science of the principles, as saṃhṛti.

29. The impression (*vāsanā*) left by them (i.e. objects) is tirobhāva and the eradication of that impression is anugraha. This destruction [3] has the propensity, like fire, to destroy everything within reach.

30. This jīva is sustained by merely an infinitesimal part of myself. I have previously [4] explained to you my illusory form in association with its relevant objects.

31. When in consequence of (the advent of) pure knowledge, the jīva discards its limitations, then freed from every shackle it becomes illuminated (with knowledge).

32. In consequence of (the advent of the divine attributes) jñāna and kriyā, it (then) becomes omniscient and omnipotent;

---

[1] The image is peculiarly Vedāntic. Another popular image of the kind is to observe the sea in a drop of water.

[2] Corresponding to the five functions of God enumerated in the ensuing verses.

[3] Grasana, to devour.

[4] See ch. VII.

and since all fetters have been removed, in acquiring my nature it even becomes non-molecular (in size, i.e. infinite).

33. As long as it is unnoticed by me, who am moved by pity, its knowledge continues to be restricted and it (continues) to experience the universe through its senses (lit. instruments of knowledge).

34. Observing objects with the eye (i.e. a sense organ), using the mind to form notions, attributing ego-consciousness by virtue of ahaṃkāra, it finally uses intelligence to determine (an object).

35. Thus from having lived in the waking state, it enters the dream state by relying then solely on its internal senses. From that state, in a state of profound sleep, it reverts to its own true nature.

36-39. These three states actually belong to prakṛti, and not to the jīva. Even the state of turya, entered during the jīva's meditative trance, does not properly belong to it. The jīva does indeed consist of pure transcendental substance (*śuddhasattva*). It is independent of all states, is unaffected by any attributes belonging to prakṛti,[1] is unlimited by the conditions (*upādhis*) and is indivisible. In fact the jīva incorporates (pure) consciousness. But although that is its essence, it becomes blinded by avidyā and hence does not see me, who am (however) clearly visible and am identical with its own self.

Śakra:—O Goddess, how can you say that you are clearly visible, when you are beyond the reach of all senses? O Ambujā, even the Vedānta (Upaniṣad) fails to clarify your true nature.

40. Śrī:—O Śakra, consider me to be intuitively realizable[2] by all embodied beings. Now hear with attention my (true) nature.

---

[1] Sattva, rajas and tamas.

[2] Realization of truth or Self-realization is intuitive knowledge, which is always direct.

CHAPTER FOURTEEN

THE TRUE NATURE OF ŚAKTI (LAKṢMĪ)

1. Śrī:—God Vāsudeva is the absolute Brahman. In essence He is (higher) knowledge; undifferentiated with regard to space, time etc.; devoid of guṇas [1] and pure.

2. His nature is bliss, He is ever immutable, possesses six (divine) attributes, is undecaying and everlasting. I am His supreme Śakti, His I-hood. I am eternal and constant (i.e. immutable).

3-5. My śakti of action (*vyāpāraśakti*) is characterized by my urge to create (*sisṛkṣā*). With a billionth fraction of myself I voluntarily embark on creation by differentiating myself in two separate (particles), of which one is conscious (*cetana*) and the other is the object of its knowledge (*cetya*). Of these two, cetana is my citśakti. In fact consciousness, consisting of myself, evolves into both sentient and insentient objects. Absolutely pure and sovereign consciousness is, indeed, my real form.

6. Like the juice of the sugar-cane, this (consciousness) becomes grosser through contact with material objects. Hence it is that in the process of cognizing material objects, the latter acquire the nature of consciousness.

7. Just as fuel, when kindled, becomes engulfed by fire, so do (perceptible material) objects pervaded by consciousness adopt its nature.

8. Polarized thinking aware of (objects such as) blue, yellow, happiness, sorrow etc., distinguishes undifferentiated pure consciousness by its variegated wealth of limiting conditions.

9. Polarized thought is also one of my forms [2] voluntarily created by myself whereby, viewed from an internal and an external angle, perceptible (material) objects become classified as subject and object.

10. Neither the external (object) nor the internal (cognition) constitutes the essence of my absolute consciousness. My selfhood

---

[1] Sattva, rajas and tamas.

[2] See ch. V, 32-85.

splits itself in two components: the (objects) capable of being known; and the (subjects) who do the knowing.

11. That self of mine, which is beyond all polarized knowledge, free from the taint of words and unaffected by any limiting condition, undergoes evolution in the form of perceptible (material) objects.

12. When the mind is free of polarized thought, those perceptible (material) objects that attain the middle mode (*madhyama vṛtti*) [1] become identified with consciousness.

13. Just as the form existing in the eye is seen (by that eye) as being the form belonging to a particular external object, so also the form existing in the knowledge observed (by the knower) appears to belong to the thing known.

14. Just as a burning piece of wood looks like fire, so also are perceptible (material) objects pervaded by consciousness perceived as consciousness.

15. When the object is related to cognition by the knower (cognizer) and he reflects upon it, it is then myself, consisting of knowledge and ever revealed (who is in fact perceived as that object).

16. I-hood is the essential characteristic of knowledge distinguishing it from the object perceived; it is unique (*salakṣaṇa*), and that is my own self. Hence I, consisting of pure consciousness, am all-pervading.

17. When in the ocean of consciousness the only foothold left on the flooded island is the term connoting 'this' (*idampada*) and perceptible (material) objects are almost submerged I then provide them with a support to hold on to.

18. Those whose impressions have all been washed away (i.e. removed) by the nectar-like flow of meditation upon me, realize me, who am (pure) consciousness engulfing the multitudinous variety of objects, as identical with themselves.

19. People are of opinion that, since I consist of knowledge alone, my function of revealing objects of knowledge (i.e. cognition) is an effect of avidyā, about which I have spoken before.[2]

20-21. According to my true nature, I am neither tranquil (i.e. inert), nor creatively active, nor do I follow the middle course

[1] The third sonic manifestation, viz. *madhyamā*.
[2] See ch. XIII.

between these. I manifest myself as such [1] to those who are able to discern me with a calm mind devoid of polarized experience even in the waking state. But even when perceived by those who seek to know me while still influenced by polarization, I make them forget me.

22. Just as an object though lying right in front of a person does not appear in his mind when preoccupied, so also am I not realized by those whose (minds) are afflicted by impressions.[2]

23-24. Just as a person desirous of understanding some particular object, stills every other movement of his mind and (through deep concentration) grasps it immediately, similarly, even during empirical existence, pure-souled (persons) realize my ever-manifest and sovereign self embodying pure knowledge.

25-26. As a garment which was originally white and is then dyed red, cannot be re-dyed in another colour without first reverting to its original state, similarly how can he who has a notion of blue etc., envisage yellow, without taking the intermediate step of reverting to me, the essential pure consciousness.

27. In the same way, whilst spelling out a sentence, how can one pass from letter to letter without pausing between letters in me, the essential pure consciousness.

28. Thus, although in essence I am pure and independent, still after assuming one form and then passing on to another, I retain my pure nature during the intermediate state.[3]

29. My true state of existence, set alight by Agni and Soma, manifests itself as my abode (*padam*) in the middle (duct, i.e. suṣumnā), when passage through the right and left (ducts) [4] is checked.

30. When (visionary higher) thought (or wisdom: *dhī*) is set free from contact with all external objects and is also not focussed on

---

[1] i.e. in the true presentation of myself.

[2] Blurred by impressions left by the experience of mundane affairs, the mind fails to reflect truth.

[3] This very interesting idea conveys two facts. The first is that Śakti is always transcendental and none of her modifications affects this fundamental trait. Secondly, even while undergoing all these modifications she reverts to her essential form in every intermediate state between two successive modifications. This implies that each modification is directly linked with Śakti's essential form.

[4] Iḍā and piṅgalā; cf. Ahi.S: ch. 33 in extenso.

any particular (symbolic) object, my true self is revealed [1] in that vacant thought.

31. That which continues to exist both in light and in darkness and reveals itself both in a positive and negative (object), is my undifferentiated form.

32. Totally unattached I-consciousness, revealed in the mind of (the adept) who has completely renounced all craving for material objects and whose mind delights in devotion to me, is indeed my true body.

33. The self of those persons, who practise that (renunciation and devotion) and who have acquired true knowledge (by distinguishing truth from untruth), remains unaffected by the imposition of body, vital airs etc. (life-principle) and completely identifies itself with my true state of being.

34. As the rays of the sun become manifest but are not created (anew), so too the essence of consciousness as such, manifests itself in various states of being but has never been created.

35. Just as the sun sometimes rises in the sky without there being any particular object (to illuminate), so also does my true form (viz. knowledge) spontaneously manifest itself, even when there is no object to reveal.[2]

36-37. In the same way as crystal etc., being extremely transparent, when tinted by flowers such as the hibiscus (*japā*) cannot be perceived in its original state, I, also being transparent,[3] cannot be perceived by people apart from the palpable objects created through my decisive will. That does not imply that I do not exist there (separately from such objects).

38-39. As the existence of gold cannot be perceived apart from the earrings made of it and cannot be separately pointed to, and yet gold undoubtedly exists as gold, so also is my existence, which consists of consciousness and is eternal, pure and unaffected by either pleasure or pain, realizable solely through self-knowledge.

40. That which relates the cognizer with both the process of knowledge and its object, is my relationship to these (= knowledge

---

[1] Enlightenment comes to a mind freed of all impressions. This state of mind can be reached only through meditation.

[2] Whether the rays of the sun are visible or not, their existence is constant. Similarly the essence of consciousness may, or may not be revealed to a particular individual, but exists nevertheless.

[3] i.e. unqualified.

and its object) characterized as the essence of perception (of objects).[1]

41. Space, time and action are well known as the three differentiating factors (*bheda*).[2] But what can distinguish consciousness (*saṃvid*), which determines the distinction between (even) these (three distinguishing factors)?

42. Even time, with its three components, past, etc.,[3] which is the fundamental cause of differentiation amongst perceptible (material) objects, becomes as it were merged in the ocean of consciousness and is identified with it.

43. When past and future merge in me, the eternally existent, the concept of the present is then also obliterated.[4]

44. I am the substratum of everything, but I cannot be enclosed in anything. Hence there is no particular area of space that can be relegated to me as my substratum.

45. I have no state exempt from consciousness. Therefore I, who am unique and of the nature of concentrated consciousness, am worshipped as the possessor of all forms.

46-54. Time, place, action (*kriyā*), subject (*kartā*), object (*karma*), instrumental object (*karaṇa*), dative object (*sampradāna*), (i.e. objects in their various positions in relation to action) and the consequences (of actions), enjoyment and the enjoyer—all these merge in the self of consciousness. Gods, demons, nāgas, gandharvas, the flocks of rākṣasas, vidyādharas, piśācas (malevolent spirits), the elements—these eight gaṇas;[5] men, who classify themselves in diverse groups according to caste and function; cattle and wild creatures (*mṛgas*), birds, serpents, plants and also insects; the fourteen worlds[6] existing in heaven and the nether regions; rivers, islands, oceans and other creations of the cosmic egg; the higher and lower realities; various collections of sounds; whatever can be regarded as being either the object, instrument, or embodiment

---

[1] *pratyayārtha*: essence of perception of an object; cf. ahamartha.

[2] These three are the basic factors distinguishing one object from another.

[3] i.e. past, present and future.

[4] Because the present is a relative term dependent upon the concept of either the past or the future.

[5] Groups of creatures other than creatures of this world.

[6] Seven higher and seven nether worlds: bhūḥ, bhuvaḥ, svaḥ, tapa, jana, maha, satya; and atala, vitala, sutala, talātala, mahātala, rasātala, pātāla.

of enjoyment; the six sheaths and everything enclosed therein consisting of both sentient and insentient objects; all existing objects whether pure or impure; and the four aims of mankind (viz. dharma, artha, kāma and mokṣa); everything connected with prakṛti and impelled by time; all these (above-mentioned) both existent and non-existent (objects), whether or not pervaded by me, merge in me (are contained in me). I, the pure and independent consciousness, pervade everything.

55-58. I am recognized by the wise as the bliss and tranquillity inherent in each state of being. Though that is my true nature, fettered by my śakti called tirobhāva, citśakti (i.e. jīva) does not discover (experience) me spontaneously. However, after receiving a mere particle of my anugrahaśakti, she (*citśakti*) discovers me (instantaneously). Then after propitiating me by various means, the jīva, known as citśakti washes away all kleśas and blows away the dust of impressions; whereby the jīva, that has (thus) already severed its fetters through meditation (*yoga*), fuses with true knowledge and attains me, who am Lakṣmī and whose nature is supreme bliss.[1]

[1] Asserting in unmistakable terms that liberation means achieving identification with the Absolute Self, in other words with Lakṣmī-Nārāyaṇa.

CHAPTER FIFTEEN

VARIOUS METHODS OF ATTAINING ULTIMATE TRUTH

1. Śakra:—I salute thee, who art born in the lotus. Homage to thee, thou lotus-wreathed Goddess. I salute thee, wife of Govinda, who dwellest in a lotus.

2. I salute thee whose hair resembleth the delicate lotus-filaments, O omniscient Goddess, who art the witness (principle) residing in the mind of every living creature.

3. I have followed all (the teaching) that has issued from thy lotus-lips, (to the effect that) everything thou hast created is succoured (sustained) by thee and will (ultimately) be merged in thee.

4. The knower, the instrument of knowledge, knowledge (cognition) and the object of knowledge, all these are essentially none other than thyself. Every soul can, as it were, only traverse the ocean of creation (life) by worshipping thee alone.

5-6. All this, O Goddess, I have fully understood. Now I am curious to know how, O lotus-born, one may please thee who art on thy lotus-throne. By what means can one attain the highest goal, which is (to procure) thy satisfaction (grace, love: prīti).[1] What is the method of pleasing thee, what is its nature, what does it entail? I salute thee, O lotus-born, deign to reveal all this to me.

7-9. Śrī:—The absolute Brahman is identified with the fourfold (deity),[2] characterized by (pure) existence, consciousness and bliss; who consists of all, transcends all, is immanent in all and flawless; who is Vāsudeva, the absolute Brahman, the great principle (*mahat*) consisting of Nārāyaṇa. I am His absolute Śakti, (His) I-hood consisting of bliss and consciousness.

[1] Man's highest aspiration is to be liberated from worldly bondage and the only means to achieve that is through securing God's or Śakti's grace. Hence it is the aim of every adept of this Pāñcarātra system to confine himself to doing what pleases Him or His Śakti, and nothing else.

[2] Caturvyūha; the manifestation of God Brahman, whose essence is Absolute Being, Absolute Knowledge and Absolute Bliss. cf. *satyaṃ jñānam anantam brahma*; *ānando brahmeti vyajānāt*; T.U. 2, 1, 1 and 3, 6. It should be noted that Brahman in this text is not devoid of personality.

10. I am identified with, and (at the same time) different from Him,[1] like the moonlight of the moon. This unique existence (reality) of ours, though single, appears to be dual.

11. There is no way for the wise to progress (towards emancipation) other than by seeking higher knowledge, that is the higher knowledge whereby the seer attains Brahman, that is Nārāyaṇa, that is myself.

12. That higher knowledge derived from discriminating knowledge (distinguishing between truth and falsehood), which is totally pure and devoid of suffering, envisages Vāsudeva as its sole aim and leads to the cessation of rebirth.

13-14. Once this knowledge (realization) is obtained, (the adept) instantaneously enters me (identifies himself with me). Pleased by these particular methods followed by the pure-souled living beings, I reveal that knowledge which throws light on the supreme Self. There are four methods [2] which gain favour.

15. Śakra:—O lady living in the lotus, lovely spouse of the Lotus-eyed One, O lotus-goddess, show me what these four methods are.

16. Śrī:—Listen Śakra to the description of these four methods of acquiring my grace, which will always cause me, the Absolute, great pleasure.

17. Performance of one's duties as befitting one's caste; knowledge of the principles (*sāṃkhya*); meditative devotion (*yoga*) and complete renunciation; these are the methods designated by the learned.

18. The three types of Vedic rites as defined by the four definitions [3] comprise obligatory and occasional rites connected with one's social rank and status (*varṇāśrama*).

19. The first method is to perform a deed not made worthless by attachment (to its fruits), wherein the wise should practice four types of complete renunciation.

20. (They should dedicate every act) either to the deity mentioned

---

[1] God and His Śakti are identical yet separate, like fire and its capacity to burn. This idea was postulated later on by Caitanya's followers as Acintyabhedābhedavāda.

[2] *Karma* or virtuously performing one's religious and social duties; *jñāna* or philosophical contemplation; *bhakti* or devotion to God; and *nyāsa* or the dedication of one's self to God.

[3] Clarified in verse 20.

in the mantra, to prakṛti, to the senses, or to the supreme God Vāsudeva, Janārdana.

21-22. First to glorious Janārdana (the adept) should surrender the idea of himself as being the performer; then he should surrender the result thereof; and finally even the very acts (functions) themselves, performing (only) the compulsory and the occasional duties enjoined by sacred scripture. Desirous only of worshipping me, the man ceaselessly ingratiates me.

23. Thus is briefly shown to you the (method) as described by Śruti and Smṛti. Now hear the second method, (i.e.) the knowledge of the principles.[1]

24-25. According to the Sāṃkhya system, sāṃkhya (knowledge) is of three types. The first is knowledge with reference to the things of this world; the second consists of carcanā (speculative knowledge); and complete intuitive knowledge (of truth) is considered the third. These three types of knowledge are collectively named sāṃkhya.

26-27. (The elements of) earth, water, fire, wind and ether, ahaṃkāra (the ego-principle), mahat and prakṛti; these are the eight principles (and) I am going to explain them to you. Prakṛti is said to be of three types, māyā, sūti (i.e. *prasūti*), and guṇātmikā (or triguṇātmikā).

28. Māyā is the name of that supreme subtle principle relating to insentient objects, which is in itself free and, at the same time, not free from attachment. It is unique, devoid of vibration (i.e. movement) and imperishable.

29. Its (māyā's) slightly less subtle (lit. swollen) state is called prasūti. The development of all three guṇas in equal proportion is (known as the state of) supreme prakṛti.

30. Avyakta, akṣara, yoni, avidyā, triguṇā, sthiti, māyā, svabhāva etc. are synonyms for prakṛti.

31. Sattva, rajas and tamas are the three guṇas. Sattva is light in weight, blissful and tranquil.

32-36. Its function (mode) is known as illumination (*prakāśa*), which reflects (lit. lifts up) consciousness.[2] Rajas should also be

[1] Sāṃkhya literally means enumeration, and hence enumeration of the cosmic principles laid down in the Sāṃkhya system. See Bh.G. 2, 39 and R. C. Zaehner, Commentary on the Bhagavadgītā, Oxford 1969, pp. 139-140.

[2] Sattva illuminates in the sense that, being pure and transparent, it reflects knowledge which is the illumination of truth. Otherwise sattva, not being consciousness, cannot be illumination.

known as being light (in weight), sorrowful and unstable. Its function (mode) is activity, which is the cause of all vibration. It is imperishable. Tamas is massive, consists of illusion and is immobile. Its function (mode) is to fetter (*niyama*) and is sometimes characterized by inducing sleep. O Vāsava, neither on earth, in heaven, nor in the space between, does any object exist devoid of these three guṇas, which are the products of prakṛti. These guṇas, governing the mind, manifesting themselves through the senses and at the same time inherent in every single object, produce pleasure, pain and illusion. It is these guṇas, evolved into the body and the senses, that are responsible for all activity. He who constantly bears this in mind, frees himself from these guṇas.

CHAPTER SIXTEEN

ELABORATION OF THE METHODS TO ATTAIN ULTIMATE TRUTH

1-4. Now listen attentively, O Śakra, to my description of mahat, the first disturbance (lit. activity) in the tranquil equilibrium of the guṇas.[1] It too has three aspects (modes, manners of manifesting itself): the sattva-aspect which is buddhi (intellect); the rajas-aspect which is prāṇa (the vital air); and the tamas-aspect called kāla (time). Now hear me explain these. Buddhi is the incentive to mental effort (*adhyavasāya*); prāṇa is the incentive to endeavour (*prayatna*); and kāla is the incentive to transform in the form of impulse and effective development (*kalana*). Ahaṃkāra results from a modification of mahat.

5. (Ahaṃkāra) also has three aspects resulting from the proportional difference in the guṇas. The five tanmātras (element-principles), space etc., are evolved from its tamas-aspect.

6-7. The cognitive senses owe their origin to predominance of the sattva-aspect (of ahaṃkāra); the conative senses to predominance of its rajas-aspect; while the mind (*ubhayātmaka*) originates from both (its sattva- and rajas-aspects). This is how the tattvas (cosmic principles) exist.[2] Amongst these, only prakṛti, the eternal, is the source of all (and not an effect).

8-9. The other seven (principles), starting from mahat, have both the aspects of being the source and the effect. The modifications of the five tanmātras (element-principles), viz. space etc., the cognitive and conative senses together with the mind,—these sixteen are referred to by scholars as being mere effects.

10-12. These are the twenty-four tattvas [3] (cosmic principles).

---

[1] When all three guṇas are present in equal proportion, the cosmic principle containing them is called prakṛti; when that balance is disturbed for the first time, the same principle is called mahat.

[2] Here tattva paddhati refers to the unconscious principles. There are two types of created objects, conscious and unconscious. The latter have twenty-four components: prakṛti, mahat, ahaṃkāra, five subtle elements, five gross elements and eleven cognitive, conative and internal organs. Conscious reality consists of two components: creatures and the creator.

[3] See note 2.

O slayer of Vṛtra, (I have already dealt with) other details and peculiarities relevant to these. O king of the gods, I have told you about this avyakta (unmanifested) prakṛti along with its own twenty-three modifications. This (prakṛti), consisting of both manifest and unmanifest objects, is characterized as continuously producing (effects, *kārya*).

13. Citśakti differs from this. It is imperishable; and the wise (respectable), who are versed in the scriptures dealing with the categories, call it jīva (the individual soul).

14. In essence this is pure, unmodifiable, unchangeable, concentrated consciousness, eternal, endless and unlimited (lit. unabating).

15. These, prakṛti and Puruṣa,[1] though by nature unattached, appear to be connected and are even higher than mahat (the highest).

16. Both these eternal (realities) are identifiable as liṅga (indicatory mark) [2] and (at the same time) are devoid of any indicatory mark (*aliṅga*). It is therefore left for the learned to deduce their common characteristics by inference.

17-19. Now listen, Śakra, while I recount their differences. Prakṛti consists of the three guṇas, eternal and ever evolving, though it is undifferentiated, impure, and invariably identified with the jīvas. It is also the unconscious (material) object subjected to the delusion of pleasure and pain. Puruṣa is the innermost ever-existing soul which, though functioning, is uninvolved and is the sākṣin (the witnessing consciousness), the knowledge and at the same time the knower, who is pure, unending and incorporating the (divine) attributes.

20-21. These are the divergences between the two. Now listen to a description of their nature. She who (That which) is devoid of positive or negative material diversity, is unchangeable, ever active (in creation), ever blissful, with a form consisting of all the six attributes, is (in fact) myself, Nārāyaṇī, the Śakti of Viṣṇu, pure Śrī.

22-25. These two (viz. Puruṣa and prakṛti) originate from me and will merge in me. Containing all these, I have evolved into various

---

[1] The jīva and the Person are identical since they spring from the same reality and merely reveal two aspects of the Supreme Conscious Being.

[2] Liṅga means a sign indicating an object's nature, but it may sometimes denote just sex.

objects and resting in Nārāyaṇa,[1] once again I become active in creation (i.e. develop myself) out of Him. Nārāyaṇa is the unique Viṣṇu, the eternal Vāsudeva. Since He is not different from (His) Śakti, He is the one and undifferentiated Brahman; the great ocean, as it were, of jñāna, śakti, bala, aiśvarya, vīrya and tejas; He is ever tranquil and embraces the entire universe containing both static and dynamic objects (i.e. living creatures and inanimate things). Thus, Śakra, the science of sāṃkhya (i.e. the knowledge of truth) has been briefly revealed to you.

26-28. The wise should first study the science of knowledge (sāṃkhya) which consists of the enumeration of the cosmic principles. Then he should master the knowledge concerning recapitulation (*carcā*) derived from the teaching of the principles set forth in scripture concerning their common and divergent characteristics, their nature and source etc. The true knowledge attained by the pure soul after mastering the speculative discussion on the revelation of existing reality, is that absolute knowledge (*sāṃkhya*) bestowed through my grace.

29-30. Thus I have given you an account of the philosophy of Sāṃkhya. After applying themselves to this philosophy according to the Sāṃkhya system, these adepts of sāṃkhya attain my state of existence. The third method called yoga will (now) be described to you. There are two types of yoga, samādhi and saṃyama.

31. Samādhi results from (practising) the components (of yoga) known as yama etc., which implies existing in a state of identity with the absolute Brahman called Śrīnivāsa, without having to return.[2]

32. This state (condition) is proper to those who have realized Brahman; it consists of intuitive realization based on the identification of the meditator with the object meditated on, and arises through grace [3] bestowed by me.

33. Saṃyama implies good deeds relating solely to the highest Self. That again is of two varieties, pertaining to the body and to the mind.

---

[1] The period of time covering from after dissolution to before creation.

[2] This is the ultimate samādhi or meditative trance, in which the yogin is perpetually united with God. This is emancipation.

[3] Liberation is attained solely through divine grace and by no other means.

34-37. I shall elaborate on both saṃyama and samādhi. The first method consists of performing (religious) duties previously described by me. It generates pure consciousness by purifying the inner organ (*antaḥkaraṇa*). When by confining himself to good deeds (the adept) receives my favour, I bestow (on him) buddhiyoga (the realization of truth through mental communion with the Highest), which (further) purifies the inner organ.[1] As already mentioned, this is the second method called sāṃkhya. It eludes observation and is based on study of the sacred scriptures. When this last mentioned realization of truth takes firm root (in the mind), it becomes (as vivid as) direct knowledge (of the Highest) and gains my supreme satisfaction.

38. Then I, recognized in my own form with my attributes and vibhavas, disclose that direct higher knowledge which is the outcome of discrimination (between truth and falsity).

39. The third form of direct (knowledge) comprised in samādhi is inviolable and firm,[2] resulting chiefly from sattva and is largely due to grace.

40. That (other) variety of the third (method of knowledge), which is described by the name saṃyama and includes the pure enjoyment derived from three different sources,[3] greatly delights me.

41. There I, the soul of the universe, Śakti of Viṣṇu the all-embracing, am worshipped directly as myself, or as God Puruṣottama (and through Him as myself).

42. Thus I have carefully explained to you the three exalted methods (of attaining the highest goal). Now listen to my description of the fourth method called complete renunciation.[4]

43. It consists of the (adept's) abandonment of every task however weighty or trifling; (whereafter) having been made thoroughly miserable (lit. burnt) by the fire of worldly existence, he (the adept) resorts to me alone.

---

[1] Contemplation on the cosmic principles clarifies the adept's mind, which then apprehends the real nature of creation; but the realization of that is not liberation.

[2] Unlike the ordinary meditative trance, this lasts for ever and he who attains that plane of meditative practice never reverts to awareness of the mundane world.

[3] These sources are explained in the ensuing verses. Pure enjoyment differs from ordinary enjoyment in that it is not centred on the individual experiencing it, but on God and Śakti.

[4] Elaborated in the next chapter.

44. When, with unwavering mind a person resorts to me, I permit him to identify himself with me after his mind has become rid of all sin.[1]

[1] The difference between ordinary devotion and total self-surrender to God is brought out by analogy. The first is called the law of the monkey-cub and the second the law of the kitten. A baby monkey clings to its mother with all its might and puts all its effort into that clinging, whereas a kitten does nothing and allows its mother to carry it in her mouth and pull it by the scruff of its neck. This complete trust without endeavouring to attract its mother's attention is the keynote of self-surrender or prapatti.

CHAPTER SEVENTEEN

THE SECRET METHOD [1] OF SELF-SURRENDER, THE FOURTH METHOD OF ATTAINING THE HIGHEST GOAL

1-2. Śakra:—I salute thee who residest in the lotus, mother of all embodied beings and wife of Padmanābha. I salute thee (again), O Lotus-goddess! Thou hast already revealed to me the three methods [2] and I have understood them. O Lotus-goddess, my mother, inform me of the supreme fourth method.

3. Śrī:—Nārāyaṇa is the one and eternal God Vāsudeva, the absolute Brahman, the flawless fourfold (God), consisting of existence, consciousness and bliss.

4. I am His absolute and unique Śakti, the eternal Goddess, performing all His functions and sharing all His states of existence.

5-6. Brahman is tranquil, ever conscious and full of bliss; absolute and constant, the repository of supreme divine majesty [3] and entirely quiescent (*samatāṃ gatam*). I am Its Śakti Brāhmī [4] consisting of tranquility, bliss and consciousness, characterized by supreme divine majesty, free from impurity and entirely quiescent.

7-8. When to reassure living beings Nārāyaṇa, the absolute Brahman, assumes a majestic form of corporeal existence which is divine and pleasing to the eye, then I too possess a corporeal form. I am Nārāyaṇa's supreme Śakti, perfect, with well-proportioned limbs and beautiful in every lineament.

9-13. Our supreme abode untouched by sorrow is the great space. The whole group of the divine attributes has voluntarily chosen to be limited by space.[5] That (abode) is attained by successful adepts

---

[1] *Rahasya* actually means esoteric rites, here the main dogma of the Pāñcarātra. See C. Rangachari, Sri Vaishnava Brahmans, p. 199.

[2] See ch. XVI (in extenso).

[3] The term *mahāvibhūti* applies to God's innate sovereign power as distinguished from *līlāvibhūti* which denotes its operation in creative activity. *Mahāvibhūti* is greater than *līlāvibhūti* which indicates a special phase of God's existence, whereas the former is His eternal natural state of existence.

[4] Brāhmī denotes that this Śakti represents Brahman's existence.

[5] Evidently God's abode has no existence of its own separate from God. It is the same as God's existence incorporating all six attributes, but expressed in spatial terms in order to start the adept off with a clear idea of the goal he aims at reaching and to make it easier for the novice to understand.

(*siddhas*) who have proved themselves unfailingly devout in the performance of their duties, are thorough masters of the Vedas and of the Upaniṣads and have purged themselves of all defilement through innumerable cycles of rebirth; who have attained success through enduring great suffering; who have gradually removed all impediments, are versed in reasoning and observance of the precepts; who have attained realization and mastered the philosophy of the principles (sāṃkhya); who have control over all their senses, who possess both dhāraṇa and dhyāna, who are yogins and have attained samādhi. That (abode) can only be attained immediately after a hundred years of ceaseless (devotion to God) by those who are wise and aware of the duties to be performed during the five divisions of the day,[1] and skilled in performing the five types of sacrifices.[2]

14-16. That ancient space is highest of all and eternal. Arriving there, those who are familiar with the principles sever all their fetters. Those who have thrown off the shackles of transient existence abide there in splendour, like tens of millions of suns and millions of full moons. They are free from all sensual defects and are surrounded with brilliance. They exude nothing and partake of no food. Their bodies are composed of the six attributes and are pure.

17. That is where, after exhausting the consequences of their

[1] The first part of the day begins with the break of dawn, when the adept awakes and worships God with japa, meditation, rites and chanting. This is called *abhigamana*. Next, in the middle of the morning, he goes out to collect the flowers, food etc. needed for the worship and dependent on the alms he receives. This is called *upādāna*. Upon returning at noon, he makes preparations for performance of the ritual sacrifice with its eight components, and then performs it. This is *ijyā*. At the fall of evening, he starts studying texts and commentaries on his own system as well as other sacred books and ponders on these. This is *svādhyāya*. Then finally, deep in the night, he starts performing his yogic exercises accompanied by japa and meditation which he continues throughout the night, snatching sleep between periods of meditation. This division of the day is called *yoga*. See J.S. *22*, 68-74.

[2] First, *brahmayajña*—studying and teaching; second, *pitṛyajña*—offering tarpana to one's dead ancestors performing the obligatory rites prescribed for their benefit; third *devayajña*—performing the sacrifice to God; fourth *bhūtayajña*—offering *bali* or food to spirits or demigods; and fifth *nṛyajña*—serving guests with dedication. These five are considered to be a householder's daily duties. Cf. Ga.P. ch. 115.

deeds[1] extending over a very long period, the highly privileged ekāntins enjoy the constant sight of us.[2]

18-25. There the Brahmās and Śaṃkaras (Śivas) along with Puraṃdaras,[3] the gods and the ever successful sages, who are ever omniscient, rejoice and directly view the supreme form of Viṣṇu. There too abide those perfect adepts who meditate on (lit. cling to) the mantra consisting of eight, twelve, or six letters; or else on the praṇava-mantra, the mantra (starting with) *jitaṃ te* etc., or on the Tārika or Anutāra-mantras.[4] In that place there is overall rejoicing amongst the pure (divine beings) including Ananta, the king of birds, Viṣvaksena etc., and all those deities who execute my commands. That is where the divine-bodied possessor of Śrī, the God of gods Janārdana, reclines on the resplendent and highly blissful couch of Ananta's coils. He is richly adorned with weapons as well as with divine and wonderful ornaments (consisting of) vijñāna, aiśvarya, vīrya and an abundance of śakti, tejas and bala. He is served by the king of birds, Suparṇa representing the five,[5] and formally attended by the glorious commander Viṣvaksena, who resembles (Nārāyaṇa) in form and bears the characteristic mark of śrīvatsa.

26-31. In order to bring well-being to all the worlds, to facilitate contemplation by the wise, to liberate all those in bondage and to furnish a form for the yogins (to meditate on), Vāsudeva, Nārāyaṇa the possessor of Śrī, the eternal (God), assumes (a body that is) delicate, young, divine, marked with śrīvatsa, four-armed, wide-eyed, wearing a crown and the jewel Kaustubha, splendidly adorned with necklaces, anklets, armlets, girdles, clothed in a yellow garment, bearing the supreme, divine vanamālā consisting of the

[1] The term adhikāra is fully explained in the V.S. 3, 3, 32 and Śaṅkara's commentary thereon.

[2] The term ekāntin is applied to Viṣṇu's devotees, cf. J.S. 22, 11-13.

[3] In each kalpa these gods manifest themselves afresh. As regards Indra, in each kalpa he has a different name. See Viṣ.P. III, 1, 8-31.

[4] For the mantras see chs. XXIV, XXV and XXVI. The eight-, twelve- and six-lettered mantras are respectively the Nārāyaṇa, Vāsudeva and Viṣṇu-mantras.

[5] Garuḍa represents the *Pañcopaniṣad*-mantras. These are: *oṃ ṣāṃ namaḥ parāya parameṣṭhyātmane namaḥ*; *oṃ yāṃ namaḥ parāya puruṣātmane namaḥ*; *oṃ rāṃ namaḥ parāya viśvātmane namaḥ*; *oṃ vāṃ namaḥ parāya nityātmane namaḥ*; and *oṃ lāṃ namaḥ parāya sarvātmane namaḥ*.

five (active) śaktis (of Śrī) [1], perfectly formed and beautiful in every lineament. He is the supreme king of the entire universe, the highest lord of creation. I, the consort of this beloved god Viṣṇu possessing all virtues, am the supreme and eternal goddess whose nature is knowledge and bliss, (I am) perfect and perfectly formed and always endowed with His (divine) traits.

32. I, lotus-eyed and lotus-garlanded, supreme lord (lit. mistress) of all beings, am ever served by the supreme eternal śaktis, viz. sṛṣṭi, sthiti etc.

33. I am covered with thirty-two thousand creative śaktis and surrounded by twice that number of divine sustaining śaktis.

34-35. And I am filled with twice that number of destructive śaktis. I am the chief of all śaktis and supreme controller of the whole world. I, the queen-consort of the omnipresent God of gods, (am) the bestower of everything that is desired. In beauty, virtue and age I equal Hari, whose mind I captivate (lit. stir).

36. In those particular states relevant to Lord Śārṅgin's (Viṣṇu's) particular requirements, I, ever endowed with all his attributes, execute His functions.

37. I rest on the knees of Viṣṇu, the God of gods Śārṅgin and very much loved by Him, I have attained (absolute) identity of essence (identification with Him).

38-39. Once on beholding the tormented living beings in the belly of blazing transient existence (*saṃsāra*), pity spontaneously arose in me, who am omniscient; (and I started pondering) how they might overcome their misery and attain happiness, and how after (crossing) the saṃsāra, they might come to me who await them on the further shore.

40-47. Thus overwhelmed with compassion, I pleaded with the God of gods: 'Adorable one, lord, God of the gods, master of the world and (my) beloved, O Acyuta, thou who art the beginning, middle and end of all, the Ultimate above All, O Govinda, the ancient and Supreme Puṇḍarikākṣa, the (sole) guide for crossing the treacherous and shoreless ocean of saṃsāra; thou who art responsible for the four states of existence known as the manifest,

---

[1] viz. *sṛṣṭi*, *sthiti*, *saṃhāra*, *nigraha* and *anugraha*, in other words the goddess's five functions. Vanamālā represents God's potential power or kriyāśakti.

the unmanifest, the knower [1] and time (*kāla*) and (art named) Vāsudeva lord of the universe, Saṃkarṣaṇa master of the universe, the most blessed Pradyumna, and the glorious Aniruddha, the invincible; who art the aggregate of the diverse Vibhavas; who art the possessor of all the various aspects of divine greatness; who possessest a form that is divine, tranquil, active, and blissful, manifesting the six-fold attributes; who art adorned with a bright crown, armlets, necklaces, anklets, kaustubha and the yellow garment; O thou great and generous one with eyes like the lotus; thou four-bodied Caturvyūha, brilliant as the autumnal lotus; O thou exquisitely beautiful Lord Nārāyaṇa embracing the whole universe! These living beings are all drowning in the ocean of suffering. O lord, by what device thinkest thou they can be saved?'

48-49. Thus addressed, the God of gods, the lord, answered with a smile: 'O lotus-seated, lotus-born lotus-goddess, I have devised methods whereby these souls may be liberated. (Such methods are) performing the rites and following the precepts of sāṃkhya and yoga according to sacred texts'.

50. So informed, I answered God, the excellent Person: 'O God of gods, it is impossible for them to follow (these methods) in the course of fleeting time (kāla).

51. Kāla is the inciter; it is independent and its essence is bhavat (becoming). Kāla severs their jñāna, sattva (pure consciousness), physical energy and also their span of life.

52. Various impressions (*vāsanā*) stored in the inner organ under influence of a particular kāla torment the embodied beings.

53. Although thou art unattached, yet thou ascribest to those who perform their functions (duties) the results of their deeds as affected by a particular kāla.

54. O merciful Janārdana, disclose to me who prostrate myself before thee the method that thou, in thy compassion, hast devised to rescue living beings.

55-56. When I had so pleaded, the beloved lord answered me with a smile: 'O lotus-goddess, thou thyself art aware of the answer, and yet thou askest me! Nevertheless, O beautiful one, listen. I have laid down rules for both meritorious and evil deeds and (the latter should be avoided) as prescribed by the religious texts.

---

[1] That is to say, the cosmic self (*jīva* or *Puruṣa*); see ch. V, 25-32.

57. Worthy deeds are those prescribed (by the religious texts); whilst other deeds are prohibited. He who pursues harmful activities is thereby (spiritually) degraded (lit. pulled down).

58-59. He who follows the prescribed methods is uplifted. (But) he who renounces both the prescribed methods and the prohibited deeds and follows a middle course [1] by relying solely on me for protection, ultimately becomes united with me. O lotus-born Goddess, hear me describe the method with six components whereby this can be achieved.

60-62. The resolution to perform only such acts as conform (to my desires); the abandonment of all acts that displease me; the firm conviction that (I) will protect him who chooses me as his (sole) protector; self-surrender and humility; these are the six components of (the middle course called) śaraṇāgati. Having thus obtained my protection, (the adept is) freed from (misfortunes such as) fear, sorrow and exhaustion, from all (selfish) activity and desire, from self-interest and pride; and sheltering in me alone (he) is, as it were, carried across the ocean of worldly existence.

63. The pure, who are intent upon confining themselves solely to the performance of meritorious (pure) deeds and those who know sāṃkhya and yoga, are in no sense comparable to even a billionth fraction of him who has (unreservedly) resorted (to me) for help.'

64. These words of the great God Viṣṇu gave me great satisfaction and I repeat to you what He said.

65. Śakra:—I salute thee, O great Goddess, the beloved of God, who art seated on a lotus. Deign to explain to me in detail what conforming to God's desires: (*ānukūlya*) etc.[2] entails.

66. Śrī:—Ānukūlya entails being benevolently disposed towards (of conforming to the interests of) all beings based on the conviction that I exist in all beings.

67. One should always be favourably disposed (*ānukūlyam ācaret*)

---

[1] The good deeds, such as the Agniṣṭoma sacrifice etc., are those enjoined by the sacred scriptures. Bad deeds, such as killing etc., are those prohibited by those scriptures. A true devotee steers clear of both categories by performing only those deeds which he is bound by duty to perform and refrains from all others, whilst he dedicates both himself and all the results of his acts to God. This is elaborated further on in this chapter as *śaraṇāgati*; cf. Bh.G. chs. 5-6; and Robert C. Lester, The concept of prapatti in the thoughts of Rāmānuja, Reports of All India Oriental Conference Srinagar session, 1961, Vol. II, Part I, pp. 271-285.

[2] The six components of *śaraṇāgati*. See verses 60-61.

towards all beings, just as one is towards me; likewise all forms of hostility towards living beings should be dropped.

68-73. Repudiation of arrogance (implies) humility achieved through sacred knowledge and good conduct. (Sometimes) upāya (the prescribed method) cannot be satisfactorily followed owing to the impossibility of procuring all the requirements for performance of the supporting rites, because of inability to officiate in the prescribed manner, or perhaps again for want of an auspicious opportunity to perform such rites on account of discrepancies in place, time or qualification; whereas as against what is prescribed, what is prohibited (*apāya*) is still more exacting. The repudiation of arrogance calls for timidity (*dainyam*) and humility (*kārpaṇyam*). Since Śakti is innate in God (*sūpasadatvāt*) who is ever merciful; and since there is a basic relationship (between God) as Master and (living beings) as His subjects, the deep-rooted conviction arises in the mind (of devotees) that, because God is benevolent, He will protect them.[1] Such implicit trust, O Śakra, destroys all demerit. Although God is the master of all embodied beings, and although He is full of compassion and capable (of showing it), yet without prayer He will not protect; (this consideration is inducement) to pray (by introducing the words) 'Be my protector', which imply throwing oneself on His protection (*goptṛtvavaraṇam*).

74. (The whole process of renunciation), which starts with waiving the right to claim the results of the deeds (performed by) those who rely solely on God's protection and which ends with relinquishing that privilege in favour of Keśava, is called self-surrender (*ātmanikṣepa*).[2]

75. Nyāsa, which is synonymous with nikṣepa, has five components. It is (also) referred to as saṃnyāsa, tyāga or śaraṇāgati.

76-77. This is the fourth method which was spoken of earlier. It achieves quick results. Those who follow this fourth method as practised by the brahmins tend to regard the three previous methods as less attractive. Practice of the ānukūlya method and the (method) other than ānukūlya (i.e. *prātikūlyasya varjanam*) ensures the avoidance of prohibited deeds.

---

[1] Literally 'God will protect us'.

[2] See ch. XVI, 42-44 echoing the quotation from Bh.G. 18.66: *sarvadharmān parityajya māmekaṃ śaraṇaṃ vraja*.

78-80. It has been said that the practice of kārpaṇya dispenses with the necessity of (adhering to) the upāyas: and yet confidence in God's protection makes it desirable to adhere to the upāya. Goptṛtvavaraṇam proclaims the adept's yearning for protection. (The need for this arises from the consideration) that although the Lord of the universe is omniscient (and) ever compassionate, yet in order not to disturb the law and order of the world He awaits being approached for protection. Dedication of oneself and all one's possessions is called ātmanikṣepa.

81. The śāstra has indicated that violence (*hiṃsā*), theft etc., are apāyas; and that karman (religious duties), sāṃkhya etc., are upāyas.

82-87. He who rejects both upāya and apāya and, convinced of God's protection, has recourse to the middle course by surrendering to God all that he possesses, will realize that Puruṣottama (God), the God of gods, is (his) protector.

Śakra:—O Ambikā, what is this middle course between upāya and apāya? Since all action springs from either upāya or apāya accordingly as the prohibitions and injunctions laid down in the śāstras are obeyed or disregarded, it would appear that every activity necessarily falls either under upāya or apāya.

Śrī:—O king of gods, there are three inscrutable types of karman (deeds); learn to distinguish between them by applying the prohibitions and regulations laid down in the śāstras. Some deeds produce harmful results, whilst others produce beneficial results; others again redeem sins. In the light of the śāstras recognize these three types of deeds.

88-90. The first two types (*rāśi*) known as upāya and apāya should be rejected. The third group that redeems sin (again has two subdivisions). (Of these the first consists of) deeds called prāyaścitta, which annihilate the evil consequences of misdeeds. The intelligent should avoid deeds of that nature, just as in the case of the first two groups. Only those duties, which when performed bring no reward, but when ignored result in harm, should be performed (by the adept).

91. This is the attitude taken by the Vedas, which endorse the middle way between upāya and apāya. He who follows this road seeks refuge in surrendering himself wholeheartedly (*prapadyate*) to the Lord of the universe, Janārdana.

92. The method prescribed by this śāstra,[1] if practised (even) once, will liberate the human being (adept); whereas by following both upāya and apāya he is bereft of that advantage (of prapatti).

93. If one intentionally commits some apāya deed, a redeeming rite should be performed without delay. But he who has sought refuge (*śaraṇāgati*), discovers that act in itself to be as efficacious as prāyaścitta.

94-98. Again, even if the upāyas are accepted as such, the position remains unchanged. In order not to dislocate the laws of dharma and to maintain the family, to govern the world (*loka*) without disturbance, to establish (social) norms and to gratify me and Viṣṇu, the God of gods Śārṅgin, the wise should not violate the Vedic laws even in thought. Just as even a king's favourite, who defiles a river—that is useful to that monarch, a source of pleasure and beneficial to the community for raising the crop—incurs the (death penalty) on the stake, even though he be indifferent to (the river in question), so also does a mortal, who disregards the norm laid down in the Vedas and thereby disobeys my command, forfeit my favour, although he be a favourite of mine.

99-103. Thus mentally giving up attachment to the upāyas, the wise adopt the fourth method, i.e. śaraṇāśraya; and having overcome all affliction (impediments, *kleśa*), enter the pure state (*padam*) of (sattva) existence. Hence the middle course that is neither upāya nor apāya is (called) śaraṇāgati; it is the foremost means (of attaining the *summum bonum*) and enables human beings to traverse the ocean of life and death. It is the only way of refuge whereby both the ignorant and the well-informed may set foot on that longed for farther shore (of ocean-like mundane existence) in order to become eternal.[2] The redemption of sinful acts must be sought through me alone, consort of the God of gods. Abstaining from upāya, (let the human being) take refuge in me.

104-105. (Thus) gradually nearer to me (Śakti) and intent on observing upāya, after harvesting the rewards of his immaculate deeds, he finally becomes detached (from all worldly ties) and

---

[1] Sāttvata scriptures.

[2] Explaining why *śaraṇāgati*, the middle or fourth course, is the best method for escaping misery. Since it entails total surrender of oneself with complete annihilation of the ego, it draws no distinction between learned and ignorant, intelligent and fool, strong and weak.

acquires the highest status. This (i.e. *śaraṇāgati*) or complete self-surrender is a means (of attaining the human goal)—simple to follow, but in my opinion [1] difficult to carry out.

106-107. (Therefore) only the cultured and the wise, who have rid their minds of all desire, choose this road (*śaraṇāgati*). Hence in order to achieve their aim, whether rid of desire or not, men should always worship my mantra-form (*mantramayī tanū*). In accordance with the ritual precepts, the adept should receive initiation from a preceptor, attain the fulfilment of his aspirations and worship my mantra-form with mantras consisting of me.

---

[1] Note use of the phrase 'in my opinion'. Is it the Goddess's opinion or that of the author of the text?

CHAPTER EIGHTEEN

THE COURSE OF MANTRAS AND THEIR CHARACTERISTICS

1. Śakra:—I salute thee again and again, O Goddess, who abidest in the lotus and art lotus-born. I have learned whatever is worth knowing and difficult to glean, even from the Upaniṣads.

2. O beloved of Viṣṇu, describe (to me) the mantra course (leading to the goal), so that I might worship thy divine mantra-form.

3. What is the source of mantras and to what do they ultimately lead (lit. in what do they merge)? O Padmā, what is the purpose of a mantra and how is it sustained during operation? [1]

4. What are its different forms and of what dimension is it? O Ambujā, what are the characteristics of the kṣetra and kṣetrajña states? [2]

5. Who is capable of abridging a mantra, what qualities should a preceptor possess and, O Lotus-born, how should one meditate (on a mantra)?

6-9. O Lotus-born I salute thee, I bow my head down to thy lotus-red feet and shelter under thy protection. Disclose to me in detail the knowledge required for such meditation; the relationship between achievement and the means of attaining it; the relevant pratyayas (experiences); how yoga should be practised and the sacred literature (*svādhyāya*) studied;[3] the methods applicable to rakṣā (protection from evil); [4] the ritual of expiation (*prāyaścitta*); the treatment of funeral rites; the special rites of initiation (*dīkṣā*) and establishment of the deity (*pratiṣṭhā*); and also the rules for drawing religious diagrams (*yantras*),—all these as well as the unseen agency (potency of deeds: *adṛṣṭam*) which is also involved.

10-15. Śrī:—Puraṃdara, the significance of the questions you

---

[1] i.e. how is a mantra to be worshipped?

[2] The field and the knower of the field. The field is the body and everything derived from matter; the knower is God. See Zachner, The Bhagavadgītā, p. 332 and Bh.G. ch. 13, 1-4.

[3] Literature to be studied for the understanding of mantras.

[4] Precautionary measures to be taken to safeguard mantric rituals.

have put is astounding (lit. unparallelled); (and) since I am fond of you, I shall instruct you in everything you need to know. Listen O Vāsava, the lotus-eyed absolute Person (Puruṣa), indicated by (the term) *aham* (I), is the essence inherent in every positive as well as negative state of being; that which permeates both existing and non-existent objects as their *idaṃtā*, (i.e.) the characteristic specific to a particular object. That specific characteristic is (in fact) merged into I-hood (*ahaṃtva*). When this island of idaṃtā becomes submerged, as it were, in the ocean of consciousness, then the infinite Vāsudeva alone, who is inert and devoid of creative activity, remains manifest. I am His absolute I-hood, His unique Śakti consisting of (His) Lord-hood (*īśvaratā*), (and I am) ever creatively active, ever blissful, ever maintaining perfect equilibrium; the source from which all existent objects (*bhāva*, i.e. objects possessing a state of existence) originate and become discernable in all that is cognizable.[1]

16. I am the state *pratibhā* (insight into transcendental truth and reality) inherent in all created (*uddhṛta*) objects and adhering to each of them through all their different phases (of existence).[2]

17. Realization (*avamarśitā*) of Self, identical with knowledge (*avabodha*), is said to be that highly blissful manifestation, Śabdabrahman.

18. I (Śabdabrahman) am essentially consciousness and bliss, the source of all mantras; the absolute; the mother of all sound; Śakti not subjected to appearance and disappearance (i.e. she is constantly present).

19. Nārāyaṇa is the perfect, all-pervading, absolute Brahman, I reflect that state of His being which is known as *śāntatā* (tranquility), (wherein) I am tranquil and (at the same time) the source from which everything originates.

20. That (beginning of) slight effort on my part called *sisṛkṣā* (urge to create) which then stirred in me, is referred to as *śānta*

---

[1] The creative state of Vāsudeva has two phases, śāntodita and nityodita. The first represents the state in which Vāsudeva is periodically inert; whereas the second represents the state in which He actively creates, sustains, destroys, deludes and graces creation.

[2] Pratibhā implies conscious reality which forms the essence of everything. The different phases of a created object's existence are enumerated by Yāska in his Nirukta (I, 1, 1) as: being, appearing, growing, changing, decaying and being destroyed.

unmeṣa (which represents both my inactive and active states) wherein sound and meaning (the object indicated) are distinguished.[1]

21. It is universally understood that indication of an object is invariably preceded by use of the sound denoting it. The nature of the gross form of śabda is that (it is obvious that) the object originates from śabda.

22-23. Śabda is the manifest knowledge (*bodha*), and (*artha*) is the object śabda (sound) manifests; (whereas) the primary manifestation of sound (arises) from Śakti in the form of śāntatā, which (aspect of śakti), known as nāda does not at that stage carry any implication (*vācyatā*). The śakti attached to nāda is called sūkṣmā.

24. The second manifestation (*unmeṣa*) after nāda arising from Śakti is called bindu which, though carrying implication, is not yet manifestly polarized.

25-26. This divine and highly efficacious state of mine is referred to as *paśyantī*. Besides these manifestations of śakti, her third manifestation is the state of madhyamā, in which *saṃgati* (the logical relation of word to meaning) transforms itself into an impression (*saṃskāra*). At this stage, the distinction between the object indicated and the sound denoting it, is (only) discernable in the form of an impression.

27. Śakti's fourth manifestation following that of madhyamā is the state of vaikharī, in which syllables and sentences (words) become clearly recognizable.

28. Alongside these śaktis of mine, I also have a concomitant śakti of activity (*kriyā*) in the form of knowledge (*bodharūpā*), which animates the progressive manifestations of my other śaktis such as nāda etc.[2]

29. Śāntarūpā [3] (i.e. *śāntatā*), paśyantī, madhyamā and vaikharī respectively constitute my fourfold form. I shall now recount to you the four objects denoted (by these sounds) that I have created.[4]

---

[1] In this śāntonmeṣa state, the distinction between sound and meaning, though not apparent, lies dormant. This special feature differentiates this state from the original inert (*śānta*) state of God, when nothing exists save God.

[2] Nāda, bindu, madhyamā and vaikharī are sonic representations of potent śaktis, while the main potent śakti continues to manifest herself as knowledge or realization.

[3] i.e. nāda.

[4] i.e. objects as comprised in the four Vyūha manifestations.

30. Vāsudeva etc. are successively the subtle objects of denotation of śānta etc. (In my sonic state), (first) I assume the form of light (*prakāśa*) and bliss, known as ekapadī.

31. Again the same (i.e. myself) am regarded as dvipadī when differentiated into the object denoted and the sound denoting. When I am classified in (four categories, viz.) ūṣma (*śa, ṣa, sa, ha*), antaḥstha (*ya, ra, la, va*), svara (vowel) and sparśa (consonant), I am called catuṣpadī.

32. When classified in eight categories (of consonants, varga) I am known as aṣṭapadī; and when associated with unvoiced sound (*aghoṣa, viṣarga* etc.) I am navapadī.

33. As the divine and absolute Śabdabrahman, I am ekapadī.[1] In the form of sonants (*ghoṣavarṇa*) I am dvipadī.[2]

34. When producing the entire range of salila (i.e. the undifferentiated creation), viz. dravya (objects), jāti (genus), guṇa (quality) and kriyā (action), described as fourfold, I am called catuṣpadī [3] by the learned.

35. Upon further subdivision into names and objects (named), I am traditionally said to be aṣṭapadī.[4] In the state of avikalpa (when undifferentiated in concept) and vikalpa (differentiated), I am said to be navapadī.[5]

36-37. In the supreme space (*parama-vyoma*) I exist as the divine, total and original I-hood, adorned with the garland of eternal akṣaras (sounds and letters of the alphabet) spanning all space. I am known as the mother of all mantras bestowing both prosperity and liberation. All mantras surge up like waves from me, the ocean, as it were, of consciousness.

38. These forms (masses) of sounds, lovely as concentrations of consciousness and bliss, evolve out of me as their substratum and repeatedly flow back into me.

---

[1] As Śabdabrahman sound is one, integral reality.

[2] When manifest or voiced, sound reveals both the aspects of non-manifest and manifest sound.

[3] i.e. sounds denoting any of these four categories of objects.

[4] Each of these four categories is subdivided into two, as the thing and its name.

[5] When these eight representations of sound are counted together with the one integral unpolarized sound, the sonic śakti is considered to have nine variations cf. Ṛg V. 1, 164, 41. For detailed exposition see V. S. Agarwala, Gaurī, American Oriental Series Vol. 47. New Haven, 1962.

39-42. Mantras that are of an efficacious and beneficial nature replete with me; phonetic units; parts of speech; sentences as well as treatises (*prakaraṇa*) and subdivisions (*āhnikas*); parts of texts such as chapters, paragraphs, cantos, ucchvāsas, paṭalas etc.; praśnas; vāks, anuvāks; maṇḍalas; kāṇḍas and diverse saṃhitās; Ṛk, Yajus and Sāman; sūktas as well as khilas; words forming śāstras and tantras; also the external (public) and internal (esoteric) āgamas and all the various languages—all these fall under direct or indirect speech (*gīr*).

43. This, Śakra, is the form of mantras. In accordance with the grade (relative strength) of the impulse (mental realization), a particular mantra is prescribed for the individual adept.

44-45. A mantra is sound (*dhvani*), which (the adept invariably) associates (with the belief that) 'This protects me', and which always protects from fear a person who (knows) the secret purport (of mantras). Every manifestation of I-hood in the graded sequence peculiar to sound,[1] based on absolute Ī-hood and inducive to the revelation of pure knowledge, is according to tradition a mantra.

46. In fact all mantras (repeated) by those who have discovered the secret of creation and dissolution belong to me. According to the level of the adept's mental realization, a mantra is addressed either to me or to some other (deity).

47. Mantras mainly founded on basic words generally belong to me. By their very nature these attain Brahman, which is both existent and the state of existence (*bhavat* and *bhāva*).

48-50. Mantras essentially founded on basic words protect and deliver. Mantras that of their own accord reach bhāva which extends beyond bhavat, such as the tāra, prāsādaka[2] etc., are known to have an emancipating influence. Mantras, such as Tārikā etc., which state that the condition of bhavat surpasses and, at the same time, equals that of bhāva, are known to be efficacious in procuring wealth as well as emancipation.[3] Some of these mantras find their destination in bhāva whilst others reach bhavat.

---

[1] Explained earlier in this chapter.

[2] Tāra-mantra: *oṃ*, Prāsāda-mantra: *oṃ hau*. These solely yield emancipation.

[3] Tārikā i.e. *hrīṃ*, etc., mantras which yield both material prosperity and emancipation.

51. It is generally recognized that the very nature of this type of mantra is directed towards the acquisition of wealth and emancipation, since it is aimed at the attainment of both bhavat and bhāva.[1]

---

[1] Implying that since Śakti is manifest in both created objects and the transcendental Self, She combines in herself two aspects: the material and the spiritual.

CHAPTER NINETEEN

THE ORIGIN OF LETTERS

1. I am the primary, total I-hood of Hari, characterized by the creative urge (*sisṛkṣā*). Being the supreme Śakti manifest as creation, I become creatively active.

2-3. O delight of the gods, I have fifteen similar (states) of existence (*daśā*).[1] The eternal essence of myself (as) speech (*vāc*) is akāra (*a*), which is primary and self-revealed, is consciousness and the root of the entire domain [2] of speech. When the same (*akāra*) develops [3] into the ānanda form (*ā*), the latter is regarded as the second svara (sound, i.e. vowel).

4. The third (vowel) appears as icchā (*i*) and the fourth as īśāna (*ī*). The fifth is unmeṣa (*u*) while the sixth is said to be ūrja (*ū*).

5-7. The four middle (vowels, i.e. *ṛ, ṝ, ḷ, ḹ*) are modifications of icchā etc.[4] Combination of the first (vowel) with icchā indeed produces ekāra (*e*); the same (vowel i.e. *icchā*) when combined with ānanda is named jagadyoni (*ai*). The combination of the first (vowel) with unmeṣa (*u*), indeed, produces okāra (*o*) which, when combined with the first (vowel), produces the (sound) sadyojāta (*au*). Thus (all) these (sounds which ultimately) relate to objects of knowledge[5] are derived from the first (vowel).

8-9. The thirteen (vowels), viz. ānanda etc., are specific elaborations (of the first sound). When these thirteen developments reach the stage of representing nothing but knowledge itself—their final and most subtle stage—the fifteenth sound (*ṃ*) emerges.[6] These

---

[1] The fifteen vowels: *a, ā, i, ī, u, ū, ṛ, ṝ, ḷ, ḹ, e, ai, o, au, ṃ*.

[2] i.e. everything that can be traced to speech.

[3] The process of cosmic creation is exactly imitated here. *a* being the root, all subsequent sounds are projections or transformations of it and each successive sound is an effect of the sound immediately preceding it.

[4] That is to say, *ṛ* is a modification of *i*, *ṝ* of *ī*, *ḷ* of *u*, and *ḹ* of *ū*.

[5] Emphasizing that in this manifest state of sound (*vaikharī*), it is totally polarized as the sound and its meaning, and no unrelated sound can be conceived in this stage. This trait distinguishes *vaikharī* from the two states of unpolarized sound (*nāda* and *bindu*) and from the state when sound is potentially polarized (*madhyamā*).

[6] The thirteen modifications of *a* represent the created states, while *a*

fifteen states represent the (results of) the (first) creative efforts (of Śakti) in (cosmic) creation.

10. Owing to the divine creative śakti's urge to create furnished with these fifteen limbs, she becomes active in (creating) each specific object.

11-12. From me (Śakti) engaged in the function of creating, emerged the twenty-five (cosmic) principles beginning with puruṣa and ending with pṛthivī, as well as (the corresponding sounds, akṣara) starting with *ka* and ending with *ma*. (It should be noted that) each principle emerges from the manifestation of its correlated sound. The four sounds viz. *ya* to *va* [1] are named the fourfold *dhāraṇā*.

13. As these are themselves composed of puruṣa, they are regarded as dhāraṇā.[2] *Yakāra*, consisting of a particle of (Śakti's) active (aspect), is called *vāta*.

14-16. Repha (*ra*), (being) vidyā (learning) which consists of a trifling fraction of (her) jñāna (aspect), is named pāvaka. Lakāra (*la*), representing māyā as a combination of insensibility (rigidity) and delusion (infatuation), is regarded as pṛthivī. Vakāra, which in essence is joy, is (called) Varuṇa and (represents) rāga (bliss) śakti. Those versed in the philosophical realities should view these four dhāraṇās as the support of man in between his two states (of existence viz.) the absolute and the relative (*parā* and *aparā*). The letters from *śa* to *kṣa* (*śa, ṣa, sa, ha, kṣa*) represent the fivefold pure Brahman.[3]

17-19. O lord of the gods, *śa, ṣa, sa* and *ha* should be regarded as

---

represents the *avyakta* or primordial state of creation. *ṃ* represents the final annihilation of creation when even the primordial nature is dissolved into the ultimate principle viz. knowledge, or in other words when nothing save Brahman exists.

[1] *ya, ra, la, va.*

[2] *ka* to *ma* represent the Self's material state of differentiated existence; *śa* to *ha* and *kṣa* its unpolarized absolute state; *ya* to *va* its intermediate state when through meditation it descends from the absolute to the differentiated state. Dhāraṇā means deep meditation with the mind fixed on a single object. Cf. *sa tapo 'tapyata* Bṛ.Ā.U. 1, 2, 6. A point of further interest is that normally these four sounds are called *antaḥstha*, which the text seeks to interpret as possessing God within themselves and to link up with dhāraṇā, which is also derived from the root *dhṛ-* meaning "to hold". See verse 15.

[3] The term Pañca-brahman is noteworthy. These are Satya and the four Vyūhas.

(representing) Aniruddha etc.[1] That wonderful form which I assume when I feel the stir of activity at the very commencement of creation, is the powerful śakti which is the soul of *kṣa*—otherwise known as Satyā. The five divine śaktis beginning with pṛthivī and ending with viyat (space) [2] represent my divine existence-principle, the five (divine attributes), such as bala etc.[3] These five śaktis emanating from me as jñāna are represented by *śa* etc.[4] when I am creatively active.

20. Visarga (*ḥ*), formerly described as possessing fifteen components (*a* to *ṃ*), represents myself when I consist of Soma and am surrounded by billions of rays.

21-22. O Puraṃdara, these two, bindu and visarga (*ṃ*, *ḥ*) representing the sun and the moon, are my (i.e. Somaśakti's) contracting and expanding state of existence.[5] The last[6] of (Somaśakti's fifteen) limbs, which I have referred to as the fifteenth, is Sūrya (the sun) which is receptive in nature and the swift destroyer.

23. Each of these two luminaries (*devayoḥ*) [7] possesses seven rays, so the remaining fourteen (*a-au*) vowels are construed as seven pairs.

24. O Puraṃdara, the first seven sounds (viz. *a*, *i*, *u*, *ṛ*, *ḷ*, *e*, *o*,) of these seven pairs are the rays of my sun-form in which I am (then) called the enjoyer, and my rays are the absorbers (*śoṣaka*: that which soaks up).

25. The last seven sounds (viz. *ā*, *ī*, *ṝ*, *ḹ*, *ai*, *au*) of (these) pairs are the cool, pleasant and nourishing rays of my moon-form. I am (then) called the object of enjoyment.

26. Light, sharpness, pervasiveness, assimilation (the mind's capacity to grasp, *grahaṇa*), projection (*kṣepaṇa*), agitation (*īraṇa*)

---

[1] i.e. *śa*, *ṣa*, *sa* and *ha* represent the four Vyūha forms from Aniruddha to Vāsudeva respectively.

[2] The five cosmic elements earth, water, light, air and ether.

[3] Bala, vīrya, tejas, śakti and aiśvarya.

[4] *śa*, *ṣa*, *sa*, *ha* and *kṣa*. It is interesting to note that these five sounds represent the original śakti and her subsequent manifestation as different aspects of kriyāśakti. In this context Aniruddha, Pradyumna, Saṃkarṣaṇa and Vāsudeva respectively represent the bala, vīrya, tejas and śakti attributes of kriyāśakti.

[5] *ṃ* represents the state of dissolution and *ḥ* the state of creation. That is why *ḥ* is said to comprise all fifteen vowels representing both creation and dissolution.

[6] [illegible]

[7] [illegible] and *m* = Sūrya.

and maturity (*pāka*)—these are the characteristics of the first seven rays originating from the sun.

27. Fluidity, coolness, calmness, loveliness, contentment, delight and bliss are the characteristics of the seven rays belonging to the moon.

28-29. The great sṛṣṭi (śakti) Mahānandā, adorned with clusters of millions of śaktis—resplendent with these rays consisting of Agni (i.e. *Sūrya*) and the moon and manifesting herself by embodying (making her own) the Person in the form of bindu (which represents the state of existence) consecutively following the Soma-form—appears actively as the final vowel (*ḥ*).

30. O lord of the gods, this fivefold Brahman, viz. starting from *kṣa* and ending with *śa*, issuing from her,[1] is now active and characterized by a (further) manifestation of Śakti.

31-33. *Kṣa* represents great agitation which precedes creation and is known as Satya. *Ha* goes by the name of Vāsudeva. *Sa* is the Saṃkarṣaṇa-manifestation. Pradyumna is represented by *ṣa* and Aniruddha by *śa*. Manifestations of these five sublime śaktis inherent in the fivefold Brahman and identical with manifestations of myself, are the causes for the appearance of the universe. (They stand in a similar relation to me, who am Brahman) as power to burn stands in relation to a mighty fire.

34-37. The four created dhāraṇās, viz. (the sounds) from *va* to *ya* represent, O Puraṃdara, the person's (four) states of existence viz. turīya to jāgrat respectively. In between the two states, viz. the Brahman state and the created state, they (i.e. the dhāraṇās) are imbued with the person. In between what is called the Brahman-state and the prakṛti-state beginning with *bha*, is the state called *ma*. The person is regarded as having various (states of existence), viz. jāgrat etc., vested in the four dhāraṇās. If he were not thus inherent during these (transitional states of existence, viz. dhāraṇā), (the person) would be either in the Brahman-state or in the created-state, and no movement (in the saṃsāra: *saṃsṛti*) would be possible.

38. Therefore at my bidding the dhāraṇās are manifested out of myself. Hence the person known as bhoktṛ (i.e. jīva) represents a fourfold state (of existence).

39. *Ma*, capable of enjoying (the fruits of the jīva's activities) and

[1] i.e. the kriyāśakti called the Agni-Somaśakti. See ch. XXIX in extenso.

at the same time capable of achieving emancipation, is a direct offshoot of myself, O Vāsava, for the purpose of creating objects of enjoyment for this person to delight in.

40. The insentient, supreme, subtle equilibrium of the guṇas—regarded as peculiar to the womb—has spontaneously emerged out of myself as *bha*.

41-42. In order to provide the enjoying sage (the jīva) with objects of enjoyment as well as the acts of enjoyment, O Puraṃdara, all manifested objects have gradually evolved from me out of the group of sounds ranging from *ba* to *ka*; these are twenty-three in number. Buddhi, ahaṃkāra and manas are created from the three, *ba* etc.[1]

43. The five (cognitive organs, viz.) the auditory and other organs, are represented by the sounds from *na* to *ta*. The five (conative organs, viz.) speech etc., are created from the sounds *ṇa* to *ṭa*.

44. The five element-potentials, such as sound etc., are created from *ña* to *ca*. The subtle elements such as space etc., are created from *ṅa* to *ka*.

45. Knowledge (insight, bodha) appears as identical with sound, and sound (as) identical with the objects connoted. Considering that knowledge (insight) is one of my aspects, it follows that all the abovementioned sounds (are projections) of myself.

46. O lord of the gods, this course of sound (i.e. sonic creation) representing the intermediate way, has thus been revealed to you. Now hear me describe the first and the last (course).

---

[1] *ba*, *pha* and *pa*.

CHAPTER TWENTY

EXPLANATION OF THE MĀTṚKĀS [1]

1. Śakra:—I salute thee, O Śakti who createst, sustainest and engulfest all, who art the self(hood) of Hari and ultimate knowledge (*jñāna*) itself.

2. O Padmā, through thy grace I have heard the great secret (of truth). Now please give me a detailed explanation of the systematic composition (i.e. method) of sounds (syllables).

3. Śrī:—O celestial man, hear the primordial disposition of the course (journey) of sound, knowledge of which enables the meditating adept to resemble me (become one in form with me, *sarūpatā*).

4. The ultimate (absolute) imperishable Brahman, undifferentiating between (the polarization of) knowledge and agent, appearing in the form of ever shining light and identical with the All, is termed aham (I).

5. Its ever active Śakti is the I-hood identified with It, and appears as inextinguishable light and is devoid of (polarization of) knowledge and its agent.

6-7. I (the same Śakti) am the essence of light and bliss endowed with perfect equilibrium. When in order to liberate the jīvas, my own śakti activates merely a ten millionth of a hundred-thousand-billionth fraction of myself, I then automatically evolve out of the great God into Śabdabrahman.

8. Consider this unmanifested eternal (Śabdabrahman) as resembling the faint sound produced by (the automatic vibration of) the strings (of a musical instrument).[2] That (faint sound) is indeed multiplied by numerous other sounds (*varṇa*) in order to sustain (creation).

9-10. As the subtle sound (*varṇa*), it represents the continuous flow (of sound immanent in all sound).[3] For he who, freed from the

---

[1] Mātṛkā is the collective term for the letters or sound units, which are named *mātṛkā*, or mother, because they form the basis or source of all logos.

[2] This attempts to describe the spontaneous sound vibration called Śabdabrahman by emphasizing its indistinct or unpolarized nature.

[3] The text here equates various aspects of Śabdabrahman with Sūtrātman. As the Self, being the essence of All, is immanent in All, so is Śab-

five courses (of creation) [1] and the five sheaths,[2] relies on me and perceives truth by favour of the Supreme Soul, it (Śabdabrahman) holds the position of integral intuitive experience (of the Highest, *anubhūti*).[3] My fourfold form (viz. the Vyūhas) is regarded as identical with it (viz. Śabdabrahman).[4]

11-14. During the evolutionary process represented by the letters *a* to *sa*, it (viz. Śabdabrahman) is characterized by sound, whereas, during the involutionary process represented by (the reverse order of the sounds from) *ha* to *ā*, it is characterized by knowledge.[5] During the evolution of the four deities (viz. the Vyūhas) *ha* represents dvādaśānta; whereas during their involution *a* (*akāra*) holds that position.[6] Thus either of these letters may stand at dvādaśānta. In this Vyūha aggregate composed of sound, it should be recognized by virtue of jñāna-samādhi that Vāsudeva (and the other deities in Vyūha-form) exist in the states of inertia (*viśrāma*), primary creative activity (*udaya*), pervasion (*vyāpti*) and manifesta-

---

dabrahman, the subtle sound, immanent in all sounds as their essence. It is to be noted that Śabdabrahman, being identical with Śakti is fundamentally one with Brahman.

[1] viz. bhuvanādhvan, padādhvan, mantrādhvan, tattvādhvan and kalādhvan.

[2] viz. māyākośa, prasūtikośa, prakṛtikośa, brahmāṇḍakośa and jīvakośa.

[3] Here Śabdabrahman is identified with the revelation of Brahman which, on the one hand, is the cause of emancipation and on the other hand, since Brahman and Its knowledge are identical, is Brahman Itself.

[4] Described later in this chapter.

[5] That is to say that in the process of creation evolving out of Śabdabrahman, the latter retains its original sonic character and hence the sound *a* represents Śabdabrahman as the sonic origin of creation; whereas in the process of involution, the ultimate reality that remains after the total dissolution of all creation is represented by the sound *ha*, and is in the form of absolute knowledge in which the identity of Śabdabrahman is merged and loses its sonic character.

[6] The whole structure of sounds or letters is here being fitted into the inner yogic body of a person, which consists of twelve lotuses starting from ādhārapadma and ending with dvādaśānta (see chs. XXXV, XXXIII and ch. XXXVI, 37-48 with editor's notes). This inner body is the microcosmic representation of the macrocosmos. The sounds also represent the cosmos and are divided into twelve groups of four sounds (14 vowels and 34 other sounds totalling 48). Each of these four sounds is respectively presided by the four Vyūha deities, Vāsudeva etc. Further on this is referred to as obverse and reverse creation where *ha* and *a* respectively represent culminating points at the end and at the beginning of creation, the primordial nature or avyakta. Note that the number of letter-groups is the same as that of the deities called Vyūhantaras, emanating from the Vyūhas. Cf. p. 60f., n. 3, supra.

tion (*vyakti*) [1] (respectively). At this point the embodiment (personification) of each deity should be recognized as linked up with one of these four states, i.e. viśrāma and the others.

15-17. One should reflect on the eternal God Vāsudeva, the eternal primary God Puṇḍarikākṣa (represented by) the sound *a*, as denoting inertia (*viśrāma*), for when dissolution comes, the principles viz. Saṃkarṣaṇa etc., will still be resting in this (Vāsudeva). Next, one should reflect on illustrious Saṃkarṣaṇa as represented by the *ā* and as being the *udaya* (primary creative activity); for he is the creative principle behind everything (created), the deity who spontaneously started creating the All. One should reflect on illustrious Pradyumna who, as (being) the *i*, underwent expansion.

18. Identical with trayīkarman,[2] he expands (i.e. manifests himself as) the variegated universe (and that) manifestation in turn should be reflected on as Aniruddha, represented by the *ī*.

19. At this juncture all the śaktis, such as the functions of creating the world etc., have become manifest.[3] Thus in structure they resemble a staff.[4]

20. Up to *sa* my fourfold nature is connected with the four Vyūha states. In reflecting on the process of evolution, the sound *ha* should be placed last in these twelve groups (of sounds).

21-24. During the process of involution (*apyaya*) however, *ha* should be identified with Vāsudeva in viśrāma (state of inertia), *sa* with Saṃkarṣaṇa in udaya. In the same way one should reflect on (the akṣaras) up to *ā* as representing the celestial state of the fourfold existence.[5] The two groups of six dhāraṇās,[6] characterized by the twelve adhyātmans (letters) serve as steps for the (spiritual) ascension to the Supreme, which (the adept) reaches at the end of (these) twelve steps. This explains the first systematic arrangement of sounds (*varṇamārga*), which is subtle, represents my fourfold

[1] These are the respective characteristics of the four manifestations of God, Vāsudeva, Saṃkarṣaṇa, Pradyumna and Aniruddha.

[2] See Schrader, p. 82. Besides his creative functions each Vyūha deity has certain moral functions. Pradyumna is the custodian of law and order enjoined by the Vedas.

[3] Here the term śaktis stands for the five divine functions, namely creation, sustenance, destruction, delusion and grace.

[4] Meaning that these twelve groups become manifest in a gradual order of progressive grossness, in a vertical form.

[5] i.e. the four Vyūha deities.

[6] Dhāraṇā = the object on which the mind is fixed in meditation.

nature,[1] is unrivalled and has the form of knowledge. The intermediary (method) has already been indicated; now hear from me its distinctive (feature).

25. Among the four dhāraṇās already referred to as reflecting my own form, *va* is described as rāga, the śakti of Aniruddha.

26. Māyā, being the other name of Mahālakṣmī, is represented by *la*. Vidyā, represented by repha (*ra*), is (also) known as Mahāvāṇī.

27-29. *ya* represents Mahākālī, the kriyāśakti, (and) is known as vāta. The triad form of Brahmā etc. (i.e. Brahmā, Viṣṇu and Rudra) whose wives are Trayī etc. (i.e. Trayī, Gaurī and Śrī), is represented by the first part of the subtle *ma*, the middle portion (of the same) represents the Bhoktṛkūṭastha Puruṣa,[2] whereas the remainder of that letter represents everyone in the empirical worlds.[3] Thus has been disclosed to you the intermediary system of letters.

30. O slayer of the demon Bala, I shall now explain to you the last method.[4] This third system of vaikharī [5] is identified with the seat of effort (*prayatnasthāna*).[6]

31-36. This is unmistakably revealed through utterance of the manifest sound. This (manifest sound) mātṛkā, which indicates to the jīvas that are fettered to bodies the right path they should follow, is a projection of Viṣṇuśakti. It is said that, like Viṣṇu, the mātṛkā also has fifty śaktis resting in it making up a garland of sounds. The twelve (deities) such as Keśava and the others associated with the four Vyūhas of Vāsudeva etc.,[7] are the presiding deities of the (vowels). Now hear (the names of) their śaktis. (These are) Lakṣmī, Kīrti, Jayā and Māyā, called the Vyūhaśaktis. Śrī, Vāgīśvarī, Kānti, Kriyā, Śānti, Vibhūti, Icchā, Prīti, Rati, Māyā, Dhī and Mahimā are the (names of the) śaktis of Keśava etc., referred to

---

[1] i.e. Vyūha nature.

[2] The cosmic Person.

[3] *ma* is viewed in the three states of existence: the absolute—representing the divine triad and their consorts; the subtle or intermediary—representing the cosmic Person; and the gross —representing each and every living being.

[4] Apparently sounds from *ha* to *śa* represent the paśyantī state of sound; from *va* to *ya* the madhyamā state; and from *bha* to *ka* the vaikharī state; whereas *ma* represents all three states together.

[5] That which is manifest.

[6] The place in the mouth touched by the tongue in order to produce a sound.

[7] i.e. Vyūhāntaras.

as the vowel śaktis. Now listen to a description of the deities that reside in *ka* etc.

37-43. The afore-mentioned (Vibhavas) of Viṣṇu, such as Padmanābha etc., are the (presiding) deities of (the sounds) *ka* etc. (They are as follows:) Padmanābha, Dhruva, Ananta, Śaktīśa, Madhusūdana, Vidyādhideva, Kapila, Viśvarūpa, Vihaṃgama, Kroḍātman, Baḍabāvaktra, Dharma, Vāgīśvara, the god Ekārṇavaśaya immersed in the general flood, Kūrma the supporter of pātāla (the nether regions), Varāha, Narasiṃha and Amṛtāharaṇa; Śrīpati of celestial form, Kāntātman the bearer of amṛta, Rāhujit, Kālanemighna, the mighty Pārijātahara, Lokanātha, Śāntātman, the powerful lord Dattātreya, Nyagrodhaśāyin, the much loved Ekaśṛṅgatanu, in the form of a dwarf and Trivikrama pervader of the universe, Nara and Nārāyaṇa, Hari and also Kṛṣṇa; Rāma with the blazing axe, and the other Rāma with the bow, Vedavid, lord Kalkin and the lord Pātālaśayana.

44. The last mentioned group, viz. Rāma etc., also preside over the (sounds) raṅga (nasalization), yama (transitional sound before a nasal), jihvāmūlīya, and upadhmānīya (substitutes for the visarga).[1]

45-50. Dhī, Tārā, Vāruṇī, Śakti, Padmā, Vidyā, Saṃkhyā, Viśvā, Khagā, Bhū, Go, Lakṣmī, Vāgīśvarī, Amṛtā, Dharaṇī, Chāyā, Nārasiṃhī, Sudhā. Śrī, Kīrti, Viśvakāmā, Mā, Satyā, Kānti, Saroruhā, Māyā, Padmāsanā, Kharvā, Vikrānti, Narasaṃbhavā, Nārāyaṇī, Haripriti, Gāndhārī, Kāśyapī, Vaidehī, Vedavidyā, Padminī, Nāgaśāyinī—all these goddesses together with the deities presiding over the mātṛkā, who are instrumental in the functioning of the phenomenal world, (deities such as) Śrīkaṇṭha, Ānanda, Sūkṣma etc., śaktis such as Lambodarī etc., the Vināyakas, Durgās, Kṣetreśas, Mātaras, all the conventional deities (belonging to this system) as well as the others belonging to the Buddhist and Jaina systems form part of me and should be regarded as the śaktis of (the sounds) *ka* etc.

51. As hungry children resort to their mother, so do all these deities resort to the goddess mātṛkā.

52. This (mātṛkā) is the source of all mantras, the origin of all sciences and the soil from which all the principles, all sages and all knowledge are born.

---

[1] See Ṛgvedaprātiśākhya, I, 10 and VI, 29, 30, 32-34.

CHAPTER TWENTY-ONE

ANALYSIS OF THE STRUCTURE OF A MANTRA AND THE QUALITIES LOOKED FOR IN A PRECEPTOR AND IN A DISCIPLE

1. Śakra:—I salute thee who art the (differentiated) revelation of sound and object (*śabda* and *artha*), who traversest the six courses (of creation), who art called the illuminating knowledge (*avabodha*) that lies beyond these ways and who art the beloved of Hari.

2. O goddess, (the system of) sounds from which all else springs has been fully dealt with. Now please duly explain the system (usage) of the mantra.

3. Śrī:—The greatest Person (*Puruṣa*), the possessor of Śrī, is the one absolute God who is the ocean of the six attributes; who is the divine, inner principle underlying and pervading All.[1]

4. I, Śrī, am His supreme Śakti identical with His I-hood, the substratum and śakti of everything, omniscient and all-pervading.

5. Through me the universe becomes visible, in the same way as a mountain (is reflected) in a mirror. My essential nature (*svarūpa*) is intelligence (*bodha*) characterized by pure bliss.

6. Without hindrance I follow the dictates of my will. Evolving that part of myself which represents bodha I become Śabdabrahman; and continue to evolve (further) through the course of kalās.[2]

7. The term kalā denotes the six qualities, viz. jñāna etc., belonging to the supreme God. With these, arranged in three pairs, I evolve by means of the tattvas.

8. O thou most valiant of all gods, the deities Saṃkarṣaṇa etc. are represented by the tattvas. Again I evolve by means of mantras through sound combinations.

9. Now attend whilst I reveal the system of the mantras. This (science) has developed out of Śabdabrahman and is endowed with millions of rays.

---

[1] Lit. facing all directions: *sarvatomukhaḥ*.

[2] The divine attributes: jñāna, aiśvarya, śakti, bala, vīrya and tejas.

10. Consciousness is its (mantra's) main characteristic; infused with the six (divine) qualities it can be classified in four types. Sometimes it is bīja, sometimes it is piṇḍa, sometimes it is saṃjñā and at other times it is pada.[1]

11-12. O lord of the gods, (the four stages of development of the individual soul, viz.) turya, suṣupti, svapna and jāgrat are respectively (represented by) bīja etc. A bīja(-mantra) may contain either one vowel or two vowels; it may be formed by coupling a vowel with a consonant, or it may even contain several vowels. The haris (consonants) inserted between (the bīja and the remainder of the mantra) are known as the piṇḍa section in which the consonants are sometimes connected with vowels.

13-14. The saṃjñā is the name of a particular deity addressed in association with (the words) *namas* and *praṇava*. A laudatory and vocative combination of verbal utterance with nominal concepts, fraught with recollections from the past and used to further the purpose envisaged, is the essential form of the pada-mantra. Together these four (sections) of mantras make up a whole that bears relation to the nature of the deity addressed.

15-16. The latter, approached by means of a mantra composed of these four sections grants (the adept) the fulfilment of his desire. O lord of the gods, the wise should refrain from applying these mantras until they can clearly distinguish between *kṣetra* and *kṣetrajña* mantras (those pertaining to the body and those pertaining to the soul).

17. Śakra:—O Ambujā, please elaborate on the distinction between *kṣetra* and *kṣetrajña* mantras, which safeguards (an adept from delusion) and enables him to achieve speedy fulfilment of his aspiration.

17-21. Śrī:—(In mantras containing a bīja) the bīja refers to the soul (*jīva*, life principle, i.e. *kṣetrajña*); the rest of the mantra refers to the body. In the case of mantras without a bīja, the first sound represents the soul and the rest represents the body. (In the case of

[1] Although bīja, piṇḍa, saṃjñā and pada together form a complete mantra, each of these is in itself efficacious as a mantra. Especially the first is often used independently. Therefore it is safer to say that these four together form a mantra-complex appropriate to a particular deity; but one, two, or three of them may also serve for purposes of meditation. It should be noted however that the bīja invariably constitutes the essential part of a particular deity's mantra, cf. verses 13-21.

mantras consisting of only) a bīja or a piṇḍa section, the *a* is regarded as the soul and the rest as the body. In cases of (mantras) without an *a*, another vowel is taken to represent the soul. In the case of (mantras containing) only vowels, the first mātrā (*mora*, prosodic unit) refers to the soul, whilst the body is represented by the second etc. When there is only one mātrā in a mantra the saṃskāra (i.e. the subtle sound: *madhyamā*), characterized as transcendental, is considered to represent the soul, while the uttered sounds relate to the body. In the case of piṇḍa mantras that contain no vowel, the first (letter) represents the soul and the rest the body.

22-25. Thus I have revealed which portions of a mantra relate to the body and which to the soul. If a piṇḍa or a bīja appears in all three positions of a mantra, viz. the beginning, middle and end, or in any one of these, that mantra is regarded as *sarvakālika* (applicable at all times).[1] When there is no bīja in a mantra, the bīja should be formed by taking the first sound and joining *ṃ* to it;[2] in this way the (mantra) can be made into a complete formula. Mantras have the effect of making the soul (*puruṣa*) sport[3] when it is weighed down with passion (feeling) whilst on its journey through the material world with its fourteen divisions (i.e. whilst passing through the fourteen worlds), and also when it passes through the pada-course of creation consisting of suṣupti etc. excepting in the turya state.[4]

26-27. Mantras that bestow grace lead a person (adept), who is under the direct guidance (lit. glance) of a preceptor and whose senses have been brought under proper control, beyond the course of the phenomenal world and the course of pada by instilling into him a sense of complete detachment; and those mantras eventually guide him step by step along the courses of tattva, kalā and varṇa.[5]

28. Having finally obtained grace through the mantras and having

---

[1] A sārvakālika mantra, e.g. *oṃ kṣīṃ kṣiḥ namaḥ, nārāyaṇāya viśvātmane hrīṃ svāhā*, can be meditated on for all purposes.

[2] As for example the mantra *oṃ gaṇapataye namaḥ*, in which *gaṃ* is the bīja.

[3] i.e. be active. Cf. V. S. 2, 1. 33 '*lokavat tu līlākaivalyam*'.

[4] Although padādhvan consists of all the four footsteps of the Soul, turya, suṣupti, svapna and jāgrat, the first has been exempted here since that is the Soul's natural state of existence.

[5] In other words, mantras lead the adept beyond all the courses of creation by assisting him to become completely detached and so achieve the state of absolute liberation.

shaken off all the fetters (of worldly existence), (the adept) enters [1] that eternal Brahman known as Lakṣmī-Nārāyaṇa.

29-30. Śakra:—O goddess, what are the qualities required of a preceptor and of a disciple? Which of the mantras is most efficacious for attaining the Ultimate (absolute); and how should that be taught (to a disciple)? I salute thee, please tell me.

30-33. Śrī:— (A preceptor should be) endowed with all auspicious attributes. He should be a brahmin well-versed in the Vedas; infallible in performing his six duties; [2] unperturbed; engaged in performing the rites prescribed for the five different times of a day; [3] of a pure nature; master of the knowledge concerning the purpose of the Pāñcarātra system. He should be silent and exert himself in (studying) the nature of the akṣaras and the mantras. He should be neither fat, thin, nor short. He should not be blind in one or both eyes, neither should he be diseased, deaf, an idiot, bald, crippled or with defect in any limb, or in possession of an extra limb. He should not be a leper, verbose (*ḍāmbika?*), passionate, suffering from any skin-disease, or easily overcome by greed.

34-35. One should avoid a preceptor who comes from a low family, is a rogue, cheat, or dishonest. (He) should possess kindness, self-control, calmness, firm devotion and should never overlook (his religious duties); he should be truthful, well-mannered, skilled in drawing diagrams (of yantras), completely rid of all sensuality, contented and with a mind filled with compassion.

36. He should have all the characteristics of a gentleman, be straightforward, and have an engaging smile. A preceptor possessed of all these qualities may be recognized as being a (true) Vaiṣṇava (guru).

37. The disciple, too, should possess similar characteristics and be favourably endowed. He should be of a forbearing nature, keenly intelligent and devoid of anger and greed.

38. He should always be intent on (performing his duties such as) bathing, [4] worshipping [5] etc., and should be ready at all times to

---

[1] The adept becomes identified with Lakṣmī-Nārāyaṇa, or the Supreme Being. This is in fact what absolute liberation means.

[2] Studying, teaching, performing sacrifices, officiating as a priest, giving presents and accepting gifts.

[3] See ch. XVII, 13.

[4] Religious bath.

[5] Worshipping Vaiṣṇava deities.

obey his preceptor; he should respect brahmins, fire, gods and forefathers and be disposed to gratify (gods and the dead).

39. He should be of good family, have wisdom and apply himself consistently to the study of the sacred scriptures. He may be a brahmin, kṣatriya, vaiśya or śūdra [1] devoted to Lord (Viṣṇu).

40-41. After regarding himself as (the disciple's) preceptor (and ascertaining) that he (the pupil) possesses all the necessary qualifications,[2] the preceptor who is God Himself [3] should teach him all the mantras. (And he should accord the same treatment even) to a woman who respects her husband, never neglects her religious and social duties, has a clear notion of truth and has obtained her husband's permission (to become an adept).[4]

---

[1] The Pāñcarātra system admits even a śūdra as an initiate, provided he is dedicated to Lord Viṣṇu.

[2] This actually means acceptance of the disciple by the preceptor.

[3] To the disciple, especially when undergoing purificatory rites *bhūtaśuddhi*, the preceptor is God Himself. See ch. XXXV in entirety.

[4] Unlike traditional Brahmanic religion, Pāncarātra admits the right of a woman to become an initiate, provided she has her husband's permission. The exalted position of a pious woman is discussed further on in the text. See ch. LXIII, 61-79.

CHAPTER TWENTY-TWO

DESCRIPTION OF LAKṢMĪ'S MANTRA-FORM

1. Śakra:—O goddess without beginning and without end, omniscient and beloved of Hari, how are these mantras imparted and what are their forms?

2. Are they of equal importance, or is their significance of different grades? Asking thee this (question) I salute thee, O Padmā. Please tell me (all this).

3. Śrī:—O Pākaśāsana, listen attentively to what I tell you about my mantra-form and how I reveal (the mantras).

4-5. The absolute Brahman, the ultimate resort (*dhāman*) of all, embodiment of the resplendent six (divine) attributes, unlimited by time or place, formless and unrivalled—that Brahman, the I (*aham*) itself, perfectly conscious of its own being, is devoid of the guṇas (sattva etc.), is beginningless and endless, and is the great celestial Lakṣmī-Nārāyaṇa.

6. (Brahman) is the essence of consciousness and bliss, divine, without defect, decay or death. It is in the state of unmanifested existence where there is no polarization of subject and object.

7-8. When this Brahman is motionless, I am that motionless state of Its being. Then once in a while by virtue of differentiating between the being and the state of being (*bhavat* and *bhāva*), the absolute Brahman manifests Itself of Its own free will, without relinquishing (changing) Its form.[1] I am the I-hood of the Supreme Ātman, identical with Its being and should be worshipped as such.

9-12. Of my own free will, I emanate from the radiant God who is (pure) being. Supporting the entire assemblage (of creation) which I have voluntarily created and after having created writing (sound)[2] emanating from myself,[3] I reveal my power during the six courses

[1] In the Lakṣmī-Nārāyaṇa state, or in other words, in *bhāva* and *bhavat*, the integral nature of Brahman is not changed and no duality is involved.

[2] *Likhitam* primarily means writing, hence the alphabet but also sound in general.

[3] *Ātmabhittau* literally means 'on the basis of myself, or with myself as the support' and so implies that sound evolves out of Śakti.

(of creation). These six courses are known as the ways of sound, kalās, tattva, mantras, pada and worldly existence (*bhuvana*). The supreme I-hood, which is flawless consciousness, first shows signs of activity during the course of sound. O Pākaśāsana, I have already given you a detailed description of that journey.

13. The most exalted manifestation of mine infused with consciousness and power, undergoes a seeming transformation so as to undertake the course of creation as kalās consisting of jñāna etc.

14. The kalās such as jñāna etc., (i.e.) the qualities (attributes) of the Supreme Ātman, have been precisely explained to you earlier along with their number and characteristics.[1]

15. Together with the (first) two courses (viz. of sounds and kalās), that aspect of mine which consists of consciousness is revealed during the course of the tattvas, when I assume the forms of Vāsudeva etc.

16. The Vyūhas and Vibhavas and all the other (emanations) of God are regarded as the seeming transformation of the supreme Ātman during the course of the tattvas.

17. That same aspect of myself revealed during the first two courses of creation, which is in essence consciousness, appears to undergo a lasting transformation during the most significant of all my courses of creation, i.e. the mantras.

18-20. During my highly exalted mantra-course when I am marked as consciousness, I assume the embodiments of Vāsudeva and the other (related) deities in order (firstly) to guide across to safety the jīvas drowning in the ocean of worldly existence; (secondly) in order to provide objects of enjoyment for those who (still) are in the throes of worldly existence and to stimulate a sense of detachment in them; and (lastly) in order to ensure the efficacy of worship and encourage mental disciplines (*mānasālambana*).[2] All these mantras are representations of consciousness, unrestricted in range and in achievement of purpose.

21-24. These mantras should be regarded as pure embodiments of myself (and hence) of lord Śārṅgin (Viṣṇu). They protect (adepts) who meditate on them.[3] According to the śāstras their formulas are

---

[1] See ch. II, 23-36.

[2] Discussed at length in the Viṣ.P. VI, 7, 38-60.

[3] Traditionally using the term *mantra* in two senses derived from its double 'root': *man* = to meditate, and *tra* = to protect.

secret and they promote worldly enjoyment and at the same time lead to liberation. The (four padas) jāgrat, svapna, suṣupti and turya lie on the route followed by the course of the mantras. In the state of jāgrat (waking), the senses register external objects. When the senses operating on external objects become fogged by darkness (sleep) and lose their power, the inner organ starts functioning by registering mere impressions (*saṃskāra*). This is the state of svapna (dream). When even that does not function, the state of suṣupti (deep sleep) occurs.

25-27. When a wise person, whose mind is not fogged by darkness (ignorance) and whose being is wholly saturated with sattva, has completely stilled the functioning of both his senses and his mind (*bāhyāntaḥkaraṇa*), (he enters the state of) pure sattva's tranquility (*prasāda*) (and is then) said to be in (the state of) turya. This is a definition of the four footsteps called *pada*.[1] (It should be realized) that (all these states), excepting the turya, form part of the impure course of creation.

The so-called course of the world (*bhuvanādhvan*) begins with māyā and terminates with the dissolution of the world (*kṣiti*).

27-31. The course of bhuvana is impure and soiled by filth. (During it) these mantras [2] always make the passionate man sport (in this world). (The man is) enticed by the lure of the spell cast by various forms of pleasure. Then by resorting to a preceptor who discretely casts a compassionate eye on his disciple, (these mantras) [3] rescue the latter by awakening a sense of detachment in him during his progress along pada (viz. jāgrat etc.).[4] From there, (the mantras) gradually lead him to the way of purity and (make) him a master in the (science of) Śabdabrahman, thus finally guiding him to the (realm) of absolute Śrī. In themselves the mantras do (indeed) have a powerfully purifying effect.

32-35. They are of three types, viz. the inferior, the intermediary and the superior. Those mantras, which are associated with the concrete forms of gods instrumental in producing phenomenal

---

[1] The footsteps of the Soul are its different stages of existence.

[2] These are not emancipating mantras, but mantras for fulfilment of a worldly desire harboured by the adept.

[3] But the same mantras, when worshipped with a sense of perfect detachment, are capable of leading the adept to emancipation.

[4] Helped by mantras the Soul retraces its footsteps back to the original turya state of existence.

existence and that envisage a given result as their objective, are regarded by the wise as belonging to the inferior type. Mantras, which are related to Vibhava manifestations of God and their śaktis, belong to the intermediary type; whilst the superior (mantras) relate to the Vyūhas. Mantras that envisage complete absorption in the supreme Brahman whose nature is identical with Lakṣmī-Nārāyaṇa, and which do not differentiate between the state of becoming and the state of existence, are finally the supreme mantras. The relative significance of mantras should be thus graded by the wise.

36. The mantras of superior type fall solely within the Pāñcarātra (system); the intermediary type pervades the Vedas; whilst from the standpoint of sacred scripture, mantras belonging to other systems (tantras) are of inferior type.

37-39. Mantras whose auxiliary elements (limbs, *aṅga*) are the kalās (i.e. *jñāna* etc.) are to be regarded as superior; those that have other 'limbs' are intermediary; while mantras without 'limbs' are inferior.[1] Once more listen to me, O Indra: mantras with both bīja and piṇḍa are called superior; those possessing either a bīja or a piṇḍa are called intermediary; but those with neither a bīja nor a piṇḍa [2] are called inferior. The preceptor, familiar with the various types of mantras and whose eyes are the śāstras [3], should at the disciple's request adapt his instruction to the latter's requirements.

---

[1] According to this system of classification, mantras with aṅga mantras, such as jñāna etc., are graded as superior; with upāṅga mantras as intermediary, and without such auxiliary mantras as inferior.

[2] This means when neither the bīja nor piṇḍa is obvious, e.g. the Gaṇeśa-mantra.

[3] i.e. he who interprets everything correctly in the light of sacred scripture.

CHAPTER TWENTY-THREE

DESCRIPTION OF MĀTṚKĀ

1. Śrī:—I am the supreme Śakti of Nārāyaṇa, the I-hood of the all-pervasive absolute Brahman, the supreme Lakṣmī-Nārāyaṇa.

2. In order to help the world, I become the preceptor and, in the form of Saṃkarṣaṇa, I radiate the sacred texts.[1]

3-4. Again, dwelling in the frame of the (mortal) preceptor and equipped with true knowledge I, through my glance full of śakti [2] and by means of compassionate mantras, protect the disciples who approach me. Hence disciples should always regard their (mortal) preceptor as identical with myself.

5-11. Now learn how to impart mantras to a disciple. First, a small earthen pitcher should be worshipped by a mere offering of pure flowers on ground that is undefiled, level, smooth, free of impurities, painted according to the social class (of the worshipper),[3] coated with (liquid) cow-dung rendered fragrant by incense, weeded clean of thorns, decorated with fragrant flowers, saturated with the five cow-products, and smeared by unguents such as sandal paste.[4] This ritual should be accompanied by my own mantra (i.e. *Tārā*) preceded by praṇava and followed by namas.[5] Then repeating the (*mantra*) along with the first vyāhṛti (also) preceded by the praṇava,[6] clay should be spread over the ground that has already been scented with perfume and incense. Whereafter a well-built and regular

---

[1] The first part of the sentence voices the notion that a preceptor should be regarded as a manifestation of God Himself. The second part alludes to Saṃkarṣaṇa's moral function of teaching the Vedas to mankind. Each of the Vyūha deities has two aspects, the one cosmogonic, the other moral. Discussed fully by Schrader, pp. 36-41. But the point of this sentence is that Śakti as Saṃkarṣaṇa is the eternal teacher of religion, and a preceptor is an incarnation of that Saṃkarṣaṇa manifestation of Śakti.

[2] This is the divine attribute śakti or omnipotence.

[3] White for brahmins, red for kṣatriyas, yellow for vaiśyas and black for śūdras.

[4] Although the ground is sanctified with various purifying objects, the pitcher is worshipped with flowers alone. A diagram of Mātṛkāpīṭha is given in P.S. edited by U. Ve. Govindacharya, Srirangam 1953.

[5] *Oṃ hrīṃ namaḥ.*

[6] *Oṃ hrīṃ bhūḥ.*

mātṛkā-pīṭha (pedestal) should be made, either square or well rounded in shape and measuring one or two cubits across. The same goddess (i.e. Mātṛkā) represented by fifteen letters can be traced in different groups (of letters, such as *ka* etc.).[1] She is the mother of all mantras (and represents) my manifestation in sound. The mantra-worshipper (adept) should draw (a diagram) in the form of a lotus or a disk.

12. (When the mantra) refers to Puruṣa, (the diagram should) be in the form of a disk; but if it refers to the goddess Lakṣmī, the prescribed form is the lotus. Śakti, pervaded by Agni and Soma has sixteen components [2] and is called *visṛṣṭā* (created).

13-20. To the east (of the design), (the adept) should draw petals (in the case of the lotus) or spokes (in the case of the disk) to represent her (mantra-mātṛkā) called svara (vowel). The five groups (of letters), viz. *ka* etc., (representing principles) starting with pṛthivī (*ka*) and ending in puruṣa (*ma*) should be drawn as petals or spokes in the directions starting with Agni and ending in Vāyu.[3] The four (letters) starting with *ya* and ending in *va*, which represent the dhāraṇā within (the mind), should be drawn by the wise on the north side in the form of either spokes or petals as (described) before. The group of letters starting with *śa* and ending in *kṣa*, which terminates in turīya and is said to represent the five Brahmans, should be drawn in the form of either spokes or petals to the north-east (of the diagram). The supreme and pure Brahman, consisting of light (and) known as Śabda, should be meditated upon as splendour circumscribing the diagram of the disk or of the lotus (as the case may be). In the diagram the wise should worship me —the prakṛti in the form of the tattvas—with the letters known as tattvas that start with praṇava and end in namas.[4] Then in the pericarp (of the lotus diagram), meditation should focus on the mother of mantras (Mantra-mātṛkā), who is beginningless and endless, the goddess I-hood (of Viṣṇu), the wife of Puruṣottama, the goddess Padminī holding the noose and the goad, wearing a wreath of lotuses, gracious, with a complexion like the heart of a

[1] Mātṛkā is a single entity represented by the fifteen vowels, but nevertheless manifest in all sounds variously grouped (*varga*) according to their mode of utterance.

[2] *ḥ* and the fifteen vowels including *ṃ*.

[3] South-east, south, south-west, west and north-west.

[4] e.g. *oṃ bhaṃ namaḥ, oṃ baṃ namaḥ*, etc.

lotus, the great mistress of all the worlds, whose body is composed of letters and decorated with ornaments (made of) letters.[1]

21. Her body represents Śabdabrahman; her head praṇava; *a* and *ā* form her eyebrows, while *i* and *ī* are her eyes.

22-23. *u* and *ū* form her ears, *ṛ* and *ṝ* her nostrils, while *ḷ* and *ḹ* are her cheeks, *e* and *ai* her lips, *o* and *au* the two rows of her teeth, *ṃ* is her tongue and *ḥ* her voice; the group of *ka* and the group of *ca* are her two hands, while the two groups of *ṭa* and *ta* form her two legs and the wise regard *pa* and *pha* to be her two sides.

24-25. *ba* and *bha* are the hind and fore parts of her (body), *ma* is her navel, *ya* and *ra* are her vital airs (*prāṇa*) and (body-) temperature; *la* is her necklace, *va* is her girdle, *śa* and *ṣa* represent her earrings, *sa* is her heart, while *ha* is (her soul) in the heart.

26. (The adept) should recognize *kṣa* to be (her) lightning bright radiating halo; *raṅga* (the nasal modifications of vowels) represent the tip (of) her nose and the 'twin-letters' [2] (her) heart.

27. Then the (letters) formed at the root of the tongue (*jihvāmūlīyaka*) remain at the root of (her) tongue, and the letter *upadhmānīyaka* (i.e. the visarga before *pa* and *pha*) in graded order lingers between her lips.

28. (Mantramātṛkā is to be visualized as) wearing the vanamālā consisting of beautiful (auspicious) lotuses made of letters containing Agni and Soma and reaching from shoulder to feet.

29. The learned should regard *ha*, belonging to the great Lord, as the crown (of the goddess) radiant as millions of flames, moons and suns (put together) and adorned with glittering jewels.

30-33. So envisaging the goddess Mātṛkā, the mother of mantras, (the adept) should worship her (Mātṛkā) with (offerings of) flowers, arghya etc. accompanied by (the mantra) containing the words *oṃ namo mantra-mātṛke idam arghyaṃ gṛhāṇa* ('O mantra-mātṛkā, be pleased to take this offering, humbly presented for your gracious acceptance'), (and) likewise with (offerings of) items of food in due order. Then, with palms joined, paying obeisance in a prostrate position where eight parts of the body touch the ground (the adept should propitiate the goddess with these words:) 'O Padmā, whose

---

[1] This is how Lakṣmī is envisaged as Mantra-mātṛkā.

[2] The consonant not actually written but pronounced as if inserted between a nasal immediately preceded by one of the four other consonants in each group. See Monier Williams, Dict., p. 846.

seat is the lotus, whose abode is the lotus, beloved of the lotus-eyed Viṣṇu, container of all the tattvas, goddess-mother of all mantras, reveal thyself to me in thy supreme form as the divine Lakṣmī'. By uttering this prayer after due ritual preparation, (the mantra-worshipper) will become identified with Lakṣmī.

34. (The preceptor), who has thus arranged (the letters beginning with *a* and ending in *kṣa*) on the mātṛkā (-*yantra* or diagram) and who himself has (thus) become identified with Mātṛkā, should then invoke the desired mantra and teach it to his disciple.

35. O Śureśvara, those (mantras) that possess both bīja and piṇḍa are considered the best of all mantras. Among these, bījas are even superior to piṇḍas.

36-37. O Vāsava, the jewels among the bījas are the (following) seven. The first is tāraka, the second is Tārikā, the third is Anutārikā, which is equal in power of brilliance (*tejas*) to the two previous ones, the fourth is jagadyoni, which is regarded as the great bīja.

38. The fifth bīja pertains to Pradyumna; the sixth is known as Sārasvata; and the seventh is called the one that contains Mahālakṣmī.[1]

39. The subtlety or grossness inherent in each mantra will be treated when describing the various mantras separately. (Now) O Śakra, listen attentively to their respective descriptions.

---

[1] These are the basic bīja-mantras of the *Pāñcarātra* system.

CHAPTER TWENTY-FOUR

THE STRUCTURE OF TĀRAKA WITH ITS PARTS AND THE METHOD OF INITIATION IN THE PRACTICE OF MEDITATION

1. The absolute Brahman, the ultimate presence (*dhāman*),[1] the supreme and incomparable (mass of) brilliance, Brahman which is (identical with) Lakṣmī-Nārāyaṇa is faultless and pure.

2. It alone exists, pervading this entire (world). It is the highest and greatest. I am the absolute I-hood of that Brahman, the supreme soul.

3. In order to help all living beings, I voluntarily manifest myself in the forms of mātṛkā-mantras, containing Śabdabrahman.

4. In the form of the mantra, I follow each particular (deity) referred to in it. In the beginning (the adept) should evoke me in my original tāra-form.

5. First (the adept) should take the (letter) *dhruva* (*a*), then add the (letter) *karṇa* to it (*a* + *u*), then he should add the (letter) *nābhi* (*m*) to that and finally unite them together (*a* + *u* + *m*/*om*).

6-7. Having thus constructed *om*, the adept should first decorate that Brahma-tāraka [2] with bindu, thereupon with nāda. Then, as accompaniment to this tāraka he should meditate on the eternal Brahman made up of these three letters in the Vaiṣṇava form (the mind flowing towards it incessantly) like the (continuous) flow of oil.[3]

8. Here (in this tāraka), *a* represents Aniruddha, the fifth vowel (*u*) represents Pradyumna, *m* (represents) Samkarṣaṇa and bindu (represents) Vāsudeva.

9. O Śureśvara, the indivisibility (i.e. integral nature) of these four (letters) is the nāda. The highest perfection of nāda is the I-hood (of God), who is the highest goddess.

10. She is the most subtle Śakti called the space [4] that exists

---

[1] See J. Gonda, Dhāman, passim.

[2] Tāraka is identical with Brahman.

[3] i.e. meditate uninterruptedly on tāraka.

[4] Nāda represents the supreme Brahman which is also the essence or

inside nāda. She, who is (identical with) myself, is subtle, pervaded by Śabdabrahman and is all-pervasive.

11. When the nāda ceases to (be actively present), the absolute and luminous Brahman called Lakṣmī-Nārāyaṇa becomes spontaneously manifest.[1]

12. Thus (I) have (now) told you about the supreme Vaiṣṇava presence (*dhāman*) of the Person. Listen now to the description of the essential traits of its form which is tranquil (inert).

13. First, taking the visarga (*ḥ*), (the adept) should add sūrya (i.e. *ṃ*) to it. When these are firmly joined together there arises the power (i.e. mantra) *oṃ*.[2]

14. (As this praṇava contains both visarga and bindu), this is the highest presence representing both Śakti and dissolution[3] which, if constantly contemplated upon, reveals (to the meditator) the unalterable, absolute reality.

15-18. Dissolving all objects belonging to both the pure and impure ways (creations), Śakti, who is (again) ready to start creating, arranges the further movement on Sūrya, (i.e.) Puruṣa, who is eternal, supreme and is in the form of the enjoyer (*bhoktṛ*), then, she reappears out of that state of existence which contains Agni and Soma (and) attains the perpetual intermediary coupled condition (*dāṃpatya*) consisting of bindu and nāda. Śakti attains the subtle coupled condition identical with the divine inertia and exists in the divine, pervasive supreme Self. According to the learned it (i.e. the coupled condition, *oṃ*) has three and a half measure-units.[4]

---

soul of everything. The space that surrounds this soul is called *daharākāśa* (see Ch.U. 8, 1, 1). This is the legendary abode of Brahman or, in other words, Brahman's very presence in so far as It can be grasped by the human mind.

[1] Śabdabrahman represents the dawning of God's creative activity which, though astir, has not as yet created any object. It is the state of existence when God or Śakti is potentially creative.

[2] According to the phonetic law of Pāṇini, when *aḥ* and *aṃ* are joined together, the former develops into *o*. See editor's note.

[3] Visarga is the natural inert pure Existence unrelated to creation, whereas bindu represents the state of dissolution when the creation is dissolved, or lies dormant in primordial nature or matter (*prakṛti*), which is also the beginning of creation.

[4] One measure for each of the three sounds *a*, *u* and *m*, while *ṁ* counts as only half a measure. Note that the Māṇḍukya Upaniṣad admits only three measure-units and omits the half. There the first three measure-units

19-20. O Śakra, the three fires,[1] three worlds,[2] three Vedas,[3] three guṇas,[4] three gods,[5] three Vyūhas,[6] three social classes [7] and the three (basic) vowels,[8] whatever group of three you find in this world you should consider it to be (representing) the first three (components of *oṃ*), while the half measure-unit (*bindu*) stands for the pure (existence).

21. All words have emanated from the letter *a*. From *u* have emanated the three brilliant energies (i.e. sun, moon and fire). O Puraṃdara, out of *m* emanate (all the cosmic principles) starting with the earth and ending in prakṛti.

22-25. The brilliant half measure-unit is the supreme kalā (*nāda*), consisting of consciousness. Among the two sets of six vowels (viz. *a-ū* and *ḷ-au*)the even numbered vowels (i.e. *ā*, *ī*, *ū*, *ḹ*, *ai*, *au*, representing) the six (divine) attributes of knowledge etc. should, along with the bindu at the end of (each of) them, be placed on the body of the preceptor.[9] Then again, O Pākaśāsana, he (preceptor) should place the (same) attributes (each) preceded by tāra, on (his own) navel, back, arms, thighs, knees and feet.[10] Having thus placed the mantra along with aṅga and upāṅga (-mantras), the preceptor should meditate on Puruṣottama existing in his own self. (Now) learn from me the accurate (description of the process of identification of the preceptor) with (the cosmic jīva), starting from its Viśva (state of existence) until the dissolution (of its separate existence as jīva).

---

are respectively identified with the waking, dream and deep sleep phases of the Self and the fourth phase is not allotted a measure-unit. Mā.U. 8-12.

[1] Gārhapatya, āhavanīya and dakṣiṇa.

[2] *bhūḥ*, *bhuvaḥ* and *svaḥ*.

[3] Ṛg, Yajus and Sāma.

[4] sattva, rajas and tamas.

[5] Brahmā, Viṣṇu and Rudra.

[6] Saṃkarṣaṇa, Pradyumna and Aniruddha.

[7] brahmin, kṣatriya and vaiśya.

[8] *a*, *i* and *u*.

[9] *Oṃ āṃ hṛdayāya namaḥ*; *oṃ īṃ śirase svāhā*; *oṃ ūṃ śikhāyai vaṣaṭ*; *oṃ ḹṃ kavacāya huṃ*; *oṃ aiṃ netrāya vauṣaṭ*; *oṃ auṃ astrāya phaṭ*. These aṅga-mantras are symbolically placed on various parts of the preceptor's body by touching them as and when mentioned in the mantras themselves.

[10] The upāṅga-mantras: *oṃ jñānāya namaḥ*, *oṃ aiśvaryāya namaḥ*, *oṃ śaktaye namaḥ*, *oṃ balāya namaḥ*, *oṃ vīryāya namaḥ*, *oṃ tejase namaḥ*, are also respectively placed on the upāṅga of the preceptor's body by touching these whilst uttering the mantras.

26. Viśva is the lord in the state of waking, who stimulates all the organs of sense into action and who is the enjoyer of the five objects, (viz.) śabda etc.[1]

27-28. (The adept) should meditate on him (Viśva), who is identical with Aniruddha, as the first sound (*a*). Then he should dissolve that deity with all his accessories, in *a* and then dissolve *a* in the Taijasa deity Pradyumna, who travels through the way of dream and stimulates all functions of the internal organ.

29-31. Then he should merge that deity along with his accessories in *u*. That *u* again (should be merged) in lord Prājña existing in the form of Saṃkarṣaṇa the omnipresent ruler, who abides in the state of deep sleep and ever stimulates the activity of breathing. After having merged him, the Lord of the gods, in the half measure-unit that stands for turya,[2] the divine Vāsudeva in whom knowledge and bliss inhere, (he should) merge that turya in that which is beyond turya [3] and consists of Lakṣmī-Nārāyaṇa.

32-34. Then merging his own self (therein, the preceptor) should dissolve (his own individuality) into her, the divine I-hood belonging to Viṣṇu. Having become identical with her and having reached the state of laya,[4] he should come down gradually to the state of waking. Then after initiating the disciple, the good preceptor, who has become identified with me, should himself first teach the disciple during a long period of time, the tāra(-mantra) along with all its branches and accessories and (also the method of attaining) samādhi[5] (by meditating on *oṃ*). He (i.e. the disciple) should give himself together with money to the preceptor as a dakṣiṇā.[6]

35-36. Then obtaining his (the preceptor's) permission, he (the disciple) should practise the ritual performance called puraścaraṇa[7]

[1] i.e. material objects. Śabda etc. refer to the five element-potentials or tanmātras, namely sound, touch, form, taste and smell.

[2] cf. Mā.U. 6-8.

[3] The concept of turyātīta is peculiar to this system and differs from turya in that the latter is the soul's state of existence just beyond material influence and polarization; whereas turyātīta denotes its supra-Vyūha state of existence where the soul's infinite divine majesty and splendour are fully manifested.

[4] *laya* denotes complete identification with Śakti, the presence of God.

[5] Deep meditative trance when the adept is so absorbed in what he is meditating on that he is completely unaware of everything else.

[6] Gratuity due to a preceptor or officiating priest.

[7] Collective term for the five rites which enhance the divine power of a mantra and are performed after initiation in the worship of a particular

etc., betaking himself to the bank of a great river, or to the temple of a siddha [1] etc., or to a forest of palāśa,[2] from where the (rest) of the world is (screened) out of sight. There the ascetic (adept), completely controlling his senses, should daily practise (the duties) of bathing and savana (ablutions) three times a day.

37. He should eat only once (a day), either milk or barley grain or (such food as he may obtain by) begging; he should have only grass as a seat; he must wear coarse garments made of grass and should lie on kuśa grass.

38-39. He must always hold a staff of palāśa wood and cover himself with a black (deer-)skin. Then with his mind fixed on me, he should remain completely pervaded by me and then, following the method directed by the preceptor, he should constantly practise yoga, culminating in the attainment of true knowledge and samādhi. (Whereafter) remaining silent, he should repeat the tāra (-mantra) a million times, which saves souls from worldly existence.[3]

40-41. He should (then) perform sacrifice (offered to the deity of the mantra) a hundred thousand times (*daśāṃśaṃ*) with leaves (possibly tulsi), wood for the sacrificial fire or purified butter.[4] Then I, the absolute I-hood belonging to Viṣṇu, being pleased (with him) manifest myself to the mind of this adept, which (i.e. the mind) has accurate distinctive knowledge of the truth. (And) that (accurate knowledge of the truth) reveals the (absolute) identification (*sāmarasya*) (of myself with God), which state is known as Lakṣmī-Nārāyaṇa.

42-43. (Such an adept) becomes emancipated while still alive (*jīvanmukta*), sanctifies the world with his eye [5] (glance) and all his mantras, (both) popular and Vedic, become efficacious; he becomes a master in the Vedas, in all (other) sciences, in all systems and (in the knowledge of) sacred places.

44-45. All applications and methods of application of all the

mantra. These are: japa, sacrifice, libation, ritual bath and offering food to brahmins.

[1] Established by an adept who has achieved liberation from the bondage of transient existence and rebirth. Other kinds of temples are ārṣa, daiva and laukika.

[2] Butea frondosa.

[3] i.e. perform japa, the first component of puraścaraṇa.

[4] Apparently the sacrifice includes all four of the other components of puraścaraṇa.

[5] The adept's eye has become identical with God's, and his glances possess as much divine grace as God's own. See J. Gonda, Eye and glance.

mantras are (in fact) an application of this (i.e. praṇava). The three vyāhṛtis [1] emanate from its three letters and the Sāvitrī,[2] the all-purifying (mantra), emanated from its feet.

46. From her (Sāvitri's) feet emanate the three Vedas, known as Ṛg, Yajus, and Sāman. Thus all speech, (both) secular and Vedic, consists (only) of it (the praṇava).

47. As the (tiny) seed of the banyan tree contains the germ of the whole big tree, so the entire world of speech is ever contained in it (praṇava).

48. This (*oṃ*) is the primary great bīja, the primary source of sound, Śabdabrahman, the supreme presence and the purest and highest principle (*mahat*).

49-50. Oṃkāra, praṇava, tāra, haṃsa, Nārāyaṇa, dhruva, vedātman, sarvavedādi, āditya, sarvapāvana, mokṣada, muktimārga and sarvasandhāraṇakṣama,—these and (many) others are the different names of it (used) by the learned in different śāstras.

51-52. The highly auspicious aspects of the excellent oṃkāra have (now) been mastered (by you). It is the protector of the ignorant as well as of the learned. For those who seek heaven and want to cross (the saṃsāra), it (*oṃ*) serves as a boat. As it is a combination of the letter *ha* and the letter *au*, this is called *prāsāda*.[3]

53-56. This eternal concentrated (mantra) is the essence of all realities. O lord of the gods, consider the means (of attainment, *sādhana*), attainment (*pratipatti*), application (*viniyoga*) and deep concentration (*dhāraṇā*),—(all these) as belonging to this bīja (called) *prāsāda*. Haṃsa, the great mantra, is its saṃjñā (i.e. the addressing) mantra. Consider its (viz. haṃsa-mantra's) first letter (to represent) the enjoyer, and the second the object of enjoyment. The first letter (*ha*) contains Nārāyaṇa, while the other (letter, *sa*) contains Śrī. Consider, O Śakra, these two eternal letters to be consisting of Agni and Soma, (and) in between these two exist bindu and dharma.[4]

57-62. Let the bhoktṛ-letter (*ha*) be brought forth (i.e. breathed

---

[1] *bhūḥ, bhuvaḥ* and *svaḥ*.

[2] The famous Gāyatrī-mantra: *oṃ tat savitur vareṇyaṃ bhargo devasya dhīmahi dhiyo yo naḥ pracodayāt.*

[3] The prāsāda-mantra is *oṃ hau*, which is the bīja-mantra of tāra, whereas haṃsa is its saṃjñā-mantra.

[4] Bindu is creation, and dharma (a name of the deity of death) is dissolution.

out) from the ādhārasthāna (mūlādhāra, i.e. the place below the navel) to the mūrdhan (the top of the palate, by drawing the air from deep down near the navel up to the top of the palate), then the second letter called bhogya (*sa*) must be breathed out from the mouth. By the utterance of the haṃsa, the entire creation is reconstructed. This science (*vidyā*, i.e. mantra), which is perfect in every part, is known as *ajapā*. This mantra utters itself (i.e. is uttered automatically) in the eighty hundred million and sixty-four types of living beings and all the individuals belonging to each type. This vidyā glowing inwardly, surges up (spontaneously) together with breathing. Its appearance and disappearance are like the inhaling and the exhaling of breath. Prāṇa contains sixty breaths; six prāṇas are counted as one nāḍikā. Sixty such nāḍikās make one whole day and night. These are the divisions of time.[1] O king of the gods, know that when this haṃsa (-mantra) is awakened, it is as potent as twenty-one thousand six hundred times of repetition of (any mantra).

63-65. But at the beginning of each day, the intelligent (adept) should resolve to do a certain number of japa (repetitions of this mantra) and he should then arrange its (i.e. the mantra's) five limbs (accordingly).[2] Now hear (from me) the form of these (five limbs). The faultless and illusionless Sūrya and Soma (*ha* and *sa*) having the ending of the fourth case (dative), are connected with *namas* and *svāhā*, then (follow) *vauṣaḍ huṃ phaṭ* and then the mūla-mantra followed by *phaṭ* i.e. the astra-mantra (*namo haṃsāya svāhā vauṣaḍ huṃ phaṭ*). These are the five limbs of the mantra.

66-70. This very (mantra), when reverted (*so 'ham*), is called the paramātma-mantra. Having envisaged Śakti (*sa*) along with all the auxiliaries, connect it with Sūrya (*ha*), the enjoyer; the rest must be considered to be like praṇava, (and) this is the method of (forming) the saṃjñā-mantra. According to the Pāñcarātra injunction, this

---

[1] So every day each embodied being repeats (japa) this mantra twenty-one thousand and six hundred times.

[2] Stressing that no mantra is efficacious unless the adept resolves to repeat it a specified number of times whilst observing the accompanying ritual. Thus even if some one casually repeats a mantra twenty-one thousand and six hundred times every day, it lacks efficacy for that person for want of the necessary conscious effort on his part, which is an essential factor in all mantras. The complete form of the mantra is *oṃ namo haṃsāya svāhā vauṣaḍ huṃ phaṭ*, followed by the adept's basic mantra ending with *phaṭ*.

has three pada-mantras, (viz.) *Viṣṇave namo, namo Nārāyaṇāya*, and *Vāsudevāya* preceded by *namo bhagavate*. O Puraṃdara, *jitaṃ te Puṇḍarīkākṣa namas te viśvabhāvana namaste 'stu Hṛṣīkeśa mahāpuruṣa pūrvaja* constitutes the fourth pada-mantra of the praṇava. The masters of ancient sciences knew (the mystery) of these mantras along with the oṃkāra.

71. The aṅga-kḷpti (i.e. aṅga-nyāsa) should be performed with words expressing guṇas e.g. jñāna etc., joined by praṇava and ending with a *namas*. In the same way (the adept) should perform upāṅga-nyāsa.

72-73. While performing upāṅga-nyāsa, if the mantra to be used possesses less letters (than is required),[1] then the last letter (is to be repeated till the required number is reached) along with the appropriate guṇa-word. Similarly, in the case of mantras possessing too many letters,[2] then the excess number of letters (coming after the first) twelve letters (inclusive) should be used all together with (the guṇa-word) tejas in the final upāṅga-nyāsa.

74. The single tāraka(-mantra) and the four (mantras) preceded by it are considered to be the vyāpaka-mantras in the Pāñcarātra (system).

75. There is nothing impossible (to attain) in this world through (the power obtained from worshipping) these excellent mantras. Together they serve as the ladder (*niśreṇī*) consisting of five steps to ascend to the (state of) absolute Brahman.

76. This divine and highest existence, consisting of five mantras verily consists of me (Śakti). (The adept) who has properly acquired skill in the application of mantras through their worship (*arcana*), repetition (muttering: *japa*) and meditation (*dhyāna*), achieves, after having attained my own essence belonging to Viṣṇu, the absolute Brahman.

---

[1] In this instance twelve is the minimum number of letters required, so for example in the mantra *namo viṣṇave*, the last letter has to be repeated until the desired number is obtained.

[2] e.g. in the mantra *jitaṃ te* etc.

CHAPTER TWENTY-FIVE

TĀRĀ- AND ANUTĀRĀ-MANTRAS

1. Śrī:—Thus, O Śakra, I have told you in detail all about the tāraka(-mantra). Now listen to me describing the way of Tārikā, who saves the world.

2. In order to determine the rules regarding the letters (which are the basis of mantras), first hear their characteristic names which, when properly learnt (by the adept), give (him) the key to the system of mantras.

3. The letter *a* is (called) aprameya and is also known as prathama and vyāpaka. The letter *ā* is called ādideva, ānanda and gopana.

4. The letter *i*, called rāma, is also known as iddha and iṣṭa. O Puraṃdara, the letter *ī* is (called) pañcabindu, Viṣṇu and māyā.

5. The letter *u* is known as bhuvana, uddāma and udaya. The letter *ū* is called ūrja, lokeśa and prajñādhāra.

6. The letter *ṛ* is (called) satya, ṛtadhāman and aṅkuśa. The letter *ṝ* is called viṣṭara, jvālā and prasāraṇa.

7. The letter *ḷ* is traditionally known as liṅgātman, tāraka and bhagavān, while the letter *ḹ* is called dīrghaghoṇa, devadatta and virāṭ.

8. The letter *e* is called tryaśra, jagadyoni and avigraha. The letter *ai* is traditionally known as aiśvarya, yogadhātā and airāvaṇa.

9. The letter *o* is known as otadeva, odana and vikramin, and the letter *au* as aurva, bhūdhara and auṣadha.

10. The letter *ṃ* is famous as trailokyaiśvaryada, vyāpin and vyomeśa. The letter *ḥ* is named visarga, sṛṣṭikṛt and parameśvara.

11. The letter *ka* is called kamala, karāla and parāprakṛti. The letter *kha* is (called) kharvadeha, vedātman and viśvabhāvana.

12. The letter *ga* is (called) gadadhvaṃsin, govinda and gadādhara. Then the letter *gha* is (named) gharmāṃśu, tejasvin and dīptimān.

13. The letter *ṅ* is called ekadaṃṣṭrā, bhūtātman and bhūtabhāvana. The letter *ca* is said to be (named as) cañcala, cakrī and candrāṃśu.

14. The letter *cha* is (called) chandaḥpati, chaladhvaṃsin and chandas. The letter *ja* is (named) janmahantṛ, ajita and śāśvata.

15. The letter *jha* bears the names jhaṣa, sāmaga and sāmapāṭhaka. The letter *ñ* is called īśvara, uttama and tattvadhāraka.

16. The letter *ṭa* is (called) candrin, āhlāda and viśvāpyāyakara. The letter *ṭha* is called dhārādhara, nemi and kaustubha.

17. The letter *ḍa* is (called) daṇḍadhāra, mausala and akhaṇḍavikrama. The letter *ḍha* viśvarūpa, vṛṣakarman and pratardana.

18. The letter *ṇa* is famous as abhayada, śāstṛ and vaikuṇṭha. The letter *ta* is known as tālalakṣman, vairāja and sragdhara.

19. The letter *tha* is (called) dhanvin, bhuvanapāla and sarvarodhaka. The letter *da* is known as dattāvakāśa, damana and śāntida.

20. The letter *dha* is known as śārṅgadhṛt, dhartā and Mādhava. The letter *na* is said to be Nara, Nārāyaṇa and panthā.

21. The letter *pa* is (called) Padmanābha, pavitra and paścimānana. The letter *pha* is called phullanayana, lāṅgalin and śveta.

22. The letter *ba* is referred to as vāmana, hrasva and pūrṇāṅga. The letter *bha* is known as bhallātaka, siddhiprada and dhruva.

23. The letter *ma* is named mardana, kāla and pradhāna. The letter *ya* is called caturgati, susūkṣma and śaṃkha.

24. The letter *ra* is called aśeṣabhuvanādhāra, anala and kālapāvaka. The letter *la* is called vibudha, dhareśa and puruṣeśvara.

25. The letter *va* is known as varāha, amṛtādhāra and Varuṇa. The letter *śa* is named Śaṃkara, śānta and puṇḍarīka.

26. The letter *ṣa* is (called) Nṛsiṃha, agnirūpa and bhāskara. The letter *sa* is called amṛta, tṛpti and Soma.

27. The letter *ha* is called Sūrya, prāṇa and paramātman. The letter *kṣa* is (called) ananteśa, vargānta and Garuḍa.

28-29. Thus I (conclude) my detailed description of the letters. O Śakra, highly intelligent one, (this enumeration of) letters (in a mantra) described in successive or reverse order [1] (dependent on whether they are mentioned by) name (*saṃjña*) or by numeral (according to their position in the alphabet) merely gives a general (*sāmānya*) description (of them) and in fact all these letters possessing luminous forms are parts of (absolute) consciousness.

30. Letters are the source of all mantras. They are made strong

[1] When the letters in a mantra are mentioned by name, they follow each other as named. When on the other hand they are referred to by a numeral representing their position in the alphabet, their position in the mantra is reversed. This is illustrated in the Vi.S. ch. V.

by the Lakṣmī-śakti. They are reverentially praised, worshipped and meditated upon (by the adept) by means of (their) names.

31. They bestow great prosperity (on the adept) and produce (promote) the highest knowledge (in his mind); when used in mantras they become parts of each other.

32-33. There is nothing in this world of movables and immovables that is not produced by them. Although the forms of the mantras are divine and eternal, yet mantras are thus conceived to be produced by letters. According to the sacred scripture, such mantras are full of efficacy.[1]

34-37. And, O highly intelligent one, in this way they become the basis for inspired thought. Just as human thought imagines divisions in the sky (space) though it is indivisible, so for the sake of convenience are the divisions of letters assumed in a mantra.[2] As soon as he has performed the worship of this mental expansion of letters three times (viz.) on the ground, on the lotus (diagram) and on the body of the goddess, (the adept should) reconstruct the mantras (in the following way). Taking paramātman (*ha*) let him connect kālavahni (*ra*) to it, and (then) let him join māyā (*ī*) to it together with trailokyaiśvaryada (*ṃ*). This (resultant form, viz. *hrīṃ*) is the supreme Śakti of Viṣṇu, which bestows (on the adept) all desired objects.

38. This is my state of integral existence, the constant form containing consciousness and bliss; this is that supreme state which becomes everlasting to the knower of Brahman.

39. In order to abide in it (i.e. *hrīṃ* or *Tārikā*) the knowers of the realities enter Brahman, which is identical with me. It is thus that in all sacred scriptures the leading savants of the cosmic principles look upon (*Tārikā*).

40. The entire world consisting of words and their objects is woven through and through with her (*Tārikā*). It is through her that I, the eternal, am always explained by the philosophers (*sāṃkhya*).

41. It is by her aid that those who aspire to the meditative trance

---

[1] Implying that mantras are eternal, integral manifestations of Śakti's different aspects. The motive for teaching the adept how a mantra is constructed comes from the conviction that such knowledge will strengthen and ensure fulfilment of his aspiration.

[2] Sound is an integral concept like time or space. Its divisions are artificially conceived in order to provide objects for adepts to meditate on.

are meditatively absorbed in me. It is through her that I am called by the Śaivas the final one of the thirty-six.[1]

42. It is through her that I am considered by the Sauras to be the great queen in their maṇḍala, the supreme trayī containing Ṛg, Yajus and Sāman.

43. It is through her that the Lokāyata adepts often seek (me, in the form of) a young handsome girl, attractive in every single limb.[2]

44. (It is through her that) the advocates of the theory of momentary existence[3] contemplate me as being the indeterminate (supportless) wisdom. It is through her that the Jainas always call me the Yakṣī.[4]

45-48. Paramā Tārikā, Śakti, Tāriṇī, Tārikākṛti, Lakṣmī, Padmā, Mahālakṣmī, Tārā, Gaurī, Nirañjanā, Hṛllekhā, Paramātmasthā-śakti, Bhuvaneśvarī, Cicchakti, Śāntirūpā, Ghoṣaṇī, Ghoṣasaṃbhavā, Kāmadhenu, Mahādhenu, Jagadyoni, Vibhāvarī, —these are the names of Tārikā that (are explained) by the wise in all sacred scriptures and by the learned in all the Vedas. Anutārikā is, one should know, another form of her.

49. Instead of the aforesaid paramātman, insert śānta (*śa*), the rest is just the same as before; and this is my Anutārikā form (*śrīṃ*).

50. Consider her (Anutārikā) as the great power to be equal to that of Tārikā; O Puraṃdara, these two highest divine śaktis are my (two) forms.

51. Whatever is within the capacity of the one will also be within the capacity of the other. They accept by mutual consent their rank as first and second, but both (possess equal efficacy to) fulfil the adept's desires.

---

[1] The thirty-six categories are pati + śakti, paśu or jīva, kalā, [illegible]la, niyati, vidyā, rāga, prakṛti, guṇa, the five tanmātras, five bhūtas, ten sense and motor organs, manas, buddhi, ahaṃkāra and the four pāśas.

[2] T[illegible] pure materialists and empiricists are worshippers of material pleasu[illegible]ed, for instance, from women, food and drink etc.

[3] [illegible] philosophers.

[4] [illegible]e deity assuming various esoteric forms in Jaina tantras. The [illegible] the verses from 39 to the end of this chapter is to stress tha[t] eve[illegible]ait that is highly esteemed by any religious or philosophical sec[t] is [illegible]y traceable to Śakti.

CHAPTER TWENTY-SIX

ELUCIDATION OF THE SEVEN VIDYĀS, VIZ. TĀRA, TĀRĀ, ANUTĀRĀ, VĀGBHAVA, KĀMA, SARASVATĪ AND MAHĀLAKṢMĪ BĪJAS

1. Śakra:—O Padmā, absolute Brahman, absolute presence, residing in the lotus, garlanded with a lotus-wreath, born from the lotus and consort of Govinda, I salute thee.

2. O goddess, these two ever-existing forms of thine have been enumerated. Are they distinct from thy subtle form?

3. Śrī:—There is (but) one original, supreme and absolute reality consisting of Lakṣmī-Nārāyaṇa, wherein all the six (divine) attributes exist motionless (unmanifested). It is pure, spontaneous and consists of concentrated consciousness.

4. I am its supreme Śakti existing in union with it in all its states of existence. That goddess (i.e. myself) is the supreme divine (Śakti) known to be the gross, the subtle and the absolute (in the gradual process of elimination).

5. These two śaktis (viz.) Tārikā and Anutārikā are my (mantra) forms. O Puraṃdara, (the fulfilment of) all desires is milked out of these two.

6. Both are considered divine, both are known as supreme states; all things are regarded as existing in these two (i.e. all manifestations are these two) and both are consorts of Viṣṇu.

7. (Adepts) achieve the highest goal by meditating on both of them. Now listen to my account of the absolute and the subtle reality.

8. Primary (reality) is the absolute Brahman, then comes śānta and then nāda; this is the sequence (of the gradual manifestation of reality). I remain (an integral part) of every state (of reality) in the form of *nimeṣa* and *unmeṣa* (twinkling of reality's eyes).[1]

9. The primary state (i.e.) the absolute Brahman, subtle and

[1] Co[illegible] to the idea tha[illegible] [illegible]ing [illegible] God's [illegible] [illegible] [illegible] cr[illegible] [illegible] sustenance, whereas [illegible] [illegible]sing [illegible] [illegible] [illegible] dis[illegible] of crea[illegible]n. This simile underlines th[illegible] [illegible] God [illegible] [illegible] process is as fleeting and continu[illegible] [illegible] auto[illegible] [illegible] His [illegible]

with Śakti, who is (as yet) motionless (unmanifested), is the base on which Tāra [1] expands (into) the extensive way (of creation).

10. The first manifestation of the absolute Brahman, the existing (*bhavat*), the supreme self, contains (both) *bhavat* and *bhāva* (the state of existence) (and) Tārikā inheres therein.

11. Anutārikā inheres in the inert state [2] called *śānta*, which is Brahman's first descent caused by Its creative urge that is chiefly characterized by existence.[3]

12. O Vāsava, bījas such as vāgbhava etc.[4] exist in the second descent of (the reality) called śakti,[5] wherein the (creative) state of existence (*bhāva*) abounds.

13. Thus I have explained to you the difference between these two (viz. Tārikā and Anutārikā), which (is based on the) subtle wisdom that pervades them. Now listen to my description of bījas such as vāgbhava etc.

14. Take the letter called aiśvarya (*ai*) and connect it with the letter called trailokyaiśvaryada (*ṃ*). This bīja (viz. *aiṃ*) is the source of creation and is known as vāgbhava.

15. Now listen to the description of the śakti known as Kuṇḍalinī, which contains the entire creation in a coiled (i.e. concentrated) form and which is identical with śabdaśakti.[6]

16-20. The letter *ī* is māyā, the supreme śakti, the pure jagadyoni (source of the creation). She is Śrī, the wife of the inscrutable householder (god Viṣṇu). With subtle vision let (the adept) place the letter *i* before this (letter *ī*). Thus the letter called iṣṭa, that (brings about) all desired objects, is established (within the bīja). Next, (the adept) should direct his thoughts with subtle vision towards ānanda (*ā*) to precede it and, with the same subtle vision,

---

[1] Representing Śabdabrahman.

[2] This is the state of Brahman's existence which immediately precedes the beginning of creation. The qualification 'inert' points to the relation between this state and Brahman's creatively active state. This concept of relationship is the first step forward or downward towards Brahman's state of actual creativity.

[3] Since bliss and knowledge, the two other aspects of Brahman, are not emphasized in this stage.

[4] Vāgbhava, kāmabīja, Sarasvatī, Mahālakṣmī.

[5] Paśyantī. See ch. XVIII 20-29.

[6] For a detailed description of Kuṇḍalinī see Ahi.S. ch XXXIII (in extenso) and Sir A. Avalon, The Serpent Power, passim.

(he) should join aprameya (*a*) before it (*ā*).[1] This śakti (*ai*) is the source of creation (*jagadyoni*), the giver of wealth to the three lokas (*trailokyaiśvaryada*), bright, the concealer (of the direct vision) of all beings from (the realization of) the unfathomable (all-)pervading absolute self without beginning and end; the śakti that is full of bliss, and containing volition, knowledge and action, (the traits) belonging to the letter *i* (incorporated in the letter *ai*).

21. He should meditate on Abjā (i.e. Lakṣmī), who is the object (*vācya*) of the bīja jagadyoni,[2] (envisaging her) as the goddess, the wife of Viṣṇu, the bestower of sovereignty over the three worlds and the source of creation.

22. The word rati (the name of *i*) means sport in the worldly sense and my activity is but my sport. (The word) *indhana* (meaning) illumination (and that also means) knowledge as well as will (*icchā* i.e. *iṣṭa*), is also indicated (accomplished) by the (letter) *i*.[3]

23. (The word) trailokya meaning three lokas (indicates) the three states of existence of living beings (i.e. baddha, mukta and the nityamukta).[4] As she (śakti) brings about aiśvarya (prosperity) to them, she is called *trailokyaiśvaryadā*.

24-25. She, with the unfathomable (*aprameya*) etc. unfolds the worlds through the journey of creation (*bhuvanādhvan*), and again in that same highest, the vyomeśa (that is) the absolute self,

---

[1] Thus *ai* is derived from a combination of the four vowels *a* + *ā* + *i* + *ī*. The first two letters, namely *aprameya* and *ānanda*, as their names suggest, represent Viṣṇu; while *i* and *ī* form *iṣṭa* representing the object of desire, and *māyā* representing Śakti. Hence *ai* combines both God and His creative śakti, and thus represents the primordial source of all creation.

[2] *aiṃ* is another name for the vāgbhava-bīja-mantra. Vācya actually means the sonic form of the deity whom the mantra represents.

[3] This explains how divine volition, action and knowledge are represented by the vowel *i*. *Rati*, or *Rāma*, another name for *i*, connotes sport that gives pleasure and its secondary meaning is function or activity, which construed together mean that creative functions is the sport of the divine. *Iṣṭa* (another synonym) is derived from the root *iṣ*- to wish, which in this context means divine volition. *Iddha* means kindling or lighting the fire and illumination, hence knowledge. The names *iddha*, *iṣṭa* and *Rāma* indicating knowledge, volition and action actually refer to the first three divine attributes jñāna, aiśvarya and śakti. See ch. II, 27-29.

[4] Living beings are classified in three categories: i) those who are still bound to their karma and transient existence, ii) those who are delivered from such bondage, and iii) those who are never subjected to such bondage. Great sages such as Kapila, or devotees such as Nārada, belong to this third category.

she finally comes to rest; such is the course of my rising and setting (i.e. my creative existence and my inert existence). This is the description of the mahāvidyā-(bīja) (called) *jagadyoni*,[1] which is the source of speech.

26. The fifth vidyā, otherwise called *kāmabīja*, is the producer of the fulfilment of desires. This is the great śakti of Pradyumna; learn her form from me.

27-30. Paścimānana,[2] which is said to be the middle one of the guṇa tattvas (i.e. rajas) is delightful (*rañjana*), which is somewhat tinged with the enjoyment of sattya and tamas. It (represents) the same absolute prakṛti called (the letter) *ka* which regulates the cosmic process. Joined by puruṣeśvara (*la*) she is determined to create, (and) manifesting the threefold forms (viz.) avyakta, puruṣa and īśa, the same goddess (i.e.) Māyā (*ī*) (or) Śrī resides in vyomeśa (*ṃ*). Thus (I) have revealed both the form and the might of kāmabīja.[3] The sixth (bīja) is the Sārasvatī vidyā (bīja), now listen to my account of that.

31. O Śakra, I am prajñādhāra (*ū*), the place where excellent knowledge becomes manifest. The same myself, the source of knowledge, is connected with udaya (*u*) of Viṣṇu (i.e. the active state of Viṣṇu).

32. Then with subtle vision (the adept) should add ānanda (*ā*) to precede that (letter *u*) and through the (same) subtle vision aprameya (*a*) should be inserted before that (letter *ā*).

33-34. She (this mantra who is verily) myself, arising from aprameya, contains great bliss and is auspicious, and as the container of knowledge, (she) again resides in vyomeśa (*ṃ*) whereafter, in order to be connected with dissolution, she comes to parameśvara (*ḥ*).[4] (Thus) the sixth vidyā has been duly recounted to you, both in its wording and in its meaning.

35-36. This mantra(-complex, *vidyā*) consisting of the trio of bījas, is referred to as Tripurā. (When it is practised first) in the

[1] The bīja starts with *a*, *aprameya*, the inscrutable existence which is the source of All, and ends with *ṃ*, *vyomeśa*, the absolute reality wherein at the time of destruction All is dissolved. This bīja represents the complete cycle of creation and dissolution.

[2] Fierce-faced, or wearing a malevolent expression karāla, one of the names of the letter *ka*.

[3] *klīṃ*.

[4] *a* + *ā* + *u* + *ū* + *ṃ* + *ḥ* = *auḥ* is the kāma-bīja-mantra.

reverted order (*vyutkrama*) (and then) in the regular order (*anukrama*),[1] it also brings about identity with the Self. This vidyā, when successfully practised with japa and homa (i.e. accompanied by repetition of the mantras and proper rites), is said to fulfil all desires. (The wise) know that it has many different forms arising from the combination of various consonants and vowels.

37. The seventh, viz. the Mahālakṣmī-vidyā (bīja), is the source (for satisfying) all the four aims of human life (*puruṣārtha*),[2] both individually and collectively and is capable of accomplishing anything.

38-39. Taking the absolute prakṛti (*ka*), (the adept) should join bhāskara (*ṣa*) (to it) and then having added mardana (*ma*) to that, he should join it to kālavahni (*ra*). (Then) he should decorate it with māyā (*ī*). (The resulting) complex akṣara should be made to terminate with vyāpin (*ṃ*).[3]

40-41. While performing japa with this bīja, the adept should envisage me as settled in vyomeśa (*ṃ*) and engaged in the phase of creative activity through the brilliance of my own power, after having passed through the state of pradhāna (prakṛti) and having manifested the three forms (avyakta etc.) and having created all that exists.

42. These vidyās such as Anutārā etc. are to be regarded as the rays of the vidyā in the form of Tārikā and so they consist of Tārikā.

43. Those who worship this Tārikā-vidyā [4] according to the ritual precepts enjoy imperishable pleasures, both in this life and in the life to come.

---

[1] Vyutkrama: *auḥ, klīṃ, aiṃ*; and anukrama: *aiṃ, klīṃ, auḥ*.

[2] Sexual gratification, wealth, religious merit, and liberation.

[3] The Mahālakṣmī-mantra: *kṣmrīṃ*.

[4] Either in the pure Tārikā form i.e. *hrīṃ*, or in any other manifest form, such as *śrīṃ* etc.

CHAPTER TWENTY-SEVEN

DUTIES OF AN ADEPT

1. Śakra:—I bow down before thee, O mistress of the world, beloved of Puṇḍarīkākṣa (Viṣṇu), almighty goddess of the entire creation, omniscient (one) existing in all states of existence.

2. I have heard in detail the excellent principles of the vidyās. Now explain to me the mode of (worshipping) Tārikā.

3. Śrī:—The original, unique and absolute Brahman is omniscient and consists of existence and consciousness. Active through Its own Śakti, (Brahman is) divine and (the same as) the great Lakṣmī-Nārāyaṇa.

4. I am that supreme Śakti, called I-hood, eternal and ever vested with all (God's) attributes like the pure rays of the sun.

5. O son of Aditi, I, possessing the form of Its creativity, do indeed incessantly perform God's five functions.[1]

6. O Puraṃdara, hṛllekhā, the supreme vidyā (i.e. the Tārikā-mantra) is identified with me; she is my divine, absolute śakti, perpetually endowed with all my attributes.

7. You, who have approached me faithfully and devoutly (by surrendering yourself), may receive this account of her with a constantly alert mind.

8-9. (That) which is regarded (by the Vedas) as the absolute self (principle) of (all) dynamic and static (creation), the source of creation, sustenance and absorption named Sūrya, which continuously activates the eternal (force) called *prāṇa*; consider It, (viz.) the excellent Person (*puruṣa*), as the first letter *ha* (i.e. the first letter of hṛllekhā, i.e. *hrīm*).

10-11. Consider that which is its first active state (*unmeṣa*), which embraces the three worlds and is the substratum of the entire creation, which possesses a glowing form and is not limited by anything else, to be the letter *ra*, whose form is luminous and eternal, being the real active state that pervades the entire way (i.e. all the cosmic stages of creation, modes of existence: *gatim*).

---

[1] Creation, sustenance, destruction, delusion and grace.

12-13. Displaying the five activities, the pañcabindu (*ī*) characterized by creation etc.,[1] having the form of wonderful knowledge and successively (representing) the closing and opening (twinkling) of the eyes (of the creator expressing both the states of creation and non-creation); displaying the form possessing (the attributes) icchā, jñāna and kriyā (*iddha, iṣṭa, māyā*) and the order of expansion [2]—this is the eternal condition of the pair (of letters) *i* and *ī* (appearing in the bīja hṛīm).

14-15. Hence one should know that it is myself in the form of the exalted creatively active state, who manifest the creation containing (the attributes) icchā, jñāna and kriyā and fulfil the five functions of the (all-)pervading (Lord), perform various miracles, consist of concentrated consciousness, possess the form of bliss, exist in the supreme Self, am omnipresent and beloved of Viṣṇu.

16-17. I, who am the bestower of power upon the three worlds and am devoid of any parts, after performing all the (five) duties, (ultimately) dwell again in the divine supreme Self, vyomeśa, contracting (within me) the entire (world of) objects. Those versed in (the science of) realities say that she (myself as Tārā) has five forms.

18. O Sureśvara, listen to me while I describe those forms. The one form that ends with vyomeśa has (already) been described.

19-21. Some like to place parameśvara (*ḥ*) after vyomeśa (*ṃ*).[3] Others prefer to replace vyomeśa by pradhāna (*ma*), followed by both bindu (*ṃ*) and nāda (*ṁ*) to resemble praṇava.[4] Some wise persons say that only pradhāna should be at the end.[5] Other followers of the Vedas hold that there should be sṛṣṭikṛt *ḥ* (alone) at the end.[6] The learned recognize as such these five forms of Tārikā.

22-25. O Sureśvara, these forms of the one (Tārikā) dwelling in śānta (God), viz. the one ending in pradhāna, the one ending in visṛṣṭi, the one ending in vyomeśa and the one ending in vyomeśa and visṛṣṭi —these four forms (bring about) glorious fulfilment of all individual desires both in this life and in the life after death; while

---

1 The five divine functions discharged through Śakti.

2 i.e. creative evolution.

3 *Hrīṃ* + *ḥ* makes little difference as to the sound.

4 *Hrīm* + *ṃ* + *ṁ* produces a prolonged nasalization similar to that heard in *oṁ*.

5 *Hrīm*.

6 *Hrīḥ*.

the form that ends with pradhāna, bindu and nāda (brings about) the unique bliss of emancipation.[1] Thus having ascertained the real nature of Tārikā, the preceptor should teach the vidyā, which is the essence of the absolute Brahman, to the disciple who is honest, possesses good manners and who is well disposed towards the preceptor and towards Brahmins.

26. First, he (i.e. the preceptor) should perform (the rite of) consecration (nyāsa) on his own hands, body and limbs (and) after performing the same rites on the body of the disciple, he should teach him (the disciple) the mantra (Tārikā).

27. He (i.e. the preceptor) should place the mantra, preceded by bhāva,[2] on the heart of the disciple. Thereafter he should place the excellent mantra on his own heart.

28. After having received vidyā from the preceptor preceded by initiation (*dīkṣā*), the intelligent disciple should perform all these (consecration ceremonies).

29. (The disciple should thereafter) offer himself as a dakṣiṇā to the preceptor, along with (all his) wealth or one half of his possessions, accordingly as the preceptor desires.[3]

30-31. (The adept) should fulfil all the duties enjoined by the Vedas and by convention, behave attentively towards his teacher, superiors and Brahmins, consistently practise non-malice (*adroha*) towards all the four types of living beings;[4] he is always adorned with the qualities of the ātman [5] and pursues all that bears the stamp of virtue (*dharma*).

32-33. He should be consecrated by all the pure sacramental rituals, observe his duties towards the gods, pitṛs and guests; he should be learned in the divine (sacred) scriptures and the nigamas that belong to the Vedas; he should carry out the injunctions (of the sacred scriptures) with a detached mind and try to acquire knowledge about each individual object.

34-35. He should not abuse the sacred scriptures and should try to follow their (injunctions) about the appropriate means of

---

[1] Evidently *hrīṁ* is the noblest of all Tārikā-mantra's five forms as it is conducive to liberation.

[2] *Oṁ*.

[3] This signifies the disciple's total self-dedication to his preceptor, but leaves it to the latter's discretion to allow provision for the disciple's family.

[4] Mammals; birds and reptiles; insects and plants.

[5] Bliss etc.

acquiring knowledge. He should perform the daily devotion (*āhnika*) [1] according to the precepts of the sacred scriptures in the order prescribed for rituals, starting from the beginning of the day (continuing) throughout the course of the day and night until (ending with) the close of the night, successfully (without distraction) and always adhering to the aforesaid order.[2]

36-37. He should never fail to observe the rites (that are) to be performed five times a day and should always carry out the five (obligatory) sacrifices;[3] he should be vested with (qualities such as) self-control, charity, truthfulness and non-violence and, after having performed (all) vidyās in the aforesaid order, he should maintain a tranquil attitude towards matters that concern himself and others.

38. He should always strive after absolute perfection and reject incidental occult power; he should sanctify all beings with his mind, glance and speech.[4]

39. Practising the four (virtues personified as) goddesses (viz.) maitrī etc.[5] which produce tranquillity of mind aimed at securing peace, he should occupy himself with performing the sacrifice (called) japa.

40. He should fulfil his own duties without fail and with regard to (mistakes committed through invisible influence, *daivata*, he should observe) the expiatory rite (prescribed) for each particular fault.[6]

41. Devoutly, he should always seek the protection of Janārdana, the God of all gods and of myself who possess the same divine attributes as He has, (dedicating himself) through each activity of body, mind and speech.

42. If he observes an excellent man and an excellent woman, he should worship (in them) the (divine) couple, thinking of me and without relinquishing thought of their (inseparably) coupled existence (as Lakṣmī-Nārāyaṇa).

---

[1] See Rangachari, The Śrī Vaiṣṇava Brāhmans, p. 60.

[2] See p. 89 n. 1 supra.

[3] See p. 89 n. 2 supra.

[4] i.e. be so pure that his very presence has a purifying effect.

[5] Maitrī, friendliness; kāruṇā, sympathy; muditā, happiness; and upekṣā, detachment.

[6] It is worth noting that, unlike most other Saṃhitās of this nature, the Lakṣmī Tantra does not devote a lengthy discussion to expiatory rites, although these have been mentioned as an important topic. See p. 98 supra.

43. Wherever in the nature of words or in (their) meaning there is any trace of manliness, he should always take it for granted that womanliness also resides there, because he bears in mind (the inseparability of) Lakṣmī-Nārāyaṇa.

44. When he sees a surpassingly virtuous, beautiful young woman, bearing me in mind he should look upon her without any lust.

45-48. He is never moved by passion for women, he never utters harsh words; he avoids mistakes and (if) he commits one, then without argument he expiates it by (performing) purifying rites. He never despises abnormality in any woman such as a hunch-back or other disfigurement; consistently adhering to the precepts of the sacred scripture, he performs deeds that please women. The person who thus performs virtuous deeds, who is free of sin and a devotee of mine habitually performing deeds that please me, who worships me and is wholly devoted to me, attains the highest place—the abode of Viṣṇu.

49. O Śakra, thus I have concluded describing the nature of Tārikā. Now tell me what else you want to know about the other vidyās.

CHAPTER TWENTY-EIGHT

DAILY DUTIES OF AN ADEPT

1. Śakra:—I bow down before thee, O dweller in the lotus. I prostrate myself before thee, who existest in the Trayyanta (i.e. Vedānta); through thy grace and through samādhi I have duly heard (all about) mantras.

2. (I have also) attentively (listened to) the explanation of their (meaning) and of their true forms. Now pray tell me the duties (of a devotee) during each day and each night.

3. Śrī:—Nārāyaṇa is the unique (one), the possessor of Śrī; He is beginningless, lotus-eyed and the great ocean (i.e. repository) of jñāna, aiśvarya, mahāśakti, vīrya and tejas.[1]

4. He is the self of all living beings, haṃsa, Nārāyaṇa, and the controller (of all). I am His potency and I possess all His attributes.

5. When worshipped, the same I, repeatedly producing all conditions, viz. creation etc., guide all (beings) safely across the ocean of life.

6. Pleased by the adept's (adherence to his) duties, I bestow on him various (objects of) enjoyment. My form of sattva etc. abides in (persons, who) fulfil their duties (*saddharmapara*) properly.

7. These duties are forms of ritual conduct and their characteristic (feature consists of) rites. (Now) I am going to describe that ritual conduct which is observed by the virtuous.

8. Abandoning the state of sleep that is yoga and waking up when the night ends, (the adept) should obtain the protection of Hṛṣīkeśa, (i.e.) Hari, the husband of Śrī.

9. O Sureśvara, you have already been informed about the nature of self-surrender (*prapatti*). (But) I shall go over that once more so that it may remain firmly (imprinted) in your (mind).[2]

10. After having sipped water and having become internally pure (clean), (the adept) should reflect on the astra(-mantra) [3] which has a blazing form and, through its brilliant power, he should become

---

[1] Bala is omitted, probably because it is included in mahāśakti.

[2] Repetition of this topic indicates its importance.

[3] *oṃ hrīṃ astrāya phaṭ.*

purified by (mentally) merging himself in, and (then) emerging out of, it.

11-16. Then he should perform prapatti in all its five parts. (These are), 'I have rejected all feelings of antipathy and have adopted an attitude of friendliness towards all beings to the extent that my ability and mental capacity permit. Since I am lazy, of limited capacity, and ignorant about the nature of things, the means (that I adopt) can never (be adequate to) save me. Therefore I am downhearted and poor, without ties, without possessions; (I also know) that all doctrines (*siddhānta*) and Upaniṣads (Vedānta) proclaim that Hṛṣīkeśa along with Lakṣmī, who is the very embodiment of compassion, is the guardian (source of emancipation). Whatever I possess that is difficult to forsake, such as wife or sons, all these, O husband of Śrī, I offer at thy feet along with myself. O my lord, master of the gods and consort of Lakṣmī, be my protector'. When once the adept surrenders himself in this way, no further duty is imposed on him.

17. For the man who, because he possesses little intelligence,[1] is barred from (the use of) good means (of attaining liberation) and (yet) is not hindered (from achieving it) and who thus stands between (the two of these), the proper course is to resort to other means.

18. Now learn the proper duties (of an adept) as I enumerate them. (The adept) should rise in the morning with the desire that happiness may dawn for all living beings.

19-22. Wishing well-being to everybody in thought as well as in utterance (with the following words), 'Let all beings abide in the pure way of sattva, let them worship Śrīpati for ever and consequently enter the supreme abode (of Viṣṇu)'; he should purify his body as instructed by the sacred scripture; then, after having washed himself thoroughly, he should clean his teeth. Next, he should rinse his mouth according to the instructions about methods of purifica-

[1] This is what is termed the middle course which is open to a devotee who lacks sharp intelligence enabling him to discriminate between the [illegible] and the harmful activities in which people get involved. It takes watchfulness to follow the narrow road of proper duty, [illegible] what is [illegible] appears as [illegible]dutary and vice versa. Moreover this con[illegible]ness [illegible] a man prone to forget its purpose and carries him still [illegible] away [illegible]. So the true devotee does not bother about that and t[illegible] himself [illegible] on God's mercy.

tion enjoined in the scripture and then, pouring (water, i.e. washing the place), he should worship Sandhyā,[1] who is the purifier of the three worlds, who consists of myself and who is the threefold śakti in the forms of Sūrya, Agni and Soma.

23-24. The function of the goddess Sandhyā is to purify all beings. After having worshipped the shining, supreme Person existing inside (the disc of the sun), he (the adept) should then perform agnividhi [2] and (then) he should start upādāna (which primarily consists of begging for the necessary requirements for worship). (But), if they are rich, the wise should omit performing upādāna.

25. There are seven lawful ways of obtaining money, (viz.) through inheritance (*dāya*), profit (*lābha*), purchase (*kraya*, of land etc.), victory (*jaya* in contests), application (*prayoga*), a vocational job (*karmayoga*) and lawful gifts (*satpratigraha*).

26. After taking the three types of daily baths according to the precepts of the scriptures, he should perform bhūtaśuddhi and the internal sacrifice.[3]

27-28. He should sacrifice to me, to Viṣṇu, or to both of us, offering objects either produced by himself, or which are abundant,[4] or brought by the disciples, and he should follow the method (of performance) in eight parts that ends with the anuyāga.[5] In the afternoons, the wise (adept) should engage in studying the scriptures.

29-30. He should study the sacred scripture (of his own system) and the Vedic nigamas as well as other scriptures (belonging to other systems) with a view to realizing the self, without (being distracted by) greed, attachment or hatred. He must never abuse a scripture, whether high or low, either in thought or word.

31. (Nevertheless) he should only accept that much of such scriptures as (depicts) something about himself. (The reason is that) all sacred scriptures are developed to promote the welfare of all living beings.

32. Step by step these (scriptures) reveal the ultimate good (by) commencing with an indication of purpose, (by continuing) ... the

---

[1] Twilight and dawn, junctures of day and night.

[2] See ch. XL, in extenso.

[3] See chs. XXXV and XXXVI, in extenso.

[4] The reading *krītaiḥ*, purchased, is more appropriate in this context.

[5] See chs. XXXVIII and XXXIX.

middle (to expound a justification of method) and (by finishing) at the end (with confirmation of the doctrine expounded).

33-35. (One should remember that) it is the illustrious Nārāyaṇa, who is described in (these) in their own way. Existent in Nārāyaṇa, I am omnipotent and all-seeing and, like a physician familiar with the causes and symptoms of diseases, by way of the teachers of particular (religions) I introduce various scriptures, each (based) in its own way (on) particular sources of knowledge suited to (men of) a particular capacity; hence no scripture should ever be rejected.

36. The ultimate good is easily discernable in all (scriptures); sometimes but faintly revealed, sometimes revealed to a fuller extent. Hence, one should not be antagonistic, (but) should accept them in so far as one has access to their contents.

37. (Yet one should be cautious) about adopting their specific practices and about undergoing initiation (according to their customs). After that (study of the scriptures), (the adept) should perform the rituals of the late evening (when) the sun is half set (in the western sky).

38-39. After performing the rituals of fire etc. and after purifying himself by observing (yogic disciplines such as) yama and the like, (the adept) should engage in meditation in some completely isolated place which is undefiled, thornless and attractive, covered with a soft sheet of cotton, hide or kuśa-grass and consecrated both within and without.

40-44. After sitting in a posture of either cakra (disc), padma (lotus) or svastika,[1] as he pleases, and after controlling the artery-way of (the vital air) as well as all (the five vital) airs,[2] he who has conquered his sense-organs by pratyāhāra[3] should carefully perform the rites of concentration (*dhāraṇā*);[4] and then, when firmly in the meditative trance (*samādhi*),[5] he should (continue) to meditate on me, as the peerless, inscrutable, undifferentiated, pure, omnipresent Lakṣmī, who abides in every cognition; or the meditator (may meditate on me) in the form of Padmā, the supreme (goddess), with her hands held in the attitude of granting a boon

---

[1] For a description of these see Ahi.S. 31, 31-46.

[2] System of controlling breathing and its total suspension etc. known as prāṇāyāma. See Yog.S. 2, 29 and 49.

[3] See Yog.S. 2, 54.

[4] Ibid. 2, 53.

[5] Ibid. 3, 3.

and protection, with a complexion like the heart of a lotus, holding a lotus in her hand and adorned with (all) auspicious marks; or (he may meditate on me as) the goddess existing (seated) on the lap of Nārāyaṇa, completely identified (with Him), and consisting of knowledge and bliss; and also on the husband of Śrī in the same state.

45-46. O Sureśvara, these are the various ways of meditating and one may follow any of these methods (*dharma*) that one specially likes (and has faith in); and after having reached the deepest point of meditation, one should continue in the state of meditative trance where the distinctions between meditator, meditation and the object meditated on merge into oneness.

47-50. At such a time it is myself alone that am left revealed, I who am the eternal and absolute I-hood (of God). When in the ocean of consciousness the meditator achieves identity with me, there appears at that time nothing else but me, the absolute. Wearied of meditation (*yoga*), he must mutter prayers (*japa*), wearied of japa he must practise yoga.[1] Thus when he is constantly engaged in japa and meditation, I very soon bestow my grace upon him. Having thus spent the first part (*yāma*) of the night, the intelligent and sober (disciple) should, without interrupting his meditation, then sleep for the two (remaining) portions of the night. Waking up in the latter half of the night (i.e. in the morning), he should repeat the aforesaid programme.

51. Thus I have recounted to you, O slayer of Bala, (the duties) combined with various rites. (An adept) should spend all five divisions of (the day) continuously performing services to God.

52. O slayer of Bala, there is no difference whatsoever in merit between an initiate well versed in the duties of the five sections of the day and one who is engaged in pronouncing the mantras of Lakṣmī.[2]

53. Both of them are accepted as devotees, both become bearers of (the holy marks of) the conch-shell, lotus etc., and he who steadfastedly continues to serve Lakṣmī becomes one with me after death.

[1] Repeatedly alternating japa and meditation.

[2] Implying that the adept has abandoned all other religious practices and confines himself to the continuous performance of japa and meditation on the Lakṣmī-mantra.

54. (The adept) should be loyal to his wife, should practise self-restraint at all times, should worship my mantra daily with his mind fixed on me and should always (be faithful) in my service.

55-59. He should recognize all words, whether ranking high or low,[1] as manifestations of that (i.e. of myself as Śabdabrahman). The person, who possesses knowledge of the difference between Agni and Soma and who can also differentiate between kriyā(śakti) and bhūti(śakti);[2] who realizes correctly (the reality) in the gross, subtle and absolute states (of śakti);[3] who possesses knowledge of the tantras along with their subordinate and auxiliary subjects and knows the science of the different mudras;[4] who has at his command knowledge of the requirements for internal and external sacrifices, japa and homa; who is familiar with different modes of puraścaraṇa [5] and has knowledge of reality as the goal and at the same time the means of attaining it; who is familiar with the precepts regarding names and forms and also with their modes of worship; who recognizes the reality of śarīrādhāra (i.e. *ādhāra cakra*),[6] is skilled in the methods of yoga and can also discern other (hidden) meanings in the sacred scriptures; who (possesses virtues like) sobriety, intelligence, non-violence (etc.) and who habitually practises self-control and generosity; such a person will love (serve) me, i.e. Śrī.

---

[1] The term 'words' here stands for mantras which—whether they rank high as praṇava-, Tārā-, Viṣṇu- or Lakṣmī-mantras, or are graded lower as mantras of secondary deities—are all ultimately manifestations of the supreme Śakti.

[2] See ch. XXIX, 4-11.

[3] See ch. XXXII in extenso.

[4] See ch. XXXIV in extenso.

[5] See p. 130, n. 7.

[6] See pp. 289 f.

CHAPTER TWENTY-NINE

DISTINCTION BETWEEN KRIYĀŚAKTI AND BHŪTIŚAKTI, OTHERWISE CALLED AGNI AND SOMA RESPECTIVELY

1. Śakra:—I bow to thee, the basis of the variegated (painting) of the creation called the six courses, comprising both the pure and the impure (creation); (to thee) who art the beloved of Śrīvatsa and who art the remover of the miseries of this world.

2. O Padmā, pray explain to me the precise difference between Agni and Soma and also the ways of the kriyā(śakti) and the bhūti(śakti) and everything that concerns knowledge of Tārikā.

3. Śrī:—I, representing both the all-pervasive absolute Brahman and the Śakti of Nārāyaṇa, evolve into the form of praṇava.

4. O dear to gods, listen to (my explanation of) the differentiation between Tārikā as Agni and as Soma. I shall also explain to you the ways of the kriyā(śakti) and the bhūti(śakti).

5. As I have already told you, I am the Śakti (of Viṣṇu), the sustainer of every object, and I represent Viṣṇu's supreme creative state consisting of the six (divine) attributes and consciousness.

6. As such, while engaged in creating the whole universe I become manifest in two forms characterized by my two activities, (namely the act of sustenance and the act of creation), primarily (revealing two different attributes, viz.) aiśvarya and tejas.[1]

7. (Of course, even then) my form consists of all the six attributes, (but) in this state (of creation) (i.e. Agni) tejas becomes somewhat prominent; (similarly) my form consists of (all) the six attributes (yet in the state of Soma it is considered) to incline towards the supremacy of aiśvarya.

8. The form when tejas is predominant is known as kriyāśakti; the same is called Agni since it burns away all miseries.

9. My form which is inclined towards aiśvarya is called bhūti (śakti) (or) Lakṣmī; that śakti of mine abounding in aiśvarya is my form containing Soma.

---

[1] Aiśvarya is the śakti's sovereign will (see ch. II, 28), whereas tejas is omnipotence (see. ch. II, 33-34).

10. As she dries up (destroys) all evils, Agniśakti consists of action (kriyā). The other (śakti, viz.) bhūti, which gladdens the creation, is called Soma in this world.

11. These two of my forms with icchā, jñāna and kriyā in predominance are manifested from my Vyūha-state of existence; while in my form that contains (all) the six attributes (in equal proportion) I am the highest goddess manifested in the Vyūhas.[1]

12. My special śakti called kriyā, containing the six attributes, bright with (an abundance of) tejas, has three components (*Vyūha*) viz. the śaktis (of) Sūrya, Soma and Agni.

13. The first of them is the supreme, divine and resplendent śakti called Sūrya, who is ever evolving, performing (the function of) creating the world.

14. O lord of the gods, this (śakti) called Sūrya has three aspects, (viz.) that concerning the self, that concerning divine powers and that concerning the elements.

15. In her aspect concerning the self, (the śakti) named Sūrya passes (during the Yogic process) through the (duct) piṅgalā. (In her aspect) concerning the elements Sūryaśakti proceeds (manifests herself) as light.

16-19. The śakti existing in the disc of the sun (as the presiding deity) is her (aspect) which is concerned with divinity. O Sureśvara, look upon those rays which belong to the disc of the sun as the Ṛg (-mantras) that, being identical with the heat of the sun, warm us. Consider my brightness that exists there in to be the Sāman. Consider the supreme (Śakti) that remains enclosed in the body of the Person to be the divine, charming Person (*puruṣa*) consisting of Yajus. He is the master of Śrī, carrying the conch-shell and disc, possessing long, rounded arms and a gracious face. He sits on the lotus and has eyes like lotuses.

20. O Sureśvara, this Person (*puruṣa*), who abides in (the body), has the *daśa hotṛ* [2] for his head. The (hymn called) *catur hotṛ* [3] constitutes the legs and hands of this deity.

21. O Sureśvara, his hair, flesh, bones, marrow and blood are

---

[1] The absolute Śakti manifests herself in the pure creation, whereas the partial śaktis in the form of Agni and Soma manifest themselves in the impure creation.

[2] Tai.Ā. 3, 3.

[3] Ibid. 3, 2.

made up of (the hymn called) *pañca hotṛ*.[1] (The hymn called) *ṣad hotṛ* [2] forms his breasts, testicles, manhood and anus.

22. The seven vital airs that exist in the head are said to be the (hymn called) *sapta hotṛ*.[3] *Dakṣiṇā* [4] forms his beauty and the *saṃbhāras* [5] are considered to form his joints.

23. (The hymn called) *devapatnyas* [6] constitutes (his) arteries, while (the hymn called) *hotṝṇāṃ hṛdayam* [7] is (considered to be) his mind. The Puruṣa-sūkta [8] is known as his consciousness and his śakti is called the Śrī-sūkta.[9]

24. Oṃkāra, Praṇava (and) Tāra are (his) secret names, which are eternal, while his gross (i.e. unconcealed) names are Yajus, Rudra and Śukra.[10]

25. The person who practises the divine Puruṣa-mantra and the Yajurmaya-mantra (i.e. the Sāvitrī) after (pronouncing) the vyāhṛti (-mantras) is even released from the sin of (practising) abhicāra (rites for malevolent purposes).

26. Thus the supreme śakti, Trayī, who is called Sūrya blazes in the sky. This absolute śakti, famous as Sūrya, is known in three aspects.

27-29. Sāvitrī, who is the mother of the Vedas, evolves (into sound). She has the three-lettered praṇava as her substratum; *bhūḥ*, *bhuvaḥ* and *svaḥ*, (i.e. vyāhṛtis) as her three (yogic) ducts; the words *tad* etc. (*tad savitur vareṇyam* etc. of the Gāyatrī-mantra) as her (vital) air, and her head is decorated with the *śiraḥ* [11] (-mantra); her body consisting of manifestation and bliss (contains) the letters from *kṣiti* (*ka*) to *puruṣa* (*ma*). She arises from Brahman and reverts back to Brahman. This same mother of the Vedas is (also) the absolute mother of the letters (sounds).[12]

[1] Tai Ā., 3, 3.
[2] Ibid. 3, 4.
[3] Ibid. 3, 5.
[4] Ibid. 3, 10.
[5] Ibid. 3, 8.
[6] Ibid. 3, 9.
[7] Ibid. 3, 11.
[8] ṚgV. 10, 90, 1[d].
[9] ṚgV.Kh. 5, 87, 1[a].
[10] Tai. Ā. 4, 5 and 1, 10, 1[a].
[11] *oṃ āpo jyotī raso amṛtam brahma bhūr bhuvaś suvar oṃ*, Tai. Ā. 10, 15, 1. See Rangachari, The Sri Vaiṣhnava Brahmans, pp. 31-32.
[12] See Ahi.S. chs. 58 and 59 for further details.

30-32. O handsome one, (the śakti) belonging to Agni is here described in successive and reverse order.[1] The same, possessing the form of the sun, is my role of Sāvitrī. (She is called) Gāyatrī (because) she saves from terror those who chant (her mantra), [2] (by) absorbing in her rays, life (i.e. water) from the earth, rivers and living beings and, after retaining it in her rays for nine months, releases it back in (the form of) clouds. Thus I have described (to you) the śakti consisting of Sūrya; now listen to the (description of the absolute śakti) consisting of Agni.

33-35. O Śakra, my śakti consisting of Agni also has three states. The celestial one (i.e. lightning) [3] has water as its fuel, the other (terrestrial) existing on the earth [4] has earthly fuel (e.g. wood etc.), the third remains inside the abdomen [5] and has food as its fuel. These are the three states of my śakti consisting of Agni. The same (śakti) representing all deities is called the mouth of all deities.[6] The wise (people) who are occupied with the three purposes of life (*trivarga*)[7] praise her and call her Triṣṭubh.[8] Those are who engaged in taking themselves across (to the other side of the ocean of life) are helped across by her on the difficult journey.

36-37. The other śakti which consists of Soma is also described as having three states. One is in the sky, (where) she is identified with the disc (of the moon). The other (is on the earth) in the form of the plants. In the (third form) she moves inside living beings through the (duct called) Iḍā which is in the nature of nectar.[9] When she is praised with (mantras) in anuṣṭubh (metre), she is called Anuṣṭubh.

---

[1] Implying that in the process of creative evolution Śakti is represented by the letters *a* to *ha*, and in the process of involution leading to dissolution by the letters *kṣa* to *ā*.

[2] The word gāyatrī is treated here as derived from two roots, *tṛ* = to save and *gāy* = to sing or chant.

[3] Lightning is closely connected with rain clouds, hence water is considered to be its fuel.

[4] i.e. fire in the ordinary sense.

[5] i.e. fire in the digestive sense.

[6] Cf. ṚgV. II, 1, 13.

[7] Sexual pleasure, wealth and religious merit.

[8] A Vedic metre, especially the metre of the Gāyatrī-mantra.

[9] Note that here again the text adopts the Vedic tradition of assigning three aspects to these luminaries, namely the celestial and the terrestrial, but for the third aspect abandons the spherical and resorts to the physical body. See A. Bergaigne, La Religion Védique, Paris, 2nd ed. 1963, pp. XIII-XVI.

38-39. This mantra (in anuṣṭubh: *vidyā*) is called *mṛtyuñjaya* and it overcomes death.[1] O Puraṃdara, Sūrya, Soma and Agni, all these are its (i.e. this mantra's) different forms. As the performer of (the oblation), her (i.e. kriyāśakti's) Soma aspect is manifested as arising from Sūrya and as identified with the butter offering. Then she eats that butter (*havis*) under the name of Agni, being the mouth belonging to Agni, the Brahmin.[2]

40. The entire system of creation is conducted day and night by these three (śaktis). This is the essence of the three Vyūhas[3] that consist of the kriyā (śakti).

41. This supremely profound śakti of mine, manifested with a predominance of tejas, is as bright as multimillions of suns, moons and fires in profusion.

42. She (śakti) is (identical with) the disc named Sudarśana, which destroys enemies. This highly powerful weapon made of fire belongs to Viṣṇu.

43. Its essence is supreme effort (*udyama*) and it is the dominating life-principle (*prāṇanam*) of prāṇa etc. All weapons and all śaktis arise from it (viz. Sudarśana).

44. Of all Hari's modes of activity based on his five functions this is the most effective. No single act on the part of the great Viṣṇu can (be performed) without (the aid of) this (Sudarśana).

45. This (śakti) is identical with Viṣṇu's resolve (to become active: *saṃkalpa* etc.) and starts functioning at the moment of creation. She adheres to her disc-form even when sustaining and absorbing creation.

46. This supreme kriyāśakti born from a part of myself, belonging to Viṣṇu and identical with Agni, pervades (the whole of creation) from Brahmā to a tuft of grass in six (different) courses (of creation).

47-49. Among these, O Vāsava, listen first to the (description of) the cycle[4] (of creation) consisting of letters. (In this cycle, which is represented as a wheel) the pair of Tārikā (-mantra) and tāraka (mantra) belonging to Viṣṇu is present in the axle (of the wheel). The sixteen svara letters, possessing the form of the light of Sūrya

---

[1] This refers to the Vedic hymn ṚgV. VII, 59, 12. See Rangachari, p. 75.

[2] Or, the flickering one (*vipra* denotes that which trembles).

[3] Saṃkarṣaṇa, Pradyumna and Aniruddha.

[4] Here *adhvā* (course) has been replaced by the word cycle (*cakra*) to emphasize the identity between kriyāśakti and Sudarśana.

and Soma, occupy the hub (of the wheel). The twenty-four letters, (viz.) from *ka* to *bha* and the other letters (viz.) from *ma* to *ha*, (occupying the spokes) reach the inner circumference. The (letter) *vargānta* (*kṣa*), which is identified with Agni and appears like a round form (*piṇḍa*), extends up to the periphery (of Sudarśana). In this way the divine cycle of letters extends itself over the course of the letters.

50. O Śakra, the cycle of kalā (exists) in the (following) way. Jñāna occupies the axle, śakti the hub, aiśvarya the spokes, while the threefold bala etc. (i.e. *bala*, *vīrya* and *tejas*) occupy the inner circumference etc. (i.e. the inner circumference, the section adjacent to this circumference and the periphery).[1]

51. O Śakra, (in the cycle of the) tattvas, Vāsudeva (occupies) the axle, the hub is bright with Saṃkarṣaṇa, Pradyumna is the spoke, while Aniruddha takes the form of the periphery.

52. The cycle of pada consists of turya and the others (viz. *suṣupti*, *svapna* and *jāgrat*) occupy the axle, hub, spokes and the inner circumference (respectively). (In the cycle of) mantra, the axle etc. are occupied by bīja, piṇḍa, saṃjñā and pada (respectively).

53-55. In the last cycle of bhuvana, extending as far as the worlds and their objects, kāla occupies the axle, avyakta the hub; mahat etc. occupy the rib-like spokes; and the mind, the auditory organ (and other sense organs) along with their objects etc. which are modifications (of prakṛti), occupy the circumference (of the disc). Kriyāśakti, (called) Sudarśana, possessing the form of the Person and belonging to Viṣṇu, exists in the centre of the disc and holds in her hands the six cycles (of creation). (Now) listen to the (description of) her (mantra as) the bīja, the piṇḍa, the pada and the saṃjñā.

56-60. First taking the letter soma (*s*), one should join on the letter prāṇa (*h*) at the end of it (*saha*). Then taking also the letter amṛta (*s*), one should add the letter kālapāvaka (*ra*), to it. Next one should join the letter anala (*ra*) to it and then place beside it the letters māyā and vyāpin (*īṃ*). This (*sahasrāra īṃ*) is the bīja of Sudarśana, a manifestation of my kriyāśakti. This bīja consisting of seven [2] letters brings about great prosperity. The same (mantra)

---

[1] Implying that the outer circle of the wheel, being solid, has thickness with an inner and an outer circular edge.

[2] Usually referred to as the six-lettered bīja by omitting *oṃ*.

is (called) the great piṇḍa, when it is devoid of the letters *māyā* and *vyāpin* (*īṃ*). This great piṇḍa, consisting of five letters, possessing a form resembling (in brightness) ten thousands of the fires of destruction together with the sun, with a voice like a thunder-clap difficult for (both) gods (and) demons to bear, is to be envisaged (only) once by the pure, but cannot be visualized by those who have no control over their senses; after that, one should recollect my two bījas (viz.) Tārikā etc. (Tārikā and Anutārikā), in order to pacify (Sudarśana).

61. The letter called kālānala (*ra*), that stands in the latter part of the piṇḍa, burns the demon kings and the worlds at the end of a cycle (of creation).

62. The fire is ignited by the flame that exists in the second śakti. It is this second śakti that is enlivened by the life-principle filled with amṛta and energy.

63-67. O great celestial person, thus I have recounted to you the form of the piṇḍa(-mantra of Sudarśana). Its saṃjñā-mantra is this piṇḍa with the interspersed insertion of the five vyāpakas (*ṃ*) and joined by the letter dhruva (*a*) at the beginning and the mantras varma (i.e. *kavaca*) and astra at the end.[1] The letters soma and sūrya (*sa* and *ha*), forming the first part of the piṇḍa, should be joined with two vyāpakas (*saṃ haṃ*), while at the end of the combined letters soma and agni (*sra*) another vyāpaka should be introduced (*srāṃ*). (The remaining) two vyāpakas are recorded to be at the beginning and at the end of the last letter (of the piṇḍa). The varma(-mantra) composed of the letters *prāṇa* (*h*), *ūrja* (*ū*) and *vyoma* (*ṃ*) [2] is efficacious in destroying evil calamities. The sound *phaṭ* represents Saṃkarṣaṇa, who destroys everything at the end of a kalpa, and the letter *āhlāda* (*ṭ*) at the end of it (*phaṭ*) is capable of evoking a sense of peace. In this way, O handsome one, the mantra belonging to Soma and Agni is traditionally conceived as having developed from its piṇḍa form.

68. This powerful mantra of Sudarśana is formed with its own letters (since the whole mantra is an elaboration of sahasrāra) and is instrumental in procuring all the objects of enjoyment, whether pertaining to heaven, to the atmosphere or to the earth.

---

[1] *oṃ saṃ haṃ srāṃ raṃ hūṃ phaṭ.*

[2] *hūṃ.*

69-71. O Puraṃdara, this mantra acts like a wish-fulfilling tree for those who have taken shelter under its (protection). O killer of Vṛtra, thus I, who am eternally manifest (emanating) from Nārāyaṇa for benefit of the world, have explained the distinction between Agni and Soma. (I have also told you) about the difference between kriyā(śakti) and bhūti(śakti) and about the efficacy of kriyā (śakti) according to the variation in the bīja, piṇḍa etc. Now listen again, O Śakra, (to the description) of the expansion of kriyāśakti.

CHAPTER THIRTY

THE TWO ASPECTS OF ŚAKTI, VIZ. SOMA AND SŪRYA, AND FURTHER ELUCIDATION OF THE SUDARŚANA-MANTRA

1. Thus, O Śakra, I have explained my kriyāśakti to you. I have also told you about her developments as distinguished by Sūrya, Soma and Agni.

2. I have also described to you her complex (mantra-form), distinguished by the bīja and piṇḍa (forms of the mantra). Now, Śakra, learn from me (the structure of) her pada-mantra.

3. The first piṇḍa (*jraḥ*) is a combination of (the letters) *ajita, anala* and *sarga* (*ja, ra, ḥ*). The second piṇḍa (*kraḥ*) is a combination of (the letters) *kamala, anala* and *sarga* (*ka, ra, ḥ*).

4-5. The combination of (the letters) *śveta* and *āhlāda* is called the third piṇḍa (*phaṭ*). The fourth piṇḍa (is a combination of the letters) *sūrya, ūrja* and *vyāpin* (*hūṃ*); then between these, three astras (*phaṭ*) are (inserted) and followed by (the words) kālacakrāya and the name for the wife of the god of fire (*svāhā*). It has tāraka (*oṃ*) at the beginning. This cycle (of letters) is the king of all pada-mantras (*oṃ jraḥ kraḥ phaṭ hūṃ phaṭ phaṭ phaṭ kālacakrāya svāhā*).

6. O Vāsava, there is nothing that cannot (be achieved) by this mantra. Those who have concentrated their minds on it never (again) experience defeat.

7. O Vāsava, I shall again explain (to you) all the efficacies of this (mantra which is) the best of all the mantras (and) which contains three pairs of letters (*sahasrāra hūṃ phaṭ*) that I have already mentioned.

8. This cycle has neither name nor form. It shines with the splendour of the six (divine) attributes. The adept who meditates on it, repeating this mantra with (its) bīja, becomes emancipated from the bondage (of saṃsāra).

9. This great mantra is the immediate form (embodiment) of my kriyāśakti. It consists of six letters supported by the wheel (*cakra*) existing in the essence (*vedānta*) of the Atharva Veda.[1]

[1] See Ahi.S. ch. 18 in extenso.

10. The wheel of Sudarśana extends over the six journeys (of creation); it is full of power and is supreme (of all). One should meditate on (its) various luminous parts, viz. the axle, the hub etc.

11. The letters of the mantra starting with *amṛta* (*sa*) should be envisaged (as existing) in each part (of the wheel), axle etc., i.e. the axle, the hub, the spokes, the felly (= inner circumference of the wheel) and the periphery (outer circumference of the wheel) including its edge.

12. The periphery represents the (cosmic) principles, starting with prakṛti[1] and ending with viśeṣa. In the (wheel of) Sudarśana the felly represents māyā, prasūti and the combination of the three guṇas.

13-14. The pada course forms the boundary enclosing the spokes, mantras form the one-thousand spokes, the ends of the spokes depict the course of Vyūha, whereas the hub depicts (the course of) kalā. The course of the sound (extends) up to the axle and in the very centre (of this) I, the absolute Śakti, exist, and within me exists the supreme Brahman, devoid of polarization (of knowledge).

15. One should reflect on the tāra (-mantra) as contained within (the Sudarśana) and one should envisage Tārikā as falling outside it (= tāra). Beyond that one should meditate on the bīja (-mantra) of the kriyāśakti and the first letter that follows it.

16. Thus, one should understand (how) the four bījas keep their regular order within the hollow of the axle. The hub of the cycle and the spokes (should contain) Sūrya etc. in the manner previously mentioned.[2]

17-20. The (mantra) which essentially is *hra* and *sra* has a thousand variations. (These are constructed) by adding (each of the sixteen vowels) *aprameya* (*a*) etc. (separately) to the pair of *sūrya*[3] and *kālānala*[4] as well as to that of *amṛta*[5] and *anala*.[6] To (each) of these vowels, pervaded by Agni and Soma,[7] the thirty-one letters[8]

---

[1] This implies the gross course of creation called the *bhuvanādhvan*.

[2] See the previous chapter.

[3] *ha*.

[4] *ra*.

[5] *sa*.

[6] *ra*.

[7] See ch. XXIII in extenso.

[8] *ka* — *ma* = 25 + *ya*, *la*, *va*, *śa*, *ṣa* and *kṣa* = 31 × 16 vowels × 2 categories viz. sūrya and soma = 992.

(that is, all the letters of the alphabet) excepting *sūrya* (*ha*), *soma* (*sa*) and *anila* (*ya*) are (separately) joined, which immediately add up to eight less than a thousand in number, whereafter the addition of the eight bījas,[1] joined with *hra* and *sra* (completes thousand variants). After that (these thousand letters) are arranged (in the circle diagram) starting from the north-eastern corner and proceeding through the south-eastern corner up to the north-western corner.[2]

21-24. Placing two threads diagonally across, one divides the circle (diagram) into four (equal) sections. In each section, one arranges the spokes that are five times fifty in number. This makes the number of the spokes one thousand. Thereafter one places on these one thousand letters (in their proper order), starting at the eastern (quarter) and ending at the soma [3] (northern) quarter. Thereafter, starting from the south-east and ending at the north-east, one successively places on the diagonal threads (placed obliquely to divide the circle) the four attributes of Agni, (viz.) Jayā, Vijayā, Ajitā and Aparājitā, the deities who preside over the mantra. The periphery of the Sudarśana circumscribes the spokes.

25-26. O Vāsava, all the weapons (i.e. astra-mantras) (are placed) within the periphery of the spokes. O Puramdara, the adept should meditate on all the pravartakas [4] (mantras) placed in front (of the weapons) and the nivartakas [5] are placed beyond (these last). One should envisage them as of equal number and as situated on the two sides (of the diagram). Their heads are marked with the (relevant) śastra (sword)-sign, their hands are joined and they display a spirited disposition.[6]

27-28. The space (covered) by the felly of the wheel is occupied by Mahālakṣmī in the eastern quarter, by Mahāmāyā in the south, by Sarasvatī in the west and by Mahiṣamardinī [7] in the north. Encircling them exist the triad forms of Brahmā etc. [8]

[1] The seven main bījas mentioned in ch. XXVI and the Sudarśana-bīja.

[2] The description of the thousand letters is quite different in Ahi.S. 23, 81-85.

[3] Cf. verses 27-28.

[4] Explained in ch. XXX, 35-48.

[5] Ch. XXX, 35-48.

[6] The verses 25 and 26 seem to be corrupt. Whether the weapons are separate from the pravartaka and nivartakas or not, is unclear.

[7] The special form of Durgā, cf. Br.P. IV, 25. 75 and 88.

[8] Brahmā, Viṣṇu and Maheśvara, see ch. V, 6-23.

29-33. Next are placed the manifestations of Turya etc.,[1] along with their śaktis. The twenty-four realities starting with prakṛti and ending in the elements are arranged in successive order in the inner edge beyond the felly of the wheel. The deities presiding over material for creation (i.e. cosmic principles) occupy the middle part of (the felly), while the objects of the worlds along with the worlds, viz. *bhūḥ, bhuvaḥ, svaḥ* etc.,[2] are placed at the outer edge of the felly. (These worldly objects consist of) all the mountains such as Meru etc., all the rivers such as Gaṅgā etc., all the oceans such as the milky-ocean etc., all the islands (i.e. countries) such as Jambu [3] etc., all the groups of objects of the firmament, the planets such as the sun etc., the nakṣatras (such as Rohiṇī etc.),[4] the stars and the departed souls who have become stars.

34. O Puraṃdara, the thirty-three hundred million gods occupy the circumference just as bees swarm around honey.

35. O lord of the gods, twice ten thousand fires (called) pravartakas and nivartakas encircle the two sides of the felly of the wheel.

36-37. There, the pravartaka fires, bright with a thousand fires of dissolution formed by hosts of glowing flames, burn the demons and titans. The nivartaka (fires, on the other hand) are restrained, steady and sober, with rays that are luminous and pleasant (and), guided by me, they pacify the pravartakas.

38-39. That particular mantra (viz.) the lāṅgalāstra (*phaṭ*), which comes after the Sudarśana-mantra traceable to Saṃkarṣaṇa,[5] is very terrible and a destroyer of all. The pravartaka (fires) are born out of the fore-part of it (the weapon-mantra) which exists in an oblique position at the end of the felly, while the nivartaka (fires) are born out of its other part.

40-41. These pravartaka and nivartaka (fires) consist of Agni and Soma. These weapons filled with Agni and Soma produce (other) weapons twice ten thousand in number. Now listen to the description of the forms of these various fires, remembering which men can cross even the terrible ocean of calamity.

42. The piṇḍa (mantra), consisting of (the letters) *aśeṣabhuva-*

[1] These incarnations and emanations are Vāsudeva etc., the Vyūha-forms, which preside over the states of jāgrat etc.; cf. ch. X, 18.

[2] These are bhūḥ, bhuvaḥ, svaḥ, tapaḥ, janaḥ, mahaḥ and satya.

[3] See Viṣ.P. ch. 1-2.

[4] These are the bright stars belonging to various constellations.

[5] Saṃkarṣaṇa (Balarāma): a plough is his natural weapon.

nādhāra (*ra*), *caturgati* (*ya*), *ūrja* (*ū*) and *bindu* (*ṃ*), (preceded by) the tāraka (*oṃ ryūṃ*), is called the form of the former fires (i.e. pravartaka).

43. The piṇḍa (mantra), consisting of (the letters) *amṛtādhāra* (*va*), *vahni* (*ra*), *ūrja* (*ū*) and *bindu* (*ṃ*) with tāraka before it (*oṃ vrūṃ*), is called the divine form of the nivartaka (fires).

44-46. Having divided the felly into ten parts to represent kāla, Puruṣa, avyakta and the seven manifested (svaras), the form of the pravartaka (mantra) should be written with the pair of *sūrya* and *anala* (*hra*) preceded by the first and last of the vowels that characterize its forms (*ryuṃ*), and then it (the pravartaka-mantra) should be arranged (on the circle diagram) starting from the easterly direction onwards and accompanied by the eight main bījas viz. *ka* etc. with tāra (-mantra at the beginning) and followed by *namas*. The form of the nivartaka (fires) should be written in the same way (except for substitution of) the pair (of letters called) *amṛta* and *agni*.[1]

47-49. Each (group of) fire has, according to the seven pairs of the separate vowels, seven terrible and (seven) tranquil flames.[2] (And to form the mantras these should be added to) the letters, such as the pair of *sūrya* and *agni* (*hra*) and the pair *amṛta* and *agni* (*sra*), *vargānta* (*ha*), *pradhāna* (*ma*), *siddhida* (*bha*), *vāmana* (*ba*), *śveta* (*pha*), *tattvadhāra* (*ñ*), *jhaṣa* (*jha*), *śāśvata* (*ja*), *chāndaḥpati* (*cha*), *cakrī* (*ca*), *kāla* (*ma*) etc. each combined with the *bindu* (*ṃ*).

50-54. The points where the ends of the spokes are joined to the hub are occupied by the four (forms) belonging to God, (i.e. the Vyūhas). The (Vibhava) deities starting with Keśava and ending with Dāmodara encircle (the circumference enclosing) the spokes, and should be meditated upon in association with their personally appropriate emblems, such as the lotus (mark) etc. All the deities viz. Padmanābha etc., each accompanied by his personal śakti, crowd around the external border of the felly of the wheel. The goddess Kamalā occupies the eastern side, the resplendent Kīrti the southern side, while Jayā occupies the western side and Māyā the northern side. Each of them is surrounded by a retinue of ten millions of śaktis (and) they reside in the thousand-spoked Sudarśana (or, in *sahasrāra*, i.e. the bīja of Sudarśana), which is the wheel of

[1] Cf. J.S. ch. 26 in extenso.

[2] See Ahi.S. ch. 23 in extenso.

time and their power is described as without beginning and without end.

55-62. The five divisions (of time) called year, season, month, half-month and day plus night, that are associated with the axle, hub, spoke, the inner edge of the felly and its periphery, as well as the five times five (letters or principles), viz. *pumān* etc.[1] (i.e. from *ma* to *ka*), are held in position by the thousand-spoked disc, the wheel of time which is adorned with the inner edge of the felly, spokes and its periphery, (and which also) holds the six courses (*ṣaḍadhvānaḥ*) viz. varṇa, tattva, kalā etc. The supreme Person,[2] belonging to Viṣṇu, pervading this instrument (*yantra*) holds together and moves this great form (of His), which consists of all the principles. Within this disc, which has a thousand spokes radiating from the spherical section of the hub and (encircled by) the felly, are the ogres, the demons and titans killed (by God). When this (Sudarśana) composed of various mantras has been thoroughly mastered by the mind (of the adept), recollection of it brings about the immediate destruction of an enemy. This Sahasrāra (-mantra) when continuously repeated by some one, instantaneously dispels all demerits that are the source of all miserable karman.[3] The disc Sahasrāra which is without beginning and without end, along with the four (accessories, viz.) bīja, piṇḍa, saṃjñā and mūrti, sustains this world containing (objects) both movable and immovable, by pervading it (i.e. the world) with Sūrya, Soma and Agni.

63. The primary form of the divine śakti, called kriyā(śakti) belonging to Agni, creates, protects and destroys (the creation) by attaining the form of the thousand-spoked (disc).

64. O Sureśvara, this (śakti), named kriyā, (has) a complex form owing to the combination of Sūrya, Indu (i.e. Soma) and Vahni (i.e. Agni) and is in the creative state. O lord of the gods, realize her again (through) my (instruction).

65. Thus I have (concluded) the enumeration of the group (of śaktis) in the form of Sūrya, Soma and Agni. Now learn from me about the kriyāśakti, who presides over this group.[4]

---

[1] See Ahi. S. ch. 23.

[2] The construction of this sentence is ambiguous.

[3] Cf. *kleśakarmavipākāśayair aparāmṛṣṭaḥ puruṣaviśeṣa īśvaraḥ* (Yog.P. 1, 24).

[4] Vyūhinī i.e. the presiding goddess of the Vyūha.

CHAPTER THIRTY-ONE

THE SUDARŚANA (KRIYĀŚAKTI)

1-2. The kriyāśakti exists (as the essence of) the six (divine) attributes (with a leaning towards) tejas and, as (previously) explained, assumes the form of the Person. She originates from Sūrya, Soma and Agni [1] and consists of the body of Agni, who combines (in himself) all weapons and sharp instruments.[2]

3. In the heart of (Sudarśana) exists Śakti in the form of the Person, identical with Soma and Agni, who acts according to the specific requirements of the moment.[3]

4. (I have) already explained to you the four [4] sacred sounds that express this (śakti). Among these the saṃjñā-mantra is all-powerful.

5-9. O Śakra, listen whilst I give you a detailed account of that (i.e. the saṃjñā-mantra of Sudarśana). That śakti, consisting of Soma, who represents the primeval active state of Hari, is myself (viz.) Śrī, the principal Śakti existing in the first letter (of the mantra sahasrāra, i.e. *sa*). (She is) the amṛta; (she) incorporates tṛpti, is identified with Soma, and she is the mistress of All. Abiding in the moon-digit, she infuses the creation with amṛta. The mantras śiraḥ or padma [5] etc., when joined by her (*sa*), to which (the sound of) parameśvara (*ḥ*) is added, bring about satisfaction and success. The same (*sa*) with the addition of (the letter) sṛṣṭikṛt (*ḥ*) is the everlasting jīvaśakti. In order to destroy (an enemy) one should add to her (*sa*) the sound containing vāyu (*ya*) with trailokyaiśvaryada (*ṃ*) added to it (*syaṃ*) and envisage her as Tārā standing on the enemy's head.

10. The brilliant hymn of Puruṣa [6] originates from this śakti,

---

[1] Because the bīja-mantra, viz. *sahasrāra*, contains letters called soma, sūrya, and agni (*sa, ha, ra*).

[2] Cf. Ahi.S. ch. 20 in extenso.

[3] i.e. in her Soma form she gratifies her devotees; in her Agni form she punishes the wicked.

[4] viz. bīja, piṇḍa, saṃjñā and pada.

[5] *oṃ saḥ śirase svāhā, oṃ saḥ śrīnivāsapadmāya svāhā*; cf. J.S. ch. 6, vv. 111-163.

[6] Ṛg. V. 10, 90.

who is hidden in (the letter) aprameya (*a*) and which dwells in everything that contains Agni and Soma.[1]

11. A thousand (innumerable) sages know the hymns which start with this (i.e. the Puruṣa-sūkta). This mantra, (infused) by me who reside in Agni, invariably gratifies (the worshipper).

12. There is nothing in the three worlds [2] that cannot be attained by this (śakti), who dwells in every single ritual and who abides in each of the three śaktis [3] belonging to the letter.

13-14. She produces all the śaktis, appoints all of them (to their duties) and again dissolves them (within herself); hence she is considered to be the (Śakti identical with) the highest Self, the sovereign power, the eternal Hetideva (Sudarśana), who dwelling in his own creative state becomes active for the benefit of the world.

15-16. Adopting the state of the enjoyer, sūrya (*ha*) is regarded as the life-essence bringing forth life.[4] In combination with (the letter) trailokyaiśvaryada (*ṃ*), with the speed of an arrow shot (from a bow-string), on reaching its target it (*ha*) reveals to the yogins, who attain it through proper meditation the self within the lotus of the heart.

17-19. It is called prāṇa, since it invigorates the life-essence (*prāṇa*). The (same),[5] hidden within the disc of the moon, combined with (the letters) *vyāpin* and *aprameya* (*ṃ* and *a*) [6] and meditated upon as coming from the root of the tongue,[7] produces the act of speech. The same, meditated upon as existent in the circle of (the sound) *aṃ*,[8] dripping nectar (*sudhā*), removes poisons from the world. Verily, the hymn of Śrī has originated from this (letter) when it was coupled with (the letter) *rāma* (*i*).

20-22. This and other hymns are familiar to thousands of sages. Each hymn was at some time or other imbued with one of the three

---

1 Cf. Ahi.S. 18, 33.

2 The expression usually means the entire creation.

3 viz. Sūrya, Soma and Agni.

4 This refers to the name Prāṇa given to the letter *ha*. Prāṇa usually means the vital air breath, but, in this case, the proximity of the word *prāṇayan* more appropriately suggests that *prāṇa* is understood to mean the life-essence.

5 i.e. the letter *ha*.

6 *ahaṃ* or *so 'haṃ*.

7 *jihvāmūlasthita*.

8 Evidently the dot symbol of the nasal sound.

śaktis of the letters.[1] There is nothing in the three worlds that cannot be achieved by this (sound *ha*). It (will) destroy (all)[2] and (can) lead (the adept) to the pure state [3] (of existence). It (helps) practitioners of yoga to progress (towards their spiritual goal) casting away all afflictions (*kleśāḥ*). Those who live righteously, who cling to the right explanation, say this about *ha* (the śakti).

23-24. The same śakti of the supreme self possessing the letter (called) *aśeṣabhuvanādhāra* (*ra*), which intensifies her volition is recognizable (in the sound *sra*). All movable beings flow out of her and all take shelter under her (protection).[4] The same (śakti) existing in (the sound) pṛthivī (*ka*), having flowed into the static root (of creation), occupies herself (with the function of preservation).

25. (The sounds) *sahas* (in the mantra) meaning *bala*, sport (*ramate*) in a thousand different ways (or, in the form of *sahasra*).[5] Thus my (śakti) consisting of Agni and Soma becomes a thousand (*sahasrati*)[6] and is called *sahasrā*.

26-28. The same śakti of mine (viz. *ra*), consisting of Agni and Soma, is capable of performing all activities. Enkindled by good intention and effulgent with a mass of power, she becomes the embodiment of fire and attains the state of the fire of destruction. In the pure state of *ra* she is incessantly active and blazingly radiant. (Coupled) with (the letter) parameśvara (*ḥ*), she performs miracles. *Ra* is indeed my primary supreme śakti, called *kriyā*.

29-30. *Sahasra* (that is) a countless number and that refers to the innumerable spokes.[7] O Puraṃdara, I have already revealed to you the nature of her varma and astra [8] (mantras). I have observed before that praṇava [9] (i.e.) dhruva is her origin. In this way this great mantra represents the concentrated (śakti) originating from Śabdabrahman.

---

[1] Viz. Sūrya, Agni and Soma.

[2] The letter *ha* is taken here in the sense of *hanyate*, from the root *han-*.

[3] The same root *han-* may also mean movement or mobility.

[4] *sṛ-* may mean movement or attainment. Like *ha* from *han-*, here *sra* is considered to be a derivative of the root *sṛ-*.

[5] *sahasradhā* literally means in thousand different ways, but here the context seems to indicate the meaning conveyed by the combination *sahas-ra*.

[6] This is a play on the letters *sahasrā*.

[7] *sahasra* here denotes countless. Thus *sahasra* + *ara* means innumerable spokes of the disc Sudarśana.

[8] See ch. XXIV, 64-65.

[9] Ibid. verses 4-14.

31-32. The great śakti, belonging to the Atharvan, is the precious body of kriyāśakti. The supreme Śruti called the Atharvan contains five divisions.[1] This is the essence of the Trayī (the three Vedas) which are nourished by this mantra similarly as a tree is nourished by manure. Those conversant with the rules about the structure (of the scripture) say that it has six parts.[2]

33-36. (It) also (has its own) Gayatrī-mantra, called *cakra*, the encloser known as Agni. (This runs as follows). (The letter) *gopana* (*ā*) is combined with (the letter) *varuṇa* (*va*), and (the letter) *amṛta* (*sa*) with (the letter) *udaya* (*u*).[3] Following these come (the words) *cakrāya ca svāhā*. Next (the first three aṅga-mantras) starting with *hṛdaya* and ending with *śikhā* are added, followed by (the letter) *sūrya* (*ha*) and (the word) *jvāla*. Thereafter comes the word Sudarśana preceded by the word *mahā*. After that, (the words) *cakrāya svāhā* follow along with (the remaining three aṅga-mantras) starting with the varma and ending with the astra. At the end of it stand the four pairs (of letters), viz. *namaś cakrāya* to which the (word) *vidmahe* is added. Further, the (word) *jvālāya* is placed at the end of the (word) *sahasra* coupled with (the word) *dhīmahi*. This (mantra) consists of nine letters. This is followed by the eight letters contained in the words *tan naḥ* and *pracodayāt* whereby the word *cakra* is inserted between them.[4]

37-39. Bending all fingers excepting the forefinger into a fist and holding the forefingers (poised) in the gesture of warning, (the adept should) while engaged in meditation make a circular movement with his hands to encircle the (sacred) fire that exists in the enclosure. (And then) placing the right and left palms face to face, with the little fingers and thumbs touching at the tips whilst still keeping the rest (of the fingers) erect, he should make a circular movement (with his hands) which is called cakra-mudrā.[5] The aṅga-mudrās [6] will be described later. Now listen to (the explanation) of the mantra (called) śaktigrāsa.

---

[1] viz. nakṣatra, vidhāna, vidhividhāna, saṃhitā and śānti.

[2] The six aṅgas viz. hṛdaya etc.; see ch. XXXIII, 2-11.

[3] Thus: *vāṃ suṃ*.

[4] *vāṃ suṃ cakrāya ca svāhā, oṃ haṃ namaḥ, oṃ hāṃ svāhā, oṃ hiṃ vaṣaṭ haṃsāya namaḥ, hraṃ mahāsudarśanāya cakrāya svāhā, oṃ huṃ oṃ vauṣaṭ oṃ phaṭ namaś cakrāya vidmahe sahasrajvālāya dhīmahi, tan naḥ cakraḥ pracodayāt.*

[5] Cf. J.S. 8, 39-40.

[6] Cf. J.S. 6, 105-134.

40-44. Let (the sound) *pavitra* (*pa*), that comes after praṇava, be coupled with (the sound) *anala* (*ra*) to which (the sound) *vyāpin* (*ṃ*) has been joined on. Thereafter come (the words) *mahāsudarśana, cakrarāja, mahādhvaga,* followed by (the words) *asta gata sarvaduṣṭabhayaṅkara chindhi chindhi,* and then *bhindhi bhindhi* should be uttered along with (the word) *vidāraya* (pronounced) twice, *paramantrān grasa grasa,* then *bhakṣaya* (pronounced) twice, then *bhūtāni* with (the word) *trāsaya* (pronounced) twice (ending) in the varma (*huṃ*) and astra (*phaṭ*) and the name of the wife of fire (*svāhā*).[1] This is the mantra called śaktigrasanakṛt. Identifying oneself with Sudarśana whilst pronouncing this mantra, one should suck out the enemy's power from his heart and mouth. O Puraṃdara, listen (to the description of) the meditation on the mantra which contains six letters.[2]

45-60. (The adept) who has performed the consecration of the limbs (*nyāsa*) with the application of cakra-mudrās, having entered the sacred place of fire, should meditate on the thousand-spoked great disc, which is as terrifyingly brilliant as a combination of ten thousands of fires, which pervades the six courses of (creation), is unlimited and expanded from my śakti. Lord Nārāyaṇa, who is flawless and exists in the axle (of the disc), should be envisaged as the Lord in the disc, saffron-complexioned, wearing yellow-coloured apparel, who is divine and adorned with pearl ornaments. In times of grave danger he should be visualized as possessing eight arms and knees raised,[3] multifariously weaponed and as very handsome. In his four right hands he holds the disc, the invincible mace, the goad and the lotus; while in his four left hands he holds the conch-shell, the bow and arrow, the noose and the heavy club. He possesses a benevolent divine face, (the beauty of) which is emphasized by the lustre of the teeth, tawny eyes, thick tawny hair and (he is) surrounded by a wreath of flames.[4] Also in situations when one suffers irremediable defeat from an enemy, to enable one

---

[1] *oṃ praṃ mahāsudarśana cakrarāja mahādhvaga astagatasarvaduṣṭabhayaṅkara chindhi chindhi bhindhi bhindhi vidāraya vidāraya, paramantrān grasa grasa bhakṣaya bhakṣaya bhūtāni trāsaya trāsaya huṃ phaṭ svāhā.*

[2] Sahasrāra. In ch. XXIX, 56-58 this is counted as five but the vowel *ā* is not accounted for there. In Ahi.S. 18, 9-12 all the vowels are counted thus making it a ten-lettered mantra.

[3] The typical posture of a fighting warrior.

[4] The word *pariṣkṛtam*, which may also mean "adorned", is not very clear.

to punish enemies (even if they are) absolutely safe, or when one is very much afraid of (an attack from) a thief, tiger or leopard etc., God Sudarśana should be envisaged as possessing sixteen arms, standing in the posture of pratyālīḍha [1] facing the enemy. He is decorated (in this form) with muscular arms raised, as it were, to strike (the enemy); in his right hands proceeding upwards from the lowest, he holds the flaming spear, the sword, a hundred-flamed fire, the goad, the staff, the burning dagger, the axe and the disc, (respectively), while his left arms proceeding from the uppermost downwards are (decorated with) the blazing weapons viz. the conch-shell, the bow and arrow, the noose, the plough, the thunder, the weapon (called) mace, the club and also a lance. He is enwrapped in a profusion of flames from the fierce fire caused by (the lustre of) his teeth and is encircled with the heavenly vanamālā, which effuses the realities.[2] He drives away the frightened king of the demons and titans with his fierce laughter. A man living in great fear should meditate on this deity in this form, who is (the presiding deity of) the incomparable disc belonging to the proprietor of the disc (i.e. to Viṣṇu) who resides in the disc, where the flames are smoky due to the burning fat of the demons in the disc, which is the repository of brightly burning flames extending over the six courses (of creation).

61. After meditating on (Sudarśana) in (the above manner), one should once more meditate on Sudarśana as possessing only four arms. Otherwise, the power of Hari (i.e. the disc) is such that there would be no peace again.[3]

62. Thus, O powerful god, I have recounted to you the (method) of meditating on the Person in these two different states, (viz.) the fierce and the tranquil; now listen to me describing the (nature) of meditation upon other (deities of mantras).

63. All the various states of the Person pertaining to me, as stated in this (description) of meditation, should be reflected upon, so as to bring about quick success.

---

[1] *Pratyālīḍha*, a position peculiar to shooting, the left foot being advanced, the right drawn back, is the technical term for the fighting posture.

[2] Thus the vanamālā consists of the twenty-four cosmic principles. It is curious to see that the vaijayantīmālā of Viṣṇu later on got mixed up with the vanamālā of Kṛṣṇa. The name suggests a simple garland of wild flowers. But this has been sublimated into an abstract cosmogonic idea.

[3] See Ahi.S. ch. 47 in extenso.

64. O Śakra, this is a marvellous secret (lore), which I have described to you. O celestial man, now listen to me (describing) yet another secret (lore).

65-69. My śakti, consisting of Agni, that I have previously described to you and which is as bright as billions of suns and fires, is (identical with) my form consisting of vibration, which resembles millions of moons. (This is) the mantra (that runs as follows): (The sounds) *amṛta* (*sa*), *paramātman* (*ha*), and *aśeṣabhuvanādhāra* (*ra*) are (together) connected with (the sound) *pañcabindu* and *vyāpin* (*īṃ*).[1] This śakti, arising from the great Self to help all beings, is to be contemplated upon as forming the axle (of Sudarśana cakra), while the halo (of the śakti) forms the circle of the hub. The (six) sounds of the mantra (should be regarded) as the six spokes. The (sounds) *sūrya*, *uddāma* and *bindu* (*huṃ*) should be meditated upon as being firmly fixed over the felly and the rest of the mantra (i.e. *phaṭ*), as pervading the circle, which is the periphery. One should meditate on one's own self as existing in the middle of Māya [2] and of the supreme self.

70-71. Having removed the Person (self) (from the manifested creation), one should meditate upon him as existing in Sūrya and Agni. The yogin engaged in meditation eradicates all the flaws of life through his meditation and experiences supreme devotion towards me, finally taking shelter in me.

72. The intelligent (adept), who is engaged in muttering (the letters called) *paramātman* and *amṛta* (*sa* and *ha*) [3] should continuously bear in mind how pleasant is (the taste of) nectar.

73-76. Inundated by the nectar flowing from within the śakti,[4] enlivened by *prāṇa*,[5] all the yogin's defects having been burnt by the flame of fire (*anala*),[6] he attains supreme power (*aiśvarya*) through the efficacy of pañcabindu; through constant practice of yoga (he acquires self-)mastery, concentration (of mind) (and) command over his senses. Casting away all affliction, he obtains my form (*veṣam*). Through his deeds the elated yogin becomes

---

[1] This refers to the mantra called Sudarśana i.e. *sahasrāra īṃ*.

[2] Māyā is here Lakṣmī herself.

[3] This means the entire Sudarśana-mantra.

[4] i.e. the letter that is called *amṛta*.

[5] Reference to the letter *ha*.

[6] The letter *ra*. All these letters including *ī* (*pañcabindu*) refer to the letters used in the Sudarśana-mantra.

powerful and self-controlled in all respects. Identified with the supreme Īśvara, he attains through my grace my state (of existence, *dhāma*), which is, indeed, identical with myself.[1]

77-78. That which is (called) *kriyā* is also named *cit* (consciousness) and that which is (called) *cit* is (indeed) the supreme *kriyā* (action). These two, together with divine bliss, are recognized as constituting one integrally supreme śakti, identical with consciousness, action and bliss. That supreme I-hood of Viṣṇu is my (own) self, who fulfils all desires.

79-82. Through my own independent will, I expand myself into two (śaktis); one of these śaktis is called *kriyā* and the other is the great *bhūti*. O Śakra, I as the great goddess, remain common to both of them. Thus, I have shown you (the secret) of this śakti that is identical with activity, along with all its components. Now listen to the (secret of) Tārikā, in her (successive) gross, subtle and absolute (states). Bhūti, called Tārikā, possesses the form consisting of the six (divine) attributes, (but in her) the attribute of activity is subdued and the attribute of supreme power (*aiśvarya*) is emphasized. Now listen attentively, O king of gods, to me describing in detail her states (of existence), such as gross etc.

---

[1] Cf. J. Gonda, Dhāman, pp. 79-81.

CHAPTER THIRTY-TWO

TĀRIKĀ IN THE THREE STATES OF EXISTENCE VIZ. THE GROSS, THE SUBTLE AND THE ABSOLUTE STATES

1. Śrī:—Listen to the description of the three states of existence, viz. the gross, subtle and absolute (states) of (the śakti), which is the supreme science (i.e. mantra) called Tārikā, the saviour (of the devotee from the sufferings of) existence.

2. The gross form (of Tārikā, who is identical with) me, contains five sounds or (sometimes) four;[1] my subtle form possesses three sounds;[2] and (my) absolute form consists of (the sound called) viṣṇu.[3]

3-4. Each of these three states of mine (i.e. of Tārikā) is again subdivided into three conditions. The absolute condition in the gross state contains (the sound) *paramātman* (*ha*), joined with (the sounds) *aśeṣabhuvanādhāra* (*ra*), *Viṣṇu* (*ī*) and *vyāpin*.[4] This (state) contains both the enjoyer and the object of enjoyment. Now listen to me (describing) its form.

5-6. The beloved of Hari, existing (in the space) that lies behind the forehead (i.e. the *sahasrāra cakra*),[5] arising from (the letters) *aśeṣabhuvanādhāra, vyāpin, paramātman* etc.,[6] ascends to Viṣṇu's form (of existence), and regains her own form [7] adorned with the (sound) *nāda* from which tāra originates.

7. The Goddess, enfolding in her wisdom the entire world consisting of the enjoyer and the objects of enjoyment, dwells in the all-pervading supreme soul.[8]

8-9. The gross state of (Tārikā) in her absolute condition has the

---

[1] Five letters when *hrīṃ* is adorned with the sound called *nāda* (*ṁ*) after the bindu which resembles the tingling sound of a bell; otherwise four letters.

[2] *īṃ*.

[3] *ī*.

[4] i.e. *hrīṃ*.

[5] See M. V. Jhavery, Comparative and critical study of Mantraśāstra, Ahmedabad 1944, Introduction.

[6] i.e. *hrīṃ*.

[7] Cf. ch. XVIII, 24.

[8] i.e. *haṃ*; the words vyāpin and paramātman are used in double-meaning.

form of Viṣṇu (ī) and retains it. Performing the five functions,[1] expanded by the three types of divine majesty and sheltering in the Anala [2] to surge like the sea, vitalizing that deity (the goddess ī) is regarded as existing in her subtle condition.

10-11. After having accomplished the creation (of the universe), she, the goddess who is gross and marvellous in her gross state, who can perform miraculous deeds, who is the source of creation, preservation and dissolution and who is sheltered in the absolute, existing in the void (ṃ), regulates the existence of the universe in the form of *sūrya* (*ha*) and *Viṣṇu* (*ī*)[3] aided by the power of the fire of destruction (*ra*).[4]

12. Thus, O Vāsava, the three conditions of my (Tārikā's) gross state have been explained. Now, O killer of Vṛtra, listen to (the description of) the three conditions of the subtle state.

13. This subtle supreme goddess exists permanently in the (letters) *vyāpin* and *paramātman* [5] and is not governed by kāla.[6]

14. The evolved objects (of creation) are said to be of two kinds, (viz.) the category of the pure (creation) and that of the impure. The gross condition of (the subtle Tārikā) comprises the impure (creation), while the subtle condition comprises the pure (creation).[7]

15. Three conditions of this (subtle Tārikā) are noticeable as in the case of the gross (Tārikā). O Śakra, now listen to (the description of) my (= Tārikā's) form in the absolute state.

16. She is all-pervasive, divine, integral, flawless; this supreme śakti consisting of myself is described by the name Viṣṇu (ī).

17. She is the essence of Viṣṇu and is regarded as the I-hood of Hari. The yogins aspire to her and she is the goal of those who follow the Sāṃkhya (system).

---

[1] i.e. creation etc., see ch. XIII, 27-29.

[2] Agni identical with kriyāśakti.

[3] The letters *ṃ*, *ha* and *ī* are referred to.

[4] These three letters viz. *ha*, *ra* and *ī*, together form the Tārikā-Bīja-mantra *hrīṃ*.

[5] *Haṃ*.

[6] This implies that in the gross state Tārikā is governed by Kāla (the time eternal). The concept of kāla is discussed in ch. V.

[7] The difference between the subtle and the gross states lies in the fact that the subtle state comprises the pure creation, whereas the gross state is mainly occupied with the impure creation. Moreover, the subtle state of Śakti indicates her immanence in All, without emphasizing her function of creation etc.

18-26. She is the supreme form (i.e. manifestation) and is the sublime way (to achieve the Pāñcarātra goal). Śakti, Kuṇḍalinī, Ādyā, Bhramarī, Yogadāyikā, Anāhatā, Aghoṣā, Nirmaryādā, Nadodgatā,[1] Śabdabrahman, Śaktimātṛkāyoni, Uttamā, Gāyatrī, Kalā, Gaurī, Śacī, Devī, Sarasvatī, Vṛṣākapāyī, Satyā, the famous Prāṇapatnī, Indrapatnī, Mahādhenu, Aditi, Devanandinī, the divine mother of the Rudras and the Vasus,[2] Hitā (an artery), the Sister of the Ādityas,[3] the Navel of Amṛta, the absolute Dhṛti, Iḍā, the lovely Rati, the noble Gurudhātrī, the Earth, Viśruti, Trayī, Go, Prāṇavatsalā, Śakti,[4] Prakṛti, Mahārājñī, Payasvinī, Tārā, Sītā, Śrī, Kāmavatsā, Priyavratā, Taruṇī, Varārohā, Nīrūpā, Rūpaśālinī, Ambikā, Sundarī, Jyeṣṭhā, Vāmā, Ghorā, Manomayī, Siddhā, Siddhāntikā, Yogā, Yoginī, Yogabhāvinī etc.—these are the mysterious names of Śakti mentioned in the various sacred scriptures by scholars well versed in doctrines.

27. That absolute, divine Śakti exists in three forms. This threefold nature of hers as gross, subtle and absolute is now revealed (to you).

28. (The letter) *ī* is said to be its essential nature. That exists in three ways. Now listen to the description of its nature according to the *Aprameya* (*a*) etc.

29-32. When the absolute Brahman called the undecaying Vāsudeva, possessed of the six divine attributes, after attracting (to Itself) all diversities has integrated them and become one, this divine being is called by the yogins aprameya.[5] At that juncture no polarizations exists, either in the form of the pervader and the objects pervaded or in the form of the act of creation and objects created. It has no (attributes) and is not cognizable. Brahman possessing the six attributes is then virtually regarded as being in a deep sleep, appearing as void. At this stage (Tārikā) abides under the name of Viṣṇu [6] and, resembling a waveless ocean, she represents the state in which śakti is identified with the possessor of śakti.

33. When, through Its own volition, the pure (*avraṇam*) Brahman

---

[1] Here Nada means Nāda.

[2] The twelve Rudras and the eight Vasus. See Viṣ.P. 1, 15, 128-131.

[3] The number of Ādityas varies in the Vedic and in the Purāṇic texts from six to twelve.

[4] This is a repetition.

[5] *a*.

[6] *ī*.

called Vāsudeva once again awakens (i.e. becomes creatively active), (It) is then called prathama (viz. *saṃkalpa*).[1]

34. During the stage that Brahman expands (Itself) over the pure and the impure creation, this (śakti), identical with the will of Brahman, is called māyā.[2]

35-36. (All creation) starting from Saṃkarṣaṇa and ending with the earth (principle) remains in her womb. When the absolute Brahman voluntarily splits Itself in two as the pervader and the pervaded, the goddess, who performs the five functions [3] (of God), exists as pañcabindu.[4]

37-38. The form of my absolute state in its three (conditions) has thus been explained to you. It manifests (itself) in different forms to illustrate different principles vested in the sounds (denoted by the alphabet) and, (manifesting itself) of its own will in the shape of the world, it becomes the signification of each (of the letters). There it vests in each principle in its own form.

39-43. On attaining the form of each (of the relevant letters), my subtle element, called the eternal sevanī,[5] remains concealed in each (letter) in the same way as fire remains concealed in firewood. Through affinity with each individual sound, my absolute element in the form of Śakti belonging to Viṣṇu (*ī*), vests in the body of each separate (sound) and governs (the sounds) as (their) presiding deity. Then Yoginī, the imperishable and supreme goddess, becomes the object of their signification, the substratum of the entire world; she is represented by the letters manifesting the pure principles and becomes the bestower of lordship over the three worlds.[6] Every single gross principle is my eternal utterance.[7] (This is assumed on the basis) of the fact that all (gross principles) represent specific

---

[1] *a*.

[2] *ī*.

[3] Creation, preservation, dissolution, concealment or delusion and grace.

[4] *ī*. The implication is that different names for the same letter signify the different states of existence of God and of His Śakti in their absolute form.

[5] This alludes to the procedure required for the position of the tongue etc. in producing various sounds.

[6] This refers to the letter *m*. Here an error in gender has obviously been made due to the syntactic confusion.

[7] This is said in order to establish the permanence of these principles, possibly implying a covert refutation of the Yogācāra theory of their momentary existence.

states of (my) existence and also because it is acknowledged that I dominate them (gross principles).

44-45. This goddess who controls (all things) stands in a double relationship (towards them): the same (goddess) abides in the sounds *kṣa* etc., namely in the five Brahmās starting with *kṣa* and ending with *śa* which I mentioned (previously), as the bestower of dominion over the three worlds,[1] and has two forms of existence, viz. as the essence (of all things) and as their controller.

46-47. The four dhāraṇas, viz. the sounds which, as explained (before), start with *va* and end with *ya*, contain both the subtle and the absolute form (of Tārikā) who, as already (described), exists in them (these letters) in fulfilling her two functions. The letter *ma* has been referred to earlier as representing the conscious (being) in its three states[2] and (in that letter her) subtle and absolute states both exist together.

48. The sound *bha* is said to represent māyā, the source, with its threefold attributes. There also the goddess (Tārikā) exists in the two forms referred to above and bears the name *ī*.

49. The three sounds *ba* etc.[3] represent (the principles) buddhi, ahaṃkāra and manas and in those letters too this goddess exists in the two aforesaid forms.

50-51. Also in the two groups of senses represented by the (two groups of letters) *na* etc., and *ṇa* etc., (the goddess exists) in both her subtle and absolute states (as said before). The two groups of vibhūtis in their subtle and gross forms[4] are represented (by the two groups of letters viz.) *ñ* etc., and *ṅ* etc., and (there) also the goddess exists in the two aforesaid forms.

52. Assuming different bodies, like an actress,[5] śakti represented by *ī* extends herself over the pure and impure creations by means of the seventy different (principles).[6]

53. He who concentrates on this supreme goddess *ī*, who has

---

[1] The letter *m*.

[2] See ch. XIX passim.

[3] *ba*, *pha* and *pa*.

[4] The five tanmātras and the five gross elements.

[5] As an actress in her diverse costumes portrays various persons, so also the goddess, though one and the same, manifests herself as the different principles embodied in different sounds. The simile recalls to mind Vidyāraṇya Muni's concept of Naṭapradīpa in Pañcadaśī.

[6] Thirty-five in each of the pure and impure creations.

expanded herself in this manner, attains the ultimate, eternal abode of Viṣṇu.

54. Wherever this śakti existing in (the letter) *ī* goes, be it in the pure or in the impure course (of creation), she never severs her relation with Viṣṇu.

55. She exists pervading the pure and the impure course (of creation), assuming many diverse roles according to her existence in one, two, three or more vowels and consonants.

56. Again, philosophers should know her further threefold classification in gross forms etc. which is not related to *ja* or *ṭa*.[1]

57. When she is related to sṛṣṭikṛt, she is in the gross state; when related to vyomeśa,[2] she is subtle; when related to *ī* (alone) she is the spotless, absolute Śakti.

58. This supreme spouse of Viṣṇu remains steadfast in all the ādhārapadmas [3] like the unwavering flame of a lamp.

59-61. Following the course of Brahman, starting from the lower region of the abdomen and ending at the top of the head, this unique, brilliant, shining, purifying and well known (śakti) escaping through the opening at the top of the skull [4] attains the great lotus.

---

[1] This implies all the sounds represented by the alphabets.

[2] Sṛṣṭikṛt = *ḥ*; vyomeśa = *ṃ*.

[3] Of foremost importance in the system of Tantric meditation is the awakening of the kuṇḍalinī-śakti and its upward journey through the suṣumnā-column of the spine, piercing the various seats of varying degrees of consciousness till it reaches the sahasrāra-padma, the seat of the absolute and integral consciousness, and thereby annihilates all trace of polarization. The main purpose of haṭhayoga, an inseparable part of Tantric worship, is to achieve by this means the liberation of the adept from the bondage of material existence. These centres of consciousness are variously called adhāracakras, adhārapadmas, cakras or padmas. The lowest centre is called mūlādhāra, situated at the base of the spinal cord. The next is the svādhiṣṭhāna, located below the navel. The third is called maṇipura and is located in the region above the navel. The fourth is the anāhata, higher up near the heart. Next comes the ājñā which is situated close to the forehead. Finally, the sahasrāra padma (the thousand-petalled lotus), situated on the crown or more precisely above the crown, represents the culmination of the upward (spiritual) journey of the kuṇḍalinī-śaktí belonging to the living being. This is the objective of every living being that brings about his total merger in the all-pervading source, which is absolute consciousness. See L.T. ch. XL, 5-8; and M. P. Pandit, Studies in the Tantras and the Veda, Madras 1964, pp. 78-84; Jhavery, o.c., pp. 39-46; Arthur Avalon, Serpent Power, Madras 1950, passim.

[4] See e.g. Śiva Saṃhitā 5, 150 and A. Daniélou, Yoga, London 1949, p. 133.

On the path to supreme bliss she is the immanent essence of the mantras, whose essence I am, as well as of the mantras whose essence is Viṣṇu and it is she who destroys the mortality (of the adept) and saturates him with amṛta.

62. Those (mantras), five hundred in number,[1] which are supremely powerful, when muttered along with the mantras belonging to the Advaya [2] of the Sāṃkhya system bring forth both enjoyment and liberation.

63-65. These (mantras) are described as the drops (minute emanations) of the absolute (state of the goddess). Just as myriads of rays pervade the brilliance, or as permanence pervades all the (divergent) objects of the world, so the illustrious spouse of Viṣṇu, the goddess existing in *ī*, who pervades various glorious emanations (Vibhavas) and various created objects, exists as (their) external and internal states of existence, as identical with Śabdabrahman.

66. O Śakra, in this way I have shown you the different (states) of Tārikā, the gross, the subtle, etc. Now learn from me the aṅga (-mantras) belonging to her (= Tārikā).

---

[1] Anūnaśrī.

[2] Advaya is the Puruṣa of the Sāṃkhya system.

CHAPTER THIRTY-THREE

AṄGA, UPĀṄGA AND OTHER MANTRAS

1. Śrī:—O lord of the gods, my son, listen to the (description) of the mantras (called) aṅgas and upāṅgas, which contain various mantras, belonging to the Tārikā-vidyā.

2-3. The letters *prāṇa (ha)* and *anala (ra)*, joined separately to each of the five (vowels), viz. *gopana* [illegible] *ūrja (ū)*, *airāvaṇa (ai)* and *au*[illegible] *(au)*, followed by the anusvāra, form the piṇḍas.[1] These are to be regarded as the bījas[2] (*hrāṃ, hrīṃ, hrūṃ, hraiṃ* and *hrauṃ*) of the (five) aṅgas, starting with the heart and ending with the eyes.[3]

4-5. After the bīja of the heart (*hrāṃ*) one should add the words *jnānāya hṛdayāya namaḥ*. This mantra brings about (the yogic mental stage called) dhāraṇā.[4] Beginning with the praṇava and ending with *namaḥ*, this mantra consists of eleven letters.[5]

5-10. After the praṇava and the (second) bīja one should add the words *aiśvaryāya śirase svāhā*: this (again is an) eleven-lettered (mantra[6] belonging to the aṅga, called *śiraḥ*). After the praṇava and the (third) bīja one should add the words *śaktaye śikhāyai vauṣaṭ*. This is the ten-lettered (mantra) belonging to (the aṅga called) śikhā.[7] After Praṇava and the (fourth) bīja one should add the words *balāya kavacāya huṃ*, (and) this ten-lettered mantra (belongs to the aṅga called *kavaca*).[8] The word *tejase* is to be added after the praṇava and the (fifth) bīja (followed by the words) *netrābhyāṃ vauṣaṭ* (and this constitutes) the ten-lettered mantra belonging to (the aṅga called) netra.[9] Similarly, *oṃ hraḥ vīryāya astrāya ca phaṭ* is the astra-mantra.

---

[1] The second part of a complete mantra, see Ch. XXIII.

[2] The main part of a mantra.

[3] The five Aṅgas represent the five parts of the divine body viz. hṛdaya, śiras, śikhā, kavaca, netra.

[4] See Yoga. S. 3, 1 and the commentary Yogapradīpikā of Baladeva Miśra there on.

[5] *Oṃ hrāṃ jñānāya hṛdayāya namaḥ.*

[6] *Oṃ hrīṃ aiśvaryāya śirase svāhā.*

[7] *Oṃ hrūṃ śaktaye śikhāyai vauṣaṭ.*

[8] *Oṃ hraiṃ balāya kavacāya huṃ.*

[9] *Oṃ hrauṃ tejase netrābhyaṃ vauṣaṭ.*

In a similar way the text enumerates the following mantras:[1]

A) (11-14) The six upāṅga-mantras (connected with the minor limbs or parts of the body):

1) *oṃ hrīṃ jñānāya udarāya namaḥ*; 2) *oṃ hrīṃ śaktaye pṛṣṭhāya namaḥ*; 3) *oṃ hrīṃ balāya bāhubhyāṃ namaḥ*; 4) *oṃ hrīṃ aiśvaryāya ūrubhyāṃ namaḥ*; 5) *oṃ hrīṃ vīryāya jānubhyāṃ namaḥ*; 6) *oṃ hrīṃ tejase caraṇābhyāṃ namaḥ.*

B) (15-28) The mantras of decorations and weapons, viz. kaustubha, vanamālā, Śrīnivāsapadma, pāśa and aṅkuśa:

1) *oṃ ṭhaṃ rhrūḥ ṭhaṃ namaḥ prabhātmane kaustubhāya svāhā*; 2) *oṃ lsvīṃ namaḥ sthalajalodbhūta bhūṣite vanamāle svāhā*; 3) *oṃ bsuṃ namaḥ śrīnivāsapadmāya svāhā*; 4) *oṃ rṇāṃ kastha kastha ṭhaṭha varapāśāya svāhā*; 5) *om lṃ rkṛm niśitaghoṇāya aṅkuśāya svāhā.*

C) (29-39) The six mantras of containers (*ādhāra*):

1) *oṃ hrīṃ ādhāraśaktyai namaḥ*; 2) *oṃ rhrūṃ kālāgnikūrmāya namaḥ*; 3) *oṃ hāṃ anantāya namaḥ*; 4) *oṃ kṣmlāṃ vasudhāyai namaḥ*; 5) *oṃ svāṃ kṣīrārṇavāya namaḥ*; 6) *oṃ puṃ ādhārapadmāya namaḥ.*

D) (40-43) The sixteen ādhāreśa-mantras:

1) *oṃ dhṛṃ dharmāya namaḥ*; 2) *oṃ dhṝṃ jñānāya namaḥ*; 3) *oṃ dhḷṃ vairāgyāya namaḥ*; 4) *oṃ dhḹṃ aiśvaryāya namaḥ*; 5) *oṃ jṛṃ adharmāya namaḥ*; 6) *oṃ jṝṃ ajñānāya namaḥ*; 7) *oṃ jḷṃ avairāgyāya namaḥ*; 8) *oṃ jḹṃ anaiśvaryāya namaḥ*; 9) *om vṛṃ ṛce namaḥ*; 10) *om vṝṃ yajuṣe namaḥ*; 11) *oṃ vḷṃ sāmāya namaḥ*; 12) *oṃ vḹṃ atharvāya namaḥ*; 13) *oṃ lṛṃ kṛtāya namaḥ*; 14) *oṃ lṝṃ tretāyai namaḥ*; 15) *oṃ lḷṃ dvāparāya namaḥ*; 16) *oṃ lḹṃ kalaye namaḥ.*

E) (44-48) The mantra of avyaktapadma, the three maṇḍala-mantras viz. Sūrya, Indu and Agni and the cidbhāsana-mantra. (These five mantras with the afore-mentioned sixteen ādhāreśa-mantras (saṃjñāmantras) constitute the āsanamantras):

1) *oṃ bsuṃ avyaktapadmāya namaḥ*; 2) *oṃ sūryamaṇḍalāya*

[1] From here to the end of this chapter I have not translated the verses, but have only constructed the mantras from the text. The last aṅga-mantra is listed under the tenth verse of this chapter. Furthermore I have listed mantras in groups classified as A.B.C. . . . with references to the verses in parenthesis. At the end of the chapter, Śrī warns Śakra, that he must keep the secrecy of these mantras and should teach them only to the very worthy devotees.

namaḥ; 3) *oṃ indumaṇḍalāya namaḥ*; 4) *oṃ agnimaṇḍalāya namaḥ*; 5) *ahaṃ saḥ*.

F) (49-60) Mantras belonging to kṣetrapāla and other deities of the door (dvāradevatās):

1) *oṃ kṣmrāṃ kṣetrapālāya namaḥ*; 2) *oṃ śrīṃ śriyai namaḥ*; 3) *oṃ croṃ caṇḍāya namaḥ*; 4) *oṃ proṃ pracaṇḍāya namaḥ*; 5) *oṃ jroṃ jayāya namaḥ*; 6) *oṃ vroṃ vijayāya namaḥ*; 7) *oṃ grīṃ gaṅgāyai namaḥ*; 8) *oṃ yrīṃ yamunāyai namaḥ*; 9) *oṃ śrūṃ śaṅkhanidhaye namaḥ*; 10) *oṃ prūṃ padmanidhaye namaḥ*.

G) (61-63) Gaṇeśa mantra: *oṃ gūṃ gaṇapataye namaḥ*.

H) (61-63) The aṅga-mantras of Gaṇeśa: (*oṃ*) *gāṃ hṛdayāya namaḥ*; (*oṃ*) *gīm śirase svāhā*; (*oṃ*) *gūṃ śikhāyai vauṣaṭ*; (*oṃ*) *gaiṃ kavacāya huṃ*; (*oṃ*) *gauṃ netrāya vauṣaṭ*; (*oṃ*) *gaḥ astrāya phaṭ*.

I) (64-68) The Vāgīśvarī-mantra: *oṃ rkṣrīṃ hrīṃ sryāṃ styrāṃ a ā i ī u ū ṛ ṝ ḷ ḹ e ai o au ṃ ḥ ka kha ga gha ṅ ca cha ja jha ñ ṭa ṭha ḍa ḍha ṇa ta tha da dha na pa pha ba bha ma ya ra la va śa ṣa sa ha kṣa vāgīśvaryai namaḥ*.

J) (69-70) The six aṅga-mantras of Vāgīśvarī: *oṃ sryāṃ hṛdayāya namaḥ*; *oṃ sryīṃ śirase namaḥ*; *oṃ sryūṃ śikhāyai namaḥ*; *oṃ sryaiṃ kavacāya namaḥ*; *om sryauṃ netrāya namaḥ*; *oṃ sryaḥ astrāya namaḥ*.[1]

K) (71) The guru-mantra (the mantra for the preceptor): *oṃ oṃ oṃ guṃ gurave namaḥ*.

L) (72) The paramaguru (grand preceptor)-mantra: *oṃ oṃ oṃ paṃ paramagurave namaḥ*.

M) (73) The parameṣṭhin (great grand preceptor)-mantra: *oṃ oṃ oṃ pāṃ parameṣṭhine namaḥ*.

N) (74-75) The pitṛ-mantra: *oṃ oṃ oṃ oṃ oṃ ṭhmrūṃ svadhā pitṛbhyo namaḥ*.

O) (76-77) The ādisiddha-mantra: *oṃ oṃ oṃ oṃ oṃ oṃ āṃ ādisiddhebhyo namaḥ*. (77 The mantras from kṣetrapāla to ādisiddha (F-O) are efficacious in removing obstacles).

P) (78-88) The lokeśa-mantras: *om hlāṃ indrāya namaḥ*; *oṃ hrāṃ agnaye namaḥ*; *oṃ hmāṃ yamāya namaḥ*; *oṃ nḷṃ nirṛtaye namaḥ*; *oṃ hvāṃ varuṇāya namaḥ*; *oṃ hyāṃ vāyave namaḥ*; *oṃ dhvāṃ somāya namaḥ*; *oṃ hcūṃ īśānāya namaḥ*; *oṃ hṇāṃ anantāya namaḥ*; *oṃ hkhāṃ brahmaṇe namaḥ*.

---

[1] There is a slight difference from the same mantra recorded in J.S. 7, 53-54.

Q) (89-98) The mantras of the weapons of the lokeśas: *oṃ rjmrūḥ kuliśāya namaḥ; oṃ jmrīḥ śaktaye namaḥ; oṃ dmūḥ daṇḍāya namaḥ; oṃ ṭmrūḥ khaḍgāya namaḥ; oṃ tśāḥ pāśāya namaḥ; oṃ jvāḥ dhvajāya namaḥ; oṃ hrūḥ musalāya namaḥ; om rjuḥ śūlāya namaḥ; oṃ kroḥ sīrāya namaḥ; om vnāḥ padmāya namaḥ.*

R) (99-101) The viṣvaksena-mantra: *oṃ rhūṃ vauṃ jñānadāya namaḥ.*[1]

S) (102) The aṅga-mantras of viṣvaksena: *oṃ rhrāṃ hṛdayāya namaḥ; oṃ rhrīṃ śirase svāhā; oṃ rhrūṃ śikhāyai vauṣaṭ; oṃ rhraiṃ kavacāya huṃ; oṃ rhrauṃ netrāya vauṣaṭ; oṃ hraḥ astrāya phaṭ.*

T) (103-104) The surabhi-mantra: *oṃ svīṃ surabhyai namaḥ.* This mantra fulfils all desires for enjoyment.

U) (105-107) The āvāhana-mantra: *oṃ oṃ hrīṃ hrīṃ paramadhāmāvasthite madanugrahābhiyogodyate ihāvatarehābhimatasiddhide mantraśarīre oṃ hrīṃ namo namaḥ.*

V) (107-108) The arghya-mantra: *oṃ hrīṃ haṃ haṃ haṃ hrīṃ hrīṃ hrīṃ idam idam idam arghyaṃ gṛhāṇa svāhā.*[2]

W) (109-110) The prasādana-mantra: *oṃ īṃ hrīṃ īṃ haṃsapare parameśe prasīda oṃ hrīṃ namaḥ.*

X) (111-112) The visarjana-mantra: *oṃ hrīṃ bhagavati mantramūrte svapadaṃ samāsādaya samāsādaya kṣamasva kṣamasva oṃ hrīṃ namo namaḥ.*

---

[1] This mantra is slightly different from the same recorded in the J.S. 7, 87-89. There Viṣvaksena is mentioned by name.

[2] The J.S. records a shorter mantra: J.S. 7, 101-103.

CHAPTER THIRTY-FOUR

THE HAND POSTURES AND METHOD OF THE RITUALISTIC BATH

1. Śrī:—O Vāsava, I shall now describe to you the store of hand gestures (mudrās) [1] which (are related to) the store of mantras. The mere knowledge of them results in great success in the (science of) mantras.

2-3. The adept who knows the mantras should make such gestures: in the (holy) water at the time of bathing; when he performs his own (consecration by) nyāsa; (or) the prescribed rites connected with a maṇḍala, after a (particular) ritual (*pūjā*) comes to the end; when mantras are placed on the image (*arcā*), on the vessels containing arghya,[2] on (the offered) food after offering the 'complete oblation' (*pūrṇāhuti*), and on the mantra which exists inside.[3]

4-7. For purposes of destroying enemies and removing all barriers, one should (make the following hand gesture): the hands are kept in front of (the adept's body), joined together and fully stretched, the two arms are so posed that these (i.e. the hands) remain facing each other, while all the fingers (excepting the middle fingers of both hands) may touch the pair of middle fingers. This (mudrā) is called mahāśrī; it grants all good fortune, removes all evils, hastens the fulfilment of desires and is the embodiment of the awakening of knowledge in persons who are ignorant.

7-10. Stretching the left (hand) out, with its fingers separated (from each other) and their tips bent, one should put the thumb, like a bridge, touching the middle (finger), opposite the other fingers. Then one should touch the front of one's chest with this śakti-mudrā which bestows happiness. These two mudrās, which

---

[1] Mudrās here exclusively mean the hand postures that accompany mantras.

[2] This consists of sesame seed, darbha-grass, barley, white rice, water, milk and fruits put into two small bowls and used as a purifying agent. See J.S. 13, 65-75, also Ahi.S. 28, 33-34. There the eight purifying objects are white mustard seed, darbha, sesame seed, barley, incense, fruits and flowers.

[3] This refers to the mūla-mantra.

are great and praised by masses of yogins, occupy the place of the highest subtle (represent the highest spirit) and give satisfaction to me.

10-14. Learn now the yoni-mudrā of myself who occupies the place of the gross. Stretching out the hands firmly (and) well pressed together in front (of the body), one should reverse each ringfinger over the back of the other. From their middle and base the (two) index fingers, (each) touching its base, should be nestled in front of them (= the ring fingers). The two little fingers (of the hands) are first placed in front of the remaining two middle (fingers), touching each other's surface, while the palms are concaved in the middle. The two thumbs should be placed in the direction of the first part of the middle fingers.

15-18. (Now) are described the modifications (i.e. emanations) of the śakti-mudrā called sukṣmā. The thumb (of each hand) should be placed on the fingers (of the same hand), one by one, starting from the index finger (*pradeśinī*), like a bridge. O Puraṃdara, these four mudrās belong to my śaktis (viz.) Lakṣmī etc.[1] These goddesses (viz.) Lakṣmī, Kīrti, Jayā and Māyā are my śaktis. The right hand is to be clenched into a fist. (Then) O greatest of all gods, the thumb of the left (hand) should be placed inside (the fist) in an erect position, (and kept) in front of the heart. This mudrā, belonging to the (aṅga called) hṛdaya, increases intelligence.

19. (If) all the fingers (of each hand) are stretched out and are touched by the thumb, this mudrā belongs to the (aṅga-mantra) called śiras and it brings the mantra near (the adept).

20-21. (The mudrā formed by) clenching the fingers, with the exception of the index, into a fist, with the index finger pointed upwards, is well known as the śikhā-mudrā,[2] which is terrible to all evil influences. One should always show it to destroy all evil and hindrances. Hence one should diligently show it at the beginning (of the worship), in the house of sacrifice.

22-24. (This aforesaid mudrā) connected with (the relevant) mantra eradicates all obstacles. The fingers of both hands are projected in front (of the body), while their middle (parts, i.e.

[1] See ch. VIII 22.

[2] The mudrā that belongs to the part of the body called *śikhā*, i.e. a tuft of hair at the back of the head.

palms) are joined from the wrist. This mudrā belongs to the armour [1] (*varman*). One should touch both one's shoulders with it. The formation of this mudrā by a mantrin [2] during (performance) of a ritual makes him invincible even to a host of wicked beings, ghosts, ghouls and magicians.

25-26. The fingers of both hands are interlaced and bent towards the back of the palms. The index fingers of the two (hands) are joined at the tips to form a vertical hole.[3] The thumbs are joined together at the base and are reversed. This mudrā belongs to the eye (*cakṣus*) and (the hands in this posture) should be put near the eyes.[4]

27-28. The index fingers of both hands are snapped [5] quickly with the thumb, (and the adept should) gaze at them all the time and direct them to all the ten directions.[6] This is known as the astra-mudrā, which frightens the enemies of the gods.

This group of six mudrās belonging to (the mantras of) the parts of the body are capable of doing all (functions).

29-30. Now listen to the description of the mudrās belonging to (the mantras of) the three pairs of secondary limbs (*upāṅga*).[7] Let all the four fingers of the right hand be joined together and the thumb be placed slantingly touching their bases. This mudrā belongs to (the mantras of) the secondary limbs (*upāṅgas*) and each of them should be touched by it (in their specific) positions.

31-33. Listen now to the (description) of the mudrā pertaining to the mantras of the ornaments (*alaṅkāra*) and the weapons (*astra*).[8] The little finger, the third finger and the middle finger of

---

[1] Unlike the other parts, the "fourth part of the body", viz. the *varman*, is not a limb in the proper sense, but the armour of a warrior which is indispensable to him. The gesture associates the mantra with the body from waist to shoulders.

[2] A mantrin is an adept who, at his initiation ceremony, was allotted a special mantra of his own, which is to be kept secret by the preceptor and the initiate.

[3] This is an attempt to imitate the form of an eye.

[4] This actually means touching the outer corners of the eyes with the hands in this posture.

[5] The word *sphoṭayet* means "let it be snapped producing a sound".

[6] The four cardinal and the four intermediate regions along with the upward and downward directions form the ten quarters.

[7] These are the belly, the back, the arms, the thighs, the knees and the legs (see ch. XXXIII, 12-13).

[8] These are not the weapons that belong to the six aṅgas (cf. ch. XXXIII, 4-11) but the secondary weapons adorning the body of the deity.

both hands should be (bent) so as to reach the middle of the palms like fists. Then these two fists of the two hands are joined together. After that the two index fingers are raised and joined at the tips. The position of the tips of the thumbs is reversed and they are placed in between the index fingers. This mudrā is known as belonging to (the mantra of) kaustubha (gem).[1]

Now listen to this (description of) the mālā-mudrā.

34. One should simultaneously make a circular movement with the two index fingers over (one's own body) starting from the neck and reaching (down) to the feet across the two shoulders. This is (the mudrā) belonging to the (mantra of) vanamālā.

35. Leaving out the two thumbs, one should interlace the eight fingers (of the hands) in front (of oneself) and let the arms hang downwards. This is the alternative (mudrā) belonging to (the mantra of) vanamālā.

36. The mudrā (formed by) joining the thumbs together side by side while keeping the (other) fingers apart from each other, belongs to (the mantra of) the lotus (*paṅkeruha*), which promotes strength and good fortune.

37-39. Turning the right hand upwards, one should join the thumb and the little finger together in front (of the palm) like a bridge, while the three (remaining) fingers are kept well-pressed (against each other) and are bent like the hood (of a snake). This mudrā belongs to (the mantra of) the noose (*pāśa*).

After having first (clenched the palms) of both hands into fists with the thumb of each fist on the back of it, one should turn the left fist downwards and place the right on the back of it (= left fist). This afore-mentioned mudrā belongs to the (mantra of) ādhāraśakti, (viz.) kūrma, the fire.[2]

40-42. The third and the index fingers of the left hand, which is turned downward, should be bent and placed firmly on the back of the middle finger. The middle finger of the other hand should be straightened and turned downwards. Then the little finger and the thumb are firmly stretched out. This mudrā pertains to the anantāsana(-mantra) and the rising Ananta.[3] This is well known as the chief of all āsana-mudrās.

---

[1] The kaustubha gem adorns the chest of Viṣṇu (cf. Harivaṃśa, ch. 22).
[2] Kūrma is designated as the fire of destruction; see ch. XXXIII, 32.
[3] Ananta is the great mythological snake, an incarnation of Saṃkarṣaṇa,

43-45. The undifferentiated absolute Śakti is called ādhārādhāra. The kūrma-mudrā is her unmeṣa (state, the first state of differentiation) and the ananta-mudrā is her nāda (state).[1] One should keep her (= Śakti) in mind in this way while performing the āsana-rites. Both hands are clenched into fists with three fingers (in each) and are joined together in front (of the body). The two index fingers are made to touch the tips of their (respective) thumbs and these should again be joined together.

46-48. This mudrā belongs to the (mantra of) pṛthivī, the supporter of all created (objects).

The wrists and the tips of the finger-nails of both hands are joined together, the fingers are pressed face to face. The two tips of the thumbs are moved quickly in the hollow inside. The middle of the palms should be made hollow like a cavity. This mudrā belongs to (the mantra of) kṣīrārṇava. (The mudrā of) the padma (-mantra) has been mentioned before.[2]

49-51. After separating the two hands, one should join the index fingers against each other in front. In the same way, one after another, one should join the pairs of the middle fingers and the third fingers and then join the two little fingers face to face, while the pair of thumbs should be placed in front of each pair of fingers. These four mudrās belong to the four (ādhāreśa mantras of) dharma etc.[3] The four (mantras of) adharma etc. possess four similar mudrās.[4]

52-56. The lotus[5] that exists above them (= dharma etc.) possesses the mudrā called pādmī, which has been described before.[6]

After having joined the index finger and the thumb of the right hand, one should disjoin them slowly. Afterwards, one by one each

---

who supports the earth on his thousand hoods; cf. Bhā.P. 3. 26. 25; 4. 9,14; 5. 25. 1-11; 7. 7. 10-11.

[1] See ch. XVIII. 19-23.

[2] See verses 35-36. J.S. is more explicit here and says that the mudrā of (ādhāra-) padma is the same as kṣīrārṇava, only differing in the accompanying mantra.

[3] These are dharma, jñāna, aiśvarya, vairāgya. Adharma, ajñāna, anaiśvarya and avairāgya are the counterparts of the preceding group of four. See ch. XXXIII 40-43.

[4] It is interesting to note that the J.S., which is the model of this text, does not mention adharma etc. separately.

[5] This is called avyakta-padma. Ch. XXXIII. 45.

[6] See verses 35 and 36.

finger is made supine. This is the mudrā of the three dhāmans [1] (i.e. mantras of the dhāmans).

Listen (now) to the (description of the mudrā) belonging to the cidbhāṣana.[2] The hands should be spread out distinctly and then shaped in a cup-like form. This is the mudrā of (the mantra) of cidbhāsana, which is absolute and contains pure sattva.

Thus, O Śakra, you have heard the description of the thirty-two mudrās belonging to the (mantras of) ornaments, weapons, seats etc., which (= mudrās) destroy all evils. (Now) listen to the (descriptions of) the ten mudrās pertaining to (the mantras of) kṣetreśvara etc.[3]

57-60. Both hands (each) clasping all the fingers (of the other) should be pressed with force, while keeping the thumbs turned upwards. This mudrā belongs to (the mantra of) kṣetrapāla, which removes all evils.

O Puraṃdara, making both hands supine and placing (them) on (the body), one should bend all the fingers and put them in the middle (of the palms). Then after placing the thumbs (over them), one should open them (= the fingers) gradually. This mudrā, described to you for the first time, belongs to the Śrī-bīja (-mantra). (The mudrā of the) Caṇḍa-bīja (-mantra) should be (formed) by raising the index finger of the left hand.

61-68. The same (index finger [4] raised) from the right hand indicates (the mudrā of the mantra of) Pracaṇḍa(-bīja). When the middle finger of the left hand is raised, it (forms the mudrā of the mantra) of Jaya. (The same pose of the finger) from the right hand is known as (the mudrā of the mantra) of Vijaya. The third finger of the left hand, if (raised) in the afore(-said) manner should be known as (the mudrā of) the Gaṅgā (-mantra). (The same finger) raised from the right hand, O Vāsava, is said to belong to the Yamunā (-mudrā). The mudrā with the little finger of the left

[1] The sūrya-maṇḍala, indu-maṇḍala and agni-maṇḍala are regarded as the three dhāmans; ch. XXXIII, 46.

[2] J.S. mentions this mudrā as the bhāvāsana mudrā and the editor there names it the haṃsa mudrā. In fact all these mean the same, namely the highest plane that an adept aspires to reach in meditation. J.S. 8. 70.

[3] Kṣetrapāla, Śrī Caṇḍa, Pracaṇḍa, Jaya, Vijaya, Gaṅgā, Yamunā, Śaṅkhanidhi and Padmanidhi. See ch. XXXIII, 50-51.

[4] The word *pradeśinī* literally means that which indicates a direction; hence the index finger has obtained that name. See T. T. Bhaṭṭācārya, Vācaspatyam, Benares 1963, Vol. VI, p. 4469.

hand (in the same pose) belongs to Śaṅkhanidhi; the mudrā with the little finger of the right hand in the same pose, to Padmanidhi.

The right hand (with all the four fingers and) the thumb as well, is clenched into a fist firmly holding the index and the third fingers of the left hand. Next the middle finger (of the left hand) should be carefully placed [1] on the back of the fingers (of the right hand) posed (in the aforesaid manner), so that it (= the middle finger) looks like the dangling trunk (of an elephant). The little finger of the left hand is held not too close to the fist (but) by the side of the right thumb, and is placed (in such a position) as to resemble a tusk. The left thumb as well as the right thumb are held quite clearly in a somewhat slanting position, so that they look like the auspicious ears of an elephant. This mudrā belongs to (the mantra of) Gaṇeśvara [2] and it (= mudrā) destroys all hindrances.

69-72. After having first joined the wrists of both hands together, the pair of the middle fingers should be lifted and joined at the tips. The pair of the index fingers are (posed) in the same way and the two third fingers (are held) in a similar way. The thumbs are (bent) double and gradually lowered downwards until they touch their respective palms. (Next) the two thumbs are clearly straightened. The two little fingers (are to be held) in a similar position. This is the vāgīśvarī-mudrā, which bestows command of language.

73-79. The two hands should be cupped (and joined together) in front of (the adept). Then they (= the joined hands) should be stretched (until) touching the forehead (of the adept, whose) head is bent. This is the mudrā of the three (mantras of) guru etc.,[3] which please the mind.

After having turned the right hand upwards with the fingers joined together and slightly bent and the thumb spread out in a slanting position, one should then lower it a little. This mudrā belonging to (the mantra of) pitṛgaṇa (forefathers) is considered to create permanent satisfaction. This (= mudrā) is always more pleasing to the ancestors than (the performance of) a thousand śrāddha (the funeral rites).[4] This should always be carefully shown while worshipping the ancestors.

---

[1] *Prayatnīkṛta* literally means processed.

[2] Gaṇeśa, the god of success and the remover of hindrances.

[3] Guru, paramaguru and parameṣṭhin. See ch. XXXIII, 71-73.

[4] The statement does not imply that this mudrā should be substituted

The two hands turned upwards are to be placed near the navel, with the right (hand) on the back of the left. This mudrā belongs to (the mantra) of siddhasaṃsad.[1]

The right hand with (its fingers) well pressed together should be turned opposite (i.e. with back) to the (adept's) own self and the left hand, (also) turned opposite, should be (kept) hanging. These two mudrās (called) varābhaya are considered to belong to (the mantra of) the lokeśas.

80-84. Together with each mantra of the vajra etc. (the weapons of the lokeśas),[2] one should show the aforesaid [3] (mudrā) called astra along with the śakti-mudrā. (This is the mudrā belonging to the mantras of) the weapons of the lokapālas, which are worshipped here in (the proper) order.

The three (fingers) of the left hand, (viz.) the little finger etc., are placed on the palm of the same (hand). The index finger is to be raised on the back of them away from the thumb. Thereafter, making a fist with the right hand with the three fingers as before and placing it (= the fist) by the side of the nostril, one should double the index finger and put it at the tip of the thumb. The right arm should be poised as if about to throw a disc. This is the mudrā of (the) Viṣvaksena (-mantra), which severs all bondages (of the world).

85. The right hand should be slightly folded and placed on the chest with the thumb [4] held apart and clearly (visible). This mudrā is considered to (belong to the mantra of) invocation.

86-89. The fingers of both (hands) should be kept apart and (posed) like the blade of a sword. (Next), after having raised the two thumbs like sticks, one should gradually (close the hands) into fists, starting from the little finger. This mudrā is for the visarjana (-mantra).[5]

Having straightened both hands which are turned downwards

for the śrāddha rites, but only emphasizes its higher capacity for pleasing the pitaras.

[1] See ch. XXXIII, 77. There the siddhas are moreover called ancient (*ādisiddha*).

[2] See ch. XXXIII, 89-98.

[3] See verses 27-28.

[4] Although the text mentions 'thumbs' I have used the singular, for J.S. gives the singular form and moreover no mention is made of the left hand; cf. J.S. 8, 111.

[5] This is the farewell rite.

and held close together with the two little fingers and the two thumbs well pressed together and (each of) the two middle fingers placed on the back of the opposite (palm), one should throw the two index fingers and ring-fingers apart. This mudrā, which fulfils all desires, is said to belong to the kāmadhenu (-mantra).

90. O Vāsava, realize that there are two ways of applying the mudrās, (viz.) that pertaining to the spirit in the form of consciousness, and that pertaining to the external (activities) arising from speech, action and mind.[1]

91. The one who, being well versed in the prescribed application, practises a mudrā according to this method, makes all this display (of mudrās) to stop rebirth.

92. Thus, O Puraṃdara, I have told you everything about the group of mudrās. Now, to broach the subject of propitiation, listen to the (description of) the supreme method of ablution (*snāna-vidhi*).[2]

93. Alakṣmi[3] is regarded as being covered both inside and outside with dirt. In order to prevent (i.e. the dirt from corrupting the body of the adept), her ablution is prescribed in all (scriptures).

94. That ablution again is of three kinds, (viz.) with water, mantra and mind (according to the) order (of merit). O Puruhūta, (each of) these three excels (the preceding one) a hundred times (in merit).

95. Ablution in the holy water of Puṣkara etc.[4] is regarded as

---

[1] The external mudrā obviously combines the relevant mantra and the mental disposition. The Parama Saṃhitā is more explicit about the meditative type of mudrā and says that it is purely meditative and solely efficacious for achieving emancipation. It also claims that the mudra is the concrete form of the specific grace accorded to the adept by the particular deity invoked. Pa.S. p. 98 and 100.

[2] This should have formed a separate chapter, as in J.S. In this context it should be noted that the L.T. mentions only three types of snānas, whereas the Pāñcarātra system recognizes seven types, namely vāyavya, i.e. covering the body with the dust raised by home-coming cows; pārthiva, marking the body with sacred mud; divya, bathing in rain falling from a cloudless sky; vāruṇa, bathing in water; āgneya, smearing the body with sacrificial ash; mānasa, meditative purification of the body before the worshipper starts the actual worship; and mantra, sprinkling water with blades of kuśa-grass while uttering the Vedic mantra *āpo hi* etc. Ṛg.V. 10. 9. 7; cf. Vi. S. ch. X, 4-15.

[3] It is interesting to note the mention of this deity who, as far as I know, is worshipped by the women of Bengal with the aid of a Brahmin or some other male person. See S. R. Das, Folk Religion of Bengal, Calcutta, p. 24-26.

[4] A place near Ajmer, Rājasthān.

water (-ablution). Ablution (conducted according to the method) prescribed by the Bhāgavata [1] scriptures is a hundred times (more efficacious) than that.

96. The mantra (-ablution) performed through (the use of) mantras and the consecration of the body (*aṅganyāsa*) is a hundred times more (meritorious) than that (i.e. ceremonial ablution). The meditative (ablution)[2] consisting of pure consciousness is a hundred times more (meritorious) than that (i.e. mantra-ablution).

97. First one should perform the water-ablution following the general rules and then (one should perform the same) following the special rule. The method (of the performance of) the special (ablution) is as follows:

98. Having first performed ablution with earth [3] and water, one should apply perfumed ointments etc. (to one's body).[4] This bath, which should be combined with prāṇāyāma,[5] destroys dirt.

99. First one should inhale (*pūraṇa*) twelve times (while muttering) the Tārā (-mantra). (The breath) should (then) be held (for as long as it takes to mutter Tārā) sixteen times, and it should again be exhaled accompanied by (muttering the Tārā) twice six times.

100-101. This cycle of (the breathing of) the air, ending in exhalation and (inhaled) from left to right alternately, removes all dirt which has previously gathered in the life-artery (*prāṇanāḍī*). Having thus realized the 'true state' (*tattvamayo bhūtvā*), one should purify by means of (practising yogic) concentration (*dhāraṇā*)[6] (on) the dirty and worthless created mass (i.e. the body), which is (created through the order of the) six sheaths (*kośa*).[7]

102. One should, through the practice of dhāraṇā, gradually merge all the principles of the earth etc. in their respective origins, ending at the (stage of) avyakta.[8]

---

[1] This perhaps means the scriptures of the Bhāgavatas.

[2] This means the ablution in meditation.

[3] Fine earth is used as a cleansing agent.

[4] Sandalwood paste, saffron, musk etc. are smeared on the body to perfume it.

[5] This is an important Yogic breathing exercise which is of four kinds. It is a method to break the normal rhythm of breathing and make it very subtle through prolongation. See Yog.S. 2, 49-53 and the commentary thereon in Baladevamiśra's Yogapradīpikā.

[6] See Yog.S., 3, 1 and the Yog.P. thereon.

[7] See ch. VI in extenso.

[8] See ch. VII and ch. V, 20.

103. Then one should merge one's own self into me (Lakṣmī) like milk merges in milk (i.e. without differentiation). After having become identical with Lakṣmī, one should become identical with Nārāyaṇa.

104. Having achieved (the state of) deep meditation (*dhāraṇā-bandha*) with a mind containing pure essence, (one attains the state) which is identical with the state of Paramātman, and that (state) is considered to be the same as the supreme Śakti.

105-109. Remaining in that (state), one should burn one's body (piṇḍa) with the fire of dhāraṇā. Immediately thereafter, one should envisage consciousness, the mass of light (*tejaḥpuñja*) of fire containing particles of rays, as descending on the head (of the adept) and subsequently setting the body afire. The real (*sat*) sattva existing within (then) becomes calm, while the rajas and the tamas are burnt. Having removed the ashes containing the rajas and the tamas with the upsurging air, one should call to mind the amṛta-water as flowing through the course of creation from the great ocean, as it were, of blissful consciousness (*cidānanda*), which is waveless and the source of all guṇas. Having thus strengthened the internally existent sattva, one should embody it. Through this course of creation he (the adept) obtains a pure phenomenal body.

Thus the internal purification has been described. Listen now to a description of the external purification.

110. In the order that is about to be disclosed, step by step, one should perform the rites of the mantranyāsa. Having accomplished thus the external purification, one should perform the ablution.

111. Having obtained a bit of clay with hands that are purified [1] and consecrating it with mantras, it should be placed in three portions on the end of the left hand (at) the base, the middle and the tip (of the fingers).

112. One should first perform the purification of the holy water (*tīrtha*) with that which consists of the conscious śakti.[2] That holy water is said to be of three kinds according to (whether it is) gross, subtle or absolute.

113-114. One should worship [3] the whole gross world with the gross form (of the holy water); one should worship the (deceased)

---

[1] With a sprinkling of *arghya*.

[2] This is the jñānaśakti mentioned in ch. VIII, 23.

[3] *Tarpaṇa* means worship with water alone.

ancestors along with the gods with the subtle (holy water) which contains sattva. With the absolute (form of holy water) which is of the blissful form, one should acquire the capacity for performing my worship. That is the reason why (it is said that) one should first perform by one's own self the rites of purifying the holy water according to the rules of scripture.

115-117. Having obtained the essence of the holy water (*tīrtha-sattā*) belonging to Viṣṇu by means of concentrating thought and merging it in me, the śakti, the great source of blissful consciousness, and burning the gross (body) with the fire of knowledge, one should fill it (i.e. body) up with the bliss of Brahman. Thereafter placing the essence of Viṣṇu in the holy water imbued with the conscious śakti, the intelligent (adept) should meditate in turn with the astra (-mantra), mūla-mantra and aṅga-mantra on the first, middle and last portions of the clay (respectively).

118-119. In order to pacify (i.e. to remove) all hindrances, one should throw (the portion of clay which has been consecrated by) the astra (-mantra) to all the ten directions. The portion connected with the mūla-mantra should be thrown into the holy water. By (doing this) my proximity (i.e.) the mantra-form (is achieved) instantaneously. One should smear one's limbs with the portion of mud that (has been consecrated with) the aṅga-mantra.

120-122. Having entered the water and taken a dip and come up again, one should throw over one's head the first handful (of water after consecrating it) by uttering the astra (-mantra); the second (handful should be consecrated) with the mūla-mantra and the third with the aṅga-mantra. Then returning to the bank and performing ācamana [1] properly, one should perform the ablution with mantras and proper rites of consecration (*nyāsa*). Next one should perform the meditative ablution with an attentive mind.

123. Contemplating on the lotus-eyed Lakṣmīdhara (Nārāyaṇa) existing in one's own self, one should envisage the flow of the water as originating from his [2] (= Nārāyaṇa's) feet and falling on (one's own) head.

[1] The word *ācamana* means sipping water from the cupped right hand and then touching the ear and other parts of the body for the ceremonial purification of the body.

[2] This refers to the river Gaṅgā, which was mythologically described as originating from the feet of Viṣṇu. This flow of water came into existence

124-129. One should bathe one's entire body, both inside and outside with this (water). After entering into (the state of) meditative trance (*samāhita*), one should perform these three types of ablution at the proper times once, twice or thrice according to one's capacity. After having performed the tarpaṇa to the gods who are pervaded by me and to the sages by (pronouncing the mantra consisting) of the names (of the relevant god or sage) preceded by the praṇava and ending in namas, one should perform tarpaṇa to the (deceased) ancestors (by only substituting the mantra with) the svadhā ending After concluding the ablution in this manner, by means of pūraka [1] one should invoke the deity of the (mūla-) mantra existing in the holy water,[2] and consider it (= the mūla-mantra) to be placed in the mind. (Next) having gathered the astra (-mantra) which was formerly scattered in all directions,[3] one should collect all the sacrificial ingredients and repair to the temple to make the sacrifice. This Pāñcarātra-shrine (*vimāna*), full of all the (requisite holy) signs, may be constructed by oneself or may belong to some sage, or may be made by some successful adepts or erected by some man whose mind has become purified and identified with me.[4]

130-134. He should willingly repair to the bank of an auspicious lake, quiet and pleasant, or to a quiet garden decorated with holy trees, or to a charming broad bank of a river spread with sand, free from (strong) wind, solitary and untouched by evil, or to whichever place his mind takes a fancy.

(The adept), who possesses the supreme mantra that remains in the heart in the form of blissful realization, should not look in any other direction, should stay silent and hold his breath [5] and, having

by the melted mind of Viṣṇu that overflowed while he was listening to divine music. Viṣ.P. I, 9, 103; II, 2, 334; 8, 108-113, 120-2; III, 14, 18; IV, 4, 26-30.

[1] This is the first type of prāṇāyāma consisting of slow and deep inhalation.

[2] See verses 118-119.

[3] See verse 118.

[4] Verses 128 and 129 seem irrelevant to the topic and do not conform to the ritual sequence followed by the J.S. Ch. 10, which the present text more or less follows as a model. Possibly these two verses are a later addition. The mention of Pāñcarātra further strengthens this doubt as it is abrupt and unnecessary.

[5] This is called *kumbhaka*, the second part of *prāṇāyāma*, where the inhaled air is held for as long as it took to inhale.

reached the holy place, should through the tip of the nose emit the breath [1] (with the utterance) of my mantra, the supreme self possessing a blazing, fiery form. (Next he should) place the astra (-mantra) outside (his body) and strike the earth with (his) foot.

135. Bearing in mind me, Lakṣmī, the unique, highest goddess in mantra-form, one should find a quiet place and construct a beautiful seat.

136-137. After having (placed on a seat made of) grass, hide, cloth, or a plank of sacrificial wood and praising with devotion Hari, me and the group of preceptors, one should with bowed head mentally beg their permission (and then) mentally perform [2] all the (sacrificial) rites by means of concentrated thought (*jñānasamādhi*).

138. Whatever rites are performed through realization in the (state of) meditative trance (which is identical with the state of) Brahman, become filled with pure sattva and are surely undecaying.

139. The forms of evil generated by rajas and tamas concern external objects and accordingly their purification by action, or speech, or thought (is external too).[3]

140-141. Therefore that which is 'scented by meditation' is absolutely free from fault. Hence one should stay (in the state of) meditative realization originating from pure knowledge and perform all the spiritual rites by meditating on the (highest) knowledge. Thus, O Sureśvara, is told to you the proper method of (the rite) of ablution. Hereafter I shall recount to you places where aṅganyāsa etc. should be performed.

---

[1] This is obviously the third part of the said *prāṇāyāma* viz. *recaka*, exhaling slowly. See Yog.S. 2, 49-51 and the Yogapradīpikā thereon.

[2] *nirvapana* literally means to pour out, or to offer a libation.

[3] This verse is also confused in its language and subject matter. At the expense of clarity, apparently a whole chapter on the rules of ablution and another chapter on the adept's preliminary meditation have been condensed and inserted as an appendix to the chapter on the mudrās.

CHAPTER THIRTY-FIVE

THE PURIFICATION OF THE BODY (BHŪTAŚUDDHI)

1. Śrī:—O Śakra, in order to perform successfully (the rites such as) the internal sacrifice[1] etc., listen attentively to the description of the bhūtaśuddhi[2] recounted by me.

2. In this (system) bhūtaśuddhi is the name given to the mental process of identifying with me (the principles) starting from the earth (element) and ending in prakṛti. (This is done) by means of (the sounds representing them) starting from *ka* and ending in *bha*.

3. Consider that the existing eight principles[3] (earth etc.) have two forms differentiated by being gross or subtle.

4. That which comes within the range of the eye is described as having the gross form. Its dormant existence in its source is called the (subtle) element-potential (*tanmātra*).

5. According to the difference of grossness and subtlety these principles are (classified as) sixteen in number. One should suspend their relation (*vṛttī*) with their respective objects and organs.

6. One should bring the three (sets) of the (senses of) smell etc., (i.e. cognitive organs), (the organs of) excretion and procreation etc., (i.e. the conative organs) and fragrance etc., (i.e. the qualities therein) to rest in the (respective) element-potentials such as the

---

[1] This will be described in the next chapter.

[2] Bhūtaśuddhi is the process of purifying the five elements of the adept's body. This rite makes the body fit to worship God. The method, as described in the second verse, is to dissolve each element into its source. This process of dissolution is conducted in meditation and finally it reaches the point of the primordial source, prakṛti. Thus the adept merges into the Śakti, the ultimate source, and emerges, with a spiritual body which consists of Śakti alone. This is total identification with the basic mantra which is accomplished by uttering a series of mantras with their appropriate mudrās. The final merging is with the mūla-mantra representing God. This ritual of visualizing the identification of the adept's material body with the mantric manifestation of the supreme deity totally eradicates the adept's impurities. The performance of bhūtaśuddhi is preliminary to all forms of ritual worship, and is compulsory for all followers of the Tantric tradition. See Agehananda Bharati, The Tantric Tradition, London 1965, p. 112.

[3] See ch. XV, 26-27.

earth (element) etc., following the course that is opposite (to that of creation).

7-10. Just as waves are dissolved in the sea because of the wind, so also a wise (man) should dissolve the waves of sense and objects in the ocean of the great elements through (the power of) his correct knowledge. The mind (*manas*) and the ego (*abhimāna*)[1] should be dissolved in ahaṃkāra; the vital air (*prāṇa*) and determination (*adhyavasāya*)[2] should be thrown down into the principle of buddhi; the three guṇas (viz.) sattva, rajas and tamas should be dissolved into prakṛti. That which contains the three guṇas and the unmanifested (*avyakta*) source (*kāraṇa*) of mahat etc.,[3] is threefold, viz. traiguṇya, prasūti and māyā.[4]

11. Thus, those who are well versed in (the knowledge) of the principles (*tattvas*) recognize the ten [5] sources (*prakṛtayaḥ*). These again are considered to be twenty in number according to the differentiation of gross and subtle.

12. These are considered to be the ten mantras of the gross sources, (viz.) the name of the principle (intended), ending in *huṃ phaṭ* and preceded by the Tārikā (-mantra) with the praṇava (-mantra) at the very beginning (to complete the mantra).[6]

13. One should similarly (formulate the mantra by) thinking of (the words) the flesh, the fat and the juice (belonging to the body of the adept) coming after the three letters with vyoma and the two paras adorned with the bindu and nāda.[7]

14-16. There are nine forms of the primary (Śakti), which are considered to belong to the ten subtle forms (of bhūta-mantras). After (recalling the above-mentioned mantras), one should recollect (the names of) these śaktis which are said to be (identical with) the supreme (śakti) that has become the soul (jīva) in the individual bodies, together with (the letters) māyā and vyoma.[8] Their names

---

[1] Ego is the function of the principle of ahaṃkāra.

[2] Adhyavasāya is the function of the principle of buddhi.

[3] All the other principles, proceeding from avyakta, the supreme source.

[4] See ch. VII, verses 16, 30-33, and ch. XV, verses 26-31.

[5] The five elements, ahaṃkāra, mahat, traiguṇya, prasūti and māyā: ch. XV, 26-27.

[6] e.g. *oṃ hrīṃ ahaṃkārāya huṃ phaṭ*.

[7] *Oṃ hrīṃ huṃ māṃsamedarasebhyaḥ ṭhaṃ ṭhaḥ*. This is not found in J.S.

[8] *Oṃ nivṛttaye īṃ* etc. The word *nava* is difficult to translate, since there are ten śaktis mentioned.

are traditionally said to be Nivṛtti, Pratiṣṭhā, Vidyā, Śānti, Śāntyatītā, Abhimānā, Prāṇā, Guṇavatī, Guṇasūkṣmā and Nirguṇā.

17. The mantras formulated by adding (the letters) vahni, Viṣṇu and the half-moon to the afore-said bījas of the ten (principles) are known to be those of the tutelary deities (of these śaktis).[1]

18-20. Possessing the names of Gandhaśrī, Rasaśrī, Rūpaśrī, Sparśaśrī, Śabdaśrī, Abhimānaśrī, Prāṇaśrī, Guṇaśrī, Guṇasūkṣmaśrī, and Māyāśrī, they remain inside the ten (aforesaid) śaktis as their guardian (deities). This is the way how bhūtaśuddhi has to be performed, considering it to be a part (of the method leading to yogic perfection). Now listen attentively to the description of (the method of) sthānaśuddhi (consecration of the place), which should be performed before (*bhūtaśuddhi*).[2]

21-22. Thinking of me as the smokeless burning embers glowing like thousands of fires of destruction or suns, one should (mentally) burn the earth in the fire ejected from my mouth, and then sprinkle that with the moisture derived from my face, which resembles ten thousands of moons. This is the rite called sthānaśuddhi. Now listen to the process of (performing) bhūtaśuddhi (purification of the body-elements).

23-24. Through the force of the mantra[3] attracting the earth-element—quadrangular, flat, yellow and marked with the sign of thunder—to proximity with one's body that is present in the same place, one should merge it in the smell-potential. Thereafter that should be dissolved in me, who am the substratum of it, with its own bīja (accompanying it) and then one should throw me (its śakti) in the external water-element.

25. (Then) that (external water-element) which possesses the divine form of the half-moon with the mark of a lotus, should be merged into its own place (of origin), the liquid-potential, by means of its own (bīja) mantra.[4]

26. After having established it (there) with (the relevant) mantra, it should be dissolved in me (its śakti) and I should be

---

[1] *Oṃ īṃ gandhaśriyai rīṃ* etc.

[2] The worshipper must perform five types of preliminary consecratory rites: consecration of the place, of the vessels, of the image, of his own self and of the mantra.

[3] In J.S. the mantra is mentioned as *slāṃ*: J.S. 10, 17.

[4] In J. S. the mantra is mentioned as *ṣvāṃ*: J.S. 10, 19.

thrown into the external fire (-element). This method should be pursued (in the proper order) till (one reaches) māyā.[1]

27-28. The wise should know that the process of the involution of my śaktis is not the same in each case. Just as butter churned out of milk may be thrown into the same milk, (or) (the butter) may sometimes be thrown into some other milk, or it may be thrown into other butter, so the wise think that the tutelary śaktis may be thrown (into their sources) till the (attainment) of the prakṛti-state (in a different order of dissolution).[2]

29-30. Thus I, the supreme Śakti associated with this nine śakti (group), who am meditated upon as the end of the attributeless (state, *nirguṇānta*) and who constitute the basis of māyā, the tenth (śakti, called Nirguṇā), should be taken to the next śakti existing in the eleventh (principle)[3] (who is) Lakṣmī (Herself), filled with great activities (lit. vibration) and is endowed with the form (of the state where she is) manifested as Vyūhas.[4]

31. (Then) dissolving this eleventh śakti into the twelfth (śakti), which is identical with the great self, undefinable and peerless, one should merge this twelfth śakti into me.

32. Thus, after having raised it (the śakti of the individual) to the position (called) dvādaśānta[5] one should meditate on this supreme twelfth śakti which consists of all, as merged in me, who consist of the sounds.

33. My subtle body, which consists of the sounds, is as (bright as) millions of fires and moons and suns, possessing eyes, heads and faces in every direction, resembling in form an ever-flowing stream (of nectar).

34. This (śakti) first appeared (actively) from Viṣṇu, as the luminous (flash of) lightning (appears) from the (dark) cloud, fully equipped with all completeness (in order) to help all living beings.

35. Śakra:—O Lotus-born (goddess) deign to speak to me about

[1] See verse 10.

[2] The idea seems to be that the effect may go back to its immediate source or to its ultimate source or to another preceding effect. This allows for considerable flexibility in the process.

[3] See IV, 4-32. This is the Vyūha-Śakti or Śuddha-śakti. The word *nirguṇānta* means māyākośa.

[4] See ch. V, 7-10.

[5] A place above the top of the head, i.e. the seat of māyā. Cf Prakāśa on Varīvasyārahasya by Bhāskararāya, The Adyar Library Series, Vol. XXVIII, 3rd ed. 1968, p. 91.

the places of the body where one should practise gradual involution, and also (to explain to me) the nature of the images of the elements, the earth etc.[1]

36-37. Śrī:—The place of the earth(-element) is up to the knees. The place of the water(-element) is considered to be up to the waist; the place of the fire(-element) is up to the navel; and that of the air (-element) is up to the heart. The place of the ether(-element)[2] is up to the ears. The place of ahaṃkāra is up to the hole (the cavity of mouth or the hole on the crown). The place of mahat is up to the brows, and in the space (above the head) is said to be the place of the absolute. [3]

38-39. Then, one step higher (than the place of the absolute) four fingers above the crown, is the position of prakṛti. The place of the avyakta (principle) is situated sixteen fingers higher up above that (location of prakṛti). Twelve fingers higher up (than the location) of the eleventh is the seat of akṣaraśrī (i.e. Śabdabrahman).[4]

The great image of the earth(-element) is quadrangular (in shape) possessing the mark of the thunder.

40. (The image of the) water(-element) is considered to be like the half-moon (in shape), white and possessing the mark of the lotus. (The image) of the fire(-element) is said to be triangular (in shape) possessing the mark of svastika and red (in colour).

41. (The image) of the air(-element) is said to be a grey circle possessing six dots, while that of the ether(-element) is black in colour like collyrium and possesses only the image (i.e. without any definite shape).

42-43. Having thus dissolved the (cosmic) principles, one should conduct the individual (self)—which exists within the dvādaśānta,[5]

---

[1] The word *bimba* means an orb or disc; it may also denote an image. Dictionaries give a number of meanings. Here I have taken the meaning 'a copy' of the imagined shape of the elements.

[2] The text has *nabhas*.

[3] It is difficult to determine the exact meaning of this word *para*. In chapter VI no less than thirty-five principles are enumerated. It may mean here cosmic intelligence or the life-principle or the group of pure undifferentiated sattva, rajas and tamas.

[4] Four fingers above the crown is the position of prakṛti. The position of avyakta is sixteen fingers above that. The place of the eleventh category, viz. māyā, is eleven fingers higher than that. Twelve fingers higher is the place of the supreme Śabdaśakti, a position also called dvādaśānta.

[5] See above, p. 205, n. 5.

appears from the cavity of the heart [1] and is the support of the series of cognition, and which passes through the duct of suṣumnā upwards from the knees—over the steps (consisting of) śaktis [2] and dissolve it in me, who remain inside.

44. At the end of that (viz. dvādaśānta), there exists the great lotus possessing a thousand petals, which is as brilliant as millions of suns and as lustrous as millions of moons.[3]

45. The form that contains Agni and Soma, which abides in (all), which consists of great bliss and is indefinable, incomparable and identical with consciousness, (is regarded as) absolute and belonging to me.

46. A partial projection of it (i.e. of the above-mentioned form of blissful consciousness) is the excellent stream of the blissful individual (consciousness). One should bring the bliss in oneself back to (me,) the great blissful one.[4]

47. Then the body (of the adept), which is (dissoluble) like a heap of salt, should be thoroughly burnt in the great and swiftly moving fire of consciousness, which comes out of my mouth.

48. Those who possess śāstric vision should consider the dāhapāvaka (*ra*) together with the rasa (*tha*) and the sixth (vowel, viz. *ū*) and bindu (the mantra of dāhapāvaka) as standing between Tārikā and (the word) for salutation (*nati*).[5]

49. Then one should sprinkle it (the body of the adept) with the (flow of the) nectar originating from my mouth, who am pervaded by Soma. The refreshing (mantra) is considered to be the candra (*ṭa*) and sūkṣma (*ya*) (together with) vyoma (*ṃ*).[6]

50. (Next) one should contemplate the śaktis (formerly) sent (as cosmic principles) by me—who was actively manifested with a will to create and who dwelt in the consciousness and in the life-

[1] Cf. Ch. U. 3, 12, 8.

[2] The above-mentioned twelve śaktis of the twelve cosmic principles or categories.

[3] This lotus is here identified with the great śakti in the state immediately prior to the state of creation. It grew out of Viṣṇu's navel, and manifested Brahmā. L.T. V, 22-23 and VI, 5.

[4] This is the dissolution of the inner individual self in the cosmic śakti.

[5] *hrīṃ rthūṃ namaḥ.*

[6] *ṭyaṃ.* The entire mantra should run as follows: *hrīṃ ṭyaṃ namaḥ.* These two processes, in which the body is first consumed by spiritual fire and then bathed in the nectar, makes it thoroughly pure like burned gold. The second mantra is cited differently by J.S. as *vsaṃ*: J.S. 10, 78.

principle (the two cosmic principles)—as merged in me, who consist of sound.

51. Then one should recall (these principles) starting with māyā and ending with the earth(-element) as being recreated together with their own śaktis, preceded by the (creative) impetus.[1]

52-55. Then (the adept should recall) the creation of (his own) body, bright (i.e. cognizable) due to the cognizance of the instruments (of creation). After having (re-)created the body in this manner, which (now) consists of the pure Lakṣmī and is 'great', the adept should bring the heart, i.e. the individual self, through the same channel. The mantra of the body is said to be the complex of the three sounds anala (*ra*), soma (*sa*) and candrī (*ṭa*) which is placed not too near the middle (of the mantra).[2] The (adept) who possesses a pure body should practise mantranyāsa so that he may acquire the capacity to worship, please worshippers, dispel demons etc. and overcome obstacles.[3]

56-57. The adept should recall each (object), the wooden plank etc., which was previously[4] laid on the ground, through its own mantra, and visualize these in five different forms namely ādhāraśakti, kūrma, the earth, the milky ocean and the lotus. (He) should then meditate on Tārkṣya [5] as being there, existing as one whose essence is the bīja kharva [6] (i.e. who exists in the kharvabīja).

58-60. After being seated there and having meditated on the spouse of Lakṣmī as (identical with) one's own self, around the seat (of meditation) one should set up a boundary (which consists as it were) of a wall (made from) the repeated (utterance) of the astra (-mantra) [7] and which resembles a thicket of arrows. One should (then) protect that place and the wall with the kavaca(-mantra).[8]

The performance with (mantras), which remain in the sky,[9] is necessary in order to make a (mantra)nyāsa invisible.

---

[1] *Codanā.*

[2] *hrīṃ ṛtsaṃ namaḥ.*

[3] This is the praise of the mantranyāsa ritual. It is customary to praise and give information about the usefulness of the object discussed.

[4] See ch. XXXIV, 135-136.

[5] Name of Garuḍa, the vāhana of Viṣṇu.

[6] *Khaṃ.*

[7] *Oṃ vīryāya astrāya phaṭ.*

[8] *Oṃ balāya kavacāya huṃ.*

[9] Nyāsa is not a visible process and the placing of mantras is done in the void. See Agehananda Bharati, The Tantric Tradition, London 1965,

(Next), one should perform (in the following manner) the rite of dehanyāsa, which is preceded by the hastanyāsa.[1]

61-63. One should (start the hastanyāsa by) placing Tārika on the thumb and all her other śaktis [2] on the (remaining) four fingers. Lakṣmī should be placed on the index finger, Kīrti on the middle finger, Jayā on the ring finger, while Māyā is placed on the little finger. The order of (words in these) is as follows: tāraka, Tārikā and the (respective) names (of the śaktis),[3] starting (the process) from the little finger.

One should next perform the nyāsa of the five parts of the body (aṅga),[4] starting with the heart and considering the eyes to be one of the aṅgas.[5]

64. The (mantra called) kaustubha [6] (should be placed) on the palm of the right hand and (the mantra called) vanamālā [7] on the palm of the other hand. The (mantra called) padma [8] (should be placed) in the middle of the palm of the right hand as well as on the palm of the left hand.

65. The (mantra called) aṅkuśa [9] should be placed on the palm of the right hand, (the mantra called) pāśa[10] on (the palm of) the left. This is the way how (the adept) should first perform the hastanyāsa (the nyāsa of the hands).

66-67. Listen now to how the dehanyāsa (i.e. the nyāsa rites of the body) should be performed. (The mantras of) the two tāraka and Tārikā,[11] resembling the sun and the moon, should be placed (all over the body, i.e.) from the crown to toes and from the feet to the head. Then the (mantra) of Lakṣmī[12] is to be placed on the left shoulder and (that of) Kīrti on the right.

p. 91-92: M. B. Jhavery, Comparative and critical study of Mantrasastra, Ahmedabad 1944. p. 79-81.

[1] All aṅganyāsa should follow the hastanyāsa.

[2] Lakṣmī, Kīrti, Jayā and Māyā.

[3] *oṃ hrīṃ lakṣmyai tarjanībhyāṃ namaḥ*, etc.

[4] Hṛdaya, śikha, śiras, astra and kavaca.

[5] Netra should be added to the above list of aṅgas.

[6] Ch. XXXIII, 15-17.

[7] Ch. XXXIII, 18-20.

[8] Ch. XXXIII, 21-23.

[9] Ch. XXXIII, 26-28.

[10] Ch. XXXIII, 24-25.

[11] *oṃ* and *hrīṃ*.

[12] The mantras of Lakṣmī, Kīrti, Jayā and Māyā are discussed in ch. XLV.

68. The (mantra of) Jayā is put on the right hand and that of Māyā on the left hand. The mantra of the heart exists inside the nose and the mantra of the head on the head.

69-70. The (mantra of) the śikhā (the tuft of hair on the top of the head) is placed on the tuft of hair, while the (mantra) of the armour remains on the shoulders. After having placed the mantra of the eyes on the eyes and (the mantra of) the weapon on the two palms of the hands, the noble holder of mantras (adept) should place the six (mantras of the) upāṅgas [1] on the navel, back, the pair of hands, thighs, knees and feet.

71. The (mantra of) kaustubha existing inside the breast (should be placed) on the middle of (the body) and (the mantra of) vanamālā on the neck. Two (mantras of the) lotus should be placed on the two hands by repeating each mantra twice.

72-73. (The mantra of) pāśa (is to be placed) on the left hand and (the mantra of) aṅkuśa on the right. The (mantra) of the gross Tārikā [2] on the feet and the subtle (Tārikā) on the joints (*upasandhika*). The final (i.e. absolute) Tārikā should be placed on the brahmarandhra (the cavity of the crown) because this is the best of all mantras. (Hence) with each individual nyāsa [3] the adept should think of this mantra (as being luminous) like moonshine.

74-76. The adept should mentally construct the appropriate hand postures (accompanying each nyāsa). He should meditate upon all the mantras used in all the nyāsas as being pervaded by Tārikā, the absolute goddess, in the form of a deluge. When all the mantras, relating to the different courses [4] are thus meditated upon, they merge into oneness just as all the (streams of) water reaching the ocean become one. When he who practises the mantra has thus performed nyāsa, he directly becomes pervaded by Lakṣmī.[5]

77. The (adept) possessing power (*bala*), which has been acquired by means of meditation, enjoys then (after the performance) the privilege of being capable of all (religious practices). Success in all (endeavours) comes to him who meditates.

---

[1] Ch. XXXIII, 11-13.

[2] See ch. XXXII, 1-37.

[3] This means that the mantra *hrīṃ* should accompany all mantras used in performing nyāsa rites.

[4] This indicates the different courses of creation.

[5] Thus the performance of bhūtaśuddhi sublimates the material body of the adept by transforming it into pure sattva.

78. The person, whose body has gone through (the process) of nyāsa, can remain undaunted in places infested with evil. He may also overcome (the peril of) accidental death and all incidental calamities.

79. The (adept) whose body has been consecrated (*nyasta*) and who practises the mantras in the proper way, should, with a mind such as is prescribed by the sacred scripture, meditate on me, who am the great goddess possessing the form containing (all) mantras.

80. The yogin, who possesses the knowledge that I am God Viṣṇu and that I am the eternal Lakṣmī, will never again be reborn.

81. O Śakra, (the process of) bhūtaśuddhi has thus been described to you. Now listen to (me) describing the (process of) inner sacrifice.

CHAPTER THIRTY-SIX

DESCRIPTION OF THE IMAGES AND THE PROCESS OF THE MENTAL SACRIFICE

1. Śrī:—O Śakra, the one who is full of absolute bliss (*brahmānanda*) and who exists within the heart should be worshipped with (spiritual) offerings relating to supreme truth. This is considered the inner (or mental) sacrifice (ritual worship).

2-5. (The adept) should sit in the posture of either padma, svastika, or yoni[1] and (then start) meditating on ādhāraśakti,[2] the goddess, who is not to be supported by any, who is devoid of any (definite) form and is luminosity itself. (He should) concentrate (his attention) on her (as occupying) the region between his navel and genitals. The (position of) kālakūrma, which possesses a spotless, brilliant body in the form of a turtle, is above it. (This) supreme deity carries the conch-shell, the disc and the mace. The lord of the serpents (i e. Śeṣa) is situated on top of this. He possesses a face resembling a full moon, has a thousand hoods and eyes rolling with intoxication, and he holds the disc and the plough.[3] One should pay obeisance to him who is higher than the high (the supreme = absolute).

6-8. One should contemplate on the goddess earth (located) above him. She is (ocre) as the paste of saffron, her body (is) variously decorated with gold and jewels, (she) possesses a face and eyes with a benevolent (expression), her palms (are) joined and placed on her head as she remains meditating on the Omnipresent (God). One should meditate on these deities (viz.) ādhāraśakti etc. (located) in the space between the navel and the genitals, which is divided into four parts.

---

[1] See Ahi.S. ch. 31, verses 34 and 40 for the padma and svastika postures; the yoni posture is described in B.K.S. Iyengar, Light on Yoga, London 1965, p. 333. The latter is not so commonly mentioned in Pāñcarātra texts.

[2] This is the basic śakti existing as the jīvaśakti in the lowest bodily region called mūladhāra. See Agehananda Bharati, The Tantric tradition, p. 263.

[3] The plough is mentioned because the serpent Śeṣa is an avatāra of Balarāma, who also indulges in getting intoxicated.

8-9. One should meditate on the milky ocean (*kṣīrārṇava*) (as located in) the navel (and) possessing a form (white) as the kunda (flower) or moon,[1] surrounded by the rays (as it were) of the streams, (and) having a face (beautiful) as a full moon. One should meditate upon this (one) as being of inscrutable form, the formless possessor of a form.[2]

10-12. Thereafter one should meditate on the lotus appearing from inside the milky ocean, (resembling) the unwavering (mass of) fire and full of lustre like the rising sun, with a pendulous belly (and) disclosing white teeth in a smiling and auspicious face. It has two arms and is ever surrounded by a variety of auspicious bees. It has a thousand petals and is covered with thousands of rays like the sun (the thousand-rayed one). (Hence) one should put the seat (*āsāna*) on the back of it.

13. Dharma, jñāna, vairāgya and aiśvarya are in succession considered to be the legs of the seat situated respectively in the direction of Agni etc.[3]

14. All of them have human forms, a fair complexion, a lion's face, and (they are) very energetic, highly valorous and full of vigour owing to (the duty of) holding my (seat).

15. The opposites of the (seat-supports) dharma etc. are placed in the direction of the east etc.[4] (They are called) adharma, ajñāna, avairāgya and anaiśvara.

16-17. These (adharma etc.) are of human form and (are red in colour) like the bandhūka flower.[5]

The four (sacred scriptures), Ṛgveda etc.,[6] possessing the (combined) form of horse and man[7] and yellow (in colour), stay on the (four) corners, viz. between the east and north-east, between east

---

[1] *Kunda* is a species of jasmine. Both kunda and the moon are used as similes to indicate a pleasing, fair complexion.

[2] This is beyond both that which has form and that which has no form. Here the adjective *arūpin* probably means without definite form.

[3] These are the four corners, south-east, south-west, north-west and north-east.

[4] East, south, west and north.

[5] Pentapetes phoenicea (a red flower).

[6] Ṛg, Yajus, Sāman and Atharvan respectively.

[7] This is a reference to god Hayagrīva, the bestower of learning and the restorer of the four Vedas when he recovered them from the demons. He is described as having a horse's face but human body and represents the Vedas. Pau.S. XXXIV, 35; Hayaśīrṣapāñcarātra 1, 8-23; H. Daniel Smith, Vaiṣṇava Iconography, Madras 1969, pp. 193-196.

and south-east, between west and south-west and between west and north-west.[1]

18-22. The group of (four) yugas, viz. kṛta etc., which possess dark and (combined) forms of bull and man, are placed at the (four corners viz.) between the north and north-east, between south and south-east, between south and south-west and between north and north-west.

All of them [2] possess four arms. With two of these they hold the seat, while with the (remaining) two folded together they salute the (deity) seated thereon.

One should think about the supreme seat consisting of intelligence as being above them, (and) over that, one should recall the eight-petalled white lotus, which is the unmanifested. The orb of the sun, which is as bright as ten million suns, (is contemplated upon) above that. On top of that, the orb of the moon, as brilliant as ten million moons, is (contemplated upon). The orb of fire, as bright as ten million fires, is (visualized) above that.

23-24. One should remember that tamas, rajas and sattva are their (i.e. the sun's, moon's and the fire's) respective guṇas. The mantras of the principles starting with the (principle of) intelligence (*buddhi*) and ending in sattva are considered (to be constructed by) placing the names of the principles between the praṇava and the word of salutation.[3]

Thereafter one should offer the seat of consciousness which is identical with the absolute self-consciousness.

25-26. Of the space (between) the navel and the heart, which is divided into five sections, four should be used to (hold) (the deities) starting with the ocean and ending with the seat.[4] The seat of the lotus etc. should be placed nowhere else but in the fifth (section).

26-30. The elements exist in the ādhāraśakti; the element-potentials are in the turtle; speech etc. (the conative organs) remain in Ananta. The five (cognitive organs) viz. hearing etc. remain inside the earth. The mind exists in the milky ocean; the

[1] Instead of naming the directions, the names of their protecting deities are given. These are Indra, Agni, Yama, Nirṛti, Varuṇa, Vāyu, Kubera or Soma and Īśāna, guarding respectively east, south-east, south, south-west, west, north-west, north and north-east.

[2] All the sixteen deities, viz. Dharma etc., supporting the seat of Śakti.

[3] *oṃ sūryabimbāya namaḥ* and so on.

[4] The milky ocean, the lotus, the supports and the seat.

ego-principle should be meditated upon in the lotus. The intelligence (*dhī*) is regarded as (occupying) the sixteen ('supports') dharma etc. and the seat. Avyakta (occupies) the pure lotus (existing) above that (seat). The three guṇas, tamas etc., are considered to consist of three lotuses. Some call it time (*kāla*) [1] which consists of the three (principles) viz. the ego-principle (*bhūtādi*) etc. (mahat and pradhāna). Others hold the seat of consciousness to be the person called Ananta. Some hold that Garuḍa exists above the seat of consciousness.[2]

31. O lord of the gods, kharva joined by vyoman and followed by (the words) *khagānana* and *namas* constitutes the mantra (of Garuḍa). The learned say that this is the ninth mantra.[3]

2-34. Thus after having taken the steps to establish the seat with the various mantras, (the adept) should meditate on Viṣṇu-Nārāyaṇa, the flawless resplendent one who consists of the universe (and is) the supreme Self, who holds conch-shell, disc and mace and possesses four arms. His dress is yellow and He has eyes like the lotus. He is to be recalled as actively roused by His śakti which consists of vibration [4] (i.e. creativeness).

Now learn from me (the method of His worship) so that you may meditate on Him in the correct way.

35. After having accurately performed the nyāsa of the mantras and the parts of the body and after having correctly established the internal seat [5] (of God) and after having shown all the mudrās, one should recall the majesty of the mantras.

36-38. The absolute Brahman is the absolute state, which is situated beyond darkness (*tamas*). It is the supreme (integral pair)

---

[1] Here the text is somewhat confused. What is meant is that the white lotus is the seat of the unmanifest which, together with the three orbs, consists of a group of lotuses which the Pārameśvara Saṃhitā calls the cycle of time (kālacakra, P.S. 5, 14) and which J.S. calls simply time (kāla, J.S. 12, 19).

[2] Vide J.S. 12, 20.

[3] *Khaṃ khagānanāya namaḥ*. The ninth position of the mantra is found by counting the mantras of ādhāraśakti, kūrma, Ananta, bhū, kṣīrārṇava, padma, the supports and the āsana jointly, then the Avyakta-padma and finally Garuḍa. It would appear from verses 29 and 30 that avyakta-padma and the bimbas are often counted together. J.S. assigns to Garuḍa the eleventh position. J.S. 12, 20.

[4] *Spanda*; the first manifestation of the creative energy of God.

[5] See the preceding verses.

Lakṣmī-Nārāyaṇa [1] (existing) as the Śakti and the possessor of Śakti. It is (identical with) the All, It transcends the All, It abides in the All and It regulates the All. It is the concentrated consciousness and bliss and the immortal embodiment of the complete group of the six (divine) attributes. Because It is the inner soul of all existing objects (whether) conscious or unconscious, positive or negative, It is the support of all individual ego-hood (*ahaṃkāra*).

39. For some inconceivable and unaccountable reason, It (Brahman) differentiates so as to be twofold as the Śakti and as the possessor of the Śakti.[2]

40-44. That which is the object of the word I and the idea conveyed by it, is Nārāyaṇa. That which is His absolute self-consciousness, possessing all His characteristics, is Lakṣmī, the Śakti, in the form of (His) state of existence. The same omnipotent Śakti, resorting (by an act of her will) to[3] the possessor of Śakti, like the beam of the moon to the moon, expands (herself into) the world. Formerly, being desirous of expansion as (identical with) Śabdabrahman, she stretched her expanding self through the course of the (created) objects. The first, which is indeed the primary creative state (of the Śakti) as Śabdabrahman, is flawless and consists of the course of kalā [4] and is experienced by those meditating in yoga (*yogasthaiḥ*). He (Śabdabrahman), who contains a steady flow (of sounds), is called the course of sound.

45-46. Resorting to [5] the course of kalā, he (Śabdabrahman) again actively manifests himself through the mantra-course in three absolute forms as described to you before,[6] together with the whole group of Viṣṇu's supreme and brilliant śaktis,[7] who are characterized by blissfulness.

47. The same absolute form extends in the form of the stream (i.e. of the manifested) mantras through the course of the subtle (creation), and that is what I am (going to) relate to you.

---

[1] See ch. II, 10-15.

[2] This is the first awareness of the creative urge in the absolute state and this changes It into duality in which God and His creative urge are recognized as distinct. See ch. II, 9-29.

[3] For *adhiṣṭhāya* (taking as its seat, depending on) compare Bh.G. 4, 6; 15, 9; 18, 14.

[4] See ch. XXII 13-14.

[5] *adhiṣṭhāya*, see above.

[6] See ch. XXXII, 2-16.

[7] Viz. Lakṣmī, Kīrti, Jayā and Māyā.

48-49. Again, that subtle (state of Śakti) exists in three states along the course of the gross (creation). The gross state is that primary form of Lakṣmī and Nārāyaṇa increased by the six (divine) attributes, in which the limbs and other parts of the body (of the divine couple) become distinguished. One should, indeed, find here all the conscious and unconscious (objects).

50. The learned should know that the Vaiṣṇava[1] embodiment of each mantra is its power to bestow particular majesty (on the adept) and to be its presiding deity.

51. The śakti who is effective for the particular function belonging to each particular (mantra) is my own self, the lotus-goddess, who the consciousness belonging to (each) mantra is called the person (*puruṣa*).

52. The feature (of the mantra) which has the capacity for producing (successful) results belongs to prakṛti. The feature of determinateness is the attribute of mahat.[2]

53. The association of the mantras with the ego-sense is the quality belonging to the ego-principle. The mental vision of the mantra is the cause for its sensuous knowledge.

54. Whatever is in the form of sound in the mantra should be considered as existing in the ether. The tremor (*kampa*), which occurs at the advent of the mantra, is said to be the form (characteristic) of the air(-element).

55. The quality of revelation in the mantra during meditation is contained in the fire(-element). The satisfaction derived from the actualization of the mantra should be known as (the quality) of the water(-element).

56-59. The state of existence belonging to the mantra is said to be the quality of the earth(-element).

In this way the holder of the mantra (the adept) should concentrate his thought on the all-pervasiveness of the mantra, (and) by the power of the mantra he will soon become (endowed with) that condition.[3] Thus, by the capacity of one's own consciousness one should visualize the pervading and vibrating Tārikāśakti in front of

---

[1] The mantras bear the form derived from the majesty of Viṣṇu; hence they belong to Viṣṇu and are subordinate to Him.

[2] Mahat is the first principle, which is (also) an effect in the gross creation and, as such, it is the first determinate state of creation.

[3] *tena bhāvena* here refers to the cosmic qualities of the mantra.

(oneself) (spread) over the sky like lightning. (Then) within the lotus of the heart, on the aforesaid (seat of) glowing consciousness,[1] one should meditate on the eternal divine pair inside the luminous form of Tārikā (as) Śabdabrahman. Listen now to the proper method (of such meditation).

60-61. (The adept) should meditate on the flawless Nārāyaṇa who is the repository of integral parts of Sūrya and Anala, who is seated on the seat of consciousness, who possesses large eyes which resemble the lotus, who has yellow garments, who has noble limbs and is adorned with girdle and anklets and dazzling with necklace, ear-rings, armlets, crown and golden bracelets.

62-63. His complexion either follows the (particular) yuga [2] or is (dark) like the blue sky. The deity carries conch-shell and disc, and bestows (on devotees) boon and protection. He is brilliant like a gem and deep like the full ocean. He is glowing like the sun and shining like the moon.

64-66. After having first meditated on Hṛṣīkeśa, possessing a pleasant lotus(like) face, one should first worship the excellent Person (Hṛṣīkeśa) with eighteen (items of) offerings [3] with the Puruṣa-sūkta and the praṇava (mantra). Then, O Vāsava, after worshipping likewise the divine Lord with the Puruṣa-sūkta, the praṇava and (the mantras possessing) twelve letters and eight letters and six letters, and the (mantra beginning with) *jitaṃ te* (etc.),[4] (the adept) should meditate on Lakṣmī as pervading the entire body (of the adept). Then after worshipping her as identified with the destruction of the (body as has been described in the process of bhūtaśuddhi), one should invoke Lakṣmī.

67. Thereafter, with various offerings, as prescribed by the sacred scriptures, one should worship her as seated on the left (side of the) lap of god Viṣṇu.

68. Śakra:—I salute thee, beloved of God, Goddess of the gods and possessor of lotus eyes (eyes like the lotus). Deign to describe the

---

[1] See verses 24-30.

[2] In each of the four ages of the world, the colour of the image of Nārāyaṇa varies. Thus in the *kṛtayuga* it is white; in the *tretāyuga* it is red; in the *dvāparayuga* it is yellow and in the *kaliyuga* it is black. See Sā.S. V, 82-92.

[3] These are described later in verses 77-79.

[4] See ch. XXIV, 67-69. *Oṃ Bhagavate Vāsudevāya namaḥ; Oṃ Nārāyaṇāya namaḥ; Oṃ Viṣṇave namaḥ; Jitaṃ te Puṇḍarīkākṣa, namas te viśvabhāvana, namas te 'stu Hṛṣīkeśa mahāpuruṣa pūrvaja.*

method (of worship with) the Puruṣa-sūkta and the (mantras) such as Tārā.

69-70. Śrī:—God Nārāyaṇa, the possessor of Śrī, the lotus-eyed one, is the unique one. I am Hari's unique Śakti, who performs all (functions). Both of us are seated in the supreme expanse of the void for the purpose of bringing happiness to all souls, the two masters served by the sages (devotees).[1]

71. Once, there arose in our heart the intention that we should find out some means for the deliverance of the living beings.

72-74. The great ocean of Śabdabrahman is the energy which arose from us. Then two nectar-like hymns emerged from the churning of that (ocean of Śabdabrahman): the hymn of Hari, the Person, and similarly the hymn of myself (the Śrī-sūkta). Each of them is related to the śakti of the other, being furnished with each other's sound. The hymn of the unmanifested Person has Nārāyaṇa as its seer. The other, which is called the Śrī-sūkta, has me as the seer.

75. The five mantras starting with the praṇava, have been earlier shown (described to)[2] you. Now listen to the brief (description) of the order in which they are worshipped.

76-79. In the greatest of all hymns belonging to the Person eighteen ṛcs are pronounced One should perform the (offerings of) āvāhana etc., the eigh.. n excellent objects of enjoyment with these (ṛcs). These eighteen (offerings) are considered to be (as follows).[3] Āvāhana (evocation)[4] and the seat, (water) to wash the feet, together with arghya [5] and (water for) washing the mouth, (ingredients for) the bath and the dress along with the scarf and the sacred thread,[6] perfume, flower, lamp, incense, madhuparka,[7] prāpaṇa,[8] betel-leaf with camphor and the offering of a handful of

---

[1] This is obviously inspired by the Vedic statement *tad viṣṇor paramaṃ padaṃ sadā paśyanti sūrayaḥ* etc., Ṛg V. 1, 22, 20. *Vyoman* stands for *padam* (the supreme abode of Viṣṇu).

[2] Namely tāra, jitaṃ, the six-lettered, eight-lettered and the twelve-lettered mantras.

[3] The Puruṣa-sūkta (ṚgV. 10, 90) has 16 stanzas; usually there are 16 upacāras (offerings). See also J. Gonda, Viṣṇuism and Śivaism, London 1970, ch. IV, n. 196.

[4] The entire rite with āvāhana-mudrā etc.

[5] This consists of rice-grain etc. mixed with butter; see ch. XXXVII, 30.

[6] Upavīta is always given to the male deity.

[7] This consists of a concoction of curds, milk, butter and honey.

[8] Offering of foods such as rice etc.

flowers to the feet (of the deity), the dedication of the propitiation of the self and the meditation on the desired state of existence.[1]

80-86. The bright form of Viṣṇu, which is full of all (lucky) signs and consists of the substratum of all, which is supreme and eternal and possesses all the six (divine) attributes in their totality, is said to be the mantra-embodiment. (The faculty) whereby the adepts makes the deity his own through the power of his own self and by the (practice of worship) with the mantras which are identical with consciousness, is called *āvāhana* by experts in the science of mantras. The following act by which Hari spontaneously inhabits the universe (consisting of both) conscious and unconscious with a view to well-being (*svastikṛti*), is (called) *āsana*. The (adept should) think about arghya etc. (as follows): 'The blissful śakti of mine (i.e. Lakṣmī), by which the deity is strengthened, is indeed the arghya, ācamanīya and so on. The existence of all the worlds and of all living beings is based on water and both are comprised of it.[2] This is expressed by the offering of pādya (water etc. to wash the feet). I satisfy the eternal by dividing myself in six ways; as sound etc., i.e. the five external objects, and as the internal ego'.[3]

86-93. One should assiduously propitiate the Lord of the world with the objects of enjoyment relating to the 'complete sight' (*saṃdṛṣṭi*) which are actually collected. Those auspicious (objects), impressive in the forms they take (such as) lamps or vehicles the very sight of which gives rise to pleasure, are regarded as relating to saṃdṛṣṭi. The objects of offering, which bring luck and which always satisfy with a relish, (namely) prāpaṇa, ācamanīya etc. are (called) *ābhyavahārika*. Those objects offered, (such as) pādya, āsana and so on, which are pleasant, pleasantly soft to touch, and which satisfy the Unborn with (the sensation of) touch, are (regarded as) *sāṃsparśika*. Some include the perfumes such as scented air [4] in the category of sāṃsparśika, and others in ābhyavahārika. The remaining processed incenses, the offerings consisting of sound (such

---

[1] The type of liberation envisaged, such as sārūpya etc.

[2] The primordial water is the first manifestation of prakṛti: ch. V, 19-21.

[3] The material objects offered are Śakti herself manifested in two ways, viz. as the external objects such as sound, touch, form, taste and smell; and internally as the ego which should also be offered.

[4] Air circulated by fans and scented with natural scents such as sandal-wood paste etc., while incense produces perfume through being processed.

as) eulogies, instrumental (music), songs etc., and humility, folding of the hands etc. are considered *ābhimānika*. Thus, following the instruction of the sacred scriptures, one should please the Excellent Person with these four types of offerings and with the ṛcs,[1] preceded by the praṇava. At the end of the mantras [2] the offerings (should be) indicated. Thereafter the pleasure (of God, solicited by the adept, should also be mentioned).[3]

94-96. Then having pronounced oṃ, the ṛc and the five mantras beginning with the praṇava, (the adept should pronounce the mantra) "I evoke the Lord of Lakṣmī, the undecaying supreme self, the Lord of the world, the divine Nārāyaṇa, the Person; let Him abide in this image, together with Śrī, through inclination to favour me". Thus (by the power of the mantra) inducing the (deity) within the flowers of his hand to occupy the image (conceived by) himself, he should salute (the image) and after exchange of greetings, the (adept) should gratify Him with the following (formula expressing) inspired thought (*dhī*).

97-99. "Having, O Adorable One, prostrated (myself), I worship (thee) with a seat". Then uttering the (relevant) mantras and pointing out (the objects offered) by pronouncing (the word) 'this' three times and then pronouncing the name (of the object), he should thereafter perform the (rite of) soliciting (God's) pleasure (by saying) "Let God Vāsudeva be pleased".[4] (Next) he should sprinkle the arghya over the seat (*vedi*). This is the process (prescribed for) the rite of (making the) offerings. The indication of the āsana, arghya etc. among the (objects of) offerings should be made according to their gender.[5]

100. (The adept) should perform the āvāhana (rite) with the first (ṛc of the Puruṣa-sūkta), the āsana with the second, arghya should be offered with the third, together with (sprinkling) of water held in a flower on the head.

101. The pādya should be offered with the fourth (ṛc), (and) the

[1] The ṛcs of the Puruṣa-sūkta.

[2] This means the offering of the objects, a topic elaborated further on.

[3] This is also a part of the total offerings.

[4] The offering is made by saying for instance *idam idam idaṃ pādyaṃ prīyatāṃ bhagavān vāsudevaḥ*.

[5] In place of *idam* one should use other suitable forms of the pronoun e.g. *ayaṃ gandhaḥ*, or *iyaṃ puṣpāñjaliḥ* etc.

ācamanīyaka with the fifth. The bathing rites should be performed with the sixth (ṛc), the (rite of) dressing with the seventh.

102. The scarf (should be offered) with the eighth (ṛc), the fragrant unguent with the ninth, the garland and ornaments with the tenth, and the lamp with the eleventh.

103. The fragrant incense (should be offered) with the twelfth (ṛc), madhuparka with the next, prāpaṇa with the fourteenth and anuvāsana [1] with the fifteenth.

104. The salutation [2] is performed with the sixteenth, the handful of flowers (is offered) with the next. The (entire) rite of propitiation (is offered) with the eighteenth (ṛc).

105-109. (The adept) should perform the rite of ācamana (also) in (the offerings of) the bath, the dress and the lamp. The ceremony of arhana (special worship) should be performed before offering madhuparka or rice.[3] Afterwards the rites of tarpaṇa [4] and ācamana are to be performed with two praṇavas. Thus the adept should conduct the ritual of the bath etc., offerings, as befits a king, with the appropriate mantras according to place and time. Following the requirement of place and time (the adept) should always perform the three (ritual acts), saṃkalpa (intention), pradāna (offering) and prīti (propitiation) with regard to each object offered. Thereafter, being concentrated, he should hold his palms together and uttering "Oṃ bhagavan, I worship thee with the seat", he should offer the seat, pronouncing (the relevant) mantra and indicating (it) as "This is the seat".

110-113. (Next) he should fetch water for arghya (respectful reception) etc. saying *"oṃ oṃ priyatāṃ bhagavān vāsudevaḥ"* (and) then place that near the deity. (This sentence should be concluded with the words) *ābhir arghyābhiḥ* etc., (and) similarly (in the case of other offerings with) *ābhiḥ pādyābhiḥ, ābhir ācamanīyābhiḥ, ābhir arhanīyābhiḥ, tarpaṇīyābhiḥ, adbhiḥ, snānīyābhiḥ* and so on. Thus should be pronounced the propitiation and the intention. At the

---

[1] *Anuvāsana* means scented betel leaf and other such items (areca nut and herbs), which are offered for chewing after a meal. These promote digestion and remove the stale taste of food from the mouth.

[2] *Añjali*, joined palms of both the hands.

[3] This is technically known as *prāpaṇa*. *Arhaṇa* is a generic term for worship with offerings associated with reverence, such as the seat, the dress etc.

[4] *Tarpaṇa*, on the other hand, is worship with the offering of water.

moment of offering (one should) pronounce (the formulas) such as *imā arghyāḥ* in accordance with the proper gender. In case of external worship, the practice is to offer arghya etc. first.[1]

114-118. Thus (the adept) should propitiate the Lord of all gods, Janārdana, with six (offerings such as) the garland etc.,[2] or with five or with four or with three or with two or (even) with one, as place and time permit. (Next) he should meditate on Janārdana, the Lord of all gods as being indeed worshipped with me, just as the rising of the moon makes the ocean swell all over.[3] (Thereafter) the (adept) possessed of the mantras should, while concentrating his thought,[4] worship me as prescribed with the sacrifice (called) the layayāga,[5] and consider me as the undefinable, incomparable, infinite, the enduring essence of existence, inseparable from the excellent Person like the fragrance from a flower or the flame from a lamp, and the unique one. Finding out the method of Tārikā [6] worship, he should worship me, the Tārikā, with that.

119-121. Thereafter, the wise (adept) should mentally conceive me as arising from the excellent Person by His will, as the flash of lightning arises out of the cloud. He should then meditate on me as seated on the left (side of the) lap of the Lord of gods. Knowing our identity and that we are essentially soothing (lit. cool),[7] he should surrender himself to Janārdana (uttering) the two supreme ṛcs, which begin with (the word) *hiraṇya*,[8] and also appease her, who is myself, not differentiated (from God) (by uttering) the next two (ṛcs).

[1] That is, instead of saying for instance *oṃ oṃ priyatāṃ bhagavān vāsudeva ābhir ācamanīyābhiḥ*, one should say *oṃ oṃ ābhir ācamanīyābhiḥ priyatāṃ bhagavān vāsudeva*.

[2] Garland, lamp, incense, madhuparka, prāpaṇa and anuvāsana.

[3] This simile is not clear. Probably, as in mental worship, all the ingredients consist of Lakṣmī, so the one who meditates should think that God is indeed being worshipped with Lakṣmī (XXXVI, 147), whose very presence exalts God.

[4] For *bhāvayan* see L. Silburn, Instant et cause, Paris 1955, p. 308 ff.

[5] Conceiving the mantra as God with all His marks and adornments, weapons and secondary manifestations incorporated, one should worship Him with the relevant basic mantras, flowers and unguents. This is called *layayāga*. See J.S. 12, 76-81.

[6] See ch. XLII in extenso.

[7] i.e. that we are perfectly free from terrifying emotions.

[8] *Hiranyavarṇām* and *tām ma ā vaha*; these mantras are in the Śrī-Sūkta, st. 1 and 2.

122-131. Conceiving me with (visionary) thought as being gracious, (the adept) should surrender (himself) to me (uttering) the fifth (ṛc).[1] Fully cognizant of the power of Tārikā as mentioned before, O lord of gods, while pronouncing the mantra called āvāhana accompanied by (the practice of) pūraka [2] and showing the (relevant) hand-posture,[3] (the adept) should evoke me from the deity,[4] (envisaging me) as seated on the lap of the supreme self and always with a gracious face and possessing all (auspicious) marks. (I as Tārikā) possess (a complexion) like the inside of a lotus, am beautiful and have large black eyes, am decorated with glittering golden bracelets, armlets, necklace and ear-rings, and possess a deep navel, lean belly adorned with the three lines [5] (and) hard, firm, high, full, rounded and close-set breasts. (I possess) locks like moving swarms of black bees, rosy lips like the bimba,[6] teeth like rows of pearls, the shining mark on the forehead resembling a half-moon, and am endowed with all (auspicious) signs, black curls, hands in the posture of granting favours and holding a lotus [7] and am adorned with a lotus-garland. (I am) embraced by Viṣṇu with His left hand and my lotus-hand is placed on His shoulder; with the left arm (I) carry a blossom of the celestial flower.[8] (My Tārikā form) may otherwise hold the hands in the posture of granting boons and protection or may carry the noose and the goad, (whilst I am) reclined in the half-svastika position and adorned with a brilliant diadem. Having meditated on me, the eternal mantra form, he (the adept) should visualize me (as such).

132-134. Then again, as before, the adept should perform the nyāsa of the body without performing the nyāsa of the hands, accompanied by the basic mantra and other mantras. (Then he

[1] The fifth ṛc of the Śrī-sūkta.

[2] A part of the prāṇāyāma when deep breath is inhaled. See Ahi.S. 32, 51-55.

[3] See ch. XXXIV, 85.

[4] It is not clear why the ablative is used. Probably to mean "from within the image"

[5] Three horizontal shallow lines across the lower part of the abdomen are a sign of perfection in the female body.

[6] This fruit of the plant Momordica Monadelpha is a common simile for the lips because of its deep rose colour covered by a papery thin transparent skin.

[7] One hand is held in the said posture, while the other is holding the lotus.

[8] Most probably the pārijāta is meant here, as nothing has yet been said about the tulsi plant or about the branch of bilva (Aegle Marmelos).

should offer) mentally, flowers, arghya, a lamp, incense, garlands, unguents; then (he should furthermore) respectfully (offer) water for washing the feet and sipping; he should salute, or prostrate (himself)[1] mentally (uttering) the word *jaya* (victory be unto thee), and thereafter he should show the hand postures which have already been described to you.[2]

135. (He should then repeat the following words:) "Welcome to thee, lotus-eyed one. O Ambujā, deign to remain close to me, (and) accept the mental worship that has been properly conceived."

136. After obtaining my permission, he should perform the mental sacrifice, with offerings created by a constructive (realizing) mental impulse [3] and with pavitras [4] which relate to supreme truth.

137-139. Thereafter the proficient (adept: *sunişņāta*) should worship me with external rites which are to be described at length further on. Having performed (the rite) with offerings of the sāṃsparśika etc. (categories) till the prāpaṇa, he should then remember his preceptor who induced (him to perform this rite), be he alive or dead, and the knower of the mantra should offer him all his wealth and should mentally give a portion of the prāpaṇa to those alive and those dead, in due proportion.[5]

140-141. (The adept) should recall to (mind) all (my) subordinate (deities) who will be described in detail (later).[6] (Bearing) these (in his mind) as lying dormant in me—the source—just as trees lie dormant in the seeds, he should perform the sacrifice of dissolution (*laya-yāga*)[7] together with the application of their individual mantras.

142-145. Having produced the fire (consisting of) consciousness by rubbing the (pieces of) wood for kindling [8] (which consist of) meditation, (and) after consecrating it with the consecratory (procedures) [9] and illuminated thought (*dhī*) as described (later on),

[1] *aṣṭāṅgapraṇāma* is the prostrating of oneself in such a way that eight parts of the body touch the ground.

[2] See ch. XXXIV, 85.

[3] For *saṃkalpa* see Silburn, o.c., p. 202 f.

[4] This is a tuft of darbha grass with three blades bunched together with two loops. Two of these grass heads remain in the plate containing the ceremonial offerings; ch. XL, 54.

[5] These verses are not clear to me.

[6] See ch. XXXVII, 41-74.

[7] See ch. XXXVIII, 14-27.

[8] A piece of wood taken from the Ficus Religiosa or Premna Spinosa.

[9] *saṃskāraiḥ*: *vaiṣṇavīkaraṇaprakriyā*; see p. 257 f. infra.

the wise (adept) should in that triangular fire, consisting of the three guṇas (and) which exists in the location (support: *ādhāra*) of the three guṇas, perform the (mental) sacrifice which brings the wealth of liberation. (He should perform it) in the fire-place (*mahānasa*).[1] This fire of Viṣṇu having been placed in the container of that which possesses the three characteristics,[2] (the adept) should bring the purified butter (consisting of) Brahman, distilled from the (mantra of) Tārikā, from the atmosphere (which is) the seat of nāda and enter (into his body) through the (passage of) the cavity of the crown (*brahmarandhra*). Then, after purifying the (said) butter and having approached the abode of the fire, in accordance with the authoritative treatises he should perform all the prescribed rites with that sacrificial butter.[3]

146. At the end of the sacrifice, the wise (adept) whose intention it is (to perform) that (rite) should, with illuminated thought which will be described later and in the right frame of mind, surrender to me the mental rites (of the sacrifice).

147. The whole order of (successive rites) prescribed for the performance of the external (sacrifice) is applicable to this mental (sacrifice). But one should perform that carefully with all the requisites which are identical with me.[4]

148. This mental sacrifice, which is the destruction of all evils and which brings about all (expected) results, has now (been) described. (The adept) should perform this sacrifice till the end of his life.

149. After carefully preparing all the requisites pervaded by me, (the adept) should perform the external sacrifice to mitigate the impressions (of the mind) arising from external objects.

150. Thus, O Śakra, my internal sacrifice has been told to you. Listen now to the exact description of the nature of the external sacrifice, which I am about to give.

---

[1] This seems to be a highly cryptic description of the entire process of the Kundalinī-Yoga. The fire-place, or sacrificial pit, is the circle of the navel, on which the adept should fix his concentration in order to wake up his individual śakti which abides there contracted and asleep. See J.S. 12, 115 Ahi.S. 32, 11-12 'triangular fire' refers to the śakti-yantra.

[2] The "locus" of the three guṇas is prakṛti. The lotus of the heart is the container of prakṛti, bearing the characteristics of the three guṇas.

[3] Brahman or Śabdabrahman, the pure Śakti distilled from the Tārikā.

[4] The objects of internal sacrifice are all products of thought. Hence they are conceived of as the manifestations of Śakti herself.

CHAPTER THIRTY-SEVEN

EXTERNAL SACRIFICE (CONSTRUCTION OF THE PLATFORM FOR WORSHIP; MAṆḌALA OF NINE LOTUSES)

1. The external sacrifice is considered to be that in which I am worshipped (by the adept) with offerings consisting of (external) objects (of enjoyment), objects which are outside the vedi etc. and are looked at by my consecration.[1]

2-3. Impressions (*vāsanā*[2]) are said to be of two types according to whether they are produced by external (causes) or internal (causes). The excellent mental sacrifice removes all internal (impressions caused by) the external (causes), while the external sacrifice is prescribed for purification (eradication) of the 'stock' of impressions (caused by) the external (causes).

4-7. Having found the site [3] according to the (direction) of the sacred texts, one should (first) construct a pavilion there. Then, one should build a platform at the centre of it (*brahmasthāna*), possessed of all good qualities. One should then lay a thread, wholly white with its end turned eastward and measuring either eight hands,[4] half that length, or half of that (half) length, over the centre of the platform. (The line WE in diagram I). Marking off three equidistant points over it (namely), on the centre (of the line, i.e. point Y) and on the centre (points) of the two sides (WY and YE, namely points X and Z), one should then nail five wooden

---

[1] *madbhāvanekṣitaiḥ* = *madātmanā bhāvitaiḥ* ("promoted, or consecrated by my essence, by means of a gaze").

[2] Residues of deeds done remaining as mental deposits unconsciously in the mind.

[3] The topic about the ground, suitable for worship is described in the Hayaśīrṣa Pāñcarātra, ch. 5, 1-53. One might consult also the well-known handbooks on architecture, temple building and maṇḍalas.

[4] The exact measurement of a hasta is twenty-four fingers. Eight atoms make a *rathareṇu*, eight rathareṇus make a *trasareṇu*, eight of these make a *bālāgra*, eight bālāgras make a *likṣā*, eight of these make a *yūkā* and eight yūkās make one *yava*, while eight yavas make one *aṅgula* (finger). Ibid., 7, 2-5. The thread is smeared with white chalk so that when it is laid on the ground, a white line is imprinted on the ground.

DIAGRAM I

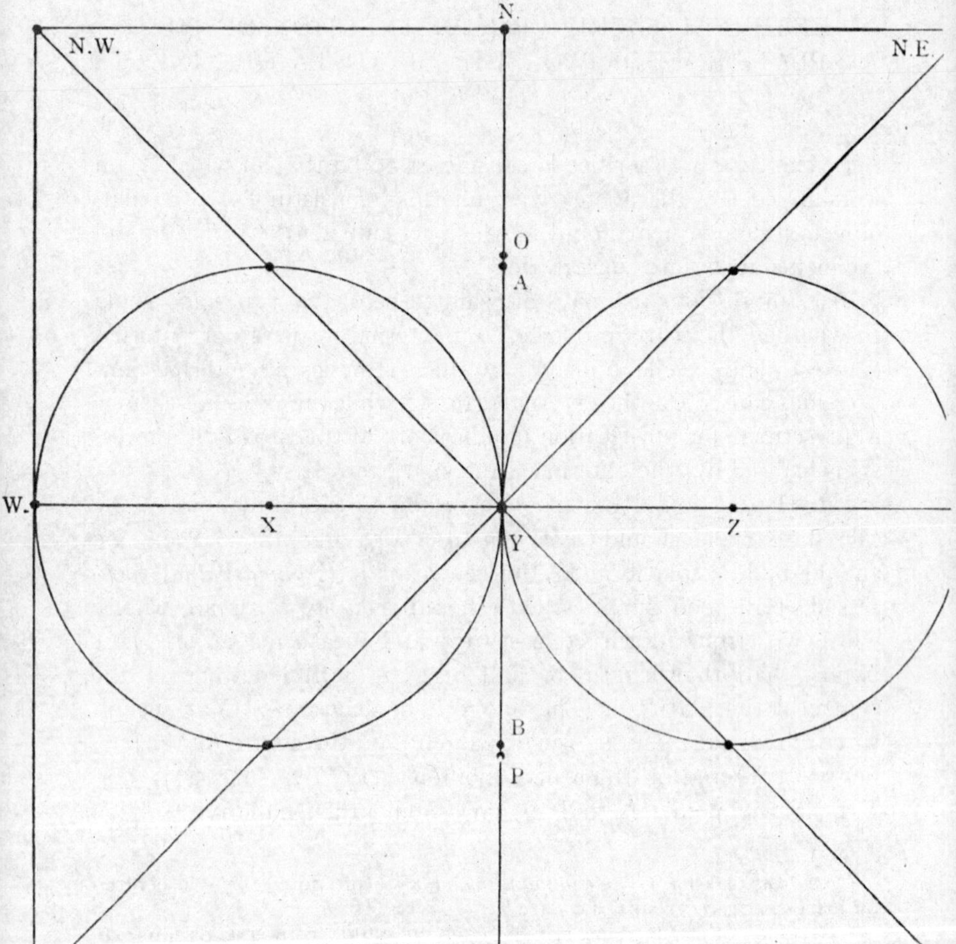

pegs [1] at the two ends (W and E) and the three middle points (of the first mentioned line, namely WXYZE). Since the centres of the two halves of (the main line) are determined by the two pegs standing on the two (points X and Z) next to the end points (W and E, through the equidistant points X, Y and Z), one should place the foot of a measuring compass [2] successively on the two centres (X and Z) and draw two (successive) circles (with it) [3] and thus determine the exact centre of (the first mentioned) line (WXYZE).

8-13. Further, (placing the foot of the compass) on the two above mentioned centres (X respective Z and taking a radius longer than the distance XY), one should draw two circles (the unmarked X and Z circles in the first diagram) and mark two points on the left and right (side of the centre Y, where the circles intersect each other, namely the points O and P in diagram I).[4] Then one should ascertain the centre points (A and B of the lines NOY and YPS, drawn perpendicular to the line WXYZE, through its centre, and both the lines measuring exactly the same), on the left and right side of the centre (Y).[5] Since the centres of the lines (NY and YS) are thus determined, one should now place the (foot of) the compass (first) on the point (Z) at the east (of the centre Y) and (draw an arc with an arbitrary radius at the south-east corner of the platform) and then on the point B at the south of (Y) and draw another (arc at the same corner with the same radius as to the first arc, intersecting it at the point SE, which determines) the south-east corner of the centre (Y). Similarly, the north-east corner of the

---

[1] *Śaṅku* is a peg, nail or gnomon. See P.K. Acharya, Mānasāra, An Encyclopaedia of Hindu Architecture, vol. VII, Oxford 1946, pp. 476-482.

[2] The same Sanskrit word is sometimes used for the pin of a gnomon or measuring compass. The change of the verb serves as a clue to determine the meaning of *śaṅku*.

[3] Viz. the X and Z circles, see diagram I. The radius of the circle is one fourth of the length of the line that is the distance between any two adjacent pegs.

[4] The method followed is obviously that of drawing a perpendicular on the centre of a given line.

[5] This means, on the north and south sides of the first line. The centre points are determined by ascertaining three equidistant points on the line NOYPS see diagram; I. It is to be noted that in the tradition of Hindu temple architecture the exact direction of the east and the west is determined by a gnomon. This process of determining these directions is known as *apacchāyānirṇaya*. Cf. Hayaśīrṣa Pāñcarātrā, ch. 8; Pau. S., ch. 3 and P.K. Acharya, o.c., vol. VII, pp. 476-482.

DIAGRAM II

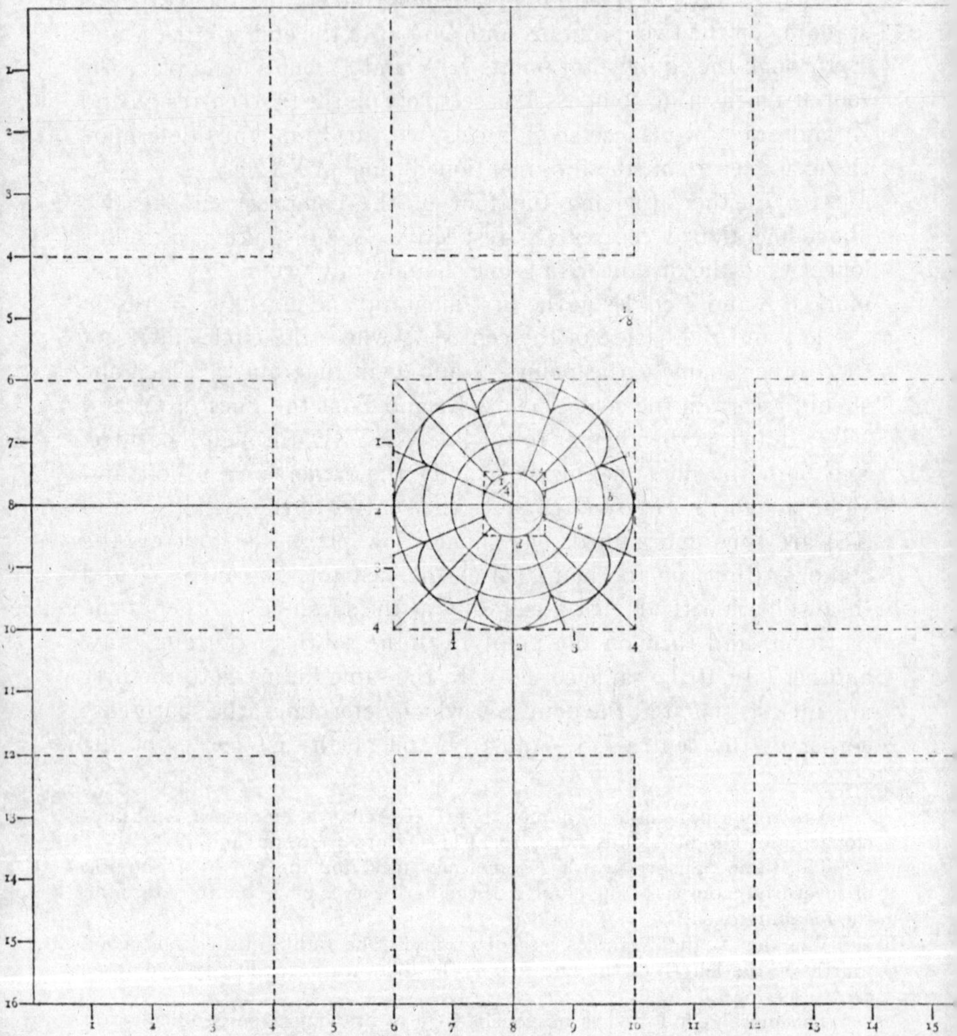

centre point should be ascertained in this way, (only replacing the southern point B) by the northern point (A). The other two corners, namely the south-west and the north-west, should be determined by drawing successive pairs of (intersecting) arcs as (shown) before, (one at each of the corners, using the points B and X and A and X respectively as centres and keeping the same radius). In order to indicate the area clearly, one should draw four boundary lines (NE-E-SE; SE-S-SW; SW-W-NW; and NW-N-NE of diagram I) on four sides (namely the east, the south, the west and the north).

After dividing the area into sixteen parts (squares),[1] (the adept) should draw nine lotuses (one on the area covered by the) four squares at the centre (of the area) and (one in each of) the directions of East etc. and the four corners (NE etc., vide diagram II).

14-15. Now listen about how to draw the eight-petalled central lotus. Four circles should be drawn on the central area in such a way, that one eighth (part of the entire area of the squares) is left out. (These circles are drawn to help the drawing of) the pericarp, d, the filaments, c, the base of the petals, b, and their sections, a, (all of these belonging to the central lotus) respectively (see diagram II). Beyond these (circles) a section measuring one fourth of the (area) should be left empty.[2]

16. Within (that encircled area for the drawing of) the (central) lotus, (the adept) should draw eight lines, (four) in the (four) cardinal and (four) in the (four) intermediary directions. Between these lines he should draw eight more lines (diagram II).

17-19. He should then draw eight petals to accord with the (cardinal and intermediary) directions with the aid of the thread attached to the (circle drawn) for the specification of the bases of the petals.[3] (These) simple and well-drawn lines are called *vyomarekhās*.[4] The other eight lotuses are drawn in the same way. This enchanting great square diagram of nine auspicious lotuses should possess gates on the outside together with śobhās and the koṇas and

[1] See diagram II, the numbers 1-16 on the two hands of the outer square indicates these squares. The J.S. clearly describes these as squares. J.S. 13, 24.

[2] This is the length of the radius of the first and the smallest of the four circles, d, which is drawn on the centre; see diagram II.

[3] According to the J.S. a compass is used to outline the petals by drawing semicircles, whereby the foot of the compass is placed on the circle that specifies the bases of the petals of the lotus: J.S. 13, 31.

[4] The meaning of this word is vague. It may imply curved lines, which tends to confirm the notion of semicircles for petals.

(the lotus should have) four colours so that the pericarp etc. are distinguishable.[1]

20-23. When for some reason worshipping (the deity), the holder of the mantra should, on a flat surface (*prastara*) made of flowers, or on (one made of) a piece of pure (unwashed, i.e. new, *ahata*),[2] wholly white, incensed and perfumed [3] cloth, or on a besmeared level sand-platform (*sthaṇḍila*), recall to his mind the nine lotuses (of the maṇḍala). In conformity with the prescripts of the scripture (he may) also carve an image of the deity of his meditation. He may (even) propitiate (the deity) in a pitcher (i.e. instead of an image), made of gold or silver etc. but avoiding metals such as iron etc.[4] which contains curds (or) milk (or) water, with any of the recommended (auspicious) leaves arranged on it and decorated with cloth and silks. The noblest among those who possess knowledge of the mantras should (in all cases) worship the (maṇḍala of) nine lotuses, visualizing it there.

24-25. In the pitcher, or in the temple, or in the image-form, (or) wherever the holder of the mantra performs the worship, he should (first) meditate on the (maṇḍala of) nine lotuses, which contains the whole world and represents the exalted home of all the gods, which encompasses all (other) loci and is the paramount abode. He should then (worship) by offering arghya etc., uttering (each time) the sounds of the name of Tārikā together with namaḥ.

26-29. Four pots, made of metals such as gold etc. and filled with purified water, with scent, garlands, jewels, herbs and water-soaked kuśa-grass are to be set in the four corners of the pedestal, facing the image. These should be arranged from south-west to south-east in the order of arghya, ācamanīya, pādya and snānīya [5] respectively, the adept reciting the relevant mantras whilst arranging them. (First) *oṃ*, then the name of the offering inserted in (the mantra) and then (the word) *kalpayāmi* ('I arrange'). In the centre

---

[1] See diagram No. III for the meaning of śobhā and koṇa. The J.S. gives a more detailed description of the maṇḍala and the scheme of colours: J.S. 13, 31-40.

[2] Cf. Vācaspatyam, vol. I, p. 576.

[3] perfumed with fragrances other than incense.

[4] Besides the two precious metals J.S. recommends copper and clay for the sacred pitcher. But there again, iron and other baser alloys such as bell-metal etc. are prohibited.

[5] See ch. XXXVI, 77-78.

one should set a pot containing arghya, which is composed of various ingredients.[1]

30. White mustard seed (*siddhārthaka*), sesame seed, panic grass, barley grains and white rice-grains mixed with water, milk and fruits are said to be the ingredients of arghya.

31. Filling (one) pot (with arghya) accompanied by (the utterance of) Tārikā in the material form of flowing nectar, (the adept) should meditate on the cycle of mantras in that (pot), the container of the Undivided (the unanalysed One).

32. (Immediately after), the Undivided (mantra-form), as existing within the (first) arghya, should be worshipped first with a flower etc. That (arghya) should be conceived (*bhāvanīya*) as being identical with the container of Agni and Soma.[2]

33-34. This is the first sacrament.[3] Now listen to the second one. (The adept) should burn that (offering) with the tremendous multitude of the sun's rays and then should extinguish (that fire) of the burnt (offering) with the cool rays of the full moon. He should (then) fill it with the waves of the nectar-ocean of Brahman's bliss.[4]

35. Having consecrated it with all the chief mantras such as Tārikā etc. he should take the water (of arghya) and pour it from that (vessel) into another bowl.

36. Such a method of (performing a) sacrament is prescribed for each bowl. One should by this (performance) bring prosperity and gratification to the bowls.[5]

37-38. (After placing the bowl of arghya), one should make the hand posture of the wish-yielding (cow) together with her own mantra called Surabhi.[6] After having meditated on Surabhi[7] who

---

[1] There are two readings of this word, viz. *anekārthaṃ* and *anekāṅkaṃ*. The latter must be rejected since it makes no sense in the present context. But J.S. records this as *anekāṅgaṃ*, which has more bearing here, and possibly *anekāṅkaṃ* is a corruption of that word.

[2] See ch. XXIX, 12.

[3] Here identification of the receptacle used for such sacraments is ambiguous, since the word dvitīya leads to an expectation for more. J.S. makes clear that the two sacraments are for the two bowls of arghya which meaning is preferable here.

[4] The process is the same as that for purification of the ground. See XXXV, 21-22.

[5] This verse seems irrelevant here and breaks up the continuity of the discourse.

[6] See ch. XXXIII, 10 for the Surabhi-mantra and ch. XXXIV, 87-89 for the Surabhi-mudrā.

[7] The mythical wish-yielding cow, daughter of Dakṣa, wife of Kaśyapa

resembles the Snow Mountain in colour and dwells at the place of the substratumless (Brahman),[1] one should attentively show her (Surabhi) the hand gesture with one's two hands anointed with perfume, imitating the udder (of that cow).

39. After sprinkling the maṇḍala and the pavilion with the water from the bowl of arghya, (the adept) should strike [2] all the ingredients of the sacrifice with the mantra of the weapon (*astra*).[3]

40-44. Thereafter, he should wash them with the basic (mantra). (Thus) these (ingredients) become (sacrificial) offerings. Then, after saluting Viṣṇu, he should worship the lotus goddess, seated on His (= Viṣṇu's) lap, by offering loose flowers etc. together with the basic mantra. Afterwards, taking the vessels containing arghya, the flowers, the incense, the unguents, the lamp and the food-offerings, he should perform the worship at the gate.

At the threshold of the gate outside the entrance in the middle, (the adept) should worship the lord of the area, envisaged as standing on that ground, by resort to meditation and other (parts of the worship). One should meditate on the lord of the ground who always keeps his left hand clenched, who is as (dark as) the inky cloud, carries a staff in his hand and has a huge body. He should also show (the deity) the (appropriate) hand posture.[4] This is the order for performing (the various rites) in all other cases (of worship).

45. He should worship Lakṣmī, placed on the door at the top door-frame; Lakṣmī, who holds the lotus in her hand and who is standing on the lotuses.

46. (He should also worship) Caṇḍa and Pracaṇḍa on the outer sides of the bottom of the door-frame facing south and north, and Jaya and Vijaya, on the inner sides (of the door-frame also facing south and north).[5]

---

and mother of all cattle and animals with cloven hoofs. See the Bhā.P., I, 17, 9; VI, 6, 26-27.

[1] For the meaning of *pada* see J. Gonda, The concept of a personal God in ancient Indian religious thought, Studia missionalia 17, Rome 1968, p. 121.

[2] *tāḍayet*: this is a form of purification; see H. Brunner-Lachaux, Somaśambhupaddhati, Pondicherry 1963, p. 100.

[3] See ch. XXXIII, 5-10.

[4] See ch. XXXIV, 57-58. The Viśvamitra Saṃhitā gives almost the same description.

[5] Jaya and Vijaya are the traditional gate-keepers of Vaikuṇṭha in the mythologies: Bhā.P. III, 16, 2 and 26-37; VIII, 21, 16. There are four pairs of chief gatekeepers in the Viṣṇu pantheon: Caṇḍa and Pracaṇḍa; Jaya

47-48. All these (Viṣṇu's gate-keepers) are known to possess four arms. They hold in their hands the mace, the disc as well as the conch-shell and they are of great strength. They frighten the non-devotees and are ever ready to destroy all evil. They should be worshipped and meditated upon in these forms and (their) hand-postures [1] should also be shown.

49-51. From left to right across the middle of the two side frames, (the adept) should then worship Gaṅgā and Yamunā, who bear in their hands pitchers containing holy water, and are pretty in their pristine youth, of white complexion and smiling countenance. Gaṅgā should be meditated upon as gracious and with a face (as beautiful) as the full moon. The river Yamunā should also be (regarded) as (possessing) similar (form), (only) she is (dark) as an inky cloud.

52-53. Following the same order [2] (the adept) should worship with arghya, flower etc. the two lords of the treasures, called Śaṅkha and Padma, who stand on the inner side of the door. Those two lords of the treasures are envisaged as being seated on the jewel-box. They are fat-bellied, tawny-eyed, two-armed and full of divinity.

54-55. Having completed the worship of the door, (the adept) should take some flowers, and holding them in front with his thumb, index and middle finger, whilst uttering the mantra of the weapon, should recall (to mind) the disc as existing on that (flower). This should be consecrated with (its) mantra.

56-57. This sharp-spoked, fire-formed, fire- and thunder-showering destroyer of all hindrances should be placed within the sacrificial chamber. Then (the adept) should point the index finger of his right hand straight upwards and recalling that lightning brilliance (of the disc), while reciting the mantra of the tuft of hair, he should enter the sacrificial chamber, twirling that (raised index finger).[3]

58-59. He should then sprinkle his own seat with water from the vessel containing arghya, and at the same time (recite) the astra-mantra. He should worship there the seats composed of mantras

---

and Vijaya; Dhāṭā and Vidhātā; and Bhadra and Subhadra. H. D. Smith, o.c. pp. 233-234.

[1] See ch. XXXIV, 60-62.

[2] The order of Gaṅgā and Yamunā, namely from left to right.

[3] This symbolizes the whirling of the disc.

such as ādhāraśakti etc.,[1] and should also demonstrate with each its respective hand posture.[2] Then, sitting down on that (seat), he should worship the lord of the gods, who dwells in his heart.

60-61. (Thereafter) he should (mentally) bring to his eyes that majestic state of the couple, which is called Lakṣmī-Nārāyaṇa, the eternal supreme dweller of the heart and identifying himself with that (he) should view all (the ingredients of the worship)[3] with a steady gaze.

61-62. Wherever (the adept) wishes to perform the worship, whether in the pavilion or on a pedestal, he should (first) worship the seats (namely) ādhāraśakti [4] etc. with arghya, flowers and so on. Afterwards, he should worship dharma etc.[5] appearing in their respective directions.

63. Then after visualizing in meditation (the containers), (viz.) the lotus, the orbs [6] of the sun etc. ending with the seat of spiritual realization (*bhāvāsana*), successively situated one above the other, one should worship them with (offerings of) flowers etc.

64-67. The area of the maṇḍala, extending from the right of the deity who is in the maṇḍala to (the location) of the yugas such as kṛta etc., should be divided into seven sections from north-west to north-east. In the first (section) the adept should worship Gaṇeśa [7] seated in the posture of the lotus [8] on the filaments and petals of the lotus (of the maṇḍala), and holding with his two upper hands the rosary (of eleocarpus seeds) and the axe, whereas the two main

---

[1] See ch. XXXVI, 2-12.

[2] See ch. XXXIV, 39-48.

[3] This process of gazing at the objects of enjoyment offered to the deity makes them identified with the great divine couple. This is known as the rite of *īkṣaṇa*, while the sprinkling of water from the bowl of arghya is called *prokṣaṇa*. See J.S. 13, 87-89. The significance of gazing is extensively discussed by J. Gonda in his monograph 'Eye and Gaze in the Veda', Amsterdam 1969.

[4] This is necessary in order to identify the material seat of the image with the spiritual seat, meditated upon, and the external worship becomes entirely symbolic of the spiritual worship through meditation.

[5] See ch. XXXVI, 13-19.

[6] See ch. XXXVI, 20-31.

[7] This text is obscure and perhaps corrupt. J.S. describes a square to the left of the maṇḍala, which falls outside the area of the deity's main seat and beyond the position of the corner seat-supports such as kṛta etc. J.S. 13, 95-97.

[8] See the Ahi. S. 31, 34.

hands are held in the gesture of granting boons and protection. Or, these hands held in the posture of granting boons and protection may also be envisaged in the pose of discourse (*vyākhyā*) by joining the index finger to the thumb.

68-72. The wise should place the plump and pendulous-bellied, stout elephant-headed (deity) with only one tusk along with the six aṅga(-mantras) on the six filaments of the lotus, while reciting his (= Gaṇeśa's) own mantra and making the appropriate hand gestures and offerings of flowers etc.[1]

The wise next worship goddess Vāgīśvarī with her personal mantra. She is envisaged as seated on the white lotus within the orbs of the sun, the moon and fire, unfettered by any limitation whatsoever, yet assuming embodiment; she is the first manifestation of my power consisting of sound. She is white, has two eyes and two arms holding the conch-shell and the lotus, and is clad in garments and ornaments as (white) as the surging waves of nectar.

Thereafter (the adept) should worship his own preceptor and his preceptor's preceptor. These (should be envisaged) according to those forms which are well known in the world.

73. After that, (the adept) should worship his (= the preceptor's preceptor's) preceptor, the exalted one (*parameṣṭhin*).

Then the pitaras are to be worshipped as bodiless, devoid of form.

74. Thereafter he should worship the successful worshippers who preceded him (*ādisiddhas*), who are engaged in meditating on God and are calm in (appearance), with eyes closed, have auspicious limbs and who are full of excessive power.

75. Having successively obtained the permission (of these deities), he should then invoke and worship me envisaged as being seated on the lap of the highest god. O Sureśvara, now listen to the particulars about the formalities of (worship).

[1] See ch. XXXIII, 61-62 and ch. XXXIV, 64-68.

CHAPTER THIRTY-EIGHT

EXTERNAL WORSHIP. FURTHER DETAILS WITH A DESCRIPTION OF SOME LESSER DEITIES

1. Nārāyaṇa is the unique God possessing the form of the full sixfold attributes. I am His great Śakti, (His) eternal selfconsciousness.

2. I, the above (Śakti), underwent embodiment with the intention of obliging my worshippers. Listen (now) to a detailed description of the rites prescribed for worshipping me, who am seated on the lap of the supreme God.

3-4. After obtaining permission from Gaṇeśa etc.,[1] (the adept) should invoke (the Śakti) existing within his own heart.[2] He should (then) meditate on the supreme soul, which is worshipped (by the adept) in the internal (or spiritual) worship (*antaryāga*), which possesses all the unmanifested (*stimita*, motionless) six attributes in their entirety and which is the container of myself, Śakti. This (Supreme God) tāraka (as He is called in His mantric form)[3] should be pronounced thrice and then Tārikā [4] should be uttered thrice.[5]

5. He should (then) invoke the lotus-eyed Person, possessing a strong and noble (form) with four arms, by uttering the mantra in masculine gender (*praṇava*).

6-9. Following the method of recaka,[6] (the adept) should invoke the lord of Lakṣmī, coexistent with the divine Śakti, to descend from the seat of anāhata,[7] by using the intermediary (duct) between

---

[1] See the previous chapter, verses 65-75.

[2] This is the inner principle, known as *jīva-śakti*, or *anugraha-śakti*. See ch. XIII, 2-15 and 24-27.

[3] oṃ is the māntric form of the supreme God and utterance of the mantra ensures the presence of the deity.

[4] Here also the utterance of *hrīṃ* ensures the presence of the deity.

[5] *oṃ oṃ oṃ, hrīṃ hrīṃ hrīṃ.*

[6] Recaka is the third part of prāṇāyāma, when air is exhaled slowly over a period of sixteen smallest units of time (*ṣoḍaśa-mātrā*). This can be counted by slowly tracing a circle around the left knee-cap with the left hand. The exhalation is done either through the iḍā duct or through the piṅgalā duct. The first runs from the left nostril to the complex of ducts near the navel, the other runs from the right nostril to that complex. See the Ahi.S. 32, 8-29 and 32, 44; 51-55.

[7] The twelve-petalled lotus at the heart.

the two (other ducts) Agni and Soma [1] which has its outlet within the nose (of the adept), or he may visualize the resplendent (God) as (already) freed (from his heart), like a flash of lightning bursting out of a cloud and then subsiding into complete tranquility (afterwards).[2] He should next envisage Him as existent in the handful of flowers (to be offered) and enthroned on the spiritual seat (*bhāvāsana*) whereafter he should perform the rite of nyāsa.[3] The rite (of nyāsa) should be duly performed step by step in his (= the adept's) mind accompanied by the four hand postures, saṃnidhi, saṃnirodha, saṃstambhana and sthāpana.

10-11. The process of saṃnidhi (proximity) is (the position) made by turning the hands upwards with fingers pressed tightly together, and placing the thumb of each (hand) over its own little finger. When in the same (gesture) (instead of the little finger) the ring-finger and the middle-finger are (successively) covered (by the thumbs), the two (hand gestures) of saṃstambha and saṃnirodha are (respectively) formed.

12-15. O Śakra, the four fingers of each hand should be clenched (and then) the two thumbs (of both hands) are placed diagonally, across them (= fingers). This completes the posture of saṃsthāpana. Having made these hand postures accompanied by the utterance of the mantra of Tārā etc., one should continue to meditate on Hari as being present (having arisen there) until the offering of pādya and arghya has been completed. (Also) while offering the bath, the ornaments, the garment and the garland, or in the case of other (types) of worship (*bhogayāga*), where other objects appropriate to that (particular ritual) are offered, one should visualize Hari as possessing the form stipulated by the sacred scriptures, and as being full of compassion and indulgence.

16-19. The absolute Śakti consisting of myself, who is already associated with the image and exists in its form, should as in the

[1] The duct piṅgalā and the duct iḍā, respectively. See Ahi.S. 32, 30. The intermediary duct is suṣumṇā, the most important duct for the yogins, since it reaches the Brahmarandhra and is the most effective means of lifting the kuṇḍalinīśakti from the complex of ducts. See Ahi.S. 32, 11-12. Cf. Svātmārāma, Haṭha Yoga Pradīpikā 3, 3.

[2] *Yad vā*: these two words pose some difficulty in following the ritual, but since J.S. regards the process as a continuous one, I too have preferred to do so.

[3] The ritual prescribed for placing Viṣṇu in each ingredient of the worship.

case of Hari also be visualized as entering the objects of enjoyment offered (to the deity). (The adept should then continue) the worship of the invoked (deity) by throwing a full handful of flowers mixed with arghya. (Then), with head lowered and hands clasped over his head, he should slowly worship (the deity) by reciting the two mantras of tāra and Tārā together with namas.[1] (Thereafter) he should successively offer the deity flowers, arghya, incense and unguent accompanied by the mūlamantra etc., either briefly or elaborately as the time permits.

20-21. (And then) he should, reciting the mantra of Tārā, worship the formless and peerless Śakti[2] pervading every part of the (deity's) body. After that, with their own mantra he should worship the deities of the weapon and of the ornaments as well as the śaktis etc. in their relevant positions on the (deity's) body. This is called the *layayāga*, the great fulfiller of all desires.

22-25. Thereafter with my aforesaid mantra the intelligent (adept) should invoke me as distinguishable from the body of Lord Viṣṇu, which is totally infused with (my) Śakti. (I,) the undefinable and unparalleled goddess, who am all-powerful, divine and unique, whose highly luminous body is composed of the six (divine) attributes, correspond with Viṣṇu in every respect, at all times and in all places. I have voluntarily accepted embodiment out of compassion (and) in order to benefit the adept. Without abandoning God's form, I nevertheless remain separate (from God's body).[3] After this, the wise (adept) should perform the successive rites that are enumerated for proper observance of the rite of invocation.

26. He should then meditate on my dear self as seated on Viṣṇu's left thigh. I have already described how my body should be visualized in meditation.[4]

27-28. After that, continuing to follow the process of dissolution, (the adept) should worship the śakti etc. in me (i.e. the subordinate deities of my retinue), envisaging them as gradually emerging from me like sparks from the blazing fire.[5]

---

[1] *oṃ hrīṃ namaḥ.*

[2] The spelling is irregular.

[3] This duality in perfect unity is the central postulate of the system.

[4] See ch. XXXVI, 124-131.

[5] The purport of this simile is to emphasize the fact that the minor deities belonging to the main deity's retinue are components of the one, absolute deity.

Now listen to how each (subordinate deity) is placed on the site of worship (*bhogasthāna*).[1]

29. (The adept) should envisage the lotus-eyed Person and the lotus-goddess seated on His lap as (both) occupying the seat of spiritual realization (*bhāvāsana*)[2] situated in the pericarp of the central lotus (of the maṇḍala).

30-34. Lakṣmī [3] should be visualized on the pericarp of the lotus to the east (of the central lotus), emanating from her [4] body which possesses two arms and two eyes and wears attractive earrings, a white wreath and robe. She is adorned with necklaces, armlets and all auspicious marks; she has firm and high breasts; wide eyes resembling full-blown lotuses; a face lit up with a charming smile; lovely tresses resembling a swarm of bees in flight; she has a bright mark on her forehead, lips that are red (and soft) like petals; her hair is black and curly; her teeth are like rows of pearls. She is seated in the lotus posture, holding the noose and the goad in either hand, and her (appearance) resembles the inside of a lotus.[5] She faces us.[6]

35-37. One should visualize the supreme Kīrti as existing in the pericarp of the lotus to the south (of the central lotus), who emanates from my body. She consists of renown and resembles Lakṣmī in her garb and ornaments, except that sometimes her (complexion is fair) like the kunda flower.[7] Jayā should be visualized as seated on the pericarp of the lotus to the west of us,[8] (as) emanating out of my body and possessing a body similar to (that of Lakṣmī), (but) red (in colour). One should visualize Māyā as being present in the pericarp of the lotus to the north (of the central lotus) issuing from my body, and she (also) resembles Lakṣmī but is occasionally of a red (colour).

38-39. (The mantra) of the heart (*hṛdaya*) should be placed on the lotus at the south-east corner, (that of) the head (*śiras*) on the

[1] This apparently means the maṇḍala.
[2] See ch. XXXVI, 24 and 58.
[3] One of the four principal śaktis of the absolute Śakti.
[4] The absolute Śakti.
[5] The colour is light pink.
[6] 'Us' here refers to Śrī and Nārāyaṇa.
[7] A variety of white jasmine.
[8] 'Us' here denotes the divine couple, Lakṣmī and Nārāyaṇa, visualized on the central lotus of the maṇḍala.

lotus at the south-west corner. (One should place the mantra) of the tuft of hair (*śikhā*) on the lotus at the north-west corner, (that of) the armour (*varma*) on the lotus at the north-east corner. (The mantra of) the eyes (should be placed) on the foremost petal of the central lotus, while (that of) the weapon on the corner (petal).

40-41. (The adept) should meditate on Vāsudeva as being present in front of (the mantra) of the eyes, and should envisage lord Saṃkarṣaṇa (as present) on the southerly petal of the central (lotus). Pradyumna should be visualized on the westerly petal of the central lotus and Aniruddha on the northerly.

42-43. One should visualize the elephants known as Gulgulu, Guruṇya, Madana and Śalala, who are the embodiments of nectar, on the two corner petals behind (the mantra of) the weapon; they carry a jug of nectar in their hands and are fair like the conch-shell or the kunda-flower and they have four tusks.[1]

One should place (the mantra of) the kaustubha on all the petals of Lakṣmī's lotus.[2]

44. Similarly (i.e. on all the petals), one should place (the mantra of) the vanamālā on the lotus that (contains the mantra of) the heart. (The mantra of) the decorative lotus [3] should be placed on the petals of Kīrti's lotus.

45. Likewise one should also place (the same) on the petals of all four lotuses (such as) the petals of the lotus of Jayā, the petals of the lotus of (the mantra of) the armour and (other) lotuses.[4]

46. One should place (the mantra of) the excellent goad on the petals of the lotus of (the mantra of) the head. (The adept) should place (the mantra of) Garuḍa, the best of all birds, in front of the four gates.

---

[1] *catur + radān*.

[2] The lotus to the east of the maṇḍala belongs to Lakṣmī.

[3] Ch. XXXIII, 21-23.

[4] This is a very corrupt verse. The four emblems, namely the conch-shell, the lotus, the disc and the mace should be placed on the petals of four lotuses. But since J.S., the basic text of the Lakṣmī Tantra, is already so confused on this point, where only three lotuses are mentioned for these four emblems, the redactor is here at a loss. In J.S. the lotus is placed on the petal of the Kīrti-lotus; the conch-shell on that of the śikhā-lotus; the disc on that of the Jayā-lotus. But about the mace, it states that it is placed on the petals of the lotus of that place (?). L.T. is silent about the lotus of Māyā, whereas J.S. assigns the noose to it. In short, the difficulty about deciding where to place the mace remains unsolved.

47-49. Alternatively one may place the elephants in front of their own gates.[1] One should place Balākikā on the groun ' of the east-gate. She carries a lotus in her hand, is white-complexioned, has eyes like lotus-petals, a gracious expression and a dwarfed form. The blue-complexioned Vanamālikā is placed on (the ground of) the south-gate, the red-complexioned Vibhīṣikā inside the west-gate and the multi-coloured [2] Madhudīdhiti within the north-gate.[3]

50. The eight guardians of regions, called Indra etc.,[4] together with their conveyances, remain outside the gates from the east to the north-east corner.

51. Further on, (the adept) should envisage Brahmā and the king of the serpents[5] and still further on, he should meditate on their (= the lokapālas') weapons [6], viz. the vajra etc.

52. At the north and the north-east corner (the adept) should meditate on Viṣvaksena, who has noble features and is descending from the sky.

53-59. O Puraṃdara, now hear from me about how to meditate on (the deities) who are not yet described.

(The adept) should visualize Vāsudeva as consisting of amṛta, with (a dark) body (like) a cloud and wide eyes (resembling) the lotus. (In each of his hands) he (respectively) holds the conch-shell, disc, mace and lotus, and he has the śrīvatsa on his chest, is clothed in yellow and possesses four arms.

Saṃkarṣaṇa should be called to mind as possessing (a white) body resembling a mound of snow, he is clad in blue and has four arms (the lower two of which) hold the plough and (the mace called) Saunandaka,[7] while (the other) two hands are held in the pose of granting boons and protection and he is capable of rescuing (the people) drowned (in misery).

(The adept) should call to mind Pradyumna as the red (-coloured) god clad in red, displaying the bow and arrow and the hand postures of granting boons and protection.

---

[1] The gates at the four corners. See ch. XXXVIII, verses 39, 41, 42.

[2] *Śaṃkarīm*, read *saṃkarīm*, or perhaps a proper name ?

[3] Cf. Ag. P. 308, 6-8, and M. T. De Mallmann, L'Agnipurāṇa, Paris 1963, p. 189.

[4] See M. T. De Mallmann, o.c., p. 188; also see p. 214 n. supra.

[5] Brahmā is the guardian of zenith, Ananta of the nadir.

[6] See J.S. ch. 7, 78-86.

[7] This is the special mace of Kāmapāla. See Bhā.P. 10, 66.

He should envisage Aniruddha as being yellow (-coloured), clothed in white, with the sword and the shield in two of his hands, while the other two are held in the posture of granting boon and protection. All these lotus-eyed individuals are seated (in front of us) and are looking towards us (i.e. towards) myself and Viṣṇu in a north-easterly direction, while elephants resembling mountains of snow pour (water) on us from the pitchers of nectar.[1]

60-62. The wise should meditate on the mantra of the heart as being white and red in colour, clad in a white garment, as having four arms and as sitting in the lotus posture. In (two) of his hands he carries (lit. he is decorated with) the lotus and the conch-shell, (while the right) hand (of the remaining pair of hands) is held in the posture of the heart [2] and the left hand (is held) in the posture of granting everlasting protection. He remains seated facing us, profusely adorned with white ornaments and attire, his body smeared with camphor.

63-64. The wise (adept) should visualize the lord, (the mantra of) the armour as seated before us, as red as the (flower called) bandhujīva; [3] he holds the lotus and the disc and is supreme. He is as dark as crows, bees or collyrium (alternatively, he is as dark as the raven or collyrium).[4] He is holding a lotus bud. His (main) right hand is held in the posture peculiar to himself,[5] while the other (is held in the posture) of granting protection. He is smeared with musk and is (decked) with dark-coloured flowers.

65-66. (The adept) should visualize (the mantra of) the weapon of great activity as seated facing us, coloured yellow and red, and holding the mace and the lotus respectively (in his two upper hands). His two front hands are held in the posture associated with himself.[6] He is richly adorned with golden clothing and ornaments and is fierce like the fire of destruction.

---

[1] See M.T. De Mallmann, o.c., p. 188-189.

[2] See ch. XXXIV, 17-18.

[3] Pentapetes Phoenicea. A red flower.

[4] The word can be taken as a compound of three words (*kāka, ali* and *kajjala*: *kākālikajjala*) or of two words (*kākāli* and *kajjala*). The text is confusing since in two successive verses the deity is first described as being red and then black. Moreover, he appears to be holding both a lotus and a lotus bud.

[5] See ch. XXXIV, 23-24.

[6] See ch. XXXIV, 27.

67. Alternatively, the eminent adept may conceive these (mantras) of the heart etc. to be female (deities),[1] profusely adorned with the afore-mentioned robes and ornaments and smeared with unguents tallying with (the colours) of their own forms.

68-72. Thus (I) have described how the bodily forms of the aṅga (-mantras), which dispel all sins, should be envisaged in meditation.

(The adept) should visualize (the mantra of) the kaustubha (gem) as having two hands and the brilliance of thousands of suns. He is richly clad in gleaming robes and ornaments, his hands are held close to his chest, in the posture peculiar to himself.[2]

(The adept) should meditate on (the mantra of) the vanamālā who is composed of five colours and lovely with eyes that are auspicious. She holds her hands in the posture resembling a mature man.[3]

(He) should meditate on the lotus-faced lotus, kindly and (pleasing) like the moon. He possesses two hands, is handsome in every limb (of his body) and holds his hands in the posture of the lotus.[4] (The adept should meditate on) the (mantra of) the lord of the noose, who is as dark as the new blades of the durvā grass and with the face of a snake. He has two hands, of which the right hand is held in the posture peculiar to himself,[5] while the other is held in the posture of granting boons. He is terrible and awe-inspiring in appearance.

73. One should visualize (the mantra of) the goad as being sharp, long nosed and fierce (in form). His right hand (is) held in the posture (of the goad) [6] and the left hand in the (posture) of (granting) boons.

74. The apparel, appearance and ornaments of the guardians of the quarters are well known; [7] their weapons are of human form and their heads bear their (identifying) marks.[8]

---

[1] Apparently these deities of the aṅga-mantras may be either male or female, but their distinctive features such as colours, ornaments etc. are the same in either case.

[2] See ch. XXXIV, 31-33.

[3] There are two postures belonging to the vanamālā (see ch. XXXIV, 34-35), but neither tallies with description of the resemblance to a mature woman, which may possibly refer to the deity, and not to her hand posture.

[4] See ch. XXXIV, 36.

[5] See ch. XXXIV, 37-38.

[6] See J.S. 8, 49-50.

[7] See M. T. De Mallmann, o.c., pp. 124-127.

[8] See J.S. 7, 78-86, for the names of the weapons. The descriptions of the

75. The four-armed Viṣvaksena should be envisaged as holding the conch-shell and the lotus, while the two other hands are held in the posture of Viṣṇu's own hands.

76-77. One should then visualize Garuḍa at the gate as the possessor of terrifying eyes, a red head, a huge beak and as having the colour of hot gold. He has large teeth and a vulture-face and is adorned with a circle of feathers.

Thus I conclude my brief description of how the (deities in) the retinue (of myself and Viṣṇu) should be envisaged (in meditation).

78. Above our gross (form), one should meditate on the subtle (form) of (the mantra of) Tārikā, consisting of the state of the couple both perceptible and imperceptible and free from (moral) impurity.

79-84. One should meditate on the (mantra of) the absolute Tārā above that, who possesses the complete sixfold attributes and consists of consciousness. That (is) our divine absolute (state of) the couple, consisting of the great God who has hands pointing to every direction, feet and eyes, head and face, seeing in every direction, who (= the couple) manifest both sound and meaning and are ever active by virtue of their own power. The entire circle of the mantras is reflected in that (= absolute Tārā). After comprehending her fully and adhering strictly to the ritual of nyāsa, (the adept) should worship Tārā, the all-pervasive and absolute, in both her forms of evolution and involution. He who is conversant with the mantras should first mentally worship us, who are complete (i.e. the substratum of all) and who are unblemished, with all the objects of enjoyment starting from arghya and ending with prāpaṇa.[1] Then he should worship all the (deities) of our retinue, starting with the śaktis and ending with Viṣvaksena. (But) Garuḍa and the four celestial female gate-keepers [2] (should be worshipped) first of all.

---

female door-keepers are already given in the verses 47-49. Cf. also De Mallmann, o.c., pp. 187-189.

[1] Food offered to the deity. Washed uncooked rice is arranged on a platter in a central mound surrounded by six or eight smaller mounds. Some sweet meats and fruits and often a piece of betel leave are arranged on the top of each mound. This food offering is called *naivedya*. Besides this, other food articles like fruits, roots, bulbs, sweets, cooked food etc. are also offered. All these are collectively called *prāpaṇa*.

[2] Balākikā etc. See ch XXXVIII, 47-49.

Thus, O Śakra, I have revealed to you (the process of) nyāsa, (relating to the main deity and the retinue on the nine-lotus-maṇḍala), where objects of enjoyment are offered in worship. Now hear from me the number, description and names of these objects of enjoyment.

CHAPTER THIRTY-NINE

VARIOUS REQUISITES FOR EXTERNAL WORSHIP

1. Śrī:—O lord of gods, now listen to (the description of) the objects of enjoyment which, when offered, are gratifying to me, and wherein my śakti, manifested for the enjoyment of these objects, exists.

2-3. In arranging those objects of enjoyment (offered) according to the means (of the worshipper), through her diverse and manifold powers which have become manifested in material form (my śakti has purified them), all these (= objects of enjoyment) are to be considered as wholly worthy of God.

3-4. First, the excellent seat is spread on the soft cover (of the ground) [1] followed by (the offerings of) arghya, pādya, madhuparka and requisites for sipping water (*ācamanīya*) [2] and then comes the offering of one's own self and belongings,[3] preceded by the salutation.

5-6. Having obtained permission, (the adept) should then offer (to the deity) the excellent snānāsana,[4] (consisting of) a footstool, the arghya, then the gifts of pādya (such as) the water (to wash) the feet, the slippers, the cloth (*śāṭī*) (to wear during the act) of bathing, a plate full of śāli rice, the mirror, scented water and the requisites for washing the hands.

7-13. (The snānāsana also consists of) the tooth-pick, water to wash one's face and rinse one's mouth, scented oil, mixed flour of rice (*śāli*) and wheat and powdered turmeric mixed with a little

---

[1] In the ritual for worshipping God, the Pāñcarātra enumerates six sets of objects of enjoyment as offerings to the deity, namely mantrāsana, snānāsana, alaṃkārāsana, bhojyāsana, repetition of mantrāsana and paryaṇkāsana. The details of these are now being enumerated. Cf. Ahi.S. 28, 36-50.

[2] See ch. XXXVII, 28-30.

[3] The Pād. T. cites the mantra as "O Lord of the universe, I am thy slave, together with my son etc. (members of) the family, deign to introduce me, who am attached to thee, to beneficial duties": Pād.T. 4, 3, 140.

[4] This is the second set of offerings. The Sā.S. mentions the mantra as "O God, I have made these manifest to thee, who art engaged in taking a bath. This is the highly auspicious snānāsana, which (consists of) a footstool; deign to arrive here soon in order to help me": Sā.S. 6, 26.

bit of (powdered wood of) padmaka,[1] meant for cleansing (and rubbing the body) and thereafter, tepid water together with oil-cake for bathing[2] and sandal-wood (paste) mixed with camphor for smearing (the body after the bath); (then) cow-milk, cow-curd and cow-butter (clarified), honey and juice of the sugar-cane.[3] (It is also accompanied by) scented āmalaka,[4] water mixed with (the pollen of) lodhra,[5] the red sandal-wood water, the excellent dew-water (night-dew), the water with granthiparṇī[6] in it, the tagara-water[7] and then, gradually, water mixed with priyaṅgu, jaṭila and white mustard and sarvauṣadhi,[8] water mixed with flowers, fruits and leaves, water mixed with seeds and perfume, water mixed with gold and jewels, river-water, water from sacred places and pure water. These (special) waters are to be offered together with the bathing water and one should, during the progress of the bathing ceremony, offer, from time to time, arghya from the bowl of arghya.

14-18. From time to time he should also offer a wash (*kṣālana*) with water sprinkled with flowers.

(After performing the bath), in one hand he should take the pitcher containing water left after the bath, which is mixed with turmeric, the śāli (rice), garland etc., while in his other hand he should take an incense-burner containing some white mustard seed and, moving it around his head he should throw (both of) them outside (the maṇḍapa).

[1] Padmaka is the wood of Cerasmus Puddum, which possesses the scent of the lotus. This mixture of wheat etc. is an excellent toilet article for skin-care.

[2] This is the lump of pressed oil-seeds from which the oil is extracted; a mild detergent. The use of tepid water is unusual for the Indian plain, especially in South India. Maybe this indicates a colder region of the origin of the text. Kashmir?

[3] The mixture is known as the madhuparka.

[4] The fruit of Embelic Myrobalan. A citrus berry, frequently used in various remedies.

[5] Symplocos Racemosa. The pollen of its flower is used as a face-powder.

[6] A kind of fragrant plant.

[7] Tabernaemontana coronaria. A fragrant powder is prepared from it.

[8] Priyaṅgu: Panicum Italicum, a medicinal plant and perfume. Jaṭila: long pepper. Sarvauṣadhi: a combination of different herbs, namely kuṣṭha, muṃsī, haridrā, vaca, śaileya, candana, surā, campaka, karpūra and mustā. Sometimes karpūra (camphor) is replaced by another type of haridrā (turmeric) and candana (sandal-wood) is replaced by *ṣaṭhi* (a creeper used for medicinal purposes).

After that, he should offer two nicely washed (pieces of) cloth for (the deity's) body, (one for) drying the water from his hair and (the other for) wiping the water from the body.

Thereafter, he should offer bhadrāsana (consisting) of two garments, nicely washed and perfumed with incense, (namely) the lower garment and the upper garment. He should then purify the place with a pitcher full (of water) and meditate on Hari as soaring in the sky.[1]

Next, he should offer an alaṃkārāsana[2] consisting of a soft thin coverlet.

19. There (on that carpet) he should offer all (the objects) previously enumerated, such as arghya, pādya etc. (with hairpin etc.) to part the hair and a comb to comb (the hair).[3]

20. (He should also offer) flowers that decorate the head, then other objects to adorn the crown; perfumes such as the sandalwood etc., fans to ward off (perspiration).

21-23. He should also offer wonderful adornments (for the head such as) a diadem etc. and garlands of various shapes made of flowers (that are considered) pure; offerings of a handful of flowers to (the god's) feet, surrounding them with flowers, and collyrium, cooled with scents to darken (the deity's) eyes. He should similarly (offer) other cosmetics[4] and put the mark on the forehead, and (should hold) a clear polished mirror before (the deity's) eyes.

24-26. (He should also offer) the lamp, the incense, the conveyances, whether living or otherwise,[5] eulogies, auspicious songs, dances and instrumental music; also bowls full of jewels to make up for (possible) deficiencies in the offerings, and all those special (objects of adornment and toilet) worthy of use by an emperor, fashioned by the (adept by relying on his own) inventiveness. All these objects

---

[1] This spot represents the highest seat of God in the human body known as dvādaśānta.

[2] *Āsana* here means a carpet or a piece of cloth spread out on which the ritual offerings can be placed; cf. Ahi.S. 28, 31.

[3] Obviously here the real act of hair-dressing is not intended, but the requisites with which it is done.

[4] The *ālambhana* here means cosmetics such as the lacker and saffron colourings used for painting the lips, hands and feet, the gall of the cow for painting the forehead, and the like.

[5] Means of conveyance such as the real elephant, horse, chariot etc., or gold or silver replicas of these.

of enjoyment placed on the carpet for adornment (*alaṃkārāsana*) are imbued with me.[1]

Next should be offered (to the deity) the carpet for food-offering, on which are laid out the pādya, arghya etc., as stated before.

27-28. Now, learn from me how one should worship with madhuparka. A combination of milk, honey and curd is (called) madhuparka. Having placed a bowl in front (of the deity) the (adept) should fill it with madhuparka, and he should (set before the deity) arhaṇa [2] and tarpaṇa [3] in two bowls separate from that containing arghya.

29-30. (He) should first worship (the deity) with (the offering of) arhaṇa, then with (that of) madhuparka and (after that) he should perform (the rite of) tarpaṇa with all the (waters required) for tarpaṇa and then he should do the fanning (*niṣpuṃsana*) [4] with the hands. Thereafter, he should offer ācamana [5] and a full bowl of madhuparka containing only cow products. He should perform the rice-sacrifice together with its subordinate rites, as in the case of the madhuparka (rite).

31. For the rice-sacrifice, one should offer (the deity) a bowlful of śāli-rice.[6]

(In mantrāsana, the fifth set of offered objects) one should offer (to the deity) betel with camphor and perfumes.[7]

32. Thereafter, (the adept) should offer a marvellous couch to rest on.[8] There (on the couch), he should repeat all the offerings of objects such as arghya etc., as before.

---

[1] See ch. XXXVIII, 16-17.

[2] Arhaṇa here consists of a watery substance for sprinkling, which is also called arghya. Cf. Ag.P. 34, 20: *tathāṣṭāṅgārghyam ākhyātam, yavagandhaphalākṣataṃ kuśasiddhārthapuṣpāṇi tilādravyāni cārhaṇam.*

[3] Tarpaṇa consists of the offering of drinking water.

[4] This is a special way of pleasing God: the worshipper, standing, spreads all the fingers of both his hands and, while joining the hands by the tips of the thumbs, moves them around the entire length of the image, while shaking the fingers slightly.

[5] Ācamana is the offering of water for rinsing the mouth. This water is mixed with clove, pimenta acris and jasminum grandiflorum. Cf. Ag.P. 34, 21: *lavaṅgatakkolayutaṃ dadyād ācamanīyakam* and Ahi.S. 28, 35.

[6] Śāli is a special type of rice of inferior quality with very small rounded grains. Eight types of grains are offered to the deity: śāli, mudga (lentil), nīvāra, śyāmāka, priyaṅgu, sesame, barley and wheat.

[7] The word *anuvāsana* means perfumed betel etc. which soothe the stomach after a heavy meal.

[8] This is the last set of offerings to the deity known as paryaṃkāsana.

33-34. After that, in a (quiet place) unseen by anyone he should perform japa (muttering of the mantra) with an auspicious rosary, properly consecrated by mantra. In ordinary cases, when the number of (mantra-repetitions is) over ten, one may use the knuckles of the fingers (of one's hands) for counting. But it should be understood that when the number exceeds a hundred, one should use a rosary.

35. The vācika (type of japa) [1] is (desirable) for minor rituals, the upāṃsu (type) [2] is for rituals leading to the achievement of success, the mānasa (type) [3] for rituals yielding the wealth of liberation, (while) the dhyāna (type of japa) is for achieving success in every (endeavour).

36. The rosary should be made in such a way that no ordinary man can see it. A rosary made entirely of the hard cores of akṣa (nuts) is considered the best one.[4]

37. A (rosary) made of dhātrīphala, resembling the core (of the akṣa), is said to be of medium excellence, while that made of badara nuts resembling the cores is (said to be) of minimum excellence. (A rosary) containing one hundred and eight (beads) is regarded as excellent, that (containing) half (that number of beads) is of medium (excellence) and the one containing one fourth (of that number) is said to be of least (excellence).

38-39. (A rosary with beads) made of gold is utilized in (rituals intended for) the access to some object, the attainment of prosperity, or worship of the ancestors.

(The same) made of silver or copper is (utilized in rituals intended for) acquiring intelligence, valour or victory.

(The same) made of tin (is utilized in rites intended for) mastery over female spirits (*yakṣiṇīs*), (beads) made of lead are useful (for the mastery) over the ogres and ghouls (*rakṣas, piśāca*).

40-43. (A rosary consisting of beads made of) bell-metal is (used in rituals intended for) mastery over vampire spirits (*vetāla*), while the same made of brass (-beads) is (used for) mastery over serpents and reptiles, (and) an iron(-beaded rosary is used in) minor rituals. This completes (the description of) metal beads.

For the (rituals performed in order to obtain a long) span of life,

---

[1] The *vācika japa* means the muttering of the mantra aloud.
[2] *Upāṃsu japa* is when the mantra is repeated in a whisper.
[3] The *mānasa japa* is repetition of the mantra, done mentally.
[4] Eleocarpus seeds.

cure from any diseases or to gain prosperity, the beads should consist of all (kinds) of jewels. Crystals are said to be (most efficacious) for the (rituals intended for) the attainment of liberation and tranquility, coral beads for good luck, and those made of (just) thread for liberation.

For the attainment of tranquility, liberation and prosperity beads made from the root of the tulasī plant (are most useful). Lotus beads are considered to bring about success in all (aspirations), while those made of shell bring prosperity.

44. Beads made of excellent pearls (are used in rituals) yielding longevity, children and fame.

44-47. (The adept) should use (a rosary consisting of beads) made of any one of these (aforesaid) materials at an auspicious moment which is full of good qualities.

He should then wash it with perfumed water accompanied by the (utterance) of the mantra of the weapon.

Spinning thread, fresh and strong, of jute or cotton fibre, he should take three strands of it three or four times the length required for strength. Washing that (thread) with water (consecrated by) the mantra of the weapon, he should string the beads on it. The beads should not fall short of or exceed the desired number, should be equal in size and should be tightly strung. The two ends of the string fitted with beads of the desired number (are then joined together with) a bead set there to form the Meru (centre) [1] of the rosary. This is how the rosary should be made.

---

[1] Cf. J.S. 14, 27.

CHAPTER FORTY

THE DAILY DUTIES OF AN ADEPT

(*Consecration of the rosary, japa, the significance of the bell, details of the sacrifice including subsequent duties, anuyāga*).

1. Śakra:—I salute thee, water-born (goddess), I salute thee, lotus-born (goddess); O Lotus-born One, deign to tell me how to consecrate (*pratiṣṭhā*) the rosary.

2. Śrī:—After preparing the rosary (in the aforesaid manner), one should place it on an auspicious plate. (Then the adept should first) worship it with (all the above mentioned offerings such as) arghya, flowers etc., whereafter he should subject it to a purificatory rite (in the following way).

3. First, burn the rosary with the (mantra of) the weapon [1] and extinguish (the fire) with the (mantra of) the armour [2] and then soothe it (= rosary) with (the mantra of) Śrī in the parāmṛta-form. Thereafter, (the presiding śakti of the rosary) should be visualized (by the adept as follows).

4. She has four arms, is of matchless (beauty), is pervaded by me and she indeed (resembles) my second self. (Two of her) hands are held in the position of granting boons and protection (while the other) two hands are clasped together.

5-7. (The adept) should begin by envisaging the flame-like goddess's presence in the lotus of (the cavity called) [3] brahmarandhra and then visualizing this supreme Śakti of Viṣṇu consisting of myself and the destroyer of all conceit, in (the lotus of) the dvādaśānta [4] he should envisage her gradual (descent to) the lotus of the heart and her manifestation in the rosary, after she has

[1] *oṃ hraḥ vīryāya astrāya phaṭ*. This is the first stage of purification where all impurities are burnt away by the fire of the mantra of astra.

[2] The mantra of varma, *oṃ hraiṃ balāya kavacāya huṃ*, covers and extinguishes the fire of astra.

[3] The duct of suṣumnā has five cavities, the brahmarandhra being the middle one. It is filled by the coiled up śakti (kuṇḍalinī), while the other four cavities are filled by blood. Ahi.S. 32, 23.

[4] Seat of the Self, twelve fingers above the top of the head.

(again) risen from the lotus of the heart, emerged once more through the brahmarandhra and by degrees become effusive.

7-9. O Sureśvara, when visualizing my presence in the śakti (of the rosary) (the adept) should envisage me (in my three states, namely) the gross, the subtle and the absolute Tārikā forms accompanied by the series of (mantras called) aṅgas and upāṅgas. O Sureśvara, he should envisage māyā,[1] (wherein) the beads, the thread, the rosary and even (the śakti) of Viṣṇu (who is) present in the rosary are all joined together.

9-15. Regarding this consecrated rosary as a gift from me, (the adept) should then perform the rite of japa following the method already described.[2] He should visualize it (= the rosary, as embodying) the five states (of existence) of the Self, (viz.) the Undifferentiated, the absolute, the subtle, the gross and the Lakṣmī-Nārāyaṇa state. Similarly, (he should visualize) the five conditions [3] (of the Self), viz. turyātīta, turya, the deep sleep, the dream and the waking (to be present therein). He should also (visualize) the (differentiation of the Self) as the agent capable of initiating activity (from) the first inkling of that agency (in the Self) to the state of (full) performance (as the agent), the instrument and then the objects created; the sounds of the mantras as well as the gross sound—all these he should visualize as vested there (in the rosary). He should envisage the pride-destroying śakti of Viṣṇu, consisting of sound, as present within the lotus of the heart and poured out of my lotus mouth; he should visualize the rosary as pervaded by me and then perform japa with that (rosary) which consists of (all) mantras. He should envisage all the mantras represented in that (rosary) as flowers on a creeper.

16. Whilst performing (the rite of) japa, the wise (adept) should visualize the lord, (i.e. the deity invoked) by the mantra, as manifested each time (his finger) contacts a bead and as vanishing within his heart when that (contact) is interrupted.

17. Bearing in mind this constant (alternation) of appearance and disappearance (*utkrama*) of (the one who) is the product (*saṃsyūti*) of the essential radiance of the heart, (the adept) should continue to repeat (his basic mantra) ten million times.

---

[1] See ch. VI, 18-22.

[2] See chs. XXXVI and XXXVII.

[3] See ch. XXIV, 26-31.

18. Having completed the rite of japa according to the prescribed method, he should dedicate that rite of japa to me.[1] He should (then) meditate on that śakti in the form of japa (of that mantra), whose seat is my mouth.[2]

19-21. (The adept) should ring the (hand) bell (close to) the lamp, the incense and the arghya. The wise should make the sound of the bell whilst invoking (the deity), offering arghya and madhuparka and (other objects) pleasing to (the deity).[3] Except for the (purpose of) worshipping (a deity) the expert should not ring it (= the bell), nor should those desirous of success in (ritualistic) endeavour either in this life or in the next, perform a rite (of worship) without (ringing the bell).

This is the śakti, Sarasvatī, the deity of speech, called the bell.

22-26. All the mantras are present in the sound (and) the entire world is comprehended in the mantras. When this (bell) is shaken (rung) all the mantras eagerly approach the bell, mother of all mantras, without delay, just as calves (approach their mothers when they moo). (The adept) should envisage (the dome of the bell) as the inverted cosmic egg[4] crammed full with the worlds. The wise should visualize (the handle) on the upper side (as) the stem (supporting) the circle of an eight-petalled, white, auspicious lotus adorned with pericarp and pollen.[5] Therein the (presiding) goddess (of) the bell should be visualized with eight arms. In her four main hands she holds a noose, a conch-shell, a lotus and a goad, while her remaining four hands are (adorned with) the rosary, books

[1] This echoes the famous doctrine of the Bhagavadgītā that advocates solving the problem of accumulated 'karma' and its consequences by dedicating all human activities—especially the religious duties, the resulting 'karma' and its consequences—to God and that regards every personal act in fulfilment of a duty as a conscious effort to please God devoid of selfish motive. Cf. Bh.G. 3. 30; 4. 20.

[2] The Śabdaśakti is assumed to reside in the mouth of Śrī.

[3] Offerings of this type are elsewhere termed *ābhimānika*, ch. XXXVI, 93.

[4] Brahmāṇḍa, or the cosmic egg, contains within itself all the worlds. These worlds may be three, viz. bhūḥ, bhuvaḥ and svaḥ; or they may be seven by adding four more, viz. tapaḥ, janaḥ, mahaḥ and satya.

[5] The bell is shaped like a small handbell with a stem that terminates in a circle for use as a handle. The latter, the seat of the śakti of sound, is visualized as a maṇḍala of lotus. This confirms the previous description of creation by Śabdabrahman, which gradually manifests first sound and then objects.

(on various) sciences and are held in the position of granting protection and boons (respectively).

27-29. She is seated in the posture of the lotus, has (large) eyes like a lotus (bud) and (a rosy) complexion like the colour within a lotus. She wears a garland made of lotuses and uses unguents and robes that are yellow and white in colour. She is continuously pouring forth a host of mantras and is being highly eulogized by (deities such as) Brahmā etc. Whilst reciting (the mantra of) Tārā (the adept) should go on swinging a pair of (bells). He who uses this (bell) in rites of worship never fails to achieve success with his mantra.

29-30. Thereafter, bringing in (inviting) the superiors, either those who have (through meditation) become identified with myself or those who are worshippers of Viṣṇu, (the adept) should whilst reciting my (own) mantra [1] make a gift of half of the prāpaṇa [2] to them.

30-32. O king of gods, listen now to how tarpaṇa [3] should be duly performed (to) me, the absolute one, present in the fire and composed of the totality of Agni and Soma.[4]

On ground complying with all the requirements, situated within the northern section (of the temple) or externally adjacent thereto, (the adept) should dig a pit (for the sacrificial fire), either in the shape of a perfect square, or in that of an attractive lotus (i.e. circular) [5] with (all prescribed) characteristics.

33-34. (When the adept contemplates) performing fifty sacrifices, the pit should measure twelve fingers; it should measure a cubit minus the depth of the fingers (when performance of) one hundred and eight (sacrifices is intended); a cubit (for performance of) a thousand (sacrifices); two cubits (for performance of) ten thousand, four cubits (for performance) of a hundred thousand and eight

---

[1] The mantra of Tārā (*hrīṃ*).

[2] *Naivedya*, food stuff consisting of rice and fruits, sweets and betel leaves, offered to the deity is called prāpaṇa.

[3] This indicates the libation, the offering of water etc. to a deity.

[4] See ch. XXIX, 4-9.

[5] When on a circular pit instead of the three usual ridges (*mekhalā*), eight or twelve petals are made, it is called a padma-kuṇḍa. See Varāhaguru, K.K.C. p. 62. For further details on an agni-kuṇḍa see H. Brunner-Lachaux, Somaśaṃbhupaddhati, Pondicherry 1963, part I, p. 230 and p. 232 n., and part II, Plates nos. 1-3.

cubits (for performance of) ten millions (of sacrifices). He should dig that (pit) in compliance with the scriptures.

35-36. Alternatively he may construct a triangular pit with three ridges.

Fetching (water with a ladle) whilst reciting (the mantra of) Tārā, he should then wash the ground (for the sacrifice) three times (while still) reciting that (mantra). (And then) he should with (the mantra of) Tārā duly perform (the rites of) evaporating, burning and saturating.

36-38. After having brought about the descent of the eternal one from the lotus-heart (of the adept) through the course of creation starting from the ādhāraśakti and ending with the bhāvāsana, there (in the sacrificial fireplace) he should worship the Śakti called Nārāyaṇā—who consists of fiery energy, is absolute and is identical with myself, who is an embodiment of amṛta in all forms of abundance, who is inherent in the complex of all śaktis and in all objects—(and envisage her on all the vital points of his body).

39-40. Having thus brought about the descent of Tārikā, embodied in pulsation, from the lotus-heart (of the adept), he should throw her in the fireplace, a second lotus, whilst practising recaka. (Thereafter), having worshipped her with (offerings of) incense, flowers etc., and having shown her the hand posture of the lotus, he should visualize the Śakti as having completed her monthly period and as clothed in a clean garment after her bath.

41. He should envisage this same all-pervasive Śakti's presence in the lower piece of wood for kindling fire (*araṇi*), whilst envisaging the presence of Hari completely consisting of fiery energy in the upper piece of wood.

42-45. He should diligently rub (the two pieces of firewood) together, whilst reciting (the two mantras of) Tārā and Anutārā. Whilst reciting (the mantra of) Tārā, the adept should hold the fire—offspring of the Śakti, produced (through the friction of the pieces of wood)—and shielding it with the fingers (of his hands), he should perform all the sacraments of the Viṣṇuite faith.[1] Preceded

[1] All the ten sacraments of the higher castes, namely garbhādhāna, puṃsavana, and sīmantonnayana (described in verses 40-42), jātakarma, nāmakaraṇa and annaprāsana (verse 43), cuḍākaraṇa, upanayana and marriage (verses 43-45), excepting the funeral rites, should be performed whilst worshipping the fire, replacing however the Vedic mantras by the mantras of Tārā and Anutārā in accordance with the Viṣṇuite doctrine. The entire

by the sacrament of the first introduction of solid food (grains) the sacrament of the tuft of hair is performed accompanied by the recitation of (the mantra of) Tārā.[1] The sacrament investing the fire with the sacred thread should be performed along with (the recitation of) the Tārā and Anutārā. Thereafter, (the fire) should be married to the two goddesses, Svāhā and Svadhā, while reciting (the mantras of) Tārā and Anutārā. All these sacraments starting with the birth-sacrament, naming-sacrament etc., are performed mentally.

46. If for some reason (the adept) obtains fire by rubbing (a piece of) iron with (a piece of) flint [2] or (from any other) secular (source of) fire, he should (nevertheless) dedicate all the (personal) sacraments, (namely) fertilization [3] etc. to (the fire).

47. Depositing (this fire), the husband of Svāhā together with (his wives, Svāhā and Svadhā), the goddesses, in a metal or a new earthen bowl, the intelligent (adept) should perform his worship while reciting (the mantra of) Tārā.

48. (Thereafter) he should conclude (the rites) while taking in deep breath (*pūraṇa*) [4] and (then) he should extinguish (the fire) within his own self. Whereafter it (= the fire) should be gradually merged in the destruction, (i.e.) the ānandaśakti.

49. Then once again (the adept) should bring down (the fire) step by step through the courses of creation, and, whilst reciting (the mantra of) Tārā,[5] he should deposit it in the place existing within the lotus (drawn) on the (base of the sacrificial) pit.

50. He should then worship the fire, the husband of Svāhā and Svadhā, who consists of Agni and Soma,[6] by offering three sticks of wood one by one and by reciting (the mantra of) Tārā (with each piece).

---

process is merely envisaged by the adept, not actually performed. Visualization of the Śakti and Viṣṇu in sexual congress (verses 40 and 41) engenders the fire as Viṣṇu's child. These sacraments are more clearly but slightly differently explained in J.S. 15, 130-150. The entire process is called vaiṣṇavīkaraṇam, i.e. to make the sacrificial fire a child of Viṣṇu.

1 Here mention of the rite of annaprāśana anticipates the rites jātakarma and nāmakaraṇa.

2 *Pāṣāṇamaṇi*.

3 This is described in the verses 41 and 42.

4 See Yog.S. 2, 50 and Yog.P. thereon, and Ahi.S. 32, 51-55.

5 This is the general process for purification of the beings created. Cf. *bhūtaśuddhi*, ch. XXXV, 1-54.

6 Kriyāśakti and bhūtiśakti.

51. (He should further) offer śālī,[1] sesame and akṣata,[2] followed by three oblations of purified butter. Whereafter he should twice pronounce (the word) 'be conscious' (*bodhaya*) preceded by the (mantra of) Tārā.[3]

52. The fire, when correctly worshipped, awakens by itself.

52-53. The rite of encircling the fire is performed (by the adept) with wet hands while reciting the (mantra of) Tārā.[4] Then continuing to recite that mantra, he should perform the rite of enclosing the fire within (a boundary of) panic grass, (using) three handfuls of grass for (each of the) four points of compass and closing the boundary by spreading the bunch of darbha on the north side of the fireplace.[5]

54. He should (then) arrange all (the objects needed for the rite), namely the two bowls of (sacred water called) *praṇītā*[6] and *prokṣaṇī*,[7] the ladle,[8] (the pieces of wood for) fuel, (the two spoons called) *sruk*[9] and *sruva*,[10] the plate of butter, and the two pavitras[11] there (on that grass border).

55. After having, while (reciting the mantra of) Tārā, filled the praṇītā with incensed water and purifying it thrice by (dipping) the

---

[1] A type of rice.

[2] Rice husked after drying in the sun, as distinct from rice husked after boiling paddy and then drying it.

[3] *oṃ hrīṃ bodhaya, oṃ hrīṃ bodhaya.*

[4] Picking up a bunch of kuśa-grass (*kūrca*), the adept should dip it in the water contained in the prokṣaṇī-jug and then sprinkle the water dripping from it all around the pit and platform, thus making the place a protected area. This procedure is usually accompanied by recitation of the varma-mantra. See J.S. 15, 78; and Viś.S. XI, 21.

[5] *Paristaraṇa*: the adept makes four looped bundles of kuśa-grass. With these he then forms a boundary on all four sides of the fire, laying the bladed ends in a northerly direction. On this boundary all the requirements for the sacrifice are placed in pairs, e.g. the sruk and sruva, the prokṣaṇī and praṇītā, the two darvīs, the idhma and barhis, etc.

[6] These are the two vessels holding sacred water. The praṇītā contains water used in some quantity, whereas all the sprinkling is done with water from the prokṣaṇī.

[7] See note 6.

[8] The *darvī* is the ordinary wooden ladle used in ritual.

[9] These are the two long handled wooden spoons with ornamented ends. See H. Daniel Smith, Vaiṣṇava Iconography, Madras 1969, pp. 288-294.

[10] See note 9.

[11] Two rings made of panic grass worn by the worshipper on his ring-finger in religious rites. P. V. Kane, History of Dharmaśāstra, II, part II, p. 657.

two pavitras (into the water), he should visualize me, Śrī, while (reciting the mantra of) Tārā.

56. Placing the prokṣaṇī on the northern boundary of the fire, he should fill it (with sacred water) while (reciting the mantra of) Śrī. Having purified it (as before), he should sprinkle all the objects required for the sacrifice (with water from the prokṣaṇī).

57-58. He should then fetch the plate for the butter and place the butter on it. He should visualize Brahma emerging out of the sea of butter to be present north of the fire. Lighting it (= the butter) while reciting (the mantra of) Tārā, he should place the kindled butter on the tips of the panic (grass). (Thereafter) he should again kindle that (darbha) while reciting that (mantra of Tārā) and perform the rite of paryagni.[1]

59. He should then place that (darbha) behind the fire and after purifying it with the two pavitras while reciting (the mantra of) Tārā, he should throw the pavitras into the fire.

60-64. Thereafter he should encircle the four sides (of the fire) within a boundary in keeping with the ritual.

He should (then) place two (pieces of) fire-wood at the south-east and north-east corners of the fire-pit.

Then, taking fifteen (pieces of) dried fire-wood (he should start the ritual in the following way).

Having, while reciting (the mantra of) Tārā, sprinkled the fire (with water) he should warm the sruk and the sruva and then wipe and sprinkle them (with sacred water) while reciting the (mantra of) Tārā. Next, using the sruk, from north-west to south-east and (again) from south-west to north-east he should pour (the butter) into the fire. After that he should use the sruva to make an offering (by pouring the butter) into the centre of the fire. While reciting (the mantra of) Tārā ending with (the word) *svāhā*, he should make offerings of the butter (by pouring it with) the sruva a hundred and eight times, or fifty-four times, or twenty-seven times. This (fire is thus) made fit to receive offerings (to carry them to) God.[2]

65. The intelligent (adept) should take seven (pieces of) fire-wood

[1] A handful of kuśa-grass is dipped in the melted butter and then set alight. With this the adept encircles the pit three times, and finally throws it into the fire. J.S. 15, 76-83 and Viś.S. XI, 25-26.

[2] The complete purificatory rite is condensed here. It is elaborately described in J.S. 15, 110-130.

(from) the brahma [1] and the kṣatra [2] trees, and while reciting the (mantra of) Tārā (offer these in the sacrificial fire).

66. The remaining [3] ten (pieces of) fire-wood (from any kind of) wood should also be offered while reciting (the mantra of) Tārā. (The adept) should envisage me, the absolute one, seated on Viṣṇu's lap as being present in (the fire).

67. He should visualize Lakṣmī, seated on the lap of God (*vibhoḥ*), who is occupying the pericarp of the lotus consisting of Brahma-bliss, and he should offer all (pieces of) fire-wood to her.

68. Whereafter he should offer (her) the flowers followed by the offering of incense and other objects. The wise should offer these three (types of objects) by hand.

69-70. Next, using the sruva, the intelligent (adept) should offer the madhuparka (to the deity), and with the sruk he should then spoon up rice mixed with butter as before and offer (her) this rice four times while pronouncing (the mantra of) Tārā with (the word) *svāhā* at the end of it. (After that) using the sruva he should make as many offerings of the butter as tally with the (previously) stated number of the (pieces of) fire-wood.[4]

71-76. (Then) taking a handful of flowers, he should mentally worship (me who am) present in the (sacrificial) fire. This is the form of the daily sacrifice (offered to) me. For (the fulfilment of a particular) desire (entertained by him), the adept should make further offerings (to me) as prescribed by the ritual adopted.[5] When performing prāyaścitta [6] (expiatory rite), after (first) sprinkling water over the fire with (the mantra of) Tārā, (the adept) should throw the oblation (into the fire) ten times, while mentally adding the words 'pardon me' (*kṣamasva*) to (the mantra of) Tārā. Taking the bowl (called) praṇītā to an uncontaminated place and striking the entire boundary (of the fire with his feet), he should perform

---

[1] The brahma-tree is the Palāśa, i.e. Butea Frondosa König.

[2] The kṣatra-tree is the Mucukunda, i.e. Pterospermum Suberifolium.

[3] The seventeen pieces of fire-wood required for the offering are bound with a blade of kuśa-grass called barhis and are placed ready near the fire. See verses 60-61 of this chapter.

[4] This means that the adept must offer the butter seventeen times.

[5] *Kāmyayāga* is the ritual performed for the attainment of a particular objective. It may be of various types such as māraṇa, ucāṭana, vaśīkaraṇa, ākarṣaṇa, śāntikarman, pauṣṭikakarman and vidveṣaṇa.

[6] This rite is performed to redeem some unintentionally committed sin.

(the rite of pouring water on the fire, viz.) saṃsrāva.[1] (Then) throwing the grass-border into the fire [2] and filling up the sruva with butter he should offer the final offering while reciting loudly (the mantra of) Tārā ending with (the word) *svāhā*. (Thereafter) drawing Tārā (the mantra) together with its (presiding) śakti, the absolute one consisting of myself who am seated on Viṣṇu's lap and who am present in the fire, through the passage of the nasal joint [3] by means of air-pressure, (the adept) should place (us) on the lotus of the heart.

77. He should then bring (us) to the sacrificial ground and merge in me, who am present (as the śakti) in the (maṇḍala of) the nine lotuses. Whereafter he should dedicate the entire ritual to me, who am present in the image (which is worshipped by the adept).

78-83. The adept should remove a portion of rice from the prāpaṇa before offering it (to the deity). He should (now) perform a sacrifice by offering that rice to the four-armed Viṣvaksena. After invoking him from the atmosphere and bringing him to the edge of the maṇḍala, the intelligent (adept) should gradually worship him (= Viṣvaksena) whose colour resembles the buds of the mango tree, who possesses tawny brows, beard and eyes, is clad in yellow raiment and has four teeth. (With) two (of his hands) he strikes his own pose [4] (while in the other two) he carries a club and a sword. After demonstrating the deity's (own) hand-sign together with (all the) aṅgas,[5] (the adept) should approach the (sacrificial fire-)pit and should devoutly offer Viṣvaksena tarpaṇa (consisting of) sesame seed and sun-baked rice. Whereafter he should offer (him) the final oblation reciting (simultaneously) the mantra [6] (of Viṣvaksena) with a final *vauṣaṭ* (added to it). Having thus completed

---

[1] *Saṃsrāva* is performed by filling the śruva with sacred water and pouring it over the boundary enclosing the fire.

[2] *Stara* is the border of panic grass spread at the commencement of the rite to keep the fire from contamination. This is known as *saṃstaraṇa*. All the articles required for the sacrifice are set on this borderline in pairs. See J.S. 15, 76-78. Normally the grass border is thrown into the fire to signify the conclusion of the sacrifice.

[3] This is the suṣumṇā duct and the pressure of air actually means the function of recaka. See Ahi. S., ch. 33, 51-55.

[4] See ch. XXXIV, 83-85.

[5] Ibid., verses 19-26.

[6] *oṃ hūṃ vauṃ viṣvaksenāya vauṣaṭ.*

his worship within the maṇḍala, (the adept) should perform (the rite of) visarjana [1] to the deity, making the deity's own sign with his hands, (he should perform this rite) while pronouncing his (= Viṣvaksena's) own mantra with the addition of the word 'pardon me' (*kṣamasva*). And then he should envisage him as flying off in the sky.

84. He should throw all (the ingredients used for) the worship of Viṣvaksena into some deep water. Thereafter he should wash the maṇḍala with water (consecrated by him) by reciting, in a low tone, (the mantra of) the weapon (over it).

85-86. He should then worship (*saṃpūjayet*) all the guardians of the regions (jointly) in one (collective) oblation into the fire with (all the prescribed offerings) starting with the flowers and arghya and ending with the rice-offering.[2] Alternatively, if unable to offer more, the adept (may offer only) rice [3] (whilst reciting) the mantra of each guardian. After (completing) this ritual, he should (perform the rite of) visarjana (to these deities). He should then worship all the weapons (of these deities).[4]

87-89. Next, (the adept) should worship the guardians of the grounds along with their entire retinue [5] and following the order of their position, offer (each) a libation by pouring it into the fire. (Then) completing the (ritual) worship of all the śaktis of the seats starting with the ādhāraśakti and (of the deities such as) Gaṇeśa etc.[6] and having offered libations of butter etc. to them, he should perform the final oblation, either once or three times. He should (also) worship (the śaktis such as) Lakṣmī etc., before worshipping Viṣvaksena.

90. Worship of the guardians of the regions follows that of Viṣvaksena. Whereafter, having purified the platform (for worship)

---

[1] Literally the word means abandonment but here it refers to the rite of bidding farewell to the deity after the ritual has been completed.

[2] See verses 68-71.

[3] Two different readings are possible for the first word of verse number 86, viz. *vahnibhiḥ* or *vrīhibhiḥ*. Neither of the two is altogether satisfactory; but the second reading appears to be more appropriate.

[4] These are Indra, Agni, Yama, Nirṛti, Varuṇa, Vāyu, Soma, Īśāna, Nāga and Brahmā, their weapons are Vajra, Śakti, Daṇḍa, Khaḍga, Pāśa, Dhvaja, Mudgara, Śūla, Śīra and Padma respectively.

[5] See J.S. 7, 78-86.

[6] See ch. XXXVII, 65-74.

(the adept) should spread the panic grass on the south side (of it).

91-93. He should then worship his ancestors in order of precedence, (offering) a remainder (*avaśeṣataḥ*) from the articles of prāpaṇa.[1] Preparing three soft balls (of cooked rice, piṇḍa),[2] he should offer these to the ancestors (by placing them) on the border (of panic grass). Then he should offer to each of them a handful of water (from the bowl of) arghya. (After that he should) offer (the food) [3] dedicated to the ancestors to a follower of Viṣṇu or to a distinguished brahmin, recalling each ancestor by name. The devotee should then relinquish to me all (results derived from the performance of the ancestor-worship). (Whereafter) he should visualize the disappearance of the ancestors one by one.

94. He should then remove the arghya etc. (i.e. the implements of the sacrifice), annul (the operation of the two mantras of) the armour and of the weapon,[4] abolish (the effects of) nyāsa [5] and perform anuyāga.[6]

95. (Whereafter) he should wash the site (with water out of the prokṣaṇī) while (reciting the mantras) of the weapon and of Tārā, he should sprinkle (water over the offerings) while (reciting the mantra of) Tārā, and after pouring water (over the fire), he should perform the sacrifice of prāṇa,[7] (while reciting the) same (mantra).

96-97. Those who are uninitiated (in the Pāñcarātra discipline, should) perform the anuyāga while reciting (the mantra of) Tārā together with the mantras (prescribed by their own sacred texts) and they should visualize me, the divine bliss of Soma as being present in their hearts and as gradually being evolved into food grain, who am the embodiment of vīrya (power) and taste and am identified with (the divine attributes of) tejas, vīrya and bala.

---

1 See ch. XXXVI, 79.

2 The rice offered to the ancestors is cooked in milk and called *piṇḍa* because of its sticky consistency.

3 Cf. Sā.S. 6, 167-179.

4 Brought into operation at the beginning of the sacrifice. Although L.T. does not mention this rite, J.S. gives a full account of it.

5 This is to deconsecrate the objects offered so that they may be used in the normal way and the devotee may partake of the food offered to the deity. See K. Rangachari, o.c., pp. 93-96.

6 Activities subsequent to the sacrificial rite, such as partaking of food-offerings by the devotee, deconsecration and extinction of the sacrificial fire etc. The adept's meal is in itself a separate ritual which is called Anuyāga. The entire process is described by K. Rangachari, o.c., pp. 93-96.

7 See P.V. Kane, History of Dharmaśāstra, Vol. II, part II, pp. 763-764.

98. (The adept) should (then) envisage his own self as the lotus-eyed Supreme Person (God), the undecaying enjoyer [1] incorporating (the divine attributes of) aiśvarya, śakti and knowledge.

99. Thereafter, while reciting (the mantra of) Tārā, he should pour water over the rice.[2] And after rinsing his mouth twice, he should relinquish the (result obtained from the performance of) the anuyāga to me.

100-101. The wise should then study sacred texts until the day ends. Sacred texts (are of) four types [3] and cover the whole field of established subjects arising out of them, as for instance (the nature of) Tārikā etc. (The adept) should study them with insight and objectively in order to clarify his mind.

102-104. (At dusk) he should according to the ritual injunctions perform the rite of sandhyā.[4] Then thinking of me with a pure mind, he should practise meditation according to the injunctions (of the sacred texts) at the commencement and at the close of the night, (when his) physical faculties are calm. Thus, O Śakra, have I described to you the elaborate ritual for performing the sacrifice. Now learn from me the condensed form of this ritual. Performance (of the sacrifice) should be elaborate or concise, accordingly as circumstances of time and place permit.

105-110. No distinction should be drawn (between offerings) and one may worship me with a mere handful (of water). One may worship us (my own self and God) jointly with the Puruṣa-sūkta. Similarly, (one may worship us both jointly) with my own sūkta,[5] or one may worship us separately with (both) those (two sūktas). Instead of all the different mantras it is permissible to use only (that of) Tārā. At the beginning of the ritual one should resolve (to perform certain rites in a fixed order), and at the end of the ritual to surrender (the result obtained thereby).[6] Alternatively, the

---

[1] The food offered is identified with the Śakti, while the worshipper identifies himself with God, the supreme Person.

[2] This is called *āpoṣaṇa*, or sipping of water. See P.V. Kane, History of Dharmaśāstra, Vol. II, part II, p. 763.

[3] These are the āgamasiddhānta, mantrasiddhānta, tantrasiddhānta and tantrāntarasiddhānta.

[4] The daily rite of obligatory devotion.

[5] The Śrī-sūkta.

[6] Before undertaking any form of ritual worship the adept must decide on the steps of the ritual to be followed and select from the prescribed

sacrifice may be simplified by not adhering to any fixed specification of the objects offered. (In short) performance should be according to ability. One should not neglect (one's duty to perform) the rite (even if one is obliged) to offer nothing but a handful of water. If not a single object (= offering) is available, the wise will content themselves with the study (of) Tārā, visualizing her form in every detail. (In fact) all the rites enjoined by the sacred texts are (merely) to rouse to action those who are free from sensual desire, are pure and have attained the desired state (of existence).

111. When (the adept) becomes all-pervasive and achieves complete equanimity, who is there then to act, who to receive the dedication, what is the object and to what purposes and in what manner? [1]

112. (Such a being then) leaves behind the general empirical courses of Agni and Soma[2] and, having found his way through them, traverses the course beyond.

113-116. He who has destroyed the evil course (of mundane existence) with the fire of destruction (during meditation), becomes cool (calm) and freed from all misery. He is aware of the (gradual) ascension (of the soul through the different states of existence as) the gross, the subtle, the absolute and the supra-absolute. He performs all the activities of seeing, hearing, touching, smelling, eating, moving, sleeping, breathing, raving, abandoning, accepting and opening and closing the eyes, yet in effect these acts are altogether devoid of (results of) activity. Since he becomes identified with me, he escapes identification with the category of 'This'.[3] Without any limitation of rank, place or time, he acquires identity with the category of 'I'.[4] Like the yellow fire and the yellow smoke (i.e. like the yellow colour common to both the fire and its smoke), he remains in

---

variety and number of objects those he intends to offer to the deity. This is called *saṃkalpa*. On completing the ritual he must relinquish to God all results obtained from its performance; this is called saṃnyāsa.

[1] Since such an adept becomes identified with the Śakti, the ritual, the objects offered, the deity etc., all being various facets of that Śakti, lose their significance.

[2] The kriyā and bhūti śaktis of God manifested in the creation.

[3] *Idam* represents the unconscious material creation. Cf. Śaṅkara's Adhyāsabhāṣya on the Brahmasūtra.

[4] *Aham* represents that which is one (indivisible) and eternal, the essence of God and of His Śakti. Hence in this state the devotee becomes identical with Śakti.

the middle of both the Sūrya and the Soma (i.e. he achieves identification with both).[1]

117. The yogin, who having pierced open the palate fixes his mind, which is in the state of being pervaded by śūnya[2] that is also in the state of dissolution,[3] on the eternal abode[4] in order to meditate on Tārikā, is he who (simultaneously) pursues the course of duties, the course of knowledge, the course of yoga and is a (follower of the system of) Sāttvata.[5] He should also be regarded as a (follower of the system of) Pāśupata. He is (indeed) well versed in all systems. Thus I have revealed to you my absolute state of existence. Now listen to me as I am about to tell you all other things that (you wish to learn.)

---

[1] Just as the colour yellow is visible both within the fire and in its smoke, so the devotee in this state being merged in the Śakti, achieves identification with both her aspects, namely the kriyāśakti and the bhūtiśakti.

[2] Here it is interesting to note the use of the word śūnya for the concept of Śakti's undifferentiated state, which is also the state of dissolution.

[3] See note 2.

[4] This is elsewhere described as the dvādaśānta. See ch. XXXV, 32.

[5] A follower of the Sāttvata system makes use of all the three means of attaining liberation, namely through karma, jñāna and yoga.

CHAPTER FORTY-ONE

THE INITIATION AND ABHIṢEKA CEREMONIES

1. Śakra:—I salute thee, eternal and flawless mother of all corporeal beings and the basic Śakti of all pure and impure courses of (creation).

2. I have listened (to the) detailed (description of) the ritual of worship in its external (*bāhya*) and in its internal (i.e. mental, *antara*) form. Now I wish to hear from thee about the ritual for the initiation (ceremony).

3. Śrī:—Nārāyaṇa is the unique one; He is the possessor of Śrī and shines with the glory of His six attributes. I am His one (= sole) and eternal Śakti, whose primary form (embodies) the six attributes.

4-6. O Vāsava, (although) I am one (and unique), through (the power of) my divine knowledge I express (divide) myself in five ways, (namely) in the form of sound, of objects and of action, as well as (in the role of) preceptor and in the (form) called initiation. Those versed in the Vedas call (the ceremony of initiation) dīkṣā (because) it (= dīkṣā) severs [1] (all bonds such as) kleśa, karma etc.[2] and 'sees' (reveals) all states of existence (*padam*); [3] or alternatively (because) it (= dīkṣā) destroys all evil (leading to worldy existence) and gains (for the initiates) the supreme state of existence.

7. According to (its nature whether) gross, subtle or absolute, this dīkṣā is, to begin with, of three types. Again (each of) these three types is divided into four subdivisions to suit the nature of the person to be initiated.

8. (These) are (called) (firstly) *samayin*, (secondly) *putraka*, then thirdly (*sādhaka*), and (lastly) (*ācārya*).[4] These persons are eligible

[1] Dīkṣā is here derived from root *do-* (*dyati*) meaning to cut.

[2] The root causes leading to all the miseries of existence in this world of living and dying. See the Yog.S., 1, 24.

[3] *Akhilaṃ padam*: the reality underlying all divergent manifestations of existence.

[4] Those who have undergone the first of the five forms of dīkṣā and belong to the denomination are called *samayin*. They have no knowledge of tantras and are not eligible to worship in temples. The next category consists of those who are somewhat advanced in their tantric knowledge and practice tantric forms of worship. They are called *putraka*, be-

for initiation and a detailed description of them is given elsewhere.[1]

9-14. According to the status of the rich, of the relatively poor, or of those without any means whatsoever, such initiation is respectively of three kinds, (namely) when it is accompanied by the mahāmaṇḍala-sacrifice,[2] when accompanied by (the simple sacrifice of) butter alone, or when it is accompanied solely by sound (of the mantra). The preceptor should introduce the (prospective) disciple, who is of resolute mind and who has been repeatedly tested (by the preceptor), who has prostrated (himself before the preceptor) and is weary of the fires (sorrows) of life. (He) leads in the disciples, whose sins have been absolved by expiatory rites, who are devoted to God, who have bathed, have worn clean clothes, have washed their bodies, purified (themselves by eating the) five cow-products [3] and cleaned their teeth. (The preceptor should) similarly accept girls or women with auspicious signs.[4] He should (then) first construct a new lotus (-maṇḍala, i.e. cakrābja-maṇḍala, see appendix), and worship the pitcher (of sacred water) set therein. Then, holding a handful of (loose) flowers and blindfold with (a piece) of new cloth, they should be measured by the preceptor from top to toe, with a strand of thread.

15. Then this thread (should be made of) three strands (to correspond with the number of guṇas), each strand possessing three times three knots (twenty-seven) to correspond with the number of the principles, and (the preceptor) should envisage (in that thread) the whole range of the principles as covering the body (of the disciple) from top to toe.

16. The (twenty-seven) knots should be regarded as representing

---

they are like the sons of all initiating teachers. The third type is called *sādhaka*, which includes those who have undergone tantric initiation and are engaged in meditation and the worship of a particular deity. They are entitled to officiate at all kinds of worship including temple-worship. *Ācāryas* are the wise interpreters of the sacred literature and mantras. They are entitled to initiate adepts. In fact they are the elders of the sect.

[1] L.T. does not elaborate this topic. But J. S. and most other saṃhitās give a fuller description. Cf. Pau.S., ch. 1; J.S., ch. 17; and Sa.S. Brahmarātra, V, 119-224.

[2] The ritual worship with the cakrābja-maṇḍala.

[3] The milk, curd, butter, urine and excreta of the cow.

[4] In the Pāñcarātra system the right of young unmarried girls and married women to be initiated receives special emphasis.

the twenty-seven principles starting from Īśa and kāla and ending with the earth and (the three strands of the thread) holding the knots as representing the three guṇas.

17. Consisting of māyā, avidyā and kriyā (delusion, nescience and activity) these (principles forming the body) are called the bondage (of living beings). The body, consisting of both the gross and the subtle, produces results (of deeds) both auspicious and inauspicious.

18-19. This (body) [1] is variously coloured (influenced) by (material) qualities and is the seat of all flaws. At the conclusion of the rite of the *saṃpāta* sacrifice,[2] the (disciple) should himself continually tear to bits (his) body as represented by that thread and sacrifice the pieces which action causes the destruction of all enjoyments (of the accumulated results of his deeds).

19-26. (The preceptor) should envisage Īśvara as (located) on (his own) forehead. Visualizing Him as the essence of consciousness and with His face pointing in each direction (= as omnipresent) and existing together with His own bīja,[3] he should offer Him sacrifices in keeping with the number of the principles. He should envisage pradhāna red as a lump of vermillion and located between (his) brows. (He should visualize) buddhi (bright) as the rays of the full moon, and as present on the top of (his) palate; Ahaṃkāra as (ochre) coloured like the saffron (flower) is visualized as occupying the middle of (the preceptor's) palate. He should envisage the mind, with the brilliance of a diamond,[4] as occupying the space between his palate and ear. He should visualize the five (cognitive organs), the ear etc., as endowed with the lustre of the stars and as placed equidistantly between his throat and the lotus of his heart. He should similarly envisage the five (conative organs), speech etc., as occupying the space between his heart and navel. He should envisage the five element-potentials, speech etc., as existing between

---

[1] The three-stranded thread symbolizes the disciple's body. The three strands stand for the three guṇas of the cosmic source prakṛti. The knots of the thread represent prakṛti's first evolutions, namely the principles. The word *guṇa* is used in the double sense, meaning both a strand of thread and a 'quality' of the source.

[2] This is a type of bhūtaśuddhi, which sublimates the body of the guru. The rite is described in the ensuing verses.

[3] *oṃ*.

[4] *Vajropala*.

his navel and groin. He should visualize the gross elements within the space extending from his thighs to his ankles. These also, together with their individual orbs (*bimba*), resemble the stars. (With each of the above-mentioned visualizations of the principles) he should utter the sound of praṇava followed by the bīja of the relevant principle, then name it and end with the word *svāhā* (while offering a sacrifice to the fire). This is called the oblation of *saṃpāta*. On completion of this *saṃpāta* sacrifice the preceptor himself becomes identical with Lakṣmī.

27-28. Next he should offer the final oblation while reciting the mantra of Tārā followed by vauṣaṭ. Thus completing the sacrifice (called) *saṃpāta* he should offer to me the strong knotted thread between two plates. Leading the disciple there (to the sacrificial site), he should remove the disciple's eye-cover.

29-30. The disciple should then duly salute the preceptor, who gave him his book.[1] Taking his place near the fire he should then perform the entire ritual of sacrifice step by step, while mentally reciting (the mantras of) Tārā and of her aṅgas and upāṅgas[2] and of the train of Lakṣmī etc. He is thus made fit to (perform) japa, the ritual of (sacrificing into) the fire, listening to the sacred scripture and undertaking ritual ceremonies.

31-32. In order to purify the process of initiation, he should recite his basic mantra etc. while performing the ritual of sacrifice. Whereafter he should make first one hundred and later ten offerings of sesamum seed. He should (next) throw (into the fire) the final offering of butter, whilst reciting (the mantra of) Tārā.

32-34. This initiation is the mantra-initiation, which associates the (disciple) with all the mantras (of the system). (The preceptor) should, however, permit disciples, who being vested with no great authority aim solely at enjoyment, to choose between the mantra of the source (i.e. prakṛti, the śakti) or (the mantra) of any of her evolutions. All the mantras derived directly from the source (*prakṛti*) bring about success.[3]

34-35. (Now) the ritual for purifying the principles (forming) his

---

[1] This is probably a reference to the primary teacher who taught the disciple how to read etc.

[2] See ch. XXXIII, 1-13.

[3] Prakṛti-mantra is the basic mantra of the system, namely the mantra of Tārā. All other mantras are diverse manifestations of this basic śakti.

(= the disciple's) body will be revealed. A mantra is only acceptable from (him) in whom the (embodied) principles have been purified.

This being the mantra-initiation, now hear about how to conduct the initiation of principles (*tattvadīkṣā*).

36-37. The group of principles is purified by performing ten oblations together with the visualization (of the deity) for each principle, starting with the earth-element and ending with Īśvara, whilst at the same time (reciting the mantra which is constructed as follows): first *oṃ*, followed by the bīja(-mantra),[1] then the name of the relevant principle followed by (the word) *śodhayasva* in combination with the name (of the deity of the basic mantra). However, at the beginning of the fire-ritual the (disciple) who is to be initiated should be properly invested with a name.[2]

38-40. With his disciple being seated in the lotus posture close to himself, the good preceptor should visualize the entire group of principles starting with the earth(-element) and ending with Īśvara. He should then fix both his eyes, (which are now identified with those) of Lakṣmī,[3] on the (disciple) and touch (him) with hands (which too have become identified with those) of Lakṣmī. (He should then mentally) bring about the dissolution of the (principles forming the body of the disciple) starting with the element of earth and then evolve them afresh starting from Īśa. This method quickens the awakening (of consciousness) in the (otherwise) insentient principles present within the disciple's body. This (type of) initiation consists of meditation.

41-43. Taking the knotted thread placed between two plates, he should approach the pit (of the sacrificial fire). There he should perform (once again the process of) elimination and reinstatement (of the principles).[4] (Thereafter) he should offer first a thousand and,

---

[1] The bīja-mantra of the disciple.

[2] This naming ceremony runs as follows: the preceptor should put a flower in the hand of the blindfolded disciple and let him throw that away. The disciple should stand near the lotus diagram (cakrābja-maṇḍala, diagram IV) which has been divided into nine sections. According to the position where the flower has fallen, the disciple is named after one of Viṣṇu's incarnations, e.g. Keśava. He should add as an ending bhāgavata or bhaṭṭāraka for a brahmin, deva for a kṣatriya, pāla for a vaiśya and dāsa for a śūdra initiate. See K.K.C. pp. 170-182.

[3] Performance of the saṃpāta-homa has already achieved the preceptor's identification with Lakṣmī. See verse 26 of this chapter.

[4] The entire process is somewhat clumsily described here with much repetition and confusion in the order of the rites.

later, a hundred (more) oblations accompanied by the recitation of the (mantras of) Tārā and her aṅgas. Whereafter, picking up a flower he should consecrate it reciting various mantras, and then strike the disciple on his chest with (that flower) while reciting (the mantra of) Tārā ending with (the sounds) huṃ and phaṭ. Envisaging the disciple as filled with the principle of the earth-element, (the preceptor) should visualize the action of feeding him with all the edible products derived from the earth.[1]

44-49. Having finished (feeding the disciple with) all the food obtained from the earth (the preceptor) should then identify him with the element of water. Here again he should imagine the process (of feeding [2] the disciple) in the same way. (Meanwhile) having placed offerings (in the fire) while reciting the (mantra of) Tārā together with (the mantras of) her aṅgas, he should tear (from the thread) the knot which represents the element of earth. Putting it in the sruk and adding butter to it, he should offer that as an oblation to Tārikā, the supreme presence in the blazing fire inside the pit. Then he should pass it on to the subtler principle [3] of the water-element and perform the sacrifice in a similar manner. Whereafter he should pass it on to the still subtler element of fire and perform the rite of the final oblation (offered to the deity).

Following this method for each (of the principles) in consecutive order, he should make the final offering with each (of the principles),[4] and (gradually merging it) in the prakṛti he should (merge the prakṛti) into the (cosmic) Person and merge the (cosmic) Person into Īśvara. There is not a single principle in the whole group that surpasses Īśvara. Indeed the Śakti is of the form of Īśvara in (all her three states, viz.) the gross, the subtle and the absolute.[5]

---

[1] This probably implies forms of solid food.

[2] Liquid food.

[3] Here the sequence is reversed and each successive principle is subtler than the one preceding it.

[4] This rite requires the guru to begin by envisaging the disciple's identification with the last and the grossest of the principles and to lift him step by step in the traditional order from the grosser to the subtler principle. Each time he passes from one to the other, the discarded principle represented by the previously mentioned knot in the thread is sacrificed in the fire.

[5] Puruṣa (Person) is the totality of all individual selves. See ch. VII, 11. God here means God, the creator. Creation is Śakti's function, so Īśvara is identical with the Śakti. See ch. IV, 3-5.

49-50. Since in descending downwards from Īśvara the individual becomes impure, so on regaining that supreme principle he becomes pure indeed. (It is only) then that he, having become the abiding essence and the beholder of all, becomes worthy of initiation.

51-57. In order to emphasize the enjoyment (*bhoga*) and release (from bhoga), two final oblations should now be made.

Envisaging the disciple as (both) differentiated and absolute, the preceptor, who is (himself) in the state of parātīta,[1] should take butter twice in the sruk [2] (representing the disciple's two states). Then combining both (portions of) that (butter) he should visualize (himself) as consisting of the sound-consciousness, the excellent form of paśyantī,[3] the absolute state of Tārikā, undifferentiated and undisturbed. Identifying the disciplewi th this (state), he should make the final offering (of the above-mentioned butter) accompanying it with the (recitation of) (the mantra of) Tārā ending it with the word *vauṣaṭ*. Whereafter, in order to preserve the disciple from death, he should offer many oblations while (reciting the mantra of) Tārā starting with the praṇava (*dhruva*) and ending with the namas.[4] Next the preceptor should envisage the merger of both his disciple and himself in me, the eternal Lakṣmī, in the same way as milk mixes with milk (losing separate identity), whilst he throws (into the fire) the great final oblation after the last (customary) final offering has been made. Thus having identified the disciple with Lakṣmī, he again extricates, stage by stage, this mantra (from his own heart) through the force of the air of knowledge,[5] causes it to be heard, establishes me in the (disciple's) heart and teaches him (the mantra of) Tārā.

58. He should (also teach him) all the (mantras of) aṅgas and upāṅgas and all the methods (performances of rituals) according to the sacred texts. He should advise him of all the duties enjoined by the conventions (of the community),[6] such as respect for the secrecy of the mantras etc.

[1] This is the super-transcendental state beyond the absolute state. This is the state of God's existence transcending even the absolute Śakti.

[2] The sacrificial ladle. See ch. XL, 54, notes.

[3] See ch. XVIII, 25 and 29.

[4] *Oṃ hrīṃ namaḥ.*

[5] Vital air passing through the suṣumnā duct.

[6] This is known as *samayopadeśa*. Most of the Tantras give a detailed description of these duties which emphasize the secrecy of mantras, cf. J.S., ch. 16.

59. Thereafter touching him (= disciple) on the head, back and the chest with his (= preceptor's) hand (which now represents that of) Viṣṇu, he should consecrate all the parts of the (disciple's) body [1] by displaying (relevant) mudrās [2] (and by reciting the mantra of Tārā). Whereafter he and his disciple should join in worshipping me.

60-63. Taking the pitcher (filled with water) from where the preceptor has previously worshipped, reciting at the same time the (mantra of) Tārā, he should then, favourably disposed, pour the water over the disciple whilst mentally reciting the (mantra of) Tārikā together with (those of) her aṅgas and upāṅgas. The disciple, who has thus acquired a (new) form and crossed over the ocean of life (*saṃsāra*), should then make a costly offering to his preceptor.

Preparing (a seat and equating it with the divine seats of meditation) [3] such as the ādhāraśakti etc.[4] he should seat his preceptor on it and worship him with (the offerings of) arghya etc. with all the other (previously mentioned offerings) and also with gold and jewels. After offering him food and a libation he should worship him with the following mantra.

64. Salutation to (my) preceptor, who has the form of Sūrya, Soma and Agni,[5] illuminating the deep (darkness of) ignorance and who quenches the burning fire of three types of misery.

65. And after obtaining permission, he should start practising the (japa etc. of the) mantra and freely perform (the rituals) of his choice.

66. O slayer of Vala, here I conclude the description of the rites of initiation and abhiṣeka. Now, after due consideration tell me what more you wish to hear.

67.[6] Śakra:—O Padmā, (tell me), O Goddess, whether only those initiated in the (manner) described by you are entitled to worship Viṣṇu (the enemy of Madhu), or whether others are also so entitled.

68-71. Śrī:—O Indra, because of my affection for you this is a great secret which I am now going to reveal to you.

---

[1] See J.S. 16, 334-336.
[2] See ch. XXXIV, 18-30.
[3] J.S. gives a clearer description of this ceremony. See J.S. 16, 360-362.
[4] See ch. XXXVI, 2-36.
[5] See ch. XXIX, 1-41.
[6] The verses 67-78 are found only in the Telugu printed edition, Mysore 1888, as a parenthesis.

(The right to perform the ritual) for liberation belongs to all the members of the three (higher) classes of society who have undergone initiation. But not all of these are fit to worship (God) on behalf of others. Among (the initiates of the higher classes) in this world there are one hundred and eight illustrious sages, who have placed their prayers at Viṣṇu's feet, who are supreme Ekāntins,[1] who are well versed in the contents of the Kāṇva and Mādhyandina (schools of the White Yajurveda), who are wholly devoted to (the rites) of the Pāñcarātra (system), who have realized the religion of Śaraṇāgati,[2] who have mastered the two (principal) mantras [3] and who carry out the rites and duties enjoined by the aphorisms spoken by the sage Kātyāyana.[4]

72-76. Sages such as Kāśyapa, Gautama, Bhṛgu, Āśvalāyana, [illegible]iras etc. are best (fitted) to officiate on behalf of others at religious ceremonies dedicated to Hari. Others (bhāgavatas) have no right to officiate (on anyone else's behalf). These bhāgavatas, (worthy) worshippers, are dear to me and to Hari, others do not become bhāgavatas by worshipping the two of us[5] but are bhāgavatas only through their devotion (to us). Alternatively those who are firm devotees of the glorious Hari are called bhāgavatas by ordinary people. The highest worship should be performed by appointing a member of the families of the eminent sages such as Kāśyapa etc. (to officiate as priest). If through ignorance the highest task of an officiating priest is performed by some other (ordinary) bhāgavatas, great calamity to the king and to the state will ensue.

77-78. Hence one should take good care to appoint a priest who belongs by birth to the families of Kāśyapa etc., who is a bhāgavata, an initiate, and silent.[6] He is indeed well fitted to perform religious ceremonies, he purifies others and has great knowledge of Brahman.

---

[1] This is a name for all the followers of the Pāñcarātra system. Cf. H. Raychaudhuri, The early history of the Vaishṇava Sect, Calcutta 1936, p. 21.

[2] See ch. XVII, verses 61, 75 and 101 and ch. XXVIII, 9 and 11 describing prapatti.

[3] Most probably the eight-lettered mantra and the twelve-lettered mantra. See ch. XXIV, 67-69.

[4] The Kātyāyana Dharma Sūtra.

[5] The word *Bhāgavata* is used in two senses, those who officiate in the ritual worship of Bhagavat and those who are devotees of Bhagavat.

[6] *Nirakṣara*: uneducated ?

CHAPTER FORTY-TWO

THE RITE OF PURAŚCARAṆA, THE RITUAL WORSHIP OF THE MANTRA OF TĀRIKĀ

1. Śakra:—O possessor of the two feet which (as it were) serve as the boat to cross the ocean of worldly existence, O queen of Hṛṣīkeśa, I salute thee again and again.

2. By thy grace, O Goddess, I have followed (lit. heard) step by step the gradual order, the procedure (for performing the) rite of initiation. O Lotus-enthroned, deign to reveal to me the puraścaraṇa rites [1] of the (mantra of) Tārikā.

3. Śrī:—I am called Nārāyaṇī, the Śakti inherent in Nārāyaṇa. Tārikā, mistress of the universe, is the supreme form (manifestation) of that self of mine.

4-8. Now listen (what is) my Self, which is (considered to be) the whole valuable range of religious practices (*sādhana*) (concerning the worship of her) who is the concentrated form [2] of my very Self. The period covering the eighth to the fourteenth day of the dark fortnight has been indicated by the experts in Tantras as being the (most propitious) time for the successful (worship) of Tārikā. The adept, who is untouched by (= who never committed) any grievous sin (*mahāpāpa*) [3] or (one of the) well-known heinous crimes (*atipātaka*),[4] who has overcome disbelief and is without unseemly habits, who is always friendly towards all living beings and is contrite for all sins committed, should by performing expiatory rites (first) obliterate (the after-effects of) major and minor sins. (Then) the (adept) who practises asceticism and only eats haviṣya,[5]

---

[1] *Puraścaraṇa* is the collective term for all post-initiation rites prescribed for efficacious worship of the mantra especially imparted to the adept by the preceptor at the former's initiation. It also includes performance of the thrice daily duties of japa, tarpaṇa and the feeding of Brahmins. See Kulārṇava Tantra, 15, 8.

[2] This refers to the piṇḍa mantra of Tārikā. See ch. XXIX, 49.

[3] These are murder of a brahmin, drinking alcohol, stealing, having intercourse with the wife of one's preceptor, or associating with those who have committed any of the above-mentioned crimes.

[4] e.g. incest.

[5] Haviṣya is a meal composed chiefly of boiled grain and vegetables

who is truthful and holds fast to his vow, should mentally pronounce the word oṃ a million times, while visualizing Viṣṇu (to be) near (him).

8-9. (Thereafter) he should make ten thousand sacrifices with butter, while (reciting) the three great vyāhṛtis.[1] He should then perform an equal number of sacrifices with sesame, while (reciting the mantra of) Sāvitrī.[2] These obliterate the effects of [3] the two major sins, (namely) mahāpāpa and atipāpa.

10-11. Thus he who performs these three rites accompanied by (the recitation of) the three mantras of praṇava etc. becomes absolved of undisclosed sins such as mahāpāpa etc. Similarly (he should free himself from) the disclosed sins by fasting etc.

11-14. He who is expert in the (rites connected with the mantras called) aghamarṣaṇa [4] should fast for three nights. The one (engaged in the recitation of the mantras called) the three gems (*triratna*) should enter water three times a day and three times a night with his clothes on. Every evening (the adept) should thus take three dips (in the water) while performing the japa of the aghamarṣaṇa

---

eaten with butter and sea-salt, omitting food fried in oil. Bananas and other fruits with milk and molasses comprise the dessert.

[1] These are bhūḥ, bhuvaḥ and svaḥ.

[2] The Gāyatrī mantra. See ch. XXIX, 27 and 30.

[3] *Vihāya* usually implies 'excepting', but according to the editor V. Krishnamacharya the implied meaning of *vihāya prathitau* is 'obliteration' or 'effacement'.

[4] Three mantras, namely *drupadād ivā* etc., *ṛtañ ca satyañ ca* etc., and *āpo hi ṣṭhā* etc., (AV. 6, 115, 3; ṚV. 10, 9, 1; 190, 1), are collectively called aghamarṣaṇa-mantras or triratna-mantras. He who has committed a grave sin may obtain absolution by performing special rites in which three consecutive nights are spent in fasting and making ritual dips while reciting (in a low tone) the above-mentioned mantras. See P. V. Kane, History of Dharmaśāstra, vol. II, part I, pp. 661 and 686. The Tantric aghamarṣaṇa rite differs somewhat from the Vedic. Here, after performing ṣaḍaṅganyāsa, the adept should hold water in the hollow of his left palm and covering it with his right hand he should thrice utter the formula *haṃ yaṃ raṃ laṃ vaṃ*. Then, while reciting his own basic mantra, he should display the tattva mudrā and sprinkle his head with the drops of water escaping between the fingers of his left hand. Lastly, transferring what remains of the water from his left to his right palm, he should envisage the water as full of tejas, inhale it in imagination through his iḍā duct and, after rinsing the interior of his body in the same imaginary way, bring that water out through his piṅgalā duct. The water he visualizes by now to be black with filth, and envisaging it to be the embodiment of his sins, he throws it away. See Tantrasāra as quoted by T. Tarkavacaspati, Vacaspatyam, I, p. 68 (Chowkhamba Saṃskṛta Granthamālā 94).

(-mantras) three times and he should pass the three nights dipping himself repeatedly. (At the end of three nights) on the fourth day he should make a present of a milch cow to a Brahmin. This is (also) a way to obtain absolution from all distress (as by the other way) stated above.

14-15. Alternatively, he may (perform a different expiatory rite by) sprinkling himself three times [1] a day with the five products of the cow.[2] By passing three such nights (in performing the above mentioned rites) he can obtain absolution from all sins.

15-16. He may also perform japa of the five Vaiṣṇava (-mantras) Tāra etc.[3] all together or each individually, while visualizing them as spotlessly bright and drinking (as it were, the amṛta oozing out of them). Day and night performance of these rites sets him free from all sins.

17. Or, if allowed to share a meal with those followers of Viṣṇu who are virtuous in the world because of their staunch adherence to (all the religious) duties (of the Viṣṇuite faith), seated in the same row, one is absolved of every sin.

18. Having thus obliterated all sin by (performance) of (the expiatory) rites enjoined by the great sages, (the adept) should pass on to (the worship of the) Tārikā(-mantra), which is the saviour from the ocean of (worldly) existence.

19. The adept should, according to the śāstric canon, fast on the seventh day of the dark fortnight. Then, at dusk on the eighth day, he should (start) performing japa of (the mantra of) Tārikā.

20-22. Without neglecting his religious duties and with no other desire, (the adept) should (betake himself to) an untainted Viṣṇu sanctuary (erected) by some god or successful adept or sage; or (should repair to) the top of a mountain, or on the bank of a river, or in a meadow, or in a bilva [4] grove and there, subsisting on a single daily meal of haviṣya, milk or barley, he should for seven days perform the japa of (the mantra) twelve thousand times.

22-33. Then he should offer the libation and the butter oblations (to the deity, each) a hundred times (*daśāṃśaṃ*). If on the fourteenth

---

[1] The word *trisandhyā* denotes three junctures of the day, namely dawn, noon and dusk.

[2] For a more detailed description see J.S. 25, 14-22.

[3] Praṇava, vyāhṛtis, Gāyatrī, Tārā and Anutārā.

[4] Aegle Marmelos or the wood-apple.

night of the (dark fortnight), (the adept) thus engaged in worshipping the mantra of Tārikā has an auspicious vision (i.e. a dream, such as that) of receiving a jug of wine, of drinking wine, of an erotic meeting with a woman, of the look in (her) beautiful eyes, of affectionate embracing or sharing pleasure with her, of an assurance by her of his success in the mantric practice, of the forthcoming attainment of good results, the sight of something (somebody) auspicious or of a handsome couple, of an audience with the king or the queen, of direct confrontation with Nārāyaṇa or myself, of a loyal wife, of the advent of Viṣṇu's devotees—or whatever else is recorded as an auspicious omen in the science of dreams—then having obtained that assurance, he should arise (immediately after having dreamt) and shake off sleep, feeling refreshed. Thereafter rinsing his mouth (and) duly disposed, the adept (seated on a coverlet) should, by night, meditate on me. In the morning he should quit (his bed) and duly perform the sandhyā rites.[1] He should then invite a couple equally matched in good manners, looks and age, who are beautiful and engaged in performing pious deeds, who are neither pitiable nor mean in demeanour but full of charm, intelligence and youth, and who are attractive and soft-spoken. Invoking them as Lakṣmī and Nārāyaṇa, (the adept) should bathe them and then, sparing no expense, (clothe and) adorn them with garments etc. and, after anointing their bodies with fragrant unguents, he should feed and gratify them with a present (*dakṣiṇā*). Thereafter he should beg them, who are identified with Lakṣmī and Nārāyaṇa, for an assurance that his Tārikā worship will be fruitful. When they pronounce the words 'let it be so', he should seek refuge with them.[2]

34. He (= the adept) should then persuade them to say 'We accept'[3] (your offer of yourself). Thereafter he should satisfy (with a libation) the followers of Viṣṇu, who are the greatest expounders of (the doctrines of) the Vedas and foremost amongst the twice-born (caste). Henceforth he remains in the desired wealth (of merit).

35-43. If (on the other hand), he (= the adept) fails to see a

[1] See P. V. Kane, History of Dharmaśāstra, II, part II, pp. 312-321. This is obligatory worship that every brahmin must perform three times a day.

[2] For all ritual purposes this couple is identical with the divine couple Lakṣmī and Nārāyaṇa.

[3] This exclamation indicates acceptance.

(lucky) vision in his dream on the fourteenth day (of the dark fortnight), then during the period starting from the day of the new moon and ending on the seventh day (of the dark fortnight) he should observe the vow (of abstention), eat (only) one meal (a day) and perform japa three thousand times (every day). If within (this period) (his) young wife has had her period, he should not let that pass unheeded. He should not disparage the ways of women. He should bear in mind the blessed state of married couples. He should do everything to please the woman, (but) with mind detached, so that no sin is committed. Then, when the eighth day of the (dark fortnight) has come, he should perform japa as before and carrying out all the (rituals) such as the fire sacrifices etc., he should prepare himself to see the dream-vision. Thus he should continue to act in this way until he observes (in dream) the (lucky) signs. By this means he who has mastered the (mantra of) Tārikā can achieve anything. He is an expert in performing all the (rituals prescribed) by the sacred scriptures. He has insight in the spiritual methods. He has the knowledge of all the injunctions contained in all Tantras and is a master in all Vedāntas. He has solved all problems (of religion) and is well versed in all (religious) dicta. He is truthful, sincere, frank in speech and a past master in (steering through) the ocean of religious practice. He is always ready to apply religious injunctions to himself as well as to others. And whether or not conditions are favourable he succeeds in all (his endeavour).

43-46. Śakra:—I salute thee, the embodiment of all the six attributes, O beloved of Hari, who abidest in the lotus, and O spouse of Govinda. I have heard from thy lotus-mouth about the excellent efficacious (practice) of the (mantra of) Tārikā. This has been duly (explained to me) in its (three states), namely the gross state, the subtle state and the absolute state. Now, O lotus-born, deign to tell me about the specific application of (the mantra of) Tārā in its three states after the ritual has been duly performed.

46-50. Śrī:—Lord Nārāyaṇa is unique and is essentially the aggregate of six attributes and is the soul (*haṃsa*). I am His Śakti, the female (counterpart of the) soul (*haṃsī*), the Mistress over (all creation) and the bestower of all that is desired. Together as Haṃsa and Haṃsī we jointly (manifest ourselves) in action as Tārikā.

Now listen when I (describe) the application of this (mantra) which is essentially (identical with) us. Without question its application covers all the various other applications of all the mantras of every description in each group, whether supreme or ordinary, whether external (gross) or internal (subtle). Nevertheless, O Śakra, hear trom me some particular applications (of this mantra).

51-53. I should be visualized as the one who generates instant understanding of (the four objectives of life, i.e.) duty, subsistence, desire and liberation, who wears the hide of a black deer over the upper part of her body, who is seated on and wrapped in black deer skin, who has auspicious eyes resembling a shy black fawn, who is (as lovely) as the full moon, who displays the gesture of Brahma (with one hand) and holds the rosary (in the other), whereas in each of her other two hands she holds a lotus.[1] Alternatively, the lotus-eyed Janārdana, the Lord of all gods, may be visualized (by the adept).

54-61. After (this) visualization (the adept) should perform japa of the (mantra of) Tārā a hundred thousand times (and thus) should bring his (accumulated) merit within the bounds of perception. Next, filling many prasthas [2] with śāli (rice) and an equal number of prasthas with butter and palas [3] with sugar or molasses, he should cook them together in one pot (adding) the same quantity of milk to make the oblation nice and thick (in consistency). Then, on the morning after the day of the full moon, when the sun has only half risen, the intelligent (adept) should make one offering of the contents of that big pot by sacrificing it in the big fire in the great pit, whilst (reciting) the mantra of Jātavedas etc.[4] in triṣṭubh metre, which includes the mantra of Tārikā, using the yantra [5] as well.

Thereafter, from dawn till sunset, without respite the intelligent (adept) should continue to make repeated offerings of butter by pouring it from the sruva, which has been similarly consecrated by

[1] She appears more like some Buddhistic Tārā than Lakṣmī. Cf. B. Bhattacharya, The Indian Buddhist Iconography, Calcutta 1958, pp. 226, 231, 307-309.

[2] A *prastha* is two earthenware plates full of food.

[3] A measure for liquids such as oil or melted butter. It is a small bowl with a spout and a hooked handle and holds about one ounce of oil.

[4] Ṛg.V. 1, 99, 1[a].

[5] The Tantric diagram. See Swāmi Pratyagātmānanda Saraswatī and Arthur Avalon, Sādhana for Self-realization, Madras 1963, pp. 39-69.

the (mantra in) triṣṭubh metre. From dawn onwards (he should also) go on feeding a number of brahmins, one at a time, with śāli (rice) mixed with milk, curd and butter. And when the brahmins of superior Vedic knowledge have been persuaded to pronounce (a blessing: *svasti*), he should satisfy them and the Vaiṣṇava couple with a libation addressing the latter as Lakṣmī and the husband of Lakṣmī.

62. Helped by his strenuous effort he who performs this ritual obtains ten millions of matchless imperishable jewels.

63-67. Now, O Pākaśāsana, listen to the following highly miraculous application (of the mantra of Tārā). Taking the (basic mantra of) Tārā, add on the word *subhage* to the end and finish with the word *svāhā*. This (mantra of) Tārikā has thus become six-lettered.[1] After fasting on the fourteenth day (of the bright fortnight, the adept) should commence performing (this special rite) on the day when the moon is full. Seated between a pitcher completely filled (with water) and a (burning) lamp, in a garden full of beautiful plants, and envisaging me (i.e. the embodiment of the above mantra) as possessing the colour such as possessed by the inside of a lotus and holding a lotus in each hand, with two arms, with dark (eyes) glancing sidelong and black curly hair, with a round smiling face and of an attractive appearance, with firm, high breasts, lavishly adorned with all (sorts of) ornaments and wearing two garments of exquisite beauty, he should recite this (mantra) ten thousand times.

68-71. Thus visualizing me, the auspicious and lucky one, he should (complete) his japa. He should (next) satisfy (me) with a hundred offerings and a hundred libations (to me), accompanying them with the recitation of this (mantra of) Tārā. He should then offer me food consisting of śāli (rice) mixed with milk, butter and molasses. Whereafter, the intelligent (adept) should worship and give food to a woman possessing (all auspicious) signs. He himself should have only one meal at night consisting of nothing but haviṣya (food) and must observe complete abstention. This vow must be unfailingly observed for thirty nights by performing the (prescribed rites for) japa, libations (*tarpaṇa*) and offerings, without interruption and with diligence. On the next full moon day, having performed the rites entailed by his vow, the adept may be absolved from it.

[1] *(oṃ) hrīṃ subhage svāhā.*

72-75. On fulfilment of the vow a Yakṣī, called Subhagā, who is essentially myself, appears there. She will ask the adept: 'What shall I do for you?' (He) may regard her as being his mother, sister, wife or friend. If she is approached (by the adept) as (his) mother, she protects him from all misfortunes. If she is approached as (his) sister, she bestows upon him whatever (he desires). If (he) accepts her as his beloved, he satisfies all his (passionate) yearnings for the duration of his life. If (on the other hand) he accepts her as a friend, she gives him all the quarters (lands).[1]

75. But the adept who yearns after liberation should always recite (the mantra of Tārā in its three forms, namely) the gross, the subtle and the absolute.[2] (Then) gratified (by his performances of the rituals) I lead him to the divine state (*pada*) of Viṣṇu. However, whatever be the (practical) applications of other supreme mantras which I shall tell you later, all those (practical) applications of different mantras should (also) be regarded as practical applications of (the mantra of) Tārikā.[3] Thus I have given you a detailed description of how to perform puraścaraṇa rites and have included (an explanation of) the application (of the mantra). Now, in order to complete your understanding, learn from me the method of performing a ritual worship (with mantra) efficaciously.[4]

---

[1] This may imply that the deity makes the adept a great king; cf. expressions such as *sarvadigvijaya*.

[2] See ch. XXXII, 2-37.

[3] As previously pointed out Tārikā is the source of all mantras and is immanent in all of them. The other mantras are merely various manifestations of Tārikā.

[4] The term mantra-siddhi really means that, when the adept has fruitfully completed all the rituals and meditations relating to his own basic mantra, which is a sonic manifestation of the supreme Śakti, he becomes identified with the śakti present in that particular mantra and acquires all the divine power belonging to that śakti.

CHAPTER FORTY-THREE

DIFFERENT METHODS OF WORSHIPPING THE MANTRA OF TĀRIKĀ

1. Śrī:—Listen now, Sureśvara, I shall tell you the supremely efficacious results obtained from the various ways in which the concentrated form (*piṇḍa*) of the mantra of Tārikā may be worshipped.

2. The yogin should (begin the ritual worship) by duly attaching [1] the (mantra of) Tārikā to the range (of the parts) of (his) body, (especially) to the tip of his nose and to the tip, middle and root of his tongue.

3-6. He should carry [2] the group of (cosmic) principles, from the earth-element to the (cosmic) intelligence between his throat and chest and thighs and following the natural order of (the relationship as the cause and) effect of each (of the principles) he should pass from the one to the other (while performing an equal number of) japas (of the relevant mantra); [3] (he may perform the japa) twice, four, six, eight, ten, sixteen or twenty-four times. After (cosmic) intelligence he should visualize prakṛti and should recite (the mantra of) Tārā eighty times. (Then) he should there (in the prakṛti) envisage the individual self (*jīva*)—its scope, nature and identity—and perform japa (of the same mantra) a hundred times. He should then visualize the lotus, which is the seat of unmanifested consciousness.

7. After visualizing it in the form of a lotus [4] on which the principles exist and which is the infinite abode of the (various) parts (of prakṛti) such as the principles etc., the wise (adept) should perform the (same) japa a hundred and fifty times.

---

[1] The method of aṅganyāsa referred to here is described in ch. XXXV, 60-81. See K. Rangachari, o.c., pp. 63-67.

[2] The nyāsa is extended to the cosmic principles forming the adept's corporeal body.

[3] Each successive principle ensues from the one immediately preceding it. For example the element of earth results from the element of water which, in turn, results from the element of fire and so on. For the order of these principles see ch. V, 38-79.

[4] See ch. V, 22-28.

8-9. Thereafter, (he should visualize) the stem (of that lotus) as combining in itself Time unmanifested, the individual self and the immutable being (*akṣara*), which is represented by (the unlimited) space (*khaṃ*).[1] Time is represented there in (the stem) as tamas and forms the hollow (of the stem). Reflecting upon that which contains all the three (above-mentioned realities): 'that inner consciousness is that (which abides in all)' (the adept) should duly perform two hundred japas.

10. Under the stem (of the lotus) the śakti called Aniruddha, who is pervaded by me, the divine (Śakti), should be remembered by him as (characterized by the first manifestation of) form, time etc.[2] and he should perform a hundred japas.

11. Thereunder (he should visualize) Pradyumnaśakti and (perform) the same number of japas and thereunder (visualizing) the śakti of Saṃkarṣaṇa (he should again perform) the same number of japas.

12-13. Under all (the above-mentioned śaktis) (he should consecutively visualize) Vāsudeva (śakti), who is the (divine) couple, in gross form, in subtle form then in transcendent form and lastly in the supra-transcendent form which is the incomprehensible, incomparable manifestation of Lakṣmī and Nārāyaṇa, the impeccable Śakti and the possessor of Śakti, vibrating (*spandamāna*) everywhere.

14-16. (By that time the adept feels sleepy), which (= sleep) is (itself a form of) yoga [3] and (in the course of his meditation) he falls asleep. Awaking in the late (hours) of the night he (immediately) starts practising dhāraṇā [4] (using each of these) twelve, from Vāsudeva to the element of earth,[5] following the order of their position enumerated (before). All these dhāraṇās may be (envisaged) as held in (the adept's) heart, or (alternatively) these twelve dhāra-

[1] Vyoma, Śūnya, Kha etc. represent the same undifferentiated, unmanifested supreme Self.

[2] See ch. II, 41-48 and ch. IV, 13-19.

[3] When a yogin constantly practises yoga, the little time at night which he can spare for his sleep, needed to refresh his body, is not regarded as wasted, since even then he remains in constant contact with his Self.

[4] See the Yog.S. 3. 1.

[5] Vāsudeva, Saṃkarṣaṇa, Pradyumna, Aniruddha, jīva, prakṛti, the cosmic intelligence and the five elements.

ṇās could be (envisaged as) existing in Tārikā. This is Sarvahitayoga covering all the (cosmic) principles.

17-19. Alternatively, (the adept) may make his mind totally vacant by dissolving (all the principles) forming the manifested and unmanifested creation (each in its immediate source) and he makes (his mind) supportless and arrives at the state of voidness [1] (thinking) 'I am now entering the state of mahāyoga which in form resembles the form of void, possessing the characteristic (calmness) of the void resembling a (calm) completely filled ocean' and when the yogin remains always attached to (my form) which resembles the blissfulness of a silent and dark cloud,[2] then that yogin is for ever dear to me.

20. In that state there is no finite object to concentrate on; that unknowable transcendent form is indeed my revealed form.[3]

21-23. Within himself the yogin causes all the objects of knowledge to become, at once, one with the Ātman. He (envisages) my form as a vast expanse of extensive and unflickering fire, wherein he mentally sacrifices all created objects and all the worlds. Whenceforth he attains for ever my own state of existence, which is the (true) state of being All. He mentally offers (to me) the created objects, his beads (*akṣa*) [4] and the world etc. (tendering them as it were) with the sruk and then throwing that sruk [5] (into the fire), the yogin becomes identical with me.

24-28. An object that imposes limitations on something else is (always) wider (in scope) than that (the latter). Higher knowledge (*dhī*) limits all things whether existent or non-existent, whereas in itself it is free from all limitation.[6] That (knowledge) is my flawless form. Nothing, whether negative or positive, is beyond the scope of (that) knowledge, nothing remains unembraced by (that) knowledge and that is my immaculate form. When the ocean overflowing its boundaries floods the world no dry land or lowland remains (visible);

[1] Śūnyabhāva is the state of unpolarized knowledge. Cf. verse 8 (*khaṃ*) of this chapter.

[2] Form not in the material sense; it means as she is revealed in the intuitive knowledge of the adept.

[3] Implying that the mind becomes totally free from all impressions and thereupon reveals the true essence of Śakti.

[4] Sacrificing the beads of the rosary symbolizes the adept's attainment of the final goal.

[5] Denoting the end of the ritual.

[6] Hence knowledge in its widest scope is the cognition of the eternal truth.

so (do I flood) this universe.[1] This exalted state of existence cannot be attained by beings of limited capacity. Therefore one should perform yoga in stages to attain this (state).

28-35. (The adept) should visualize the supreme God as the essence, in a more concentrated form (than even the Śakti), and as immanent in all objects, whether good or otherwise, which have existed, still exist or will exist in future. Just as bees gather only the honey from flowers, so from everything does the yogin gather (experiences) only (of) myself. In whatever his mind dwells on he perceives only Lakṣmī. If anything attempts to escape (from me), where can it run to since everything is permeated by me? The adept should envisage the (cosmic) principles as a garland strung on me (as the thread). Or else he may regard this universe as a painting of which I am the canvas.[2] Just as foam amasses on (the surface of the) calm, shoreless and deep ocean, so should (the adept) call to mind the cognizer etc., (i.e.) the four-fold universe,[3] both at the time of their creation and at that of their dissolution. All the (cosmic principles) evolve from me and again merge back into me. The Person is my first manifestation designed by my intention.[4] My second manifestation is called the mind (which is) of more concrete (nature). The external instruments of cognition which have undergone further concretization constitute my third (manifestation), while my fourth manifestation is in the objects forming the content of cognition and is the lowest in material (grossness).[5]

36-48. It is by my own will that (the adept) who constantly meditates on me, the ever blissful consciousness, should, with a mind (*dhī*) rising higher and higher, detach himself from these four

---

[1] At the final stage of yoga the adept realizes the Śakti as the eternal consciousness, the unpolarized knowledge, which is the single abiding principle pervading everything.

[2] The first image of Śakti as the honey stresses the adept's detachment from worldly objects. They are only means to experience the existence of Śakti. The second image emphasizes Śakti's immanence in all the cosmic principles, evolving into the creation, as the antaryāmin or sūtrātmā of the Bhagavadgītā. The third image is more in keeping with the Vedānta metaphysics since it underlines the illusory aspects of creation, by comparing it to a painting on the vast canvas of the all-pervading Śakti.

[3] The cognizer, the cognition, the instrument of cognition, namely the senses, and the content of cognition, in the order of manifestation's progressive grossness.

[4] *saṃkalpa*: 'creative intention, determination, constructive imagination'.

[5] Cf. Ka.U.3, 10.

(forms in which the universe is manifested) and attain my own state of being. Or else, in the thirty-two lotuses supporting true knowledge, he may visualize me as the flame of a lamp, or as a beautiful lady.

The yogins must imagine that six lotuses occupy the region that extends from the ādhārapadma to just below the lotus of the navel. Hear their names from me. (They are called) Vyucchantī, Vyuṣitā, Vyuṣṭā, Vyuṣuṣī, Vyoṣuṣī and Ramā. The five lotuses present between the lotus of the navel and the lotus of the heart are called Paśyantī, also known as the lotus of the navel, Paśyā, Paśyetarā, Dṛśyā and Dṛśyamānā. Now listen to the names of the five lotuses that occupy the region between the lotus of the heart and the lotus of the neck. Bodhayantī, Boddhrī, Budhyamānā, Budhyamānetarā and Ghoṣonmeṣā are the names of the lotuses existing between (the lotus of) the heart and (that of) the neck. Now listen to the names of those lotuses that exist between the throat and the palate: Ghoṣayantī, Ghuṣyanti, Ghuṣṭā, Ghoṣā and Ghoṣetarā. (The following) are the names of the lotuses existing between the palate and the eyebrows: Grāhayantī, Gṛhṇānā, Jighṛkṣā, Gṛhītikā and Nirṇiti. Now hear the names of those six lotuses that exist between the eye-brows and the forehead: Prāṇayantī, Prāṇatī, Prāṇā, Prāṇāvabodhinī, Parā and Bodhā. The yogin should call me to mind as rising step by step (from the lower to the higher lotuses) as the flame of a jewelled lamp, whilst uttering me (i.e. the mantra of) Tārikā, loudly and long like the sound of a ringing bell. The yogin, who visualizes me as such, or as a beautiful lady, discards all misery and attains my own state of being.

49-50. Alternatively, (the adept) may visualize (Tārikā) as existing in the nine lotuses and as successively rising (from the lower to the higher lotus). The arrangement of these nine lotuses is as follows: three are located at the ādhāra (*padma*), three are below the lotus of the heart and three are below the forehead. Or, (he may envisage Tārikā as existing successively) in the twelve lotuses, (counting) two (lotuses) at each location (of the six vital parts of the body), (namely) the forehead etc.[1]

51. Alternatively, (he may envisage her) in the six primary lotuses.[2] He may also envisage Tārikā as containing tāranāda [3] and

[1] The forehead, eyebrows, palate throat, heart and navel.
[2] The traditional ṣaṭcakra or ṣaṭpadma.
[3] Nāda, or tāra, is sound unmanifest. See ch. XVIII, 23.

as located in the three (lotuses placed) at the mūla (*ādhāra*), at the heart and between his two eyebrows.

52-54. (The adept) should first envisage the bindu [1] as a shining, minute (atomic) grain of lentil,[2] growing in size to that of a mustard seed, and then as assuming the form of various and unspecified objects such as a pitcher, bowl etc. to represent the content of the mind (cognition). He should also envisage all the (cosmic) principles, whatever their number may be according to the sacred books, as contained there (in the bindu). Thereafter identifying that (bindu) with me, he should envisage (me as identical) with his own self-consciousness.

54-59. All objects of this world invariably conceived in pairs—such as those associated with (the concepts of) cause and effect, with protection and that which is protected, with transparency and opaqueness,[3] with existence and the essence of existence, with good and bad, with productivity and non-productivity, with quality and that which is qualified, with the container and that which is contained, with that which is pervaded by Śakti and the possessor of Śakti, with that which is enjoyed and the person enjoying, with man and woman, with action and its agent, with means and ends, with the inflectional forms [4] denoting masculine and feminine (gender), sound and form—should be envisaged by the yogin as manifestations of Lakṣmī and Nārāyaṇa.

59-65. O Puraṃdara, listen now to this highly secret rule (holy practice) of the tantra,[5] which, in the worship of Lakṣmī, a yogin should (always) follow. When at the very beginning, emanating from the primal God, I manifested myself in this world of systematic creation, I intentionally chose to assume this feminine form. (Therefore) a yogin, desirous of pleasing me and expert in the Lakṣmī Tantra,[6] should never abuse a woman, either in deed, thought or speech. Wherever I exist, the realities exist too; wherever I exist, the gods exist too; wherever I exist, merits exist too, and

[1] See ch. XVIII, 24.

[2] *Mudga.*

[3] *Ghana.*

[4] *Pratyaya.*

[5] Tantra may mean the secret lore in general, or may refer only to this particular text.

[6] This statement establishes the basic tendency of this tantra in which women occupy a specially honoured place.

wherever I exist, Keśava also exists.[1] Therefore I (should be regarded as) the woman(-hood) inherent in all women, that pervades the universe. He who abuses a woman thereby abuses Lakṣmī (Herself). He who praises her, praises Lakṣmī and so praises the three worlds. He who bears ill will against any woman is ill-disposed towards Lakṣmī (lit. the beloved wife of Hari).

66-73. He whose heart delights at the sight of a woman, resembling the moonlight (gladdening his heart), and who never entertains an evil thought (about her), is regarded as my most favourite (one). O Śakra, just as there is sin neither in Nārāyaṇa nor in myself, nor in a cow, nor in a brahmin, nor in a scholar of Vedānta, so, O Śakra, there can be no evil in a woman. Just as the rivers Gaṅgā, the sacred Sarasvatī and Aruṇā are devoid of stain, so also is an excellent woman revered (as being sinless). The (fact) that I, the Mother of the three worlds, am the basis (*avaṣṭambha*) of woman (-hood), makes her, indeed, my great (divine) prowess (*bala*). Since woman, as my direct embodiment, is the mother of the three worlds and the goddess full of abundance (capable of fulfilling all) desires (of everybody), how can the yogin refrain from worshipping her? One should not commit a wicked deed involving a woman; one should not (even) think about sinful acts in connection with a woman. Those who aspire to the attainment (of fulfilment) in yoga should always act so as to please a woman barring to commit a sin. One should regard her as one's mother, as god and as myself. He who, out of ignorance, hates women and does not help them...[2]

73-77. O Śakra, you are particularly dear to me, now listen (carefully) to what I am about to say. Having heard it, you too should put it in practice, (but) you should not tell anybody about it.

If a yogin should meet a beautiful and shapely (lit. fine-hipped) woman, he should visualize me in her whilst mentally reciting (the mantra of) Tārikā. He should contemplate her beauty with a mind free from lust. He should envisage her vital air (*prāṇa*) as the sun, and her soul (*hṛdayapuruṣa*) as the highest Self. He should envisage her beauty and charm as fire. He should visualize that highly gifted woman as identical with me. In this way, after seeing me (in her),

---

[1] 'I in the form of every woman' is implied here.
[2] This sentence is incomplete.

he should with his enlightened mind meditate on me [1] whilst reciting Brahma (i.e. tāra-mantra).

78-85. By and by, when he achieves the state of samādhi,[2] I enter there (in the person of that woman). The sign of my advent (in her) is a stillness and relaxation in all parts (of her) body. After duly worshipping me (as embodied in her), with a mind free from desire, he should stop (the moment) he is united and should avoid all sin.[3] The wise should never perform this with the wives of others, (because) she in whom such samādhi occurs is sure to love it.[4] (Therefore) one should perform this with one's own wife or with a common woman. (Of course) deviation from (this rule) is not wrong as (such a woman) is envisaged as identical with me.[5] The intense delight derived from the enjoyment through physical contact should be meditated on (by the yogin) with an unflickering mind as being my own person.[6] The state of pleasure obtained from stimulation and friction with some recommended object (of delight) (i.e.) the erotic enjoyment, should be cultivated (by the yogin). The pleasure derived from seeing some object with the eyes, from tasting (some object), from listening to (some sound), from inhaling some smell, is my blissful manifestation. As revealed (here), this becomes true in the case of the yogin who practises self-restraint, when (sensual enjoyment) arising from listening, tasting, touching etc. comes naturally to him (without his conscious desire).

86. Enjoyment derived from (mere physical) contact only brings misery. It has a beginning and an end, (hence) (a yogin's mind) should not find (real) pleasure in it.

87-94. The supreme delight experienced through the intuitive knowledge of (the yogin) who has conquered the rajas and destroyed the tamas (in himself) and who exists only in the state of sattva —that (experience of) bliss without a beginning or end is my body

---

[1] *bhāvayed evu māṃ dhiyā.*

[2] Meditative trance, the final stage of meditation.

[3] *Yuñjānaḥ* implies sexual union. A yogin may not prolong this lest he lapses into carnal pleasure, which is sinful.

[4] The caution is for the woman's sake, since she may become so attached to the blissful state that she may neglect her duty towards her husband.

[5] The cautious moral tone is somewhat lowered in favour of the yogin who practises such rites with a married woman, since he looks upon her as Lakṣmī Herself and thereby offers no insult.

[6] The pleasure is identical with the supreme bliss, which is the essence of Lakṣmī.

pervaded by knowledge. That (pleasure) can never be experienced (in the pleasure) obtained from (the enjoyment) derived from objects of physical contact, because afterwards these pleasure-inducing objects imprison a person in misery. What (is the use of) the honey in which poison lurks, even if it tastes sweet, since afterwards it kills its consumer? A person seeking to obtain happiness from enjoyment derived from physical contact is like one sheltering under the shadow of a vicious snake when exhausted by heat of the sun. Which happy person will be deceived by such pleasures, which are to be obtained through great hardship, which though seeming to entice hold misery, which are limited and decaying? The yogin, who has purified himself by reciting the prescribed (mantra), who eats with restraint and whose (two lesser guṇas) rajas and tamas, already diminished by his divine sattva (guṇa), are further reduced by the performance of rites pleasing to me, should never cease to discipline his mind in order to attain samādhi. Indeed, he who has conquered his mind is always able to win the world. My pure body automatically reveals itself to a mind (fully) conquered (by its possessor).[1]

95-96. Śakra:—O regulator of all these (created things) conscious and unconscious and all these tantras and yantras, creator of all that may be enjoyed, I salute thee who art enthroned on a lotus. How can the mind which always has a (natural) tendency to seek contact with (external) objects, which is so strongly inclined to be frivolous, which is difficult to bend and can wander far (out) in a moment's time and which is undeveloped, be controlled?

97. Śrī:—O Śakra, the mind is (indeed) always hard to control, difficult to restrain, atomic in size and (hence) (its workings are) improper and not easy to understand, and it is restless; all that should be checked by ceaseless effort (*abhyāsa*) and by overcoming passion (*vairāgya*).

98-105. Passion is the attachment to (material) objects arising from natural instinct or long habit. Vairāgya, which is the absence of that (passion) is generated by the realization of truth. That realization is the true understanding of the evil nature of (material) objects. A wise man should through intelligence discern that evilness (of such objects) by four means. He should ponder over the

[1] The trend of these verses is directed against the abuse of rites involving the sex-act.

object—what it is, what are its characteristics, what is its source and to whom does it belong—(consideration of these four aspects reveals to him) that the object is nothing but a shackle binding him who takes pleasure in it. These (objects that produce the feelings of) pleasure and sorrow are manifestations of the unmanifested (prakṛti). These objects (affording pleasure) to those who desire them are never self-determined.[1] They are products of a huge amount of money, effort and hardship. They do not produce any (real) happiness whereas misery flows (freely) out of them. The intelligent should mentally figure out this mixed nature of each object recognizing that whatever delight it gives is but momentary and that even that is inherently mingled with unhappiness. Thus the nature of true knowledge has been described in (both its) general and particular (aspects). The passion for (material) objects is caused by the notion that they produce happiness, and that (notion) is (what is known as) the false knowledge. That is why true knowledge removes that (false knowledge) by contradicting that notion, so that to regard them as being the source (of happiness) cannot stand scrutiny.

106-109. Nobody aspires after unmotivated objects for fulfilment of his purposes. Ceaseless effort to realize this truth is called abhyāsa by the scholars in their treatises on true knowledge.

Focussing his mind to concentrate on any of these objects, subtle, great, atom-sized or gross, immobile or mobile, as suits (him) the yogin should practise this abhyāsa and carefully following (this method of) overcoming passion and of sustained effort he surely succeeds in checking his wayward mind and make it tranquil.

109-111. Śakra:—O lotus-seated one, I salute thee who movest skillfully on these many lotus-like tattvas and abidest in the mind of Madhu's vanquisher.[2] Deign to show me the way how to restrain the mind, effectively and firmly, through abhyāsa. I salute thee (again) O lotus-born (goddess).

111-114. Śrī:—One may either fix one's mind on objects becoming progressively less distinct such as on a bird in the sky, which becomes smaller and smaller in its swift upward flight or on (the

[1] True knowledge, being absolute, is self-determined and the opposite is false. This is ascertained by the Vedānta metaphysics.

[2] The demon Madhu; see Ahi.S. ch. 41 and Jayākhya S. ch. 2.

star called) Arundhatī.[1] Alternatively, one may fix (one's mind on some vast object such as) a huge mountain or something infinite. One may fix attention on the tiny (central hole) in a whirling disc and allow the mind to swirl along with the disc's movement. One may similarly allow one's mind to vibrate along with the trembling tips of leaves of the sacred fig tree.[2] One may fix one's mind on an immobile object, or one may let one's mind travel along with a mobile object.[3]

115. O Puraṃdara, I have told you this only by way of giving a few examples of this method.[4] He who controls his mind by such a method acquires great (skill in) Yoga.

116. (The exalted form of) the Person existing in sūrya (*ha*) as polarized by (two aspects namely) that of the Master and servant, the absolute and the limited, should be called to mind as feminine when the *pañcabindu* (*ī*) is added to it.

117. Thus, O handsome one, have I revealed to you every aspect of Tārikā. He who has learned the truth in this way desires to know nothing more.

118. O Śakra, thus have I briefly disclosed to you how (the mantra of Tārikā in its) piṇḍa-form [5] can be effectively worshipped. Now listen as I explain the saṃjñā-mantra (of Tārikā) and its application.

---

[1] This is a famous dictum referred to as *arundhatī-nyāya*. The said star shines faintly near a bright star belonging to a well-known constellation and in order to discover Arundhatī one has first to fix attention on that constellation, then on the nearest bright star, and finally to pick out Arundhatī.

[2] The tips of these leaves form a slender strip and are easily agitated by the faintest breath of air.

[3] The implication is that the adept should focus attention on some object and be open to the impression received without attempting to interpret them. The mind then becomes relaxed and tenseness is avoided. Later the mind slowly and naturally gathers concentration and dives deeper into the basic qualities of such objects.

[4] There are various other methods for concentrating the yogin's mind but the main principle is conveyed by these examples.

[5] The piṇḍa mantra of Tārikā is *īṃ*.

CHAPTER FORTY-FOUR

REVEALING THE SECRET MANTRAS OF THE TĀRIKĀ GROUP

1-2. Śakra:—I salute thee who art skilful in protecting (both) the conscious and unconscious groups (of creation). I prostrate myself before thee who art the artist of the cosmic system of law and wife of Viṣṇu. The differentiation of the (mantra of) Tārā has already been revealed. Now, O Lotus-born (goddess), deign to show me the division of (the mantra of Tārā) into bīja, piṇḍa etc.

3) Śrī:—Nārāyaṇa is the unique possessor of Śrī, and embodies all pristine six attributes. I am His unique great Śakti embodying the six attributes.

4. In order to serve the world's purpose, that same I, who am manifest as Tārikā and incorporate (both my aspects of) knowledge and action, always sustain and purify (the world).

5. O Śakra, I have already revealed to you its (the mantra of Tārikā's) different forms as transcendent etc. Now listen to me as I enumerate the bīja, piṇḍa etc.

6-8. O Śakra, when I described the threefold form of her (Tārikā's) absolute state,[1] I told you that (God's) I-hood in that form is referred to as the bīja of Tārikā.[2] The concentrated (sound of) sūrya (*ha*) and anala (*ra*) together joined with viṣṇu (*ī*) with vyomeśa (*ṃ*) at the end (is the bīja)[3] and its effectiveness in the puraścaraṇa yoga has already been mentioned.[4] O Śakra, the yogins worship the saṃjñā (-form) of Tārikā. Now listen to me attentively as I describe it.

9. O Śakra, taking one pure (bīja-mantra) one should join it with *svāhā*. This constitutes the mantra of saṃjñā, which is worshipped by yogins and gods (such as) Brahmā etc.

10. O lord of the gods, the might of this saṃjñā can only be told by the yogins who practise it and by myself or Nārāyaṇa.

---

[1] See ch. XXXII, 15-37.

[2] Tārikā in the absolute form represents the Śakti's original state of being as Viṣṇu's I-hood.

[3] *Hrīṃ*.

[4] See ch. XLII, in extenso.

11-13. The saṃjñā requires the addition of the supreme undecaying *śubha* only.[1] Remembering that all fruits derived from the worship of śakti and all methods (of worship) belong to its piṇḍa form, by constantly practising (yoga) the yogin dissolves his body into me, and thus steeped in me attains my state of existence. Or, (seen from another angle), roused by (the yogin) I appear before him and fulfil, whatever the yogin may long for.

14. Thus, Śakra, I have briefly stated the mantra of saṃjñā. Now hear from me the pada-mantra which accomplishes all.

15. It should never be quoted or written in fragments. Its true form is taught so that there should be no mistake about it.

16-18. *Oṃ oṃ oṃ* . . . *śrīṃ hrīṃ oṃ*. Thus have I revealed to you the very miraculous pada-mantra. The wise who have undergone initiation should receive it (only) from the mouth of their preceptors. When (a yogin) has mastered this mantra, I then manifest myself (to him) as in a spotless mirror in all my capacities, aspects and roles.

18. (It is) appreciated by a adepts who have reached their goal and to whom the real nature of cosmic principles (forming) their (body) is revealed. Listen now to me as I enumerate its parts (*aṅga*).

19-20. The wonderful hṛnmantra should be pronounced as follows: *Oṃ prakāśānandasāre sarvadarśini satsattvavyañjike parabrahmarūpe bhagavati viṣṇupatni jñānāya hṛdayāya svāhā.*

21. *Oṃ avyāhatānandagate parameśvari sarvopari sthite jñānāya śirase svāhā.*

22. *Oṃ hrīṃ śaktisampūrṇe jagatprakṛtike jñānavaiśvānaraśikhe jñānāya śikhāyai svāhā.*

23. *Oṃ prāṇāprāṇamayonmeṣamahāspandamayi sarvāśramapadātīte jñānāya kavacāya svāhā.*

24. *Oṃ vikāravidhure svasvabhāve mahāvīryamayi jñānāya astrāya phaṭ.*

25. *Oṃ parānapekṣasāmarthye sarvaprasavini ante bodhamayi jñānāya netrāya svāhā.*

26. A group of five sounds composed of brahma (*praṇava*), māyā (*ī*) connected with śānta (*śa*) and anala (*ra*) with vyomeśa (*ṃ*) at the end: this is (the mantra) called brahmaśrī (*oṃ oṃ oṃ oṃ oṃ śrīṃ*).

27. *aṃ aṃ aṃ aṃ yrīṃ*: this is dhāraṇāśrī-mantra.

---

[1] Saṃjñā differs from the bīja by replacing the sound *ha* by *śa*. Thus it is *śrīṃ*.

28. *mrīṃ* should be known as the (mantra of) puruṣaśrī, which spreads a profusion of knowledge.

29. *bhrīṃ* is known as the pradhānaśrī(-mantra) which causes enlightenment to all.

30. *baṃ phaṃ paṃ prīṃ*: this is the antaḥkaraṇaśrī(-mantra).

31. *naṃ dhaṃ daṃ thaṃ taṃ trīṃ*: this (mantra) relates to jñānaśrī.

32. *ṇaṃ ḍhaṃ ḍaṃ ṭhaṃ ṭaṃ ṭrīṃ*: this mantra relates to karmaśrī.

33. *ñaṃ jhaṃ jaṃ chaṃ caṃ ṅaṃ ghaṃ gaṃ khaṃ kaṃ krīṃ*: this relates to bhūtaśrī.

34. These eight deities (namely) Brahmaśrī etc. present on the eight petals (of the central) lotus (of the maṇḍala) are known as the retinue of the pada form of the (mantra of) Tārikā.

35. All eight of them possess the colour that resembles the inside of a lotus, and have pleasant lotus-like faces. In each of their [1] two upper hands they carry two full-blown lotuses.

36-43. With her two primary hands Brahmaśrī displays the graceful brahmāñjali [2] gesture. Dhāraṇāśrī (Lakṣmī) with her two primary hands (indicates) the distinction between pure and impure. Puruṣaśrī with her two primary hands (displays) the gesture (*añjali*) of granting favour, while Prakṛtiśrī carries the noose and the goad in each of her two primary (hands). Antaḥkaraṇaśrī displays (with them) the gesture of reasoning (*tarkamudrā*); (the left) palm is turned downwards, its little and ring-fingers are bent while its two other fingers are held close together and the thumb stands straight. The right palm is raised and faces forward. This position of hands is called the gesture of reasoning. The gesture of explanation which is formed by holding both palms in the same manner (i.e. as the left palm in the gesture of reasoning) is displayed by Jñānaśrī. Now learn from me about (the position of the two primary hands) of Karmaśrī. The attitude prescribed for the Karmalakṣmī is, O noble one, as if both her two (primary) hands are ever occupied in performing her (own) activities. The two primary (hands) of Bhūtaśrī (Lakṣmī) are held (in the attitude of) bestowing various objects of enjoyment (on the devoted).

---

[1] All these deities possess four arms. Cf. Dhanada Tārā, B. Bhattacharya, o.c. p. 307.

[2] Here añjali is used in the sense of mudrā.

44-50. Now, O slayer of Bala, listen with attention to this complex (of sounds) constituting (the mantra of) Mahālakṣmī that produces all kinds of happiness. *Kṣaṃ . . . kaṃ krīṃ*: [1] this (sound-) complex (i.e. mantra) consists of the Mahālakṣmī(-mantra) and Mahāśri is its (presiding) deity. She is unique, yet possesses diverse characteristics. Although she is formless, she possesses form. She is the supreme being with countless faces, innumerable feet and hands. She is ever present in all places as the container and at the same time as that which is contained. She is multicoloured and carries a host of various weapons. She is both cruel and pleasant (in appearance). She remains seated and displays various (aspects of her) perfection. She should be envisaged as in every respect blessed (*subhagā*) and radiant with (a colour resembling the) inside of a lotus. O noble (god), the same (mantra) recited in reverse order ending with *kṣa* (i.e. *kam . . . kṣam krīṃ*) [2] and visualized as described above achieves the same result (i.e. all forms of happiness). The two groups of seven vowels [3] are arranged as the deity's rays. As the basis, bindu,[4] she creates the universe by projecting her own mighty form.

51-53. Thus what is known as Tārikā's pada (-mantra) has been revealed to you. You should always concentrate your mind focussing it on her. Thus from the vast Lakṣmī-Tantra containing ten hundred millions of verses I have picked out this essential portion and revealed it to you because of my affection for you. Long ago, in order to please me who am seated on His lap, the lotus-eyed Janārdana disclosed this supreme science to me.

54-56. Just as the sight of the moon delights people's heart, so also does the sight (knowledge) of this mantra (lit. science) please the mind of the yogins. Here it is not necessary to undergo the hardships (*parikleśa*) of yama etc.,[5] nor (need) the tiresome sitting postures (be practised), nor does the painful prāṇāyāma (need to be observed). Seated with ease in the posture of his choice and with a tranquil mind, (the adept may) constantly visualize (worship) this mantra and that secures his objective.

---

[1] *Kṣaṃ haṃ saṃ ṣaṃ śaṃ vaṃ laṃ raṃ yaṃ maṃ bhaṃ baṃ phaṃ paṃ naṃ dhaṃ daṃ thaṃ tuṃ ṇaṃ ḍhaṃ ḍaṃ ṭhaṃ ṭam ñaṃ jhaṃ jaṃ chaṃ caṃ ṅaṃ ghaṃ gaṃ khaṃ kaṃ krīṃ.*

[2] *kam kham gam gham . . . śaṃ ṣaṃ saṃ haṃ kṣam krīṃ.*

[3] *a i u ṛ e o ṃ* and *ā ī ū ṝ ai au ḥ.*

[4] See ch. XVIII, 24.

[5] Yama and niyama, the two preliminary stages of yogic practice.

57. Just as all rivers and streams flow into the mighty ocean, so also do all supreme mantras flow into this pada (-mantra).

58. Just as the lord of the rivers and streams (i.e. the ocean) possesses countless jewels, so also the pada (-mantra) is known to possess immense powers (*tejāṃsi*).

59-60. Just as when honey is added to rice the rice tastes sweet, so also these bīja etc. (various) states of Tārā, add pleasure to her. Seated on the lap of Nārāyaṇa, I, the great goddess of the entire universe who possess every perfection, should be meditated upon envisaged as the embodiment of the pada (-mantra).

61-62. O Śakra, the same absolute, undifferentiated and integrated Self of mine, moved by pity and desirous of helping the adepts with a view to the purification of their minds, filled with good intention divides this mantra form (of mine) in four ways.[1]

63. O Puraṃdara, you should now duly listen to my exposition of these four divisions of my manifestation.

[1] As Lakṣmī, Kīrti, Jayā and Māyā. See ch. XLV, 2.

CHAPTER FORTY-FIVE

REVELATION OF ŚRĪ'S VARIOUS MANIFESTATIONS

1. Śrī:—I am goddess Nārāyaṇī, older even than the first created objects, Lord Viṣṇu's primary Lakṣmī (sovereignty), the unchanging Śrī.

2. Through my sovereign power I divide my own self into four forms. These four manifestations are Lakṣmī, Kīrti, Jayā and Māyā.

3-4. When to benefit the world I divide myself into four forms, the first embodiment of myself, the great Śakti, I-hood of the omnipresent Hari, the absolute Lakṣmī, the supreme I-hood, is called the great and illustrious Lakṣmī who bestows (upon the worshippers) all kinds of prosperity and fruitfulness (in aspirations).

5. My second form is called Kīrti, the bestower of fame. My third form is called Jayā, the bestower of victory.

6-11. My fourth form is called Māyā, the performer of all (kinds of) miracles. Lakṣmī, Kīrti, Jayā and Māyā are thus present in Nārāyaṇa and are the highly radiant forms of myself, who am present in Nārāyaṇa. These (manifestations) are devoid of a corporeal body and are integral (i.e. not divided into separate parts). They are surrounded by the multitude of their śaktis like the rays (surrounding) the sun, or waves (covering) the ocean. Lakṣmī belonging to the husband of Lakṣmī is present in every (form of divine) sovereignty (such as) excellence etc. and is covered by various special and countless splendours.

In the same way Kīrti exists in the body of God and is not separate (from Him). Nothing exists that is not pervaded by her universal (common) form. Whenever fame is acquired by a person through his own effort, her universal form becomes manifest in that particular fame.

Similarly Jayā, God's (incarnation of) victory, has an all-pervading existence (i.e. it has a universal manifestation).

12. O Sureśvara, whatever supernatural power there exists (*māyā vidyate*) [1] in this creation headed by the celestial beings,

[1] Māyā represents the supernatural element inherent in all deities.

should be recognized as myself arising from God's power to work miracles.[1]

13. O best of gods, what independent existence can there be in this ocean of (cosmic) principles apart from the integrated fourfold form of Him and of myself? [2]

14-15. These (śaktis, Lakṣmī, Kīrti etc.)—perceived through practising yoga accompanied by (the mantras of) these powers of God and who have manifested (themselves) through their power of divine knowledge—should be visualized, offered oblations and worshipped by the best of the adepts with a view to the realization of their aspirations.

Now hear about the form of Lakṣmī, the first of these (my manifestation).

16-21. I as goddess Lakṣmī, present in the Vyūha, should be visualized as possessing a handsome face, beautiful eyes, two arms and wearing attractive earrings. Her colour is like that of the inside of a lotus and she is adorned with a chained girdle. She wears a white garland and (white) clothes and is ornamented with necklace and armlets. She bears all lucky signs and has round, high and close-set breasts. Her eyes are large like a full-blown lotus and she has a smiling expression. She has locks that resemble a swarm of bees in flight. Her forehead is marked with a decorative and charming spot, her gemlike lips are (ruby) red and her teeth are like rows of pearls. Her forehead is shaped like a half-moon and her tresses are dark and curly. The goddess, who bestows (on the devotee fulfilment of ambitions, namely) religious duties, advantage, sensual pleasure and liberation, carries (in her hands) the noose and the goad. She is seated in the lotus posture and is adorned with an excellent diadem.

22-26. Now listen to me as I recount her mantra, which as described by me (runs thus): *oṃ hrīṃ* [3] *lakṣmyai namaḥ paramalakṣmāvasthitāyai hrīṃ śrīṃ hrīṃ svāhā*. This twenty-syllabled mantra is the mūrti-mantra regarded as Lakṣmī's very self.

27-29. O slayer of Vṛtra, now listen to the correct form of its

[1] Here too Māyā represents that element of God's majesty which performs wonders and deludes, in fact, His function known as tirodhāna.

[2] Vāsudeva etc. are God's four manifestations, while Lakṣmī, Kīrtī etc. are Śakti's fourfold manifestation.

[3] The Tārikā-bīja-mantra is sometimes referred to as the heart of Tārikā and sometimes as the sign of Tārā's heart (*hṛllekhā*). Cf. ch. XXV, 48

aṅga-mantras: *oṃ ślraṃ ṭaṃ jñānāya hṛdayāya namaḥ, oṃ ślriṃ ṭaṃ aiśvaryāya śirase svāhā, oṃ ślruṃ ṭaṃ śaktaye śikhāyai vauṣaṭ, oṃ ślrḷṃ ṭaṃ balāya kavacāya huṃ, oṃ ślreṃ ṭaṃ tejase netrābhyāṃ vauṣaṭ* and *oṃ ślroṃ ṭaṃ vīryāya astrāya phaṭ*. O Vāsava, these six—starting with the heart and ending with the weapon—are known to be those (aṅga-mantras).

30-32. Now listen to the mantras of Lakṣmī's female companions. *Ṛṃ vṛṃ siṃ viṃ*—these (sounds) with *ṭaṃ* added to each of them form great bīja-mantras of (the four) (female) companions (of Lakṣmī, who are called) Ṛddhi, Vṛddhi, Samṛddhi and Vibhūti and their (full) mantras are *oṃ ṝṃ ṭaṃ ṛddhyai svāhā, oṃ vṛṃ ṭaṃ vṛddhyai svāhā, oṃ siṃ ṭaṃ samṛddhyai svāhā* and *oṃ viṃ ṭaṃ vibhūtyai svāhā*.

33-34. All four of these companions possess two arms. They are handsome and have the colour of the inside of a lotus. They carry (in their hands) the symbolical (branch of) a woodapple tree and a fly-whisk,[1] are seated in the lotus posture and they gaze at my face. This is how these companions should be visualized. Now hear about (Lakṣmī's) four attendants.

35. Lāvaṇya, Subhaga, Saubhāgya the third one and Saumanasya the fourth—these are my four attendants.

36-37. They all possess four arms, have handsome faces, wear blue silk clothing and in their four hands respectively hold a blossoming branch of the āmalaka tree,[2] a lotus, a pitcher and a lotus banner. Now listen to me as I recount their mantras.

38-39. One should know that the bīja (-mantras) of these (attendants) are: *lāṃ, suṃ, sauṃ, sauṃ* and *ṭaṃ*. The full mantra should run thus: *oṃ lāṃ ṭaṃ lāvaṇyāya namaḥ* etc.[3]

40. This ends the description of Lakṣmī's manifestation and of her retinue. Now listen to the (description of) the forms etc. of (my) second manifestation called Kīrti.

41. In form she resembles Lakṣmī (except that) her colouring resembles that of the campaka flower; [4] for the rest her form is the same as Lakṣmī's. Now learn from me her mūrti-mantra.

---

[1] The branch of woodapple tree is Lakṣmī's traditional symbol and the fly-whisk made of the tail of the yak is a traditional symbol of a companion maid.

[2] Emblic Myrobalan.

[3] *oṃ suṃ ṭaṃ subhagāya namaḥ, oṃ sauṃ ṭaṃ saubhāgyāya namaḥ* and *oṃ sauṃ ṭaṃ saumanasyāya namaḥ*.

[4] Michelia Campaka of a golden yellow colour.

42-44. *oṃ hrīṃ krīṃ traiṃ namaḥ sadoditānandavigrahāyai hrīṃ krīṃ svāhā*, this mantra of twenty syllables (belongs to her form).

45-46. Now learn the aṅga-mantras (of Kīrti by) listening to my description (of them). The aṅga-mantras of Kīrti are *krāṃ ṭaṃ, krīṃ ṭaṃ, krūṃ ṭaṃ, kr̄ṃ ṭaṃ, kraiṃ ṭaṃ* and *krauṃ ṭaṃ* etc. (like those of Lakṣmī). Now listen to the (description of) the forms and mantras of the (female) companions of (Kīrti).

47-52. Dyuti, Sarasvatī, Medhā and Śruti are said to be the companions (of Kīrti). They are all two-armed, golden coloured and (possess the other special features of) Kīrti's form, and all of them have smiling faces. They have a dainty book in their left hands and a fly-whisk in their right hands. Now listen as I enumerate the mantras of Kīrti's companions. One should regard (the sounds) *mrīṃ, srīṃ, mrīṃ* and *śrīṃ* with *ṭaṃ* attached to each of them, as the respective mantras of the companions. Now listen to the names and forms of Kīrti's attendants. Vāgīśa, Jayadeva, Prasāda and Trāṇa, (these attendants of Kīrti) should be visualized as possessing the colour of the kiṃśuka flower,[1] as being handsome, attractive, clothed in white, possessing four arms and richly adorned with ornaments.

52-56. One should visualize their main left and right hands as respectively holding a conch-shell with the brilliance of a hundred moons and (a branch of) the noble tree known as Kadamba [2] with flowers and bees hovering around. Now I shall tell you about the other two (hands). The left hand (of these deities) holds a mirror resembling the full moon while in their right hand these lovely-eyed (deities) hold a white fan made of peacock's feathers. The mantras of these attendants are (the sounds) *vāṃ, aṃ, prāṃ* and *trāṃ* with *ṭaṃ* added to each of them respectively.

57. Thus Kīrti, the second manifestation, has been described in proper order; now listen to the (description of) the form etc. of Jayā, my third manifestation.

58-64. The very beautiful Jayā resembles Lakṣmī in her form. *oṃ hrīṃ jayāyai oṃ maḥ ajitādhāmāvasthitāyai hrīṃ jrīṃ svāhā*: this is Jayā's mūrti-mantra. Now hear from me her aṅga-mantras. (The sounds) *jraṃ, jriṃ, jruṃ, jrḷṃ, jreṃ* and *jrom* with *ṭaṃ* are

[1] The flaming red flower of the tree Butea frondosa.

[2] Nauclea Cadamba.

regarded as the bīja-mantras of the heart etc., Jayā's respective aṅgas.

65. Jayantī and Vijayā, Aparājitā, the third, and Siddhi, the fourth, are regarded as Jayā's (female) companions.

66-67. (The sounds) *jiṃ*, *viṃ*, *aṃ* and *siṃ* with *ṭaṃ* and the respective names of these companions added to each (of these sounds) and each ending with *svāhā*, are known to be the mantras of these companions.

68-69. All these companions are as dark as the (indigo-)blue clouds. They have pleasant faces and eyes. They are wearing yellow raiment and golden earrings. They hold a white fly-whisk in (one) hand, while in the other hand (they) hold a brightly coloured cane. All of them gaze at the faces of Jayā and Ajita (Viṣṇu).

70. Pratāpī, Jayabhadra, Mahābala, the third, and Utsāha—this group of (four) are known as Jayā's attendants.

71-74. All these attendants should be envisaged as clothed in red, as being four-armed and of immense power. They carry the bow and arrows in (two of their) hands and the mace and disc in (the other two) hands, and their ornaments are made of flowers. O Sureśa, slayer of Vṛtra, (the sounds) *praṃ*, *jraṃ*, *mraṃ* and *uṃ* with *ṭaṃ* (form their respective bīja-mantras and) *oṃ* followed by the particular bīja and the particular name ending in *namaḥ* form their respective mantras.[1] This is the wonderful method (of worshipping) Jayā, my third manifestation.

75-82. Now listen to the method (of worshipping) my fourth manifestation (called) Māyā. This goddess, called Māyā, performs all miracles (and) is the great śakti of the highest God Viṣṇu. She (indeed) is my fourth (and) supreme form.[2] In form she resembles Lakṣmī. Now listen to (her) mūrti-mantra. *oṃ hrīṃ māyāyai namaḥ, mohātītanāmāśritāyai* [3] *hrīṃ mrīṃ svāhā*—this twenty-

[1] E.g. *oṃ praṃ ṭaṃ pratāpinyai namaḥ* and so forth.

[2] Māyā is obviously God's mysterious creative power whereby, on the one hand, He deludes people and, on the other gives a deceptive appearance to worldly objects. This being the basic philosophy of creation in this system, Śakti or the mysterious power of God has its most important manifestation in Māyā form. Cf. H. Zimmer, Myths and symbols in Indian art and civilization, New York 1946, p. 24.

[3] Here the mantra differs slightly from that given in J.S. (*mohātīta 'padāśritayai*) and would appear to be faulty since the two syllables making the difference are very confused in their relation to the essential vowel. Also use of the word *vāmabhrū* for *ā* is somewhat unusual. Cf. J.S. 6, 101-105.

syllabled mantra is considered (to be the Māyā-mantra). Now listen as I describe her aṅga (-mantras). *mrāṃ mrīṃ mrūṃ mrḷṃ mraiṃ mrauṃ* together with the other previously mentioned relevant aṅgas respectively form the aṅga-mantras.

83-87. O Sureśvara, Mohinī, Bhrāmaṇī, Durgā and Preraṇī are known to be the four female companions of Māyā, who possess the radiance of gems. All these goddesses resemble Māyā in their comeliness, prowess, beauty and energy. They are clothed in white and (smeared with) white unguent. They hold (in their two) hands a fly-whisk and goad (respectively) and they are seated in the lotus posture. O slayer of Bala, listen to me telling you their mantras. *oṃ moṃ ṭaṃ mohinyai svāhā*; *oṃ bhrāṃ ṭaṃ bhrāmaṇyai svāhā*; *oṃ muṃ ṭaṃ durgāyai svāhā*; *oṃ yraiṃ ṭaṃ preraṇyai svāhā*—these are said to be the mantras of the companions of Māyā.

88-100. Māyāmaya, Mahāmoha, Śambara and Kalīśvara are (Māyā's) four attendants, who resemble the rook or the collyrium (in their dark colour). They have four arms, huge bodies, handsome and smiling faces. They wear armlets and other ornaments and garments of yellow silk. They have necklaces and anklets and are decorated with various flowers. White as the snow-dust [1] they (hold in their two) raised hands a sword and a noose respectively and in their two other hands they (respectively) carry a bow and arrow and an umbrella. O slayer of Bala, *oṃ moṃ ṭaṃ māyāmayāya namaḥ*, *oṃ maṃ ṭaṃ mahāmohāya namaḥ*. *oṃ śaṃ ṭaṃ śambarāya namaḥ* and *oṃ kaṃ ṭaṃ kalīśvarāya namaḥ* are the mantras of these four (attendants, namely) Māyāmaya etc. Thus (ends my) general description of how all the aṅga-mantras should be envisaged. I have (also) specified the mudrās [2] of the deities connected with the aṅgas. All those (mudrās), which I described (before) should be displayed (by the adept, along with the mantras). He, who worships one, or all, of these goddesses with concentration and zeal becomes identified with the supreme Śrī. These four manifestations of mine are rays radiating from the (body of) God. When accompanied by all of them, God has His complete form. Each of them possesses innumer-

[1] An exact quotation from J.S. but contradicting their dark colour mentioned in the previous verse, cf. J.S. 27, 149. The same quotation has been repeated in ch. XLIX, 5-10, contradicting once again the statement about their dark complexion.

[2] See ch. XXXIV, 19-30.

able śaktis who, in every case, are identical with her and so they (= these four goddesses) possess retinues (of) countless (individual śaktis), so that the universe is pervaded by śaktis. (The adept) should meditate on me as the chief Śakti, who is the basic source of all these four śaktis, the supreme Goddess, Viṣṇu's I-hood, through whom all his functions are performed, who consists of the aggregate of all śaktis, the head of the group of śaktis and inherent in (absolute) conciousness and bliss. I am present within Agni and Soma and follow the middle course.[1]

101-102. The intelligent individual, who with introvert mind has engulfed the sun and the moon in his suṣumṇā duct, should introversively focus (his mind) on me.

102-103. Śakra:—O Goddess, who art pervaded by the supreme God and art present in the lotus, deign to reveal to me the mudrās of the female companions and the attendants of (these) goddesses.

103-113. O slayer of Bala, I have already revealed to you the mudrās of the goddesses.[2] Now learn from me (those of) their sixteen companions. (First) the adept should stretch his hands out in front of him as visibly as possible. (Secondly) he should pair off the little and the ring fingers (of both hands) by joining them at the nails (i.e. back to back with nails touching and pressed together). (Then) he should turn these four fingers towards the middle of the palms without actually touching the latter. (Thereafter) he should hold up both thumbs like two straight sticks and standing along the sides (of the hands) and stretch them towards the middle of the hollow (made) by the four aforesaid fingers (of his hands). (Next) he should take pains to bend his two index fingers like coiled snakes and the two middle fingers (of his hands) should be stretched up to touch at the tips. O Sureśvara, (then) the two hands should be firmly pressed together from the two straightened little fingers to the base of the wrists, while at the root of the two thumbs the wrists should be slightly apart. O slayer of Bala, this mudrā, called Mahāyoni, is the supreme mother of the three worlds. If (properly) displayed this can (empower the displayer) to have mastery over the entire world whenever he pleases. If a woman engaged in performing this (worship) fixes (her hands in this gesture) and

---

[1] See ch. XXVIII, 17.
[2] See ch. XXXVIII, 17-18.

displays it (even) from a distance, it will immediately cause disturbance in the mind of (even) a sage who has overcome all passion. If a man engaged in this (worship) displays it to women who have discarded all sensual pleasure or to the wives of sages, he would cause restlessness (even) in them who are devoid of passion, let alone in passionate women.

114. O Vāsava, this mudrā is common to all of these (companions). Now I shall briefly describe (that of) the sixteen attendants.

115-119. O noble (god), (the adept) should (first) place his two hands on his back and then release them. (Thereafter) the two pairs of the index and little fingers should be turned visibly downwards and between these the (pair of) little fingers are pressed together while that of the index fingers is kept apart. The pairs of his middle and ring fingers are joined together from nail to middle section (of the fingers) and, O greatest of gods, facing upwards these are held straight for ten palas.[1] The two thumbs are visibly turned downwards and separate from each other. This mudrā produces all that is desired. This one (mudrā) should be displayed (to each of the attendants) during (the recitation of) their individual mantras.

120-121. This is the description of the two mudrās each respectively common to the companions and the attendants (of Lakṣmī etc.). (The adept) who worships me thus identified with (in the form of) these four manifestations (of mine) together with their respective retinues, finally merges into my very self. My manifestations (*vibhūti*) consisting of both the (cosmic) principles and their products are innumerable.

122. O Vāsava, each of them (= manifestations) has a retinue of millions of attendants. The (already) described four (śaktis, Lakṣmī etc.) are said to be the chief ones. Thus I have accurately described to you my mūrti-mantras together with their aṅga-mantras. Now listen to me (describing) how they should be worshipped.

---

[1] A time unit. *dharaṇa* = 10 palas.

CHAPTER FORTY-SIX

MODE OF WORSHIPPING LAKṢMĪ-MANTRA AND RESULTS OBTAINED

1. Śrī:—O king of the gods, now learn (from me) in systematic order how to worship (the mūrti-mantras of these goddesses, namely) Lakṣmī etc. and how to perform various rituals accompanying these mantras.

2-17. Drawing, as mentioned before, a four-doored square diagram in the eastern direction, (the adept) should draw an eight-petalled lotus in white and red. He should then draw four svastika (-figures) in white at the four corners (of the square). After that he should first perform the vyāpaka nyāsa [1] of the basic mantra (mūla-mantra) only, on his hands starting from where the wrists begin and continuing on his body. Thereafter he should first perform the nyāsa of the Lakṣmī-mantra on his two hands as before (i.e. starting from the wrist). Next the should likewise perform nyāsa of its (= Lakṣmī-mantra's) aṅga (-mantras) on his hands and body. He should then perform nyāsa of the four (mantras belonging to) the goddesses who are her (= Lakṣmī's) companions [2] on both his hands, starting from the index finger and continuing on his body (i.e.) on the upper part of his body (head), chest, both thighs and both knees. O Vāsava, thereafter, having performed nyāsa of (the mantras of) the four (attendants of Lakṣmī, namely) Lāvaṇya etc. on his two hands starting from the ring finger and ending on the thumb, and on his body (i.e. on his left and right shoulders and on both sides of his neck), (the adept) seeking wealth (*śrī*) should duly perform nyāsa of Lakṣmī-mantra and applying the method of laya-yāga,[3] should worship only that (mantra) within his heart. And, O Vāsava, after performing the rite of looking etc.,[4] he should perform nyāsa of (Lakṣmī's) mūrti-mantra, combined with his

[1] The vyāpaka nyāsa entails covering the worshipper's entire body, with a mantra.

[2] See ch. XLV, 30-32.

[3] See ch. XXXVIII, 14-21.

[4] See ch. XXXVII, 61.

basic mantra on the pericarp (of the lotus) outside.[1] After that he should (envisage) the Omnipresent, both in His undifferentiated and composite aspects, as comprising all mantras and with Lakṣmī, seated on His lap, whom he has caused to descend (on that lotus diagram through the force of) his (basic) mantra. In order to achieve (his aim of obtaining material) enjoyment (or) liberation, envisaging (the divine couple) as described previously, he should perform nyāsa of the four (aṅga-mantras, namely) the heart etc., at the south-eastern, north-eastern, south-western and north-western corners (respectively). (The mantra of) the eyes should be placed (*nyāsa*) on the filaments of (the lotus in the diagram). Whereafter he should perform nyāsa of the four (mantras of) Ṛddhi [2] etc. on the front, right, back and left sides of (the lotus) respectively, (envisaging the divinities to) have two arms, to be as fair as the colour of a lotus, holding the characteristic woodapple branch and fly-whisk, seated in the lotus position and gazing at her (= Lakṣmī's) face. After performing nyāsa of the four (mantras of) Lāvaṇya etc.[3] on the svastikas (drawn) at the north-eastern etc. (four) corners respectively and (visualizing them as) having pleasant faces, four hands, wearing blue silk garments, holding a lotus and a pitcher in their (two main) hands and a lotus-banner and āmalaka plant with fruit in their (two other) hands, he should perform nyāsa of the astra (-mantra) on the doors and at the four quarters. O delighter of celestial beings, finally he should worship goddess Lakṣmī (i.e. her mantra) and his own basic mantra.

18-21. As previously stated he should also display the relevant mudrās at the appropriate moment.[4] And then he should perform japa, followed by homa (fire sacrifice) offering butter, sesame seed and akṣata rice, āmalaka fruits, wood-apples and, if available, lotus flowers. O slayer of Vṛtra, having performed homa as many times as possible, the adept, convinced of being identified with the body of Lakṣmī, should perform japa five hundred thousand times, meanwhile he should eat only pure food and practise abstinence. After japa, he should according to his capacity perform millions of homa offering woodapples, āmalaka fruits and lotus in that order.

---

[1] The lotus diagram, which is a variation of the cakrābja-maṇḍala. See diagram IV.

[2] See ch. XLV, 32.

[3] See ch. XLV, 35.

[4] See ch. XXXVI, passim.

22-28. O Śakra, at the end of homa the great goddess (= Lakṣmī) manifests herself (before the adept's mortal eye). The goddess then says 'My son, you have fulfilled (your vow of worshipping me). Disclose the wish you cherish in your mind (and I shall grant it). Henceforth, from today you are at liberty to perform undauntedly any ceremony you wish involving the use of my mantra and no contest or calamity will arise for you'. Whereupon the goddess returns to where she came from. Henceforth (the adept) may continue to perform (religious) ceremonies by my (i.e.) Lakṣmī's leave. If he is satisfied, he (is then empowered) to bestow on the suppliants the wealth they desire [1] and, if angered, to make by his mere word a pauper of a very rich man. By performing japa only once and meditating on (the mantra) he would be able to turn (even) copper into gold. If after filling a pitcher with water, milk or honey he places it on his right hand covering it (= pitcher) with the left (by putting the hand) over it and performs japa of the mantra a hundred and eight times, whilst meditating upon it (= mantra) with deep concentration in a meditative trance and fixing his mind on mercury, that water (etc. he) fetched in the pitcher, turns into mercury.[2]

29. O Puraṃdara, he who has (this) rasa (nectar) hits any target (aimed at by a weapon). He frees the body from (such disabilities as) old age or disease and renders it immortal.

30-40. If (the adept) fetches a pebble the size (and shape) of his thumb and holds it (tightly) in the hollow of his right fist, whilst he holds another (pebble) the size (and shape) of a badarī (nut) [3] and holds it in his left fist and then performs two hundred and sixteen japas of the mantra (of Lakṣmī) over those two (closed) fists, the pebble in the right fist becomes a gem and (the pebble) in the left fist becomes a pearl, both being very precious. He can produce any type of precious stone at will. So also, in function and appearance the pearl exactly resembles a real (pearl). Holding in his hand the bone of a cow, horse or elephant, if he performs japa of the mantra fifty times, that piece of bone becomes a (piece of) coral. If he

---

[1] *Abhiṣṭām* should be the correct reading.

[2] A particular sect believed that mercury duly treated with magical rites turns into nectar. See Raseśvara-darśanam of the Sarva-Darśana-Saṃgraha of Sāyaṇa-Mādhavācārya, Govt. Oriental Series, Class A, no 4, Poona 1951, pp. 202-207.

[3] The jujube nut.

performs japa of the mantra a hundred times on (pieces of) tin, lead or iron, these will turn into the purest gold or silver (at his will). O king of gods, (such a person) may transform any thing into any metal according to his (whims of) pleasure or anger. Likewise he can turn a pebble into (any precious) stone (he chooses). Whatever wealth (a suppliant) is desirous of possessing, whether in form of money, grain or cattle, (such an adept can) immediately bestow upon him. Inscribing the mantra of Lakṣmī with rocana [1] or saffron on a bhūrja leaf [2] and encasing that (leaf) in gold and wearing it on his body so as to worship and perform nyāsa, he lengthens the span of his life, triumphs wherever he goes and is treated with great honour. O most powerful amongst gods, here I have finished describing the worship of Lakṣmī, who is my first manifestation. This propitiation is especially appropriate for those who seek prosperity.

---

[1] Yellow powder found inside the skull of a cow.

[2] A species of birch tree.

CHAPTER FORTY-SEVEN

MODE OF WORSHIPPING THE KĪRTI-MANTRA AND RESULTS OBTAINED

1. Lakṣmī is the first amongst the group (of my manifestations) and is named after myself. I have just finished dealing with the efficacious performance of her (mantra). Now listen to (the worship) of the second (of the group).

2-3. Regard the nyāsa-process and the worship of the lotus (-diagram) (in the case of Kīrti) to be the same as was mentioned by me (in the worship of the Lakṣmī-mantra). Drawing a maṇḍala [1] as was already instructed (the adept) should design the white and yellow lotus within that (maṇḍala) and then perform the nyāsa of Kīrti seated on God's lap and (her aṅgas, namely) the heart etc. as previously described.

4-12. Now learn in systematic order the visualization of (her) friends. They should be envisaged as possessing two hands and a golden colour, with the same features as those of Kīrti and with smiling faces. In their left hands they hold a beautiful book and in their right hands a fly-whisk. (The adept) should envisage her four attendants as having the (red) colour of the kiṃśuka (flower), attractive features and charming forms. They have four hands and wear white garments. They should be envisaged as carrying in their main left and right hands (respectively) a conch-shell as white as hundreds of moons and (a branch of) the tree called kadamba (decorated with) flowers and bees. Now learn from me that in their two other hands they carry in the left a mirror resembling the full moon, and in the right a white fan made of peacock-feathers. After visualizing them in this way, the adept should display the mudrā required for each (rite) and then continue the worship (offering) arghya, flower etc. Next according to his capacity he should then perform japa and homa (offering) sesame seeds soaked in butter and mixed with fragrant śāli (rice). After (performing) homa he should clothe the image of the deity and adorn it with flowers and collyrium. Whereupon he should retire to a solitary,

[1] See ch. XLVI, 2.

quiet place and, eating only fruits and roots and uttering no word, should perform japa of (Kīrti-) mantra three hundred thousand times. Whereafter, O king of gods, he should perform homa a hundred thousand times (offering) a combination of rice and sesame seed mixed with butter (made from the milk of) a red cow and with milk of the same type.

13-33. Thereafter he should perform a thousand homas using each of the (six aṅga-mantras, namely) the heart etc., following which he should offer the final oblation consisting of milk mixed with butter. If this be done on a day when the moon is full, the great goddess (Kīrti) appears (there before the adept) and says 'Well done, well done, pray come to the supreme presence (of God), leave this mortal home, (or else) enjoy immortal pleasure whilst still living amongst mortal beings; O (my) worshipper, be free to perform any rite you please using my mantra', whereupon the goddess goes up in the sky. Whenceforth the adept may perform any rite he chooses which involves the use of the mantra of Kīrti and whatever he gives to any person never diminishes and so brings (the adept) fame that lasts the duration of the sun and the moon. When he discloses his knowledge amongst people of great power or lectures to whatever assembly, fame is showered upon him. Outwitting all (learned) pec,.. he establishes his own superiority. In times of scarcity and famine, if he performs japa on a pot (of magical) power, he can feed people whenever he wishes and in accordance with their desires. If he continues to give this inexhaustible (gift of food to people) for seven days, he becomes extremely famous and that fame endures until the dissolution of the universe. In time of prosperity (*subhikṣa*) should he take a tiny piece of gold and after duly performing japa a thousand times over it, lay it aside near at hand, it will greatly increase in quantity and continue to be available for lavish distributions among (many) needy people during two weeks, so that there can be no doubt whatsoever (about his power). Consequently he acquires great fame as a benefactor of mankind. Fetching a pitcher of water from a pool inhabited by a great serpent, if after having done a thousand japas he pours that water over (the sands) of a desert he has come to, or on low ground,[1] or on the top of a mountain, that giant serpent and his dependants come to live in that water and protect it as long as the earth will exist.

[1] Literally *nimne tu bhūtale* means 'On a low part of the earth'.

O Vāsava, in this way he gains great fame in this world. If the god concerned with the growth of seed does not send rain in the right period, he takes a bit of earth and soaks it with water from a pond, or he takes a bit of wet (clay) from within that (pool) and performs three hundred japas (of the mantra) over that (piece of clay). Whereafter he warms it with breath from his mouth and recalling the mantra of Kīrti throws that (bit of clay) up into the sky where it verily turns into a cloud. That cloud will cover the entire earth with water. At his bidding the king of clouds remains there pouring (rain) down for as long as is necessary and useful. This brings him great fame that travels throughout the three worlds. O excellent god, this royal mantra called Kīrti is influential in granting people whatever they desire. Writing down the mantra as described before [1] and wearing it on one's right hand brings great fame, honour, prosperity and learning to its wearer.

34. O Vāsava, this briefly describes how to worship Kīrti-mantra, my second manifestation, O you glorious one, amongst all manifested forms.

35. Following this delightful method of worshipping Kīrti-mantra, (the adept) gains pure fame and brings wealth to a multitude (of people).[2]

---

[1] See ch. XLVI, 38-39.

[2] The mudrās and mantras mentioned here are described in ch. XLV.

CHAPTER FORTY-EIGHT

MODE OF WORSHIPPING JAYĀ-MANTRA AND RESULTS OBTAINED

1. Śrī:—O slayer of Vṛtra, now listen to the description of how to worship efficaciously (the mantra of) my third manifestation Jayā, who is praised by many illustrious (holy) people.

2-4. Performing the nyāsa as before and worshipping Jayā within his heart, (the adept) should make a maṇḍala as previously described and draw a fair-petalled lotus in it, using (blue) powder resembling (the hue) of a blue lotus.[1] On the pericarp (the adept) should place Jayā (by fetching her there) from Viṣṇu's chest. He should also place other mantras accompanied by the performance of their nyāsas, in the already stated order. But listen now to how these (divinities) are to be correctly visualized.

5-6. All female companions of (Jayā) are dark in colour like an indigo cloud, and have a look of pleasure on their faces and eyes. They wear yellow raiment and golden earrings. In (one of their hands) they hold a white fly-whisk and in the other a decorated cane in raised position. All of them gaze at the faces of Jayā and of Ajita (Viṣṇu).

7-8. (Jayā's) four attendants should be envisaged as being as (white) as the colour (of the bud of a kunda flower),[2] as having pleasant lotus-like faces, red garments, four hands and great strength. They hold in their hands the bow and arrow and the mace and disc and they are decorated with ornaments made of flowers.

9-10. (The adept) should display all the mudrās appropriate to each of them as previously instructed. Then he should worship them with devotion and thereafter perform homa (offering) sesame seed mixed with white mustard seed, butter and bdellium (*gulgula*). At the end of homa the adept envisages his own form as identified with Jayā.

11-20. When the supreme realization that 'I am Jayā' awakens in

[1] See chs. XLVI-XLVII and note the use of different colours for the lotus of different śaktis.

[2] A kind of jasmine flower.

the mind (of the adept), he should betake himself to a safe, solitary bank of (a river or suchlike place). And setting up a (magical) boundary by applying (the mantras of) the weapon and armour,[1] which repels evil influences, he should start performing japa and meanwhile subsist on milk, rice and fruits. O Vāsava, first he should bow down before Hari and recite his own (basic) mantra with fervour; (the adept) who adheres to the habits of Ekāntins [2] eats light food, remains silent and practises meditation; he should perform japa (of Jayā-mantra) four hundred thousand times. After japa he should perform homa. For fuel he must use a million pieces of red sandalwood, each piece measuring a prādeśa,[3] soaked in butter; well-concentrated he should perform homa two billion times offering white mustard seeds mixed with honey. Whereafter he should perform homa either a million or a billion times, offering black mustard seeds. To end with, he should perform the final oblation three times, offering the three (items, namely) honey etc. O Śakra, he should perform these (three) final homas by offering honey, milk and butter in that order. Whereupon the illustrious goddess Jayā appears there spontaneously and speaks the following words: 'My son, your worship of me has borne result. Henceforth you may perform any ceremony you please entailing the use of my mantra and need suffer neither fear nor distress'. Having spoken thus the śakti embodying Nārāyaṇa disappears. Henceforth (the adept) may perform a host of various rites as selected by himself or by others, in this world.

20-26. Listen further, O wielder of thunder, as I give a detailed specification of these (rites).

Envisaging a rope as if emanating fire, whilst he recites the mantra of the goddess (Jayā), the adept may (with that rope) bind whomever he pleases to whatever object (he chooses) and thereby legitimately defeat (his enemy in battle) by gaining an easy victory.[4] Upon

---

[1] The so-called *digbandha(na)* rite for making a charmed boundary.

[2] Devout worshippers of Viṣṇu, the only God. See ch. XVII, 17.

[3] One prādeśa equals the length of a palm with fully stretched thumb and index finger placed side by side and measured from the root of the thumb to the tip of the index finger.

[4] The rope mentioned here refers of course to the noose which is always identified with a snake, hence spitting the fire or poison. Resort to a magic weapon of this kind was regarded as perfectly possible and legitimate and is frequently referred to in the Mahābhārata.

catching sight of someone's mighty army with elephants, horses and (heavily) armed men (drawn up) in battle array, if (the adept) performs japa (of Jayā-mantra) over a bow, sword, shield and five arrows and, handing these to a single individual, dispatches him alone to confront the enemy army, he (single-handed) destroys (the whole army) and gains a lasting victory. Envisaging on his right palm a blazing triangular fire,[1] (the adept) should visualize the goddess with her entire retinue therein. On being confronted by a mad elephant, lion, snake or a flash of lightning, he should (display that palm). At the sight of this palm, these (vicious beings) will turn tail in a great hurry.

27-30. O king of gods, holding a club made of khadira wood[2] (the adept) should perform (japa) of the mantra a hundred times. Then proceeding to the mouth of a cave,[3] which is of four colours (accompanied by persons[4] belonging to the four orders) and furnished with the Jayā (-mantra), he should leisurely strike that (cave-opening) with his club eight times. Next, he should worship the trap-entrance to the cave by using the mantra of goddess (Jayā) enclosed in a case with his own astra-mantra[5] ending with (the word) *phaṭ*. Whereupon the noble adept should enter the cave with all those who (accompanied him). In advancing he breaks open numerous trapdoors, conquers several powerful demons and settles his followers and their wives (in that conquered territory).

31. After drinking a pure drink[6] from his own hand,[7] the great powerful (adept) returns to his own home following the same route (which) he used (to enter).

32. O king of gods, if the adept sets his mind to be always indisputably victorious in all the three worlds, he need only use

[1] Symbol of the yoni.

[2] Acacia Catechu.

[3] The demons reign in the nether regions: a common theme of folklore, cf. Daśakumāracaritam of Daṇḍin, the beginning of the adventures of Prince Rājavāhana (Daṇḍin, Daśakumāracaritam, ed. M. R. Kale, Delhi, Varanasi, Patna 1966, p. 25-29).

[4] The reading is corrupt. J.S. reads correctly *janānvitam*: J.S. 27, 128.

[5] For *sampuṭita* see H. Brunner-Lachaux, Somaśambhupaddhati, Pondicherry 1963, p. 218.

[6] The term "pure drink" (*sāttvikam pānam*) poses some difficulty, and possibly denotes a non-alcoholic beverage.

[7] Using his own hand as a cup to avoid using a defiled cup belonging to the impure demons.

his hands armed with a raised club and a disc, (to vanquish an army in battle); or he need only carry a noose and a goad (for that purpose) and then alone can he gain victory by this means.[1] If one uses rocana, saffron or ink to inscribe the (mantra) on a bhūrja leaf and encloses it in a case (worn by the adept), on entering a crowd (of enemies), he gains an easy victory (aided by) all divine (powers). O Śakra, if a person writes (that mantra down on a leaf) with sandal-paste, milk or saffron and wears it (encased) round his neck, head, left or right hand, at all times and in all circumstances he becomes victorious. O king of gods, wherever and whenever an adept resorts to the mantra (of Jayā) in order to obtain victory, he always becomes victorious.

O Śakra, here I have explained to you how to worship my third manifestation known as Jayā.

[1] Obviously only these four weapons can be vested with supernatural power by using the Jayā-mantra.

CHAPTER FORTY-NINE

MODE OF WORSHIPPING MĀYĀ-MANTRA AND RESULTS OBTAINED. PRATIṢṬHĀ OF AN IMAGE OF LAKṢMĪ-NĀRĀYAṆA

1. Śrī:—O Vāsava, my fourth manifestation in a mantric body is Māyā. Now listen to the method (of worshipping her) together with (the description) of the (subordinate) mantras and rituals.

2. (The adept) should perform nyāsa of the mantras of Māyā's mūrti, aṅga, companions and attendants on his own hands (first) and then on (the rest of) his body as described before.[1]

3-4. Likewise, he should next worship her when she is within his own heart by offering her all articles of enjoyment. Then making a maṇḍala outside, he should draw an auspicious lotus in it and (envisaging) her seated on Viṣṇu's lap, he should cause her to descend from his heart (to that lotus). Whereafter he should propitiate Māyā together with her aṅga (-mantras) and companions etc.[2]

5-10. The four celestial companions (of Māyā, namely) Bhrāmaṇī etc. should be envisaged as having lotus(-shaped) eyes, clothed in white and glittering with jewels. They hold in their hands a fly-whisk and a goad and are seated in the lotus position. The four attendants, Māyāmaya etc., should also be envisaged as possessing fully developed bodies, and as being friendly, and (dark) like a swarm of bees. They have four arms, huge bodies and handsome faces wearing smiling expressions. They are decorated with armlets and other ornaments, wear yellow garments, necklace and anklets, and are decorated with various flowers. White as the snow-dust they carry (in their two) raised hands a sword and a noose (respectively), while in their (two) other hands they (carry) a bow with arrow and an umbrella. Having displayed the relevant mudrās to each of them as enjoined (by tradition), he should perform homa, offering sesame and white mustard seeds.

11-19. O Vāsava, still following rules (of conduct conforming to the vow the adept has taken), he should steadfastly envisage

[1] See ch. XLVI, 5 and ch. XXXV, 60-76.
[2] See ch. XLV, 83-91.

himself as identified with the person of the goddess. And after retiring to a solitary place, taking his wife (seat ?) along,[1] the adept (lit. the person observing a special vow) should perform seven hundred thousand japas as prescribed before. Meanwhile he should eat only fruit, root and milk, as time or place permit. He may even live on barley flour. But he should not beg and must only eat (whatever he receives) by way of alms voluntarily offered on a single occasion. Alternatively, he may eat rice collected (from begging) by his own disciples and consecrated by him with a mantra. He should eat that (rice) without salt, oil or meat at fall of dusk. He should eat until satisfied and may mix honey and clarified butter with the rice (to improve the taste).

On completing japa, the adept should then duly perform homa according to the sacred injunctions. Making a mixture of balā,[2] moṭā,[3] māṃsī,[4] cakrāṅgī,[5] nāgakesara,[6] sandalwood(-paste), powdered saffron and powdered turmeric, he should further add to it first butter of good quality, and then sesame seed, honey, ghee and a little solid rice (each separately). (Using this mixture as offering) he should perform three hundred thousand homas (and throw the offering in the fire) with only the thumb, middle and third fingers (of his right hand). O Puraṃdara, thereafter he should perform thirty thousands of homas offering nothing but pieces of firewood. The first ten thousand (pieces should be) made of rāja [7] and arka [8] wood, (the second ten thousand pieces should be made of) khadira [9] wood and the third ten thousand pieces should be made of sura-wood.[10]

20-23. He should forthwith offer the final oblation with an entirely pure mind. As soon as the final oblation has fallen (in the

---

[1] *Prauḍha* and *uttara* seem to denote either (his) main seat (as in the expression *prauḍha-pāda*), or his wife (*prauḍhā* denoting a mature married lady). Another, likewise uncertain probability would be 'mature, excellent companions'. Jayākhya reads *prauḍhayuk svāsanānvitaḥ*, cf. J.S. 27, 174.

[2] Semi-ripe barley grain.

[3] Sida Cordifolia or Sesbania Aegyptiaca.

[4] Nardoslachys Jatamansi.

[5] The gall-nut.

[6] Mesua Roxburghii (using the blossom of this tree).

[7] Plerospermum.

[8] Calotropis Gigantea.

[9] Acacia Catechu.

[10] Pinus Devadāru (a type of pine commonly called Deodar).

fire), Māyā accompanied by her retinue arrives there from the atmosphere saying: 'Well done, well done, from now on, go ahead and perform all rituals (which you may) choose to perform entailing use of my own mantra'. With these words the goddess instantly returns to the abode of Viṣṇu. Whereupon, O Śakra, the great adept immediately starts performing various rites which he in his heart longed to perform. He may perform these rites either on behalf of himself or on behalf of another. Now listen, I shall confine myself to mentioning some of them.

24-33. Performing japa just once on an āmalaka fruit and on a bilva fruit (the adept) should enter the palace of a king, and, standing wherever he pleases, throw these down in front of the (king's) treasury, whereupon the sky immediately rains down on the place the desired wealth, attractive jewelry or beautiful garments. Adopting the same method but using instead a small ball of (ground) rice or rice mixed with sesame seed, and throwing that on a closed granary, cowshed or a (mere) pit belonging to himself or to the king, the sky immediately pours down on the place where he stands the desired (food), rice or other such grain. Similarly a small ball made of cooked rice consecrated by japa and thrown on a stove instantly produces cooked rice. Making a small ball of cow-dung of the size of a badarī (nut) and (consecrating it by) reciting the mantra seven times while visualizing a great cauldron full of milk, curd and butter, if he throws the ball in a cowshed, instantaneously these actually appear behind him. Consecrating a badara (nut) or any other fruit with japa, upon throwing it into a royal pleasure-garden an abundance of fruits will appear there. In a nice flower-garden someone need only point at a particular flower and with only three japas in an instant the adept turns it into a lavish display of flowers.

33-34. (In short) whenever with specific intention (*saṅkalpa*) (the adept) takes hold of a part of any object and (consecrating it) with seven japas throws it down on a (certain) spot to which he has betaken himself, he is able to reproduce that object in whatever quantity he pleases.[1]

35. The worthy adept never falls into debt (i.e. never becomes poor).[2]

[1] Translated rather freely, since the text is somewhat ambiguous.

[2] The other reading, namely *sajīrṇo*, is closer to the reading in J.S.

35-43. If on picking up a piece of charcoal and concentratedly performing a hundred japas over it (i.e. consecrating it) the adept throws it in water, that water appears to have caught fire. (Holding a tiny) drop of water on a kuśa-blade and (consecrating it with) a hundred (recitations of) the mantra on throwing that (drop) over an expanse of fire, the latter is instantaneously transformed into something (cool) like water before one's very eyes. Confronting a wilderness of nothing but sand, entirely devoid of grass, as soon as he throws one blade of grass into it after (consecrating the blade by) two hundred mantra(-recitations), it (= the wilderness) is filled with flowers and leaves and is covered with foliage resembling (the celestial garden) Nandana containing lakes, an abundance of various birds, cities, gardens with palaces, walls and temples resounding with the sound of the chanting of the Vedas and adorned with (beautiful) girls. (The adept) should always demonstrate (such miracles) in the presence of royalty. With (mere) lumps of earth (smeared) with cow-dung and consecrated by (reciting the mantra) eight times, (the adept) can at will turn a wilderness, devoid of water and grain, into a (region overflowing with) water, rice and other edibles.

43-53. If when standing alone against a host of armed enemies who provoke him, the angry adept starts wishing intensely for a large army equipped with soldiers, chariots, horses and elephants, whilst he keeps on repeating the mantra, a vast, formidable and powerful army will immediately come (to his aid). On beholding it the enemy's army, robbed of courage, takes to flight.

O Śakra, (whatever wish comes to his mind, if the adept) visualizes it whilst uttering the mantra, that (thing) is sure to appear there whether it be real or imaginary. On beholding a dead tree, he should strike it with his foot whilst reciting the great mantra, and that tree will turn into (a live tree) lavishly bearing flowers and fruit. (If on the other hand) whilst uttering the mantra, he presses in his hands a tree in full leaf, bearing flowers and fruit, it loses its sap. If standing in front of a mountain he performs japa for its destruction, it crumbles down to whatever level he wishes. Once satisfied, he may later fetch that mountain back, even from the nether region and restore it to its imposing height.

(*saṃvinno*), but the reading *saṃno* is more in keeping with the purport of the theme as a whole; cf. J.S. 27, 197.

He should inscribe the mantra inside a lotus with the sap of sandalwood (-paste) and also write the aṅga-mantras on the petals of that lotus. Then, after worshipping it on a propitious day, he should cover it with flowers etc. and encase it in the manner described before. If he wears this yantra [1] (on his body) all powers immediately vest in him. He becomes dauntless on this earth, has good luck and a long life; beyond (death) he attains happiness.

54. O slayer of Vṛtra, here I (conclude) telling you briefly about the miraculous power of my fourth manifestation. It is indeed (almost) impossible to enumerate all my (marvellous potentialities).

55-58. This brief description of the powers (obtained through worship of) these four goddesses is given for the benefit of adepts. Besides all good things, both divine and mundane, this (worship) bestows on them unblemished purity of mind, and finally Viṣṇu's indestructible, absolute state of existence is revealed to the devotees. (Therefore) having quietened their minds (adepts) should adore me, Lakṣmī, as projected in these manifestations.

58-59. Śakra:—I salute thee, O most exalted of all divine beings, I salute thee, O beloved of the Vaikuṇṭha. O Lotus (goddess), on what should I concentrate when I worship you?

59-62. Śrī:—Nārāyaṇa is the unique Self, the ocean of amṛta as it were, embodying the aggregate of the six attributes. I am His supreme Śakti, never departing from Viṣṇu. I have already told you that I rest on His lap.[2] O Śakra, that (combined image) will indeed be the focal point of concentration that quietens your mind. Following the directives of the sacred texts, an image should be made of myself seated on Viṣṇu's lap and, after performing the ritual of pratiṣṭhā [3] in conformity with scriptural injunctions, you should worship us (in that combined image) with various forms of objects.

63. Śakra:—Adoration to thee, O abode of the universe, delight of the inner eye and embodiment of the six attributes, by what means can one ensure that thou and Nārāyaṇa are both present in the image?

64-66. Śrī:—As God Viṣṇu, the embodiment of the six attributes, is the essence of the All, so is my marvellous self, immanent in the

---

[1] A plaque inscribed with a sacred diagram.

[2] See ch. XXXVI, 124-131.

[3] *Pratiṣṭhā* is a rite to infuse a consecrated object with a divine presence. It can be performed on temples, images, dwellings, tanks etc.

essence of the All. Therefore the point is, since both myself and Nārāyaṇa are present [1] everywhere, why in fact is it necessary to reinfuse our presence?[2] It is well known that Viṣṇu pervades all. Keeping this actual situation in mind, the sages assert that (these rules regarding) the images and their pratiṣṭhā (establishment) are mere imagination.[3]

67. O slayer of Bala, listen now to the proper (method of performing) my pratiṣṭhā which, when effected, brings satisfaction to a person.

68-73. Have our images made as mentioned in Yoga [4] (by a craftsman) in conformity with the sacred texts. Next, bathe them in sacred water (consecrated) with two Vedic hymns and pavitras.[5] Whereafter covering these (images) with (a piece of) new cloth, study [6] sacred texts of the Vedas and the Sāttvata with pure brahmins who are scholars of religious texts. And while still holding the pavitras, they should recite (the mantras of) tāraka, Tārikā, Anutārikā and the Śākuna-sūkta.[7] When the sun sets, he should perform the adhivāsana [8] of water, on the image covered with cloth whilst reciting the sūktas *ṛtañ ca* [9] etc. and the Sārasvata[10] and also the (Śrī-sūkta containing the stanzas) *hiraṇyavarṇā* etc. At sunrise (they) should first perform the rite of the 'boundary making'[11] and then they should approach the pedestal with such words as 'deign to arise, O Brahman'. Whereafter remove the (covering) cloth and start bathing (the image) with pure water.[12]

---

[1] Lit. "are established".

[2] A free translation, lit. "what would, in fact, be (our) establishment?"

[3] *Vikalpa* implies imagination. Cf. *śabdajñānānupātī vastuśūnyo vikalpaḥ*, Yog.S. 1, 9.

[4] Implying the texts of the Pāñcāratra school.

[5] Tips of panic grass with three blades.

[6] Lit. "have studied".

[7] Ṛg.V. 2, 42.

[8] The ritual of adhivāsana is a consecration of the image to be performed the day before actual worship. It mainly consists of a bathing ceremony with some other minor rites. A special platform is set for this rite, often near some water resort. This rite should be done before the eyes of the image are carved. Cf. Pa.S. 18, 39-75, pp. 121-124 of the Sanskrit section and pp. 116-120 of the English section.

[9] Ṛg.V. 10, 190, 1.

[10] Ṛg.V. 6, 61.

[11] Probably the digbandhana rite, setting up a boundary of safety by reciting the mantra of the weapon and visualizing that it encloses the main place of worship.

[12] This is in fact a detailed description of the water adhivāsa.

74-80. On the right side of the platform which is covered with a soft cloth the image should be laid down with its head towards the eastern direction and this should be preceded by the performance of japa. And then taking a thin stick made of gold, (the craftsman) consecrates it with the mantra of the weapon, whereupon the eyes (of the image) should be outlined with that stick while reciting the mantra of the eyes. Then after the craftsman has bathed and changed into a clean garment and been viewed by the divine eyes, he should duly open the eyes (of the image) with the stick that has been consecrated by the mantra of the weapon. Thereupon (the adept) should fill two bowls with honey and butter and display them to the (image). At the same time he should dedicate (to the deity) two (lavishly) decorated cows. (The adept) should present all these items used for the opening (of the image's) eyes to the craftsman as a gift. Thereafter, tying a few black mustard seeds in a fair (piece of) cloth with white thread, (the adept) should tie, reciting Tārā, this charm around the (image's) right hand. Then he should set the image up on a firm pedestal (*bhadrapīṭha*) and duly worship it following the order of the ādhāra etc.[1] Henceforth he should, by means of visionary sight,[2] see that the image is infused by the six attributes.

81-82. He should strike it with (the recitation of) the mantra of the weapon and then he should guard [3] it with (the recitation of) the mantra of armour. Whereupon he should bathe it with water containing all sorts of herbs and then with ordinary (water). After wiping (drying it) with a (piece of) freshly washed cloth, he should then remove the charm. Whereafter the knower of mantras should sprinkle arghya on the head of (the image) whilst reciting the cakra-mantra.[4]

83-90. Having performed adhivāsana to the image as the reflection of the most beautiful (goddess Lakṣmī), with liquids out of brimful pitchers set on each of the sixteen petals of the sixteen-petalled pure lotus, consecrated by the recitation of mantras...[5]

---

[1] Ch. XXXV, 57.

[2] For *dhiyā* see J. Gonda, The vision of the Vedic poets, The Hague 1963, esp. chs. II and IX.

[3] Lit. 'surround'.

[4] *oṃ sahasrāra huṃ phaṭ.*

[5] The sentence is incomplete as parts of it have probably been lost. A fuller description is given by P.S. XIV, 102B-115A. A diagram is given

The first pitcher contains the five cow-products,[1] the second contains cow's urine, the third contains cow-dung mixed with water, the fourth contains water mixed with the ash from three different (ritual fires),[2] the next (contains) water mixed with soil from an ant-hill dug up by the horns (or tusk, as the case may be) of elephants, cows or bulls; the following one is filled with water from a rice field, a river, a lotus pond etc.; the seventh contains water mixed with mustard seeds; the eighth contains water mixed with all sorts of herbs; the ninth contains milk, the tenth curd and the next one butter. The twelfth pitcher is filled with honey, the thirteenth with water containing all kinds of seeds, the following one contains fruits and the next paddy. The sixteenth pitcher is full of fragrant water. First (the adept) should consecrate each full pitcher by (reciting) the mantra of the heart, (then) he should reverently bathe (the image) with the contents of all sixteen (pitchers). Thereupon he should smear (the image) with (paste made of) arghya and flowers, incense and (soot of) lamps in water, and powder of masura,[3] māṣa [4] and wheat, and then wash (the image) with milk.

Whereafter he should perform the nyāsa of the mantra of the supreme Tārikā on the head of the (image).

91-93. The wise (adept) should perform the nyāsa of the subtle and gross forms (of Tārikā) on various parts (of his body) in the order (here mentioned), viz. on his head, face, shoulders, ears, chest, navel, back, small of his back, thighs, knees, ankles and feet. And he should likewise perform the nyāsa of Tāraka and Anutārikā and that of the Puruṣa-sūkta and the Śrī-sūkta and that of the formula *śiro me śrīḥ* etc.[5] (on parts of his body) following the order indicated in (each verse) thereof.

94-95. He should also perform the nyāsa of the hotṛ-mantras,[6] as has been mentioned, on the Person who consists of Yajus and then he should do the same on me.

---

by the editor of this text. P.S., p. 9.

[1] Milk, curd, butter, cow's urine and cow-dung.

[2] The household fire, the ritual fire used for sacrifices and the fire used for ancestral rite.

[3] A kind of lentil.

[4] Phaseolus Radiatus.

[5] Tai. Br. 2, 6, 5, 3.

[6] Cf. ch. XXIX, 20-23 with relevant footnotes and Ahi.S. ch. 58.

(It should be noted that) first the Śrī-sūkta is (the object of) nyāsa, then the formulas *śiro me* etc. and lastly the nyāsa of the hotṛ (-mantras) is performed on our two bodies.[1]

96-98. After performing the preliminary rites in the firepit, (the adept) should perform the sacrifice for universal peace, accompanying it with (recitation of) all previously mentioned and present classes of mantras. This (homa) is to remove all evils. The mantras belonging to the Ṛg-veda are recited at the east side (of the pit), the Yajur-mantras at the southern side, Sāma-mantras at the western side and the Atharva-mantras at the northern side (of the pit), while mantras belonging to the Sāttvata system are recited right in front [2] (of the pit). This is how (the adept) should instruct the brahmins to recite the mantras.

99. He should first bathe (the deity) from all four sides with (fluid from) the pitchers set on the pericarp of the sixteen-petalled lotus whilst reciting the mantras of tāra, Tārā and Anutārā.

100-101. (Then in turn he should bathe the image with water) from the pitcher containing flowered water, whilst reciting the mantra *vasavas tvā* etc.,[3] (next) with water from the pitcher containing fragrant water and then with water from the pitcher containing water mixed with gold and (with water from) the pitcher containing jewelled water, whilst reciting the mantras *rudrās tvā* etc.[4] and *ādityas tvā* and *viśva* [5] etc. He who is familiar with mantras should then sprinkle the image whilst reciting (the mantras) of tāra, Tārā and Anutārā.

102. After that he should bathe the image with pure water whilst reciting the mantra of Tārā in its three aspects, (namely) *para* etc., whereafter he should sprinkle arghya on the head (of the image).

103-108. After smearing the image with unguents, such as sandalwoodpaste etc. he should worship it by offering articles of enjoyment beginning with clothing and ending with prāpaṇa.[6] Afterwards he should worship the pedestal containing the brahmaśilā,[7] whilst

[1] Cf. ch. XXIX, 18-24.
[2] Lit. 'in the vicinity of'.
[3] Tai. Br. 2, 7, 15, 5.
[4] Ibid.
[5] Ibid.
[6] See the note on ch. XXXVI, 79.
[7] The stone-base on which the image stands.

displaying the appropriate mudrās.[1] He should envisage the pedestal as containing all courses (of creation) pervaded by Viṣṇu and as being radiant. He should visualize the divine brahmaśilā as identical with ādhāraśakti. This applies when both the pedestal and brahmaśilā have been constructed together. If these have been made separately, then the (consecration of brahmaśilā through visualization) should be performed after laying down (the image). The rules for (the ceremony of) laying down a fixed image will be stated presently along with (rules about) how to approach the temple, fix the pedestal and brahmaśilā, perform the ceremonies of their pratiṣṭhā, the invocation of the image and nyāsa of the twelve parts of the body,[2] observe the three-day-festival and perform the ceremony of avabhṛta [3]—mention of all these will follow. (These descriptions are not found in the present text).

109. The pratiṣṭhā [4] (ceremony) for a movable image begins with its ablution with the water from the four pitchers (situated on the pericarp of the lotus design). Learn from me how to (perform the) invocation ceremony following the (preliminary) worship (of the deity).

110-116. It is necessary to offer three articles [5] to the deity before commencing the invocation ceremony.

The preceptor (envisaging himself as) identified with the essentially pure, calm and flawless parātīta (super-absolute Self), should then visualize in (his) lotus-heart the presence of Viṣṇu's Śakti, incorporating an existence similar to (Viṣṇu's). And then he should visualize (the Śakti) as infusing the already consecrated image. He should then visualize (Śakti's) state of existence consisting of Agni (*piṅgalā*) and Soma [6] (*iḍā*) as present in his own body. These two

---

[1] Mudrās of ādhāraśakti etc., all the seats of śakti. See ch. XXXIV, 36-48.

[2] The head, face, shoulders, ears, heart, navel, back, flanks, thighs, knees, ankles and feet.

[3] Final ablution of the adept at the end of the ceremony.

[4] Pau.S. ch. 38, 18 defines the term as whatever exists for the benefit of the devotee. This in fact entails invocation of the deity in a particular place.

[5] For instance pādya, flowers, arghya and the like.

[6] The two ducts, iḍā present at the left side and piṅgalā present at the right side of the main duct suṣumṇā. These two ducts are often regarded as parts of the main duct suṣumṇā which contains the brahmarandhra and is most important for yogic practices. Cf. Ahi.S. 32, 23-30.

great luminaries run through his body as well as the image's from top to bottom. Next, he should visualize his self as leaving his body through the right hand course (the piṅgalā duct) and entering the image's heart through its left hand entrance (i.e. the iḍā duct). Just as he feels his own excellent self within his own heart, so should he feel that same self of his within the heart of the (image). Visualizing (his own self) as filled with noble bliss, surrounded by its own glory, as being present both in (his own heart) and in (the heart of the image), he should meditate on its (= his self's) identity with absolute Brahman.

117. Having thus combined (all manifestations of) that supreme Viṣṇu-majesty (*mahaḥ*),[1] (the preceptor) should focus his concentration on it and keep his mind absolutely still.

118-119. When the mind begins to stir (again), he should (once more) reflect on his own separateness [2] from that (soul of the image) and envisage his self as moving out of the image by the right hand exit and entering his own lotus heart through the left hand entrance. This (special) yoga introduces all the ducts within the material image.[3]

120-123. Whereupon (the preceptor) should perform another form of yoga to infuse it (= image) with the nature of the supreme God. While meditating (he) should envisage his self escaping from his lotus-heart and during his recitation of the (mantra of) Tārikā, that bears people across (the ocean of life), as soaring upwards to the supreme state of perfection. He should then envisage the Absolute, of its own free will, tending to grow restless [4] (i.e. vibrating), whereupon (his own self) as identified with that vibrating Self possessing (the three attributes of) knowledge, aiśvarya and śakti [5], quietly returns through the same way into his lotus heart. Then (envisaging) both (his own self and the supreme vibrating Self) as

---

[1] *Mahaḥ* = *mahat*, here the individual Self.

[2] The reading *dvidhā* is the more plausible one, since it bears out the general trend of the argument and at the same time corresponds with the reading of J.S. 20, 218.

[3] This process is called *dhyānādhivāsana*. Cf. J.S. 20, 207-208.

[4] The reading *kṣobha* is preferred since it obviously fits in with the rest of the sentence, is retained in J.S. and is quoted in the Pārameśvara S. Cf. J.S. 20, 224 (the published edition of Gaekwad's Oriental Series, no. 54, gives a wrong reading) and P.S. 15, 451.

[5] As the process is called *īśvarānusandhāna* it therefore refers to the introduction of the creative aspect of the Absolute Self to the image.

being identical,[1] (the preceptor's self) emerges from his body through the right hand course (i.e. the piṅgalā duct) and enters the lotus-heart of the image through the left hand course (i.e. the iḍā duct).

124-128. Whereupon, having envisaged the identity (of the supreme Self, the preceptor's self and the image's self) as described before,[2] the (preceptor should visualize his own self) as rising through the (duct) leading up (to his head) and entering the (position called) dvādaśānta. Wherein he approaches the vibrating (Self) [3] and (identifying his own self with it), the wise (preceptor) should reenter the lotus-heart of the image through the same passage. Whence he emerges through (the duct called) agni (i.e. piṅgalā) and enters his own heart through the left side (i.e. iḍā duct). He should then identify his two eyeballs with the vibrating (Self) and (replete with) aiśvarya and he should fix his gaze upon the eyes (of the image). This mutual exchange of glances brings about a fusion between the two bodies (the preceptor's and the image's) which he should visualize as (his body) becoming one with (the image's). This particular yoga is known as the process of inserting God, the creator (in the image). This (yoga) introduces divine sovereignty in all images. Now (I shall state the yoga called) *śabdānusaṃdhāna* (introduction of sound), which is virtually the identification of the image with the (body of) mantra.

129-130. That (essence of the mantras) belonging to Viṣṇu is regarded as being Viṣṇu's subtle and faultless śakti. (The preceptor) should envisage (his) identification with that (śakti) and then merge his own self in the (śakti,[4] essentially) sound (*dhvani*), which is free from all determining (conditions) and from the elements of phenomenal sound (*śabda*). This state should be known as the state of rest (*śāntam*) which is absolute, subtle and consists solely of absolute knowledge.

131. The next (to the absolute state) is the state when (absolute sound) begins to vibrate actively on account of (distinguishing features) resulting from latent impressions derived from sounds and

---

[1] This is a free rendering of *parasparasahāyavān*, lit. "having (them) as each other's companions".

[2] See verse 117.

[3] This is the spandātman, the vibrating cosmic creator. This state of God has been described as His unmeṣa. Cf. ch. II, 21-24.

[4] Śabdaśakti. See ch. XVIII, 11-27.

the matters denoted and (the preceptor) should envisage this state of paśyantī as the highly subtle and active (state of sound).

132-134. He should then visualize within his lotus-heart the madhyamā manifestation of the sound, which is the active state when (the sound is) polarized, clearly influenced by each qualifying impression and differentiates itself from the (thing) expressed.

Vaikharī is known to be the state where the sound is produced by means of various forms of bodily activity through movements (lit. rippling) of organs and the process of breathing and where clearly distinguishable sounds denote syllables, words etc.[1]

135-137. Whereupon, identifying his (own) body as identified with the Conscious sound [2] in all (its states of) distinction, (namely) the absolute (transcendent), the subtle etc., (the preceptor) should envisage the image as incorporating (that sound-body). Then following the yoga of sonic dissolution (*śabdasaṃhāra*) [3] he should visualize the two bodies, his own and that of the image, as merged in the unflickering conscious sound. After which, following the previously mentioned order, he should envisage the unaffected Śabdabrahman inhering the sound(-pervaded) image, through the successive (states of) paśyantī etc.

138-141. Having thus introduced the presence of śabda (in the image) and having finished the mantra-introduction,[4] the wise (preceptor) should start the ritual yoga in the following way.

(Envisaging) the integral absolute (sound) as reaching the paśyantī state at the navel, (he should then visualize it as) approaching his lotus-heart through the middle channel,[5] which resembles the fibre of a lotus stalk. After allowing it to tarry there awhile, he should then envisage it as entering the heart of the image through the vaikharī (manifestation). Whereupon he should visualize the Lord of the world in mantra form manifested as the glorious nāda, pervading all mantras and present in the heart of the image.

(When the ceremony of) pratiṣṭhā is performed in this manner, the image bestows (upon the devotee) the rewards (of such performance) in the form of enjoyment and liberation.

[1] See ch. XVIII and XIX for the various grades of sonic creation

[2] Śabdabrahman.

[3] The process is the same as that of the cosmic dissolution, i.e. each principle is dissolved by reverting to its immediate source.

[4] Mantrānusandhāna, described in detail in J.S. 20, 244-248.

[5] The suṣumnā duct.

142-144. After that he should invoke the essence [1] of Hari in the image, by (first uttering the words) 'I invoke thee', and then he should envisage the entrance and emergence of Lakṣmī in and from God's body, of which every limb is a mantra. Her (= Lakṣmī's) invocation is regarded as (comprising) the first five *ṛcaḥ* (of the Śrī-sūkta). Whereupon (the preceptor) should perform nyāsa on the twelve parts of (the deity's) body just as it was (previously) performed on (the body of) God's (image). Lastly, he should perform the śānti [2] (rite of peace) to both (these deities) with the words: 'let our minds be at rest'.

145-146. Here ends the (description) of the pratiṣṭhā ceremony for movable images. The scholar of Sāttvata injunctions should perform the ceremony for immovable (images) in accordance with the previously set rules. All these three above-mentioned (rites of) introduction (of God and His Śakti etc. in the image) [3] are, in my opinion, applicable in both types of pratiṣṭhā.

147-149. When the pratiṣṭhā ceremony is thus conducted, the wise (preceptor) should then visualize the presence of Lakṣmī and of the husband of Lakṣmī in those two images. Focussing his mind fixedly on them, being their zealous devotee, who constantly worships them, performs japa relating to them and meditates on them, he finally surrenders himself completely [4] to them.

Here I conclude my description of the supreme pratiṣṭhā, which is directly infused with knowledge. This knowledge is considered to be the sole deliverer of mankind (from misery).

---

1 The Śakti of Hari, i.e. Lakṣmī.

2 Śāntikarman.

3 *Īśvarānusandhāna*, *śabdānusandhāna* and *mantrānusandhāna*.

4 *Prapadyate*; for *prapatti* see J. Gonda, Die Religionen Indiens, II, Stuttgart 1963, p. 139 ff.

CHAPTER FIFTY

THE POWER OF THE ŚRĪ-SŪKTA

1-2. Śakra:—I salute thee, the source of the universe,[1] adoration to thee who abidest in the universe as its glory, O primary cause of all (spiritual) ability (acquired through mantra-worship), I salute thee, who art identical with the primeval God and art Nārāyaṇa's spouse. O universally propitiated, lotus-born (goddess), I prostrate myself before thee.

3-4. By thy grace have I heard about the efficacy of all thy mantras. I have also duly learned how all of them should be rendered favourable. Now, I desire to hear from thy lotus-mouth all the rules relating to the (worship of) thy sūkta. I have approached thee (filled with faith), deign to instruct me.

5-10. Śrī:—God Nārāyaṇa is lord over (all things) movable and immovable. Embodying the six attributes and bliss, He is the Self (essence) of all worlds, the material cause of all (created things), the sovereign ruler, omniscient, omnipotent, free from all misfortune, flawless, and the repository of all that is beneficial. Being self-luminous, He illuminates both darkness and light; He is the inner lord (Self abiding in every being), the controller manifest in (both) the positive and the negative (phenomena). The possessor of Śakti and the substratum of all, my Lord is almighty. I am His unique, supreme, eternal Śakti known as Śrī. Free from all blemish, I fulfil all the Omnipresent's desires (entailing activities) and, with a fragment of my own self as the foundation, I evolve (into the creation), both in the pure and in the impure groups. I am ardently attached to Hṛṣīkeśa in (all His) functions and at the same time in the state of absolute equanimity.

10-16. In order to be merciful towards the worlds and benefit living beings, this pair of us, the ultimate parents of the world dwelling in infinite space with divine majesty (*paravā śriyā*), once (thought) out of compassion 'how can these creatures be happy and

[1] *Viśvāraṇe*: an *araṇi* is a piece of wood which, when rubbed against another, produces fire and so symbolizes a pregnant woman who is impregnated with fire, hence life. Cf. Ka.U. 4, 8, also ch. XL, 40-42.

be united with us?' While searching for a solution in profound concentration that (pair of us) churned (as it were) the vast, deep ocean of *Śabdabrahman*. When churned, out of that (*Śabdabrahman*) containing Ṛg, Sāman and Yajus, emerged the divine twin sūktas, in the same way as butter comes out of (churned) thick milk. This pair (of sūktas) is integral (*anāhata*), unambiguous, clear, undecaying, containing all majesty and attributes and possessed of flawless syllables and words. At the beginning and end these two possess identical letters, which are imbued with Śakti and with the possessor of Śakti.[1]

16-20. Of the two, the sūkta with male characteristics is adorned with all the characteristics of Brahman, that Is, has its foundation in His own glory and is acknowledged by the Lotus-eyed One to be His own.[2] The other sūkta possessing female characteristics (is also) adorned with the characteristics of Brahman, that Is, and has its foundation in my own glory and is accepted as my own [3] by me who am wholly concentrated. These two noble sūktas have been studied by great sages. When studied and meditated upon they carry one to one's final destination. Ancient (sages such as Śaunaka and the like), who are responsible for (modelling) the *kalpa*, have laid down thousands of special and simple rules about how to worship (these two sūktas). O guardian of the immortals, now listen to the rules concerning the worship of my sūkta.

21-22. I myself am regarded as its seer, its metre is said to be Śrī. I, the wife of Viṣṇu and the Goddess containing everything, am its deity. It is used for the worship of Lakṣmī and Nārāyaṇa.

22-23. (The adept) should visualize me, the noble Goddess Lakṣmī,[4] as seated on Viṣṇu's lap, perpetually embraced by the Supreme Self with His left arm (encircling me), while (one of) my lotus carrying hands rests on His shoulder.

---

[1] The text is not clear. Perhaps reference is made to the repetition of the letters *ha* and *sa* at the beginning and end of both *sūktas*, which letters represent Sūrya and Soma and together make up the *ajapā*-mantra, *haṃsa*, i.e. *Paramātman*.

[2] Implying that Nārāyaṇa is the sage as well as the deity of the Puruṣa-sūkta.

[3] Implying that Lakṣmī is the sage and Śrī is the deity. It is to be noted that the name *Indirāsutā* is mentioned as one of the four sages of this sūkta. See J. Scheftelowitz, Die Apokryphen des Ṛgveda, Breslau 1906, p. 74.

[4] Lakṣmī and Viṣṇu in combined form.

24. Then with the ṛcas of (the Śrī-sūkta) the adept, well-prepared and devout (*prayata*), should (start) worshipping me, the supreme Goddess seated on the lap of the paramount God Śārṅgin.

25-26. The (adept) should indefatigably invoke (us) with the first ṛc; with the second, he should offer a seat to the paramount God Śārṅgin. With the third, he should offer *arghya* and *pādya* to God (and to myself). With the fourth, he should offer *ācamana* and with the fifth, he should proffer an oblation.

27-31. The worthy adept should bathe us while reciting the sixth (ṛc), should offer clothing with the seventh and ornaments with the eighth. With the ninth he should offer perfumes, with the tenth flowers and with the next two (*ṛcas*) incense and lamp. *Madhuparka* should be proffered with the next (ṛc). (He should offer) *prāpaṇa* with the fourteenth (ṛc) and perform the salutation with the fifteenth (ṛc). At the end of each ṛc the adept (*mantrī*) should not fail to add regularly (the *mantras* of) Tārā and Anutārā [1] and duly perform *japa* (of these two) as many times as possible. Whereafter he should envisage the dissolution of the sūkta within the (mantra of) Tārikā. And then, after envisaging us in (the mantra of) Tārikā, he should meditate upon our omnipresence.

31-35. Alternatively, the invocation (ceremony) may be performed with the first four *ṛcas*. Then the pure-minded (adept) should resort to me, Śrī, with the fifth. The offering of *arghya, pādya* and *ācamana* should be accompanied by (the *ṛc*) starting with the words *āpaḥ* [2] etc. He should bathe me (while reciting the *ṛc*) *ārdrām* [3] etc. and offer clothing with (the *ṛc*) *kardamena* [4] etc. He should offer perfume with (the *ṛc*) *gandhadvārā* [5] etc. and ornaments with (the *ṛc*) *upaitu* [6] etc. (He should offer) incense and lamp with (the *ṛc*) *kāṃ so 'smi* [7] and an oblation with the sixth (*ṛc*). He should offer *madhuparka* with (the *ṛc*) *manasaḥ kāmam* [8] etc. *Prāpaṇa* should be offered with the (*ṛc*) *kṣutpipāsam*,[9] while with the last (*ṛc*) he should

[1] *hrīṃ* and *śrīṃ*.
[2] The twelfth *ṛc*.
[3] The thirteenth *ṛc*.
[4] The eleventh *ṛc*.
[5] The ninth *ṛc*.
[6] The seventh *ṛc*.
[7] The fourth *ṛc*.
[8] The tenth *ṛc*.
[9] The eighth *ṛc*.

perform the salutation. In other respects [1] he should follow previously given instructions.

36. This sūkta contains my fifty-three names, O slayer of Jambha. Listen now to my enumeration of these.

37-42. I am immanent in all beings and I hum like the female bumble bee.[2] From my abode in Sūrya and Candra [3] I gush forth in an unbroken flow of absolute sound (*nāda*) like the flow of oil [4] during the interval between the closing and opening of (God's) eyes.[5] As I travel (in turn through) all the centres of the body, from *mūlādhāra* to the *dvādaśānta* [6] with the brilliance of thousands of risen suns, fires and moons, I unfold (myself) from the *cakraka*, the air-repository,[7] as (manifested sound) *śāntā*, *paśyā*, *madhyamā* and *vaikharī*. On entering (this last state) I am present in the eight places [8] and become the mother of (all) sounds, showering objects of enjoyment in the same way as a cow (showers milk). Having praised me, addressing me as *Hiraṇyavarṇā*, the very wise Prajāpati obtained my grace and became the narrator of the *yoga* religion.[9] This (= *Hiraṇyavarṇā*) preceded by *praṇava* and ending in *namaḥ* [10] forms my nine-syllabled *mantra*, which is pervaded by the *Śabdabrahman* and is the direct means whereby yogins attain yoga.

43-44. Like a doe I flee farther and farther from the mind of the yogin.[11] Yogins observing their vows bind [12] me through their own devotion. Sixty-eight thousand yogins engaged in worshipping me and meditating on me as *Hariṇī* have attained complete inwardness of mind (*pratyāhāra*)

45-47. Meditating upon me, as Hariṇī who is covered with a deer-

[1] Implying the japa of *hrīṃ* and *śrīṃ* at the end of each ṛc, the dissolution of the Śrī-sūkta in Tārikā and visualization of the omnipresent divine couple therein.

[2] Analyzing the word *hiraṇyavarṇā*, *hi* stands for *nihita* = immanent, *raṇa* for *raṇana* = humming sound of a bee, *varṇā* = sounds.

[3] *Haṃsa*.

[4] Cf. Rāmānuja's Śrībhāṣya on Br. Sū. 1, 1, 1 *avicchinnatailadhāravat*.

[5] i.e. God's *Śānta* state.

[6] See editor's note, ch. XXXV, 32.

[7] The vital air which ordinarily remains within the *nābhi-cakra*. See Ahi.S., ch. 33.

[8] Namely *kaṇṭha*, *tālu*, *mūrdhan*, *danta* etc.

[9] *yogānāṃ dharmam ūcivān*.

[10] *oṃ hiraṇyavarṇāya namaḥ*

[11] A reference to the goddess's inscrutability.

[12] *badhnāti* = *harati*.

skin, seated on a deer-hide, embraced by Hari (or, is slenderwaisted like a doe), and possesses large doe-eyes, a yogin attains supreme serenity (of mind). Being Hari's creative potency I engage Hari in (all His) functions and am myself initiated to activity by Hari. Fawn-coloured, fair-complexioned as I am, I always remove misfortune from the honest. This my six-syllabled mantra is preceded by *praṇava* and has *namaḥ* at the end.[1]

48-50. My garland made of golden lotuses is always regarded as efficacious for the fulfilment of all desires, and is the best of all direct means of yoga (i.e. the adepts' identification with God). I create (all) fair letters. Or, I nicely accept the universe.[2] Innumerable birthless (souls) both bound and liberated, flow out of me. The king of the Guhyakas,[3] (worshipping me) as *Suvarṇasraj* and arriving at the centre of the earth (Meru), became the guardian of wealth and remained there ever after.

51-53. My spotless garland made of silver lotuses is ever sparkling. All creators, who create[4] the worlds are adorned with me (i.e. with my presence). In ancient times the forefather of the Rudras (propitiating me) as *Rajatasraj*, went to mount Kailāśa and became the lord of silver.[5] When these two eight-syllabled mantras with the addition of the tāra (-mantra) and *namaḥ*[6] are offered *japa*, worshipped, offered homa and meditated on, they fulfil all desires.

54-58. Ever in motion,[7] I remove all the sins of my devotees. Like the moon I unceasingly delight (lit. melt) the minds of my devotees. Characterized by the vibrating happiness in the minds of the yogins, I rise and like the (rising) moon illuminate their fourth (i.e. *turīya*) state (of existence). When the noble sage *Vasiṣṭha* was struck by the calamity hindering his yoga, reflecting on me, the pure one, the internal moon,[8] the great ocean as it were, of blissful consciousness and present in his (vital) duct (*nāḍī*), he recovered his own yogic (capacity). This mantra of mine consisting of six syllables[9]

[1] *oṃ hariṇyai namaḥ.*

[2] *Viśva* may connote either *Viṣṇu* or the universe.

[3] A reference to *Kubera*. See J. Gonda, Aspects of early Viṣṇuism, Delhi 1969^{2}, p. 223.

[4] *Sraj* derived from the root *sṛj-*, denoting the creative function.

[5] Is this a reference to Śiva, who is often compared to a silver mountain?

[6] *oṃ suvarṇasraje namaḥ; oṃ rajatasraje namaḥ.*

[7] The *ca* of *candra* stands for *cakra*, the whirling disc *Sudarśana*.

[8] See ch. XXIX, 36-41.

[9] *oṃ candrāyai namaḥ.*

produces instant bliss and ultimately brings about emancipation to those who are consumed by the flames of worldly existence.

58-61. I, the *Hiraṇmayī*, bright as the sun, who span (the region) from the *ādhārapadma* to the *dvādaśānta*, rise (become manifest) as buds of sound-conceptions.[1] For the benefit of the world I abide in the absolute void beyond (the reach) of *prakṛti*, which (void) is the golden centre (*maṇḍala*, i.e. *brahmāṇḍa*) consisting of the Vedas. Praising me as *Hiraṇmayī*, the sages who were masters of Vedic doctrines secured the best of all yogas obtainable by the yogins and longed for by them. This my seven-syllabled mantra [2] is capable of achieving all desired objects.

62-63. I, the witness (Self) abiding in all beings, notice [3] what is good and what is evil. I am Hari's eternal majesty (*lakṣmī*) and I am the object of all cognitive knowledge. I am ever bestowing (boons) and I direct all activities [4] and I activate the three (acts, namely physical, verbal and mental). I am also identical with the knowledge manifesting itself in every individual cognition.

64. I activate *prakṛti* in (all three of its functions, namely) destruction, sustenance and creation. I represent the minimum and the maximum manifestation of the trait revealing the essential character of every object.[5]

65. Inherent [6] in the (principle of) existence, whether manifested or unmanifested, I am at all times the inciter (potential element of all things). I manifest myself (as the creation), I ultimately dissolve myself (at the time of destruction) and I occupy myself with activity (when creation starts functioning).

66-67. I alone send (the creation) forth and (again) destroy it. I absolve the sins of the good. As the (mother) earth towards all beings, I pardon them (all their sins). I mete everything out. I am the thinking process and I am contained in everything. Aware of all

---

[1] i.e. *paśyantī* etc.

[2] *oṃ hiraṇmayyai namaḥ*.

[3] *lakṣayāmi*: an etymological explanation of the name Lakṣmī.

[4] The *la* of Lakṣmī is derived from the root *lā-* "to give", and *kṣmī* from the root *kṣip-* "to despatch, direct".

[5] *Lakṣaṇa* means an essential trait distinguishing one thing from another. It is comparable with the category of *viśeṣa* of the Vaiśeṣika system.

[6] The *la* is derived from root *lā-* "to dissolve", whereas *lakṣmī* is derived from *lakṣa-* "appearance".

these significations (of my name), the noble-minded sage Kapila exclaimed: 'O *Lakṣmī*, cast thy eyes [1] on me'.

68. This five-syllabled mantra [2] enables a person to descend into the Pātāla. It also produces all objects of enjoyment, whether heavenly, spheric or earthly.

69-70. My body incorporating knowledge resides in Viṣṇu's heart. This is the sacred knowledge relating to the Self and this is the absolute yogic knowledge. Just as the beauty of moonbeams is identical with the moon, so am I, Śakti of Viṣṇu the possessor of Śakti, abiding inseparably (in Him).

71-75. I alone become the element of [3] water, being its great (essential) quality, viz. liquidity. In ancient times I, as Sarasvatī, requested by Viśvāmitra, caused sage Vasiṣṭha to be carried off [4] in the waters of Sarasvatī. When thus the waters of the truthful Sarasvatī were about to wash Vasiṣṭha away,[5] the sages addressed me: 'O (embodiment of) truth, save the truth-loving Vasiṣṭha from the enemies'. Then I myself as Sarasvatī rescued him from the (hands of) enemies, and was given the name *Anapagāminī* by the sages. This nine-syllabled mantra removes all dangers.[6]

75-79. In the threefold abode, namely the intelligence, vital air and the physical body, I exist in three ways, namely as a horse (*aśva*), castle (*pūr*) and a carrier (*vāhanī*).[7] At the beginning of the meditation I produce a sound (*nāda*) which resembles the neighing of a horse. When I enter the arterial duct, I produce a sound resembling the rattling of a chariot, and when I am inside the hollow within (the *suṣumṇā*), I produce a sound resembling the trumpeting of an elephant. Yogins practising (yoga) comprehend me in these three ways. The first two mantras are eight-syllabled and the last one is eleven-syllabled.[8] All these three mantras yield whatever is desired.

---

[1] *lakṣaya*.

[2] *oṃ lakṣmyai namaḥ*.

[3] *Anapagāminī* is analyzed as *apsu* + *gāminī*.

[4] *Apsu avāhayam* is the derivation.

[5] *Apsu uvāha* is the derivation. See E. W. Hopkins, Epic Mythology, Delhi 1968, p. 183 f.

[6] *oṃ anapagāminyai namaḥ*.

[7] Intelligence is compared to a horse, because it travels from one thing to another. *Pūr* implies that she is the shelter of the vital air and she is called *vāhanī*, since she as the individual self guides the physical body. Cf. Ka.U. 3, 3-4.

[8] *oṃ aśvapūrvāyai namaḥ*, *oṃ rathamadhyāyai namaḥ* and *oṃ hastinādaprabodhinyai namaḥ*.

79-87. I listen to (*śṛṇomi*) (my devotee's) lamenting propitiation and I demolish (*śṛṇāmi*) the misfortunes of the honest. I cover (*śṛṇāmi*) the world with my guṇas and I protect (*śaraṇa*) it eternally.[1] I am *Hari*'s body (*śarīra*)[2] and the gods desire (*īpsitā*) me with faith (*śraddhā*). When in the state of *śāntā*, the substratum, I rumble (*rantī*) as *paśyā*, (sound) produced from the navel (i.e. the sound *oṃ*). (Then) as the initiative (*preraṇī*) I, madhyā, urge the minds (to activity) and I occupy the mouth in the form of the creator of sounds (*arṇas* = *varṇa*).[3] Present, thus in four manners distinguished by *śāntā*, *paśyā* etc., I take shelter (in Viṣṇu), whereas I myself give shelter to the *śaktis* (such as Jayā etc.). I destroy (*remi*) (the sins of the protected) and at the same time fulfil their wishes (*rāmi*). I am the most resplendent and most beneficent *rati* (revelling capacity) of the Śakti, desired (by all). It is thus that the masters in meaning of the Vedānta recognize me directly as Śrī. Nevertheless, the master,[4] my universal power (*vibhūti*), the three worlds, together with the creator and the gods do not account for even a sixteenth part of my sound(-body). The first three (mantras) comprising the three syllables imbued with me, namely *śrīṃ*, *hrīṃ* and *oṃ*, and then this (mantra),[5] all these four form my body.[6] If any one, two, three or all four of them are repeated (*japa*), worshipped, offered sacrifice to and meditated upon, it or they ensure the fulfilment of (the adept's) desires. Hence these four gems should be carefully stored in secrecy. Betwixt themselves they produce all (the divine) attributes.

88-89. I cognize (*mime*) and mete out (*mīye*) (the creation) with the help of all standards of measurement. At the time of dissolution the creation is engulfed within me.[7] I consist of God's essence[8] and I pervade (*meti*) the clear apprehension of Self.[9] That is why those who know me realize that I am held in highest esteem like one's own self. This five-syllabled mantra[10] yields all desired objects.

---

[1] The name Śrī is derived from the root *śru-* or *śṛ-* in three senses.

[2] Śrī = *śarīra*. Then again *śra* = *śraddhā* and *ī* = *īpsitā*.

[3] *śa* = *śānta*, *ra* = *ranti*, *paśyā*, *i* = *preraṇī*, *madhyā* and the *varṇas*, i.e. *vaikharī*.

[4] *api nātho* etc. seems to be an incomplete sentence.

[5] *oṃ śriyai namaḥ*.

[6] *śrīṃ hrīṃ oṃ oṃ śriyai namaḥ*.

[7] Lit. "corresponds in measure with me"

[8] Or "I consist of ātman and Īśvara"?

[9] *mā- iti* = *meti*. *mā* = *aham*. Hence *meti dhīḥ* = *ahaṃ pratīti*.

[10] *oṃ māyai namaḥ*.

90-91. Since I am the bestower (*pradātrī*) of all that is desired, the promoter (*avitrī*) of all activities and at the same time I am God's (*deva*) beloved, hence the sages know me as *Devī*.[1] This five-syllabled mantra [2] bestows (upon the adept) enjoyments and liberation.

91-94. I, consisting of consciousness, am ever inherent in all beings and produce sound (speech).[3] All the Vedas establish (*kāye*) [4] me. I am the object of such enquiry about 'who is she?' (*kā iti*). Wearing my hair in a matted mass and assuming the form of Brahmā,[5] I create many beings who are expert in Vedic studies, hence the sages, masters of Vedic learning, call me *Kā*. This five-syllabled mantra [6] yields the fruits of studying the Vedas.

94-95. Brahman's name is indeed represented by the letter *u* (*ud iti nāma*), whereas *smita* denotes its pervasiveness. As this pervasiveness depends on me, I am known as *sosmitā* (= *sa-u-smitam*).[7] This seven-syllabled mantra [8] procures great expansion (prosperity).

96-97. My own absolute *prakṛti* [9] is beneficial (*hitā*) and holds charm (*ramaṇīyā*). Holding on to her, who incorporates sattva, sages cross (the ocean-like) *tamas*. That is the reason why they worship me as *Hiraṇyaprākārā*. This ten-syllabled mantra[10] bestows (upon the adept) fulfilment of all desires and prosperity.

98-101. I directly dissolve (*drāviṇī*) all the shortcomings of those who approach me (and take refuge in me). I am continuously saturated (*ārdrā*) by the flow of *amṛta* oozing from the inverted lotus of the head.[11] My mind melts with pity (for the living beings). I burn for ever in the deepest sphere of everybody's mind as the pure,

[1] *dā- ava-* = *devī*.

[2] *oṃ devyai namaḥ*.

[3] *śabda* = *ka* etc. sounds.

[4] *kāye* = I am substantiated by.

[5] *Ka* is a name of *Brahmā*, the progenitor of beings. This description of the goddess vaguely resembles that of Brāhmī, one of the matṛkās. Cf. Gopinath Rao, Hindu Iconography, Vol. I, Part II, Madras 1914, pp. 383-384.

[6] *oṃ kāyai namaḥ*.

[7] She who possesses the *ut* and *smita* of *Brahman*: *uditi nāma* etc., cf. Ch.U. 1, 6, 7. *smitam* being explained as *vikasti*, *vikāsa*, *bṛhattvam*.

[8] *oṃ sosmitāyai namaḥ*.

[9] Implying that the word *prākāra* is derived from the word *prakṛti*.

[10] *oṃ hiraṇyaprākārāyai namaḥ*.

[11] In the creature's body this is the highest lotus seat of the Self, from which *amṛta* drips incessantly on the *kuṇḍalinīśakti*, who sleeps coiled around the *nābhi-cakra*. Cf. Ahi.S., ch. 32.

impeccable reality illuminating the world with my rays, sometimes with no flame at all,[1] sometimes with three [2] and sometimes with twenty-five flames.[3] In the last form I may again have only seven [4] or only three (visible flames).[5] These two six-syllabled mantras [6] yield (the states of) emancipation and realization (of truth).

102-104. I am filled with everlasting love for Hari and when pleased (lit. satisfied) I constantly shower gifts upon my devotees. I take spontaneous delight in the offerings of non-material (*aprākṛta*)[7] objects. Sages, well versed in the Vedic learning, envisaging me as the ever contented (goddess), attain to me (i.e. my state of existence) who am the source of all knowledge, the transcendent and everlasting contentment full of nectar. This six-syllabled mantra [8] sheds joy over the entire universe.

104-105. I satisfy Viṣṇu with the libation of my *guṇas* and I myself (am saturated) by His attributes. By force of the stimulant of the vital air, I am ever saturating the ocean of the (living beings') bodies with sap carried by seventy-two thousand arterial ducts.[9]

106-107. In the pure yogic mirrors (minds) of (yogins) who have ascended to the absolute state through the channel of the *suṣumṇā* duct,[10] my image (*bimba*) is reflected. (And then) I saturate the superb *sattva* (pure essence) of the yogins with the divine nectar-sap derived from the reflected Self, which is infused with consciousness.

108-111. Ever stimulating through my power (i.e. divine capacity), I invigorate the evolving principles, starting with *prakṛti* and ending with *viśeṣa*,[11] which have (already) been evolved into effects and I pour vital air into them in the same way as the rivers pour water into the ocean. Like the fat that keeps a lamp burning I lubricate the senses of living beings with my own sap of conscious-

[1] The *śāntā* state.

[2] The *paśyantī*, *madhyamā* and *vaikharī* states.

[3] All the sounds produced by the contact of the tongue with some part of the mouth.

[4] The sounds *ya*, *ra*, *la*, *va*, *śa*, *ṣa* and *sa*.

[5] The sounds *ha*, *ḷa* and *kṣa*.

[6] *oṃ ārdrāyai namaḥ* and *oṃ jvalantyai namaḥ*.

[7] *prākṛtasya vinā* = that which is not material.

[8] *oṃ tṛptāyai namaḥ*.

[9] Cf. Ahi.S., ch. 32, 20.

[10] Reference to the yogic process of self-purification. Cf. ch. XL, 115-116 and Ahi.S. ch. 31 and 32.

[11] *Viśeṣa*, the cosmic elements—ether, air, light, water and earth.

ness. Hence yogins, experts in yogic practices, call me *Tarpayantī*. This seven-syllabled mantra[1] supplies (life-)sap to the entire universe.

111-114. As time cuts off (*minoti*) all objects of knowledge (*padyamānam*), so it (= time) is called *padma* (lotus). Ever present in this *kāla* (time) I destroy all (at the end of creation); hence having praised me with this name, (the adept) who has passed beyond (even) time becomes successful (in his spiritual endeavour). Owing to my own prowess (I ever expand[2] this creation) through the Person, *pradhāna* and *Īśvara* (the creator),[3] therefore my body is adorned with the letters (or, with the colour) of the lotus (i.e. *padma*). Those who praise me as *padmavarṇā* etc.[4] acquire vast śāstric learning.

114-116. The primal ray that emerged from the ocean of milk as it was churned, is called *candra* and was the ray that heralded my radiant presence, when I was about to appear. Hence sages who recognized my power called me *Candrā*. That which is (now known as) the moon (*candra*) is produced from a million millionth fraction of my rays. This six-syllabled mantra[5] purifies the mind.

117-121. My radiance is always and in all states superb (*prakṛṣyamāṇā*). Even the (brilliance of other luminaries such as the sun etc.) with which (the latter) try to outshine (all else), is eclipsed by my radiance.[6] Because the shadow of a person's feet cannot overlap the shadow of his head, so some other (shadow) must be found to extend beyond that of his feet, if he wishes it to fall across (the shadow of his head). My brilliance, which is the ever active blissful consciousness, is always (matchlessly) bright. The brilliant śakti in the objects of enjoyment (*bhogyaśaktiprabhā*) throws *śraddhā*, *soma*, water, food, virile power and butter respectively into six fires.[7] Hence I am called *Prabhāsā*[8] by sages who are experts in the Tantra

[1] *oṃ tarpayantyai namaḥ.*

[2] Lit. "depict": *varṇayāmi*.

[3] *pa* = the Person, *da* = pradhāna and *ma* = the creator.

[4] *oṃ padmavarṇāyai namaḥ*. *Varṇa* is used in the double sense of sound and colour.

[5] *oṃ candrāyai namaḥ.*

[6] Both the analogy and the main sentence are somewhat muddled. Apparently the word *prabhāsā* is analysed as *prakṛṣṭaḥ bhāsaḥ yasyā sā* 'She who is endowed with the brightest luminosity'. The comparison aims at stressing that *Lakṣmī's* radiance is unsurpassed.

[7] Enumerated hereafter, in verse 124; cf. Ch.U. 5, 4-8.

[8] Here the word *prabhāsā* is split into *prabhā asyati* "fire" and "throws".

and Vedānta (teachings). This seven-syllabled mantra [1] endows (the adept) with uninterrupted brilliant energy.

121-123. All the glorious fame acquired in this world on account of a person's scholarship or charity etc. is a (manifestation) of myself. This (fame) may be of various types. You should realize that it is myself who am (in fact) the recipient of all fame, brilliant power and beauty (or welfare: *śrī*). Therefore the wise know me, the famous (goddess), as *Yaśasā*. This seven-syllabled mantra,[2] when repeated (*japa*) brings fame (to the adept).

124-126. Dividing myself into six forms, namely *svarga, parjanya, bhū, puṃ, strī* and *vaiśvānara* (heaven, air, earth, man, woman and fire) and respectively receiving the appropriate offering (*haviḥ*), such as *śraddhā, soma* etc. I consume them, whereupon having become fire I blaze brightly and so sages chant my name as the radiant *śakti* of the enjoyer (*bhoktṛśaktiprabhā*). When divided into *Agni* and *Soma* [3] I embrace [4] the whole of creation. (The adept) worshipping me with this *mantra* [5] can perform whatever (ceremony) he chooses.

127-130. I am loved by God *Hari* and all the gods are ever at my service. With me as support the senses (*devāḥ*) (can) contact their objects. (The senses such as) the faculty of hearing, the faculty of speech, mind etc. being different evolutions of *prakṛti* (matter), are insentient, and so (can only) make contact with objects through my śakti consisting of pure consciousness and activity. Therefore in order to function, the senses (*akṣaiḥ*) rely on me; so people recognize me as *Devajuṣṭā*. Always meditating on me (as this *mantra*),[6] the bestower of all powers and the beloved inherent sustainer of the senses, (the adept) achieves complete control over his senses.

131-132. In this world, all sublime revelation of great sages as well as all the capacities and activities of people in both the higher and lower stations of life (come from me). Moreover, I bestow (upon men) their (greatest) aim (in life, i.e. liberation), the shattering of

---

[1] *oṃ prabhāsāyai namaḥ.*
[2] *oṃ yaśasāyai namaḥ.*
[3] The two great sacrificial gods.
[4] I prefer the reading *bhavāmy aham* to *bhajāmy aham.*
[5] *oṃ jvalantyai namaḥ.*
[6] *oṃ devajuṣṭāyai namaḥ.*

bondage (of life and death). Therefore the wise know me as *Udārā*.[1] This seven-syllabled mantra [2] fulfils all desires.

133-134. I intensify (*tanomi*) my five duties [3] and spread (or protect, *tāye*) the universe by (infusing) myself (into it). Hence those who know the truth and are expert in Vedānta (philosophy) call me *Tām*. This five-syllabled mantra [4] promotes the extension of good luck.

134-135. Through my own brilliant energy I induce (*nayāmi*) *prakṛti* and the Person (to create), and I stretch beyond the reach of even the (eternal) time, hence people know me as *Padmanemī*.[5] This seven-syllabled mantra [6] is the bestower of all fortune and prosperity.

136-142. I alone make the sun brilliant with luminosity, illustriousness and beauty. Present in the sun (*sūrya*) [7] as the essence of sound, embodying the divine Vedas, I reveal all objects (of cognition), even those belonging to the past and to future. I am the eternal eye (i.e. vision) of the ancestors, of celestial beings and of human beings. Tāra, the first denotative sound, is my primordial (sound-expression). Being present therein as potential but (as yet) tranquil bliss, I delight the Self with my own self. My sound-body is the subtle flame of *praṇava* and resembles the continuing resonance of a ringing bell like a flow of oil. He who has realized *Brahman* will soon recognize my presence there (in *praṇava*) and I, consisting of sound, come together with all sounds produced from the āditya-sound (i.e. *praṇava*). (That presence of mine) as *śāntā* and *paśyā* etc.[8] manifests the vaikharī sounds and like the wish-fulfilling cow exists to produce all (created) things. The sages are familiar with all these various significations of my name *Ādityavarṇā*. This nine-syllabled mantra [9] fulfils all wishes.

---

[1] Derived from the root *dṛ-*, meaning to break.

[2] *oṃ udārāyai namaḥ.*

[3] Creation, sustenance, destruction, delusion and bestowing grace. See ch. XIII, 26-29.

[4] *oṃ tāyai namaḥ.*

[5] Padma, derived from the root *pad-* "to lead on, to induce", and *nemi* (connected with *nayāmi*) denoting that which encircles the periphery.

[6] *oṃ padmanemyai namaḥ.*

[7] See ch. XXIX, 2-32.

[8] *Parā*, *paśyantī* and *madhyamā*. See ch. XVIII, 20-27.

[9] *oṃ ādityavarṇāyai namaḥ.*

143-145. I spread (my luminous) rays (*kirantī kiraṇām*) all over this universe. I gradually manifest (*kirantī*, myself as sonic creation). Resting on the petals of each (of the twelve) lotuses I slowly soar up along with the air, the friend of gods and with the gem, the basic fire and finally attain the (state of) *dvādaśānta*.[1] Hence the wise sages praise me as Kīrti. This five-syllabled mantra produces flawless yogic power.

146-147. I flourish (*ṛddhāmi*) through Viṣṇu's attributes; I make the yogins happy (*ardhayāmi*). I gradually expand myself over all the petals of the lotuses of (the yogin's) yogic body, coming out of (the lotus called) *ādhāra*, and finally achieve the absolute (state) of expansion.[2] Hence in ancient times yogins called me *Ṛddhi*, the brilliance of yoga.[3]

148-149. Smell etc.[4] (essential qualities, of) the earth (element) etc. are gateways leading to the realization of myself. I am the ever-existing cause (that produces) all holy fragrances. The brahmins, who are masters in Vedic learning, name me *Gandhadvārā*.[5]

149-153. I am invincible against all titans, demons and ogres. Being pure consciousness and pure activity, I cannot be eliminated by any (counter-knowledge or act). Since I am myself consciousness and activity and at the same time the self of all beings, how can a person, desirous of denying me do so by experiencing a negatory knowledge or committing a negatory deed? No one is capable of going beyond my manifestation as consciousness. As there is no such (person), so the scholars of Sāṃkhya knowledge, who regard me as verily being unsurpassable consciousness, call me *Durāgharṣā*. This eight-syllabled mantra [6] destroys ignorance.

---

[1] Referring to the yogic process in which the *kuṇḍalinīśakti* is roused by the adept and by means of prāṇāyāma and other yogic practices is made to soar upwards, step by step through the adept's yogic body consisting of twelve lotuses, until it merges in the absolute Self at the point called *dvādaśānta*, or the end of the twelve (lotuses). Thus the *Śakti*, the individual self identifies itself with the Self, the supreme, sublime bliss, the goal of all yogic practice. Since this process involves *prāṇāyāma* (or controlled breathing) and *maṇi* or the basic *śakti* of the adept, these are referred to as the air (*devamitra*) and the basic fire (*ādhāra-vahni*).

[2] The state of *dvādaśānta* where Śakti is united with God.

[3] This name signifies Śakti's contribution to the *yogic* meditation.

[4] Implying that the other four essential qualities, fluidity, form, touch and sound correspond to the elements of water, fire, air and space.

[5] *oṃ gandhadvārāyai namaḥ* is the mantra.

[6] *oṃ durāgharṣāyai namaḥ*.

154-155. I am invigorated by the eternal Viṣṇu and am perpetually nourished by virtues. My transcendent body (being) absolute consciousness constantly flourishes, unassisted by any object of knowledge. It is verily this (body) that charges inanimate objects with spirit. Hence the great sages, endowed with insight in (the nature of) consciousness, address me as *Nityapuṣṭā*. This eight-syllabled mantra [1] ever deepens consciousness.

156-159. *Kariṇaḥ* (from the root *kṛ-*) denotes those who fulfil three types of functions, pure in their (= functions) three forms,[2] and I am ever eager to have a view of them and I always approach them (*yāmi*) in mind. The big elephants as white as the snow-mountains are my mount and I am ever in motion as their mistress (*īśvarā*). Since as the creator and the destroyer I constantly control (*yāmi*) all, the learned address me as *Karīṣiṇī*. This seven-syllabled mantra [3] fulfils all desires and bestows prosperity.

159-161. Together with my beloved God I have dominion over all creatures and I as supreme controller am ever granting boons and being solicited by all. Perpetually flourishing, I bestow prosperity (on the adept) and destroy distress. Therefore in the Vedas my name is laid down as *Īśvarī*. This six-syllabled mantra [4] yields all riches and prosperity.

162-164. All desires (for objects) belonging to the earth, atmosphere or heaven, as well as for the non-material Absolute, which always hold pleasure are contained in me. I am the ultimate basis, upon which all objects of longing are displayed. I surpass everything and am the object of Viṣṇu's mental longing. Therefore gods praise me as the *manasaḥ kāma* (desire). This nine-syllabled mantra [5] fulfils all desires and bestows wealth.

165-168. That which is known as speech belonging both to the secular and (to the sacred, viz.) Vedic and external Āgamas, whether unpronounced or pronounced, when produced through effort, always refers to me (alone). Therefore the scholars of the Vedas infer that I am that which is referred to (*ākūti*) in all forms of speech whose utterance involves physical effort. This eight-syllabled

[1] *oṃ nityapuṣṭāyai namaḥ.*

[2] Performing sacrifices, giving gifts and studying are the three functions, and the three types of action are physical, mental and verbal.

[3] *oṃ karīṣiṇyai namaḥ.*

[4] *oṃ īśvaryai namaḥ.*

[5] *oṃ manasaḥ kāmāya namaḥ.*

mantra ensures the fulfilment of all sought to be gained by sound.[1]

168-169. The whole creation, which true knowledge reveals as separated into the two categories of true and false,[2] is myself. Hence the sages call me *Satyā*. This six-syllabled mantra [3] yields al the true results (of good deeds).

170-173. The individual selves, the living beings (*paśu*) envisage (themselves) as existing in three states.[4] O Śakra, consciousness is truly their unblemished essential form (of existence). I myself am that form of concentrated conscious bliss. All the individual *śaktis* (which are the essences of the individual selves) are indeed merely particles of my śakti. It is my *Agniśakti* (i.e. *bhoktṛśakti*), who undergoes birth as this or that living being. That is why scholars of the Sāṃkhya (system) address.me as *paśūnāṃ rūpam* (the true form of living beings).[5] This nine-syllabled mantra [6] yields the fruit of true realization.

173-177. Objects of enjoyment are said to be of two types to be distinguished as those produced by the three *guṇas* (which are material) and those produced by the six attributes (which are non-material). The enlightened describe me as the self in all created beings, the superb manifestation of the glory of both types of created things (*anna*), those embodying the three *guṇas* and the others embodying the six attributes. All objects of enjoyment, both material and non-material, are products of my *Somaśakti* (*bhogya-śakti*). So the people engaged in speculating about reality, know me as *annasya yaśaḥ* (the glory of created things). This nine-syllabled mantra [7] bestows (upon the devotee) all objects of enjoyment.

177-181. When engaged (in creation) I limit the six courses (of creation). (Being the principle of measurement) I measure everything

---

[1] Here the word *sound* refers only to the *vaikharī* or manifested sound. Hence the importance of effort in producing sound. The mantra is *oṃ vāca ākūtyai namaḥ*.

[2] Cf. *sac ca tyac cābhavat*: Tai.U. 2, 6, 1.

[3] *oṃ satyāyai namaḥ*.

[4] As the celestial gods, human beings and the lower animals; or as the bound, the liberated and the ever-emancipated.

[5] *Paśu* denotes living beings as described by the Śaiva philosophers. It is interesting to note that both *spanda* and *paśu*, the two very typical Śaiva terms, are used in this text quite freely.

[6] *oṃ paśūnāṃ rūpāya namaḥ*.

[7] *oṃ annasya yaśase namaḥ*. Here it is interesting to note the influence of the Vedic formula *annādo 'ham . . . bhūyāsam*, cf. Āp.Ś.S. 6, 21, 1.

according to units of measurement. I am the knowledge acquired through all senses and (when the time of dissolution comes) I embrace all (creation) within myself.[1] I carry the whole of creation across the shoreless ocean of created existence; beyond the reach of the ocean of all imperfection, I float in the minds of the living beings. Transformed into clouds I flood the entire creation with (rain-) water. I am ever concerned about the happiness and welfare of all creatures and act accordingly, therefore the yogins know me as the mother of all creatures. This five-syllabled mantra [2] presents (the adept) with all objects of enjoyment and wealth.

181-188. The arterial duct called *suṣumṇā*, which is the most important in the complex of ducts [3] and which is described in the sacred texts as being the vehicle of emancipation, the mighty vehicle or the vehicle of yoga, is called the subtle *Viṣṇuśakti*, which is identical with myself. It forms the basis for all objects on which (the yogin's) concentration is focussed and runs through the human body from head down to the end. That (duct) which encases the supreme space (*brahmarandhra*) is called *suṣumṇā*. O Śakra, it is myself who am present in all embodied beings as the *suṣumṇā* duct in their bodies with the view to the final liberation of all souls who are distressed in the *saṃsāra*. Running from the bottom of the navel to the top of the head ranged over that (*suṣumṇā*)*śakti*, there are thirty-two lotuses called the supports (*ādhāra*). Since I pervade this row of lotuses, I am (envisaged as) wearing a garland of lotuses. As I incorporate prakṛti, the Person and the time eternal,[4] I am called *Padmamālinī*. This eight-syllabled mantra [5] yields the fruits of *karman* (good-deeds).

188-190. I cause all (beings) to wax in beauty, fame and wealth. I alone lead the *puṣkara*, the lotus-formed (entity) called time (eternal).[6] Hence the sages call me *Puṣkariṇī*. This seven-syllabled mantra [7] yields the fruit of all-round prosperity.

190-192. I am the cherished aim of all the gods and am always in

---

[1] *mātaram* is first split up into *mā-* (to measure, to cognize, to dissolve) and *tara-* (to take across, to save, fo flood).

[2] *oṃ mātre namaḥ*.

[3] Nāḍī-cakra, cf. Ahi.S., ch. 32 in extenso.

[4] See verse 113.

[5] *oṃ padmamālinyai namaḥ*.

[6] See ch. V, 22-23.

[7] *oṃ puṣkariṇyai namaḥ*.

union with Hari. Supporting all the worlds, I also fulfil all desires. I am the substratum of prakṛti, the Person and the other (cosmic principles). Therefore sages call me *Yaṣṭi* (the staff). This six-syllabled mantra [1] bestows (upon the adept) all the rewards of yogic practices.

193-194. Due to my complexion of pure gold I am of a tawny colour. In ancient times I gave (*lāmi*) *Piṅga*, the king of the Yakṣas, great wealth. O Śakra, formerly the king of Yakṣas addressed me as *Piṅgalā*. This seven-syllabled mantra [2] bestows yogic power and prosperity.

195-196. I delight Viṣṇu with my attributes and am delighted by Hari's attributes. When praised by all beings with (offerings of) their deeds, they find joy in me. Hence I am called *Tuṣṭi* by those who have reached the far shore of the ocean of yogic practices. This six-syllabled mantra [3] gives satisfaction to the mind.

197-199. I take the successful adepts to the conditional heaven or to the absolute heaven (Hari's sublime abode).[4] The primeval unmanifested beautiful sound denotes me. As the eternal Sarasvatī I express everything beautifully; hence the learned brahmins call me *Suvarṇā*. This seven-syllabled mantra [5] bestows (upon the adept) all (forms of) success and prosperity.

199-201. As the earth, I support the holy golden mountain studded with the moon, sun and planets to provide a (befitting) dwelling for god Vedhas (*Brahmā*). Therefore Viriñci (*Brahmā*) praised me (by addressing me as) *Hemamālinī*. This eight-syllabled mantra [6] bestows upon mankind the power of self-control.

201-204. For the benefit of all creatures I create (*prasūye*) the course of (cosmic) principles (*tattva-paddhati*). In the world, I delight (them) (*ramayāmi*) by bestowing upon them enjoyment and liberation according to their deserts. I also control the course of created cosmic principles together with the living beings through the

---

1 *oṃ yaṣṭaye namaḥ.*

2 *oṃ piṅgalāyai namaḥ.*

3 *oṃ tuṣṭaye namaḥ.*

4 *Suvar nayāmi* is the first explication. *Suvar* is heaven and also denotes Viṣṇu's supreme state. Hence *para* and *apara*. The second explication is based on *su + varṇa*.

5 *oṃ suvarṇāyai namaḥ.*

6 *oṃ hemamālinyai namaḥ.* The mountain refers to the Hemameru ranges.

(influence of) time. Beneficial to the sages (*sūrī*),[1] I am ever present in the orb of the sun in the form of *Sūrya(śakti)*. Hence the learned thinkers, the *sūrins*, call me *Sūryā*. This six-syllabled mantra [2] yields all desired fruits, both in the form of enjoyment and in the form of liberation. Here I conclude the description of the fifty-three names [3] mentioned in the (Śrī-)sūkta.

205-206. The wise, having obtained (union with) me, experience the fulfilment of each specific desire. Although I have here associated each (name and its mantra) with what they are specially capable of fulfilling, the intelligent should not assume that they are limited in their capacity to that alone. (In fact) they are capable of fulfilling all desires, including liberation.

207-209. As this (sūkta) of mine contains a string of names of myself, Śrī, its absolute deity, its significance is as unlimited as the stars in the sky, or as gems in the ocean, or as the pleasures of this earth, or as the longed-for objects hanging on the celestial wishing-tree, or as the noble characteristics of the cow, or as the brilliant energies of a brahmin, or as the countless divine attributes of Janārdana, the supreme God.

210-212. Were I to take Time (eternal), the god himself defined by his smallest and largest denominations, I should still be unable to complete listing all the attributes of this sūkta. (Hence) this same (sūkta) is the object upon which Vedic scholars concentrate and the sole resort of those who are learned in the Tantras. Men never fail to take refuge (achieve union) in me through (the aid of) this sūkta. When a person ponders on the meaning of this sūkta and devotes lengthy study to it, he attains serenity of mind and achieves the same state of existence (as) myself.

213-219. Having taken refuge in me or in God the supreme Person, (the adept) who is full of faith and self-restraint, should petition (us) in the following manner: 'As far as my ability and

[1] Another name for the Viṣṇu-devotees.

[2] *oṃ sūryāyai namaḥ*.

[3] The text of the *Śrī-sūkta* as recorded here does not always tally with the text given by Dr. J. Scheftelowitz's text in Die Apokryphen des Ṛgveda, Breslau 1906, pp. 72-73. For instance, in the third verse here we have *hastinādaprabodhinī* instead of *hastinādapramodinīm*. Again *kāṃso 'smi* instead of *kāṃsy asmi* (4), *hiraṇyaprākārā* instead of *hiraṇyaprāvārām* (4), *ṛddhim* instead of *vṛddhim* (7), and there are other minor discrepancies as well. The numbers here stand for the number of the verses in the Śrī-sūkta.

character permit, I refrain from any adverseness (harming any living being) and am well disposed (towards all creatures).[1] I have ceased (to commit) the errors and sins that abound in this ocean of (transient) existence. Despite that (conscious effort), may thou, called to mind, destroy (the effects) of whatever (sins) I may (inadvertently) commit. Since I am lazy, weak and ignorant (lit. not duly educated), the three methods (of knowing thee),[2] described in religious texts, cannot avail me. (Although I seek no gain), any function that I perform here (I regard as) in obedience to thy bidding. Hence, because (I am) helpless, (I am) poor, humble and unprotected, my only means of survival is by sheltering under thy cooling shadow. O unlimited, sovereign mistress of us all and resort of compassion, every scripture sings that thou art the sole refuge.

219-222. Whatever is considered to be difficult to relinquish, or (else) a difficult burden to carry, such as the self and whatever belongs to the self, I have placed at thy auspicious lotus-feet. In order to approach thee, who art the goal envisaged by all methods of (spiritual) endeavour, I accept thee as the (only) means. O Lotus-born Goddess, deign to aid me, deign to protect me. All my sins need to be scorched away and my intellect, focussed on thee, needs to be invigorated'. Having thus petitioned me, (the adept) should take refuge in me as being the (only) shelter, or (he should approach) the primary God, the lord of the universe, the Master and supreme Person.

223-225. O Śakra, the greatest eradicator of all evil and the remover of all bad luck (*alakṣmī*), this my sūkta should be recited on the occasion of any religious rite. It strengthens the power of the ritual acts, brings prosperity to the listener, destroys all delusion and removes all bad fortune as well as all imperfections. When (an adept) worships it employing physical, mental and verbal functions, it saves him from heinous sins and bestows everlasting prosperity on him.

226-231. Here, O Śakra, I conclude my narration of this best of Tantras, which contains all that the wise know to be truth. Just as the science of liberation excels amongst all the various sciences; the brahmin amongst all bipeds; the cow amongst all quadrupeds; gold

---

[1] See ch. XVII, 66-80.

[2] *Karman*, *jñāna* and *bhakti* (performing religious duties, realization of truth and devotion).

amongst all metals and *kaustubha* amongst all gems; a mother amongst all superiors and a son amongst all claimants; the mind (*manas*) amongst all senses and the wind amongst all that is mobile; *Meru* amongst all mountains and *Gaṅgā*[1] amongst all rivers; the householder amongst all ranks of life and Vasiṣṭha amongst all performers of *japa* (i.e. meditative prayer); absolute renunciation amongst all true states and visionary knowledge amongst all that is profitable; so is this Tantra the best of all Tantras dealing with realities.

231-233. Here (in this sūkta) the essence, traits and majesty of God Vāsudeva, Viṣṇu, Nārāyaṇa, the preceptor and myself are duly described. Those who possess a clear grasp of true knowledge adhere to this (sūkta) which is a view (knowledge) of myself. Holding on to this ladder, they climb up step by step to the supreme state (of existence). This is supreme amongst all Tantras and is stamped by a name that is identical with mine.

234-237. One should not teach this (Tantra) to a person who has not taken the ritual bath (signifying) acceptance of a vow (to observe the Pāñcarātra religion), nor to a disloyal person, nor to a person ignorant of the (teachings of the) Tantra, nor to someone who is prone to jealousy, nor to someone who is not a devotee of Vāsudeva and not to anybody who is not a devotee of mine. This (teaching) should be given only to a person of high moral standing, who is well bathed (clean), practises austerities, is well versed in the teachings of the Vedas and of the Tantras, who is especially devoted to me and cherishes great devotion for Vāsudeva Janārdana; who observes the pure vow (of Pāñcarātra), is clever and only acts virtuously. O king of gods, here I conclude my description of all the matters you enquired about. I am pleased with you, tell me what else you wish to hear.

---

[1] *Gaṅgā* courses through three planes, one is heaven, another is this earth and the last is the nether region, cf. e.g. Br.P. 2, 8, 26-42 and 50-52.

CHAPTER FIFTY-ONE [1]

A BRIEF SUMMARY OF THE COSMOGONY

1-7. Śakra:[2]—(I have) learned about the creation and dissolution and also about how certain (rites) should be performed and what (specific) results are obtained therefrom. (I have also learned) all about the five compulsory duties and about incidental duties. I have listened with due attention to the Tantra called Lakṣmī Tantra, the four sections of which deal with various aspects of Tantra, namely *caryā, kriyā, jñāna* and *yoga* (iconography and architecture, ritual ceremonies, cosmogony and philosophy and meditation). It also contains descriptions of old customs, ancient times and history, as well as of diverse secret rituals and is embellished with many (useful) sayings so as always to convince people. As it is elaborate and on account of changed times [3] is now (somewhat) out of date and as my mind is weak (dull), I cannot grasp it properly. O lotus-born (goddess), I salute thee. For the benefit of the world, deign to summarize the Tantra by picking out all the essential points from that vast ocean, filled with knowledge of thyself.

8. Nārada:—Thus addressed, her mind melted (like that of) a cow (answering) the call of her calf, the goddess Padmā said to the punisher of Pāka.

9-18. Śrī:—O slayer of Vṛtra, my son, it is well that you have drawn my attention to it. Listen now to an abridgement of this Tantra. I am the eternal I-hood of all beings and am considered to be the creator of the universe in descending and ascending order.[4] The supreme I-hood is known as the *turyātīta* (state). That is transcendent (absolute) Brahman, the absolute state of existence and (the

[1] As the editor remarks, only one manuscript contains the following chapters. These seem to be a supplement to the main Tantra and are probably of a later date.

[2] The opening verses are missing in the original manuscript.

[3] This statement confirms the later date of this supplement. It is also interesting to note that the colophons to these few chapters differ in content from those of previous chapters. Instead of *Pāñcarātrasāre Lakṣmī tantre* the colophons of these last chapters read *Pāñcarātrasāre Lakṣmītantroddhāre tantrārthasaṃgrahe*. This confirms the opinion that this is a brief summary of Lakṣmī Tantra.

[4] See ch. VII, in extenso.

joint existence of) Lakṣmī and Nārāyaṇa. There is no dualism there, since we exist (unitedly) as the existing (principle) and its state of existence. When activity stirs up there (in that state), as in the ocean when the moon rises, I, the Śakti of Nārāyaṇa, am then characterized by the creative urge, and that is my turya state coinciding with the beginning of my state of evolution. Therein both the pure and the impure creation lie dormant. The pure creation includes *Vyūhas, Vibhavas, Vyūhāntaras* and other such manifestations of God contained in those categories of the *Vyūhas*, the *Vibhavas* and the *Vyūhāntaras*. My (three) states of existence, *suṣupti* etc., should be classified under the following (headings). (The cosmic principles) *avyakta, mahat* etc. and the evolving creation are contained in the impure creation. O lord of gods, each of my three states of existence (*suṣupti* etc.) should be dealt with in its proper order. These four states are also present in the living beings. (The afore-mentioned) categories are components of the impure creation and are (of a) limited (nature).

18-23. There is another set of categories in both the pure and impure stages of the creative evolution which is (also) pervaded by me that consists of the cognizer, the medium of cognition and the object of cognition. Cognizers are of ten types and are classified according to states of the void and the living etc.[1] Classified into external and internal, the medium of cognition is divided into two. One should determine various types of the already described objects of cognition, which are cognized through both types (of the above-mentioned medium of cognition) and which appear in the state of yogic trance (i.e. *samādhi*) and other subsequent (states of the cognizer). The *turyātīta* state of these (cognizers) is when they realize their identity with God. Here ends the description of my (gradual) descent (into grosser creation). Now listen to my gradual ascension (through dissolution). Starting from the final state (of materialization) as the created objects return to rest in me through both the pure and impure courses of creation, that process is called my ascension.

23-24. Bearing in mind that these two phases, my ascension and descent, are parts of one (process), a person fixing his mind (solely)

[1] What is meant actually by ten types of cognizers and the state of void is not clear. Ch. XIV, 47-49 lists nine types of living beings. Possibly the void state refers to the emancipated.

on me and dedicating his (entire) life to me, (finally) achieves (union with) me.

24-32. O king of heaven, I am beyond the limitations of form, time or place. In fact these (limiting factors) are pervaded by me. With myself as the substratum, I voluntarily evolve this entire universe. Thus, I have briefly revealed to you the different aspects of my presence as the received and the receiving [1] and this is how I evolve as the definable (*vācya*, the material creation). Now listen attentively to my defining (*vācaka*, knowledge) aspect. Consisting of pure knowledge, I first evolve into *prāṇa*. Then through specific stages I evolve into (subsequent states) known as *śāntā*, *sūkṣmā*, *madhyā* and *vaikharī*. As *śāntā*, manifesting the four forms, the four objects of the knowledge of the four forms (*Vyūhas*), I evolve further into the subtle state. In the subtle state I remain in the dual form of *śakti* and *nāda*. Evolving from the subtle state I arrive at the state of *madhyamā*. (That is the state of) *bindu*, in which the totality of all the sounds is latent. I am that state of all sounds, *madhyā*. From there I evolve into the state of *vaikharī*. This is the state in which sounds are differentiated, manifest themselves and are divided into groups of fifteen etc. (the vowels etc.). (He) who is versed in the knowledge of *Śabdabrahman* and bears in mind my two states of ascension and descent (dissolution and creation), enters (the state of) the one who is beyond the reach of sound.

---

[1] *grāhya* and *grāhaka*, meaning the objects of enjoyment and the enjoyers.

CHAPTER FIFTY-TWO

THE MANTRAS

1-23. Śrī:—Now, Puraṃdara my son, listen to the course (of my manifestation) as mantra. I am revelation and bliss, and I am the I-hood of Hari. Know me, who am called *prāṇa* and consist of pure knowledge, as the mother of the mantras. As I become active to create all these (created objects) come out of me and again (at the time of dissolution) they surely are dissolved in me. I am the prowess (*bala*) of all these and they manifest forms of myself. I am manifest in two ways, in three ways, in four, five, six, seven, eight, sixteen, twenty-five, fifty and sixty-three ways. I, the Goddess, the wish-fulfilling gem, manifest (myself) in diverse forms. The vowels, the consonants, a combination of vowels with consonants, sounds, words, all extant sacred sciences and Tantras as well as sentences, topics, sections (*āhnikas*) and chapters, various external and internal Āgamas both popular and Vedic, and different spoken languages, consider all these as my mantra-form. I manifest myself in diverse polarized forms as subject and object (of knowledge) according to varying intellectual capacity. Similarly, my manifestation as the aggregate (of all mantras) or as one individual (mantra) depends on the varying mental capacity (of adepts). Mantras are of four types, classified as *bīja, piṇḍa, pada* and *saṃjñā*. O Vāsava, consider five gems amongst them to be the outstanding ones. All these are present in my *sūkta* as butter is present in curd or, O ruler of heaven, as *nāda* arises from *Sūrya, Soma* and *Agni* and the part (*indukhaṇḍa*). What is here regarded as (my) *Sūrya* manifestation corresponds with my waking state. *Agni* is my dream state and my state of deep sleep is *Soma* (manifestation) which is otherwise called *māyā*. The remaining part called *indukhaṇḍa* is my *turya* state.[1] *Nāda* is the state beyond that. *Śakti*, which is the state of inertia (*śāntā*), is in fact nāda's state of existence. Brahman, that exists beyond (even) that, is indeed the (state of union) between Lakṣmī and Nārāyaṇa. The group of twenty-four (*ṣaṭcatuḥṣaṭkaṃ?*) is produced from *Sūrya, Agni* and *Soma*. All other sounds are generated

[1] *hrīṃ* and *śrīṃ*.

from the vowels, and this concludes the description of sounds. This is the most powerful *bīja* (*hrīṃ*), that bestows (on the adept) the fulfilment of all desires. To those desiring sons it gives sons, and a kingdom to those desiring a kingdom, prosperity to those longing for prosperity, liberation to those aspiring after liberation. It destroys (the adept's) enemies and attracts those who are welcome. It is indeed the wish-fulfilling gem and there is no real gem that can fulfil desires. The other bījas such as *śa*, *ka* etc.,[1] fulfillers of all wishes, rank next to this one and (the adept) should perform *aṅga-nyāsa* with these two substitutes [2] of *māyā's* akṣara in combination with all the six vowels from beginning to end and at the same time he should display the *jāti-mudrā*.[3] The same method is also enjoined for the remaining four *bījas* (*aiṃ*, *klīṃ*, *ouḥ* and *īṃ*). Through the addition of the first *bīja* (*oṃ*), which infuses (them with) the total I-hood (of God), all the various groups of mantras become identified with me. The deities of the mantras, sustained by my śakti, are thus identical with me, so that I thereby become the focus of meditation. Each particular deity (presiding over each mantra) should be envisaged as possessing the female form and appropriate colour, weapons and ornaments etc. Consequently, becoming identified with me (mantras) soon yield the desired results. Thus O Śakra, I conclude my brief exposition of the system of mantras.

---

[1] *śrīṃ* and *kṣmrīṃ*.

[2] For *ādeśa*- see Pāṇini, I, I, 56.

[3] No description of this mudrā is given.

CHAPTER FIFTY-THREE

SUMMARIZING RITUAL PERFORMANCES

1-2. Śrī:—O Puraṃdara, in brief I shall now devote a section to ritual performances. (The adept), having washed himself clean and having bathed in accordance with the precepts of sacred scriptures, should retire to a solitary place. Then, O Śakra, after performing the rite to purify the site, he should through the promotion of higher knowledge perform *bhūtaśuddhi*.

3-15. The eight (cosmic principles) starting from the earth-element and ending with *prakṛti* are known as the sources. Differentiated by (being) subtle or gross, they are considered to be of two types. Those which can be seen by the eye are described as gross. When these lie dormant within their sources, they are described as subtle, or in the form of essence. Thus divided into the two groups of gross and subtle, the (cosmic) principles are eight in number. One should relate (the principles) to their relevant objects and senses. One should step by step merge the five gross elements in the five relevant triplets of (conative and cognitive senses and the element-potential, such as) the genitals, the sense of smell and smell (itself, the element-potential of the earth-element) respectively. The mind and consciousness of self should be dissolved into the ego. The life-principle (*prāṇa*) and determination are dissolved into the principle of intelligence. *Sattva*, *rajas* and *tamas* should be dissolved into the basic avyakta (*prakṛti*). O ruler of heaven, one should envisage the eight basic mantras belonging to these two groups of eight (sources) (as follows): the name of the relevant principle preceded by *praṇava* and *huṃ phaṭ* added after it (= principle). The eight subtle basic mantras should be formed as follows: *māṃsa*, *meda*, *asṛj*, *retaḥ*, *vyoman* and the three *akṣaras* (māyā, prasūti and prakṛti) each joined by bindu (*ṃ*). To each of these eight basic mantras *māyā* combined with *indukhaṇḍa* (*ī*) is added. The wise should recognize that *Nivṛtti*, *Pratiṣṭhā*, *Vidyā*, *Śānti*, *Śāntyatītā*, *Abhimānā*, *Prāṇā* and *Guṇavatī* are the respective *śaktis* of (the principles) starting from *pṛthivī* and ending with *prakṛti*. (The mantras constructed) by adding *vahni*, *māyā* and *ardhacandra* (*rī*) to the above-mentioned eight subtle basic mantras belong to these eight presiding (*śaktis*). Envisaging me as thousands of blazing fires of dissolution containing nothing but smokeless cinders, (the adept) should burn the ground with the fire coming out of my mouth. Whereupon he should sprinkle the place with the water that comes out of my mouth and resembles millions of moons. This concludes the procedure for purification of the site. Now listen to the description of the process of *bhūtaśuddhi*.

CHAPTER FIFTY-FOUR

BHŪTAŚUDDHI AND AṄGANYĀSA

1-9. Śrī:—Having attracted the earth(-element) from within his body and envisaging it as square, flat, yellow and bearing the sign of thunder, by exercising (his) mantra(-power, the adept) should merge it in its own source, the smell-potential. Then he should dissolve it in its own *bīja*-mantra. When it becomes dissolved in its own *bīja*-mantra, he should next, by means of his own basic mantra, dissolve it in me, the substratum (of everything). Then he should throw me into the outside (real) water. Taking that (water-element) of half-moon form, possessing the lotus sign, from within his own body by means of his own mantra, he should merge it in its own source, the essence of fluidity and in its own (*bīja*-)mantra. And after dissolving it in me its (final) support, he should then (throw) me into the fire and thus step by step without return (all is finally dissolved) in the revealed *prakṛti*. The wise should not conclude that the process of dissolving my *śaktis* invariably follows the same pattern. As (a lump of) butter may be dissolved either in the milk from which it was churned, in some other milk, or else in another (lump of) butter, so also the wise should call to mind the Śakti, the supreme supervisor, (of dissolution) back to the final source, (which is) *prakṛti*. Thus my greatest śakti (*prakṛti*), along with my seven other *śaktis* should be raised up to the (state of) *dvādaśānta* to become dissolved in me who incorporate the mantras. That body of mine incorporating all mantras resembles millions of fires, moons and suns in brilliance, and possesses eyes, heads and faces in every direction and exists (as such) only for the benefit of all living beings.

9-10. Śakra:—O lotus(-goddess), deign to tell me on which parts of (the adept's) body this process of dissolution should be performed and how should the images of the earth etc. be envisaged?

10-14. Śrī:—Up to the knee is the position of the earth, up to the waist is the position of water, up to the navel is the position of fire, up to the heart is the position of air, up to the throat is the position of the ether, up to the mouth is the position of the ego, up to the eyebrows is the position of *mahat* (cosmic intelligence) and t[illegible] absolute (*prakṛti*) exists in the void. The superb image of the earth is square and possesses a thunder mark on it. (The image) of water is considered to be of half moon shape, white and possesses a lotus mark. (That) of fire is said to be triangular, marked with the *svastika* and red in colour. (That) of air is said to be round and smoke-coloured, with six spots. Space is considered to be nothing but a (vague) image, blackish in colour.

15-19. When in this manner the elements have been dissolved in the cavity of the heart, supported by knowledge hanging like a string inside the *suṣumṇā*-duct, (the adept) should lead (the self) up above himself,[1] up the ladder of śaktis and should dissolve it in me, who am present inside the great lotus at *dvādaśānta*. The great lotus at *dvādaśānta* has a thousand petals and is brilliant like millions of suns and millions of moons. This body consisting of supreme bliss incorporates within itself both *Agni* and *Soma*. *Māyā*, the inscrutable, incomparable consciousness, is incorporated by me, and only a part of her is projected as the bliss (self) of living beings, the greatest of all rivers.[2] (The adept) should bring his own bliss and merge it into (me), who am supreme bliss.

20-29. Then on all sides (the adept) should burn his body, which resembles a heap of salt, with myriads of mighty flames, that consist of knowledge and proceed from my mouth; the sixth red day-lotus possesses *bindu* and is the fire of the (human) body. Whereafter he should shower it with the nectar of *Soma* that spouts from the mouth of myself who consist of *Soma*. Next he should reflect that these śaktis (inhering in the cosmic principles) that form his body, in whom the mantras are incorporated, are issued by me out of my (śakti called) *sisṛkṣā* (urge to create), when I who consist of both pure consciousness and the principle of life (*prāṇa*) am launched on creation. Then with those *śaktis* (inhering in cosmic principles), that belong to himself, (the adept) should envisage the creation of all (the principles), starting from *prakṛti* and ending with *viśeṣa*, in the order enjoined by the scriptures (*codana*). From them (he should envisage) the (re-)creation of

---

[1] Viz. *dvādaśānta*.

[2] The highest *Śakti* projects herself in various directions and in various forms, flowing out of her like countless rivers. *Jīvaśakti* is one of these *śakti*-streams and, being sentient, is the best one as it is closest to the supreme Śakti.

his body (*piṇḍa*), which shines because it reveals its source (the pure Śakti). Having thus (re-)created his body infused with matchlessly pure Lakṣmī, step by step, he should bring back his own self, characterized as knowledge and bliss, from the Absolute bliss to the place of his heart, following the same previously described course.[1] Thereafter he should perform mantra-*nyāsa* on his hands and body (in the following way). He should first perform *nyāsa* of my *bīja*-mantra on all the joints of his fingers of both hands, starting from the thumbs and ending with the little-fingers, on his palms and on the backs of both palms, on all the joints (of his body), from navel down to the ankles, and again from the navel up to the head, and then he should perform *nyāsa* of the *aṅga*-mantras such as the (mantra of) the heart and the like. Thereafter the wise (adept) should once more perform *nyāsa* of the six attributes, jñāna etc. with the aid of these six (*aṅga*-mantras) heart etc., on his navel, back, hands, thighs, shanks and feet. When the body is thus (re-) created and infused with the pure and beautiful Lakṣmī, (the adept) should then visualize, with the sight of higher knowledge, the performance of *nyāsa* of the six supports.[2]

---

[1] See verses 15-19.

[2] The *ādhārapadma* etc. See ch XXXV, 56-59.

CHAPTER FIFTY-FIVE

A YOGIN'S VISION OF HIS INNER BODY

1-6. Śrī:—O Indra, listen, I shall now describe the supports. O master of wealth,[1] the wise envisage six lotuses, (separately) situated behind the genitals (i.e. in the anus), in the genitals, inside the navel, in the heart, within the mouth and between the eyebrows. These have petals (called) *Vedas, Rasas, Prajānāthas, Arkas, Vikārakas* and the two *Aśvins*. These are as brilliant as millions of suns and contain (sounds) from *ka* to *ta* and (all) vowels with *ha* and *kṣa* added to them. (The adept) should envisage me, the Goddess, in the form of a jewel-lamp, as being present in these lotuses. He may fix his mind on any one of these (lotuses) he chooses and practise yoga. He should visualize this primeval absolute (Śakti) as present in his body and having a single form extending flame-like over all the lotuses from the first *ādhāra* (lotus) to the lotus at *dvādaśānta*. Thus meditating on her, who is absolute consciousness and proceeding step by step from lower lotus to higher lotus, when his mind becomes totally absorbed by (Śakti), that state of existence is Viṣṇu's absolute state.

7-19. Now listen to this description of my body(-image) in case you wish (to visualize me) within the bounds of your body. You should visualize in (your) heart a watery *Mahendra* hall[2] with four doors, (guarded), O Śakra, by the female doorkeepers, the dark Balākinī at the front (door), the fair Vanamālā at the southern (door), the same complexioned Vibhīṣikā at the back (door) and the smoke-coloured Śāṅkarī at the northern (door). There, within the hall, one should visualize an eight-petalled lotus resembling thousands of suns and adorned with pericarp and filaments. The eastern petal contains Vāsudeva, the southern Saṃkarṣaṇa; the western petal contains Pradyumna, and the northern petal Aniruddha. All of them carry the conch-shell and the disc; all are decorated with *vanamālā*; all are coloured according to the present *yuga* and all are visualized as facing me. On the corner petals four great elephants,

[1] Indra is here identified with Kubera.

[2] Refers to a maṇḍala.

Gulgulu, Guruṇya, Madana and Śalala, (respectively), should be envisaged as showering nectar on me. In the centre of the pericarp I, the supreme ruler of all the worlds, should be envisaged as having a complexion like pure gold, as holding two lotuses (in two of my hands), while the other two are held in the posture of granting protection and boons, and as wearing all sorts of ornaments, as the inscrutable, incomparable, flawless wife of Viṣṇu. I sprinkle the repeatedly heated three worlds with my cool rays issuing forth from my moonlight-like smile and from the corners of my divine dark eyes. (The adept) should worship the great Goddess (i.e. myself) with offerings, which are visualized in his mind, which being free of blemish consist only of the bliss of Brahman [1] (i.e. God Himself) and myself alone. Or (you may envisage her) as seated on Viṣṇu's lap, (her face) beautiful with the expression of happiness she derives from His company, her right arm always encircling Him. It is then necessary to realize (the mystery) of our etherial forms, and to comprehend that our matrimonial relationship which surpasses understanding remains hidden in the Vedas. The place of the seed . . . [2]

[1] The possessive case denotes identity.

[2] The chapter is found in incomplete condition. The next chapter is entirely missing.

CHAPTER FIFTY-SIX

(MISSING)

CHAPTER FIFTY-SEVEN

THE FOUR STATES OF SOUND AND CONCLUSION

1-8. Śrī—: . . .[1] who is God, the sustainer, comprehended through intuition, and the superior Śakti, the aggregate of the three forms —this is the nature of the supreme japa.

Lakṣmī is projected (into creation) in two ways, as sound and as meaning (the object of sound). There are four stages of sound's active state, named śāntā, paśyā, madhyā and vaikharī (respectively), and the active state of meaning (*artha*) has similar (four stages). The sonic state in which all impressions are dissolved, and there are no distinctive sounds such as vowels etc., is known as śāntā, which is the resting place (of all spiritual endeavour). The sonic state when Śakti is manifested as the revealer but is as yet unpolarized and integral, is called paśyantī. When it (= sound) is recognized as the revealer, it is called sound. When that sound is undisturbed by impressions (obtained from material objects) it is called *madhyā*. When it (= sound) is filled with impressions and has hundreds of differentiations, then as there cannot be several (of these basic sounds) inhering in all these material (sound-manifestations), it becomes differentiated into parts manifested in eight places (the eight places of pronunciation) and is called *vaikharī*, possessing diverse manifestations.

8-25. The absolute (sonic śakti) is called śāntā, when (sound) is totally unmanifested and inert. A thousand billionth part (of this sound) is the madhyamā sound, and a thousand billionth part of that again is the vaikharī sound. Vaikharī is manifested in three ways as the sounds, the words and the sentences. The (sonic śakti vaikharī) becomes more and more limited through these stages of sound etc.[2] This is the fourfold Śakti, manifesting herself in a reverse and obverse order.[3] Through these four gradual phases, namely śāntā, paśyā etc. (Śakti as sound) becomes creatively manifest and again through (the obverse) order, of four phases,

---

[1] The beginning is missing.

[2] Sound, word and sentence.

[3] Viz. tending towards creation or dissolution.

namely vaikharī, madhyamā etc. (she) gradually unmanifests herself.[1] This (vaikharī) is again recognized as having three forms, *vyaktā*, *vyaktasamā* and *avyaktā*. *Vyaktā* is that (sound) which is produced inside the bodies of the living beings, and which has a beginning and an end. Sound that is produced by means of (instruments such as) a vīṇā, a flute, a drum and so on, and which requires direct efforts on the part of living beings, is called *vyaktasamā*. Sound that is produced by the disturbance of air (caused by the movement of water or air) in sea, river, mountain-caves etc., is called *avyaktā*. Each of these (varieties of sound) is liable to the afore-said four stages (of development) classified as śāntā etc., in both their courses of creation and dissolution. The objects denoted are also of four types corresponding to the classification of sound as śāntā etc. Śakti manifesting herself in such manner is known as Tārikā. This *japa* [2] is called madhyama, which exists encircling manifested sound (like varṇa etc.). Śakti in the form of (pronounced) sound and produced from bodily contact; one who is inhered by Śakti, the polarized (*anuviddha*) one; and one who is produced by direct (human) effort—all these four śaktis,[3] which are being manifested, determine the superimposition of denoted objects on the sound and are collectively known as the last (fourth) state (of sound). (Śakti) is revealed in sound (either) as related to the objects of sound or as totally unrelated as in the three (other) phases (of sound),[4] and this realization, which is achieved by means of mantras, is, verily, the supreme *japa*. That which is defined in the Lakṣmī Tantra as consisting of *Agni* and *Soma*, which is approachable after (the adept) goes beyond (sound's) polarized expressions as the objects denoted and the (sound) denoting (them) and crosses the (sea of) night (ignorance), pervaded by Lakṣmī (as *tamas*), is manifested in the form of Tārikā. (The adept) should purify all mantras by merging them in the vast ocean of Tārā, the motionless, which is Absolute bliss infusing himself with her presence. Then he should worship them (as merged) in her, and hence illumined by her special grace. Whereupon he should meditate on the deity of the mantra by (performing) ordinary and special (rites). While engaged in this way

---

[1] This explains the terms *pratilomaja* and *anulomaja*.

[2] Tārikā, the mantra.

[3] Four aspects of the same *vaikharī-śakti*.

[4] Madhyamā, paśyantī and śāntā (parā).

he should perform the *japa* of the mantras. Since this *japa* is everlastingly worshipped, he should visualize the appearance of particular deities of mantras, their special (bodily) positions and other systematic *saṃskāras*, in conformity with the injunctions of scripture. This omniscient *japa* is considered to be the Absolute.

26-27. Nārada:—This great secret should not be revealed to the unworthy. No sooner had she said this than she disappeared into the ether like a flash of lightning. Having received this precious treasure, Śakra rejoiced and was freed from care.

27-38. Atri:—Whereupon, O lady, illustrious Nārada ceased speaking. O beauteous lady, the illustrious Śrī was worshipped by Indra. Amazed, Indra immediately betook himself to the abode f Brahmā. When asked, he duly told Brahmā everything. When questioned, the wise Brahmā narrated this to the Prajāpatis. All (renowned) sages heard it from Nārada on the Malaya mountain. Aṅgiras taught Pāvaka this excellent Tantra. Pāvaka (handed it on to) Kātyāyana and he (in turn) imparted this (knowledge) to Gautama in his hermitage. Gautama (handed it on to) Bharadvāja, and he to the great sage Garga, and Garga to Asita, Devala and the sage Jaigīṣavya. The (latter) sage taught the pitaras and consequently overcame all temptations. The daughter of Ekāñjanānnapika (?), who was created from his own mind, taught it to her son the great sage Vyāsa, and Vyāsa to his son the excellent yogin Śuka. Śuka narrated it to the Prajāpati, named Svarbhānu. Vasiṣṭha taught it to the wise Arundhatī, who taught Nārada. All the yogins, such as Kapila and others, obtained this Tantra of Lakṣmī from him. The moon-crested Śaṃkara narrated it to Pārvatī. Hiraṇyagarbha, the spokesman of yogins, (explained) it to Sarasvatī. All the loyal wives of gods, the sages who have revealed knowledge of Brahman and the yogins always regard the Lakṣmī Tantra as their means of deliverance. Learning it from Brahmā, O wise one, I have given a full account of it to you, who are cherished and loved by me.

39-55. O Anasūyā, listen again to this short (exposition) with a mind free from intolerance. Having heard it, you should practise it carefully and meticulously. Your mind should be focussed on the image of Lakṣmī and Nārāyaṇa, casting aside all the distracting sins present in this ocean of (transient) existence. If a sin be committed by chance or through ignorance, Lakṣmī and Nārāyaṇa, when propitiated, very soon spontaneously obliterate (its effect). Do not worry about how they (the divine couple) achieve their aims. Occupy yourself with protecting humanity. Consciously and spontaneously practise humility, which comes from the conviction that always, in all places, in all circumstances and by all means, Hari, the possessor of Śrī, will protect those who take refuge with Him. (In problems of life) regard Lakṣmī's husband as the only means to achieve (anything) and the only end (worth achieving), and lay yourself and everything you own at the feet of Śrī's consort. Dear lady, here I conclude my narration of this scripture, of its meaning and its results obtained, of this sublime knowledge, the Lakṣmī Tantra, together with its secret implications and a short summary, which I have done with care. On no account should you pass it on to a non-devotee of Vāsudeva. You should teach this excellent Tantra to him whose mind is solely occupied with Lakṣmī and Lakṣmī's husband. It should never be studied in front of an infidel, or before anyone who has not taken the bath (preliminary to the taking) of a vow, or before those who are hostile towards parents, who abuse sacred scriptures and contradict their teachers, who are against married couples, or who hate women. Only those who have taken a bath (preparatory to) vowing (to study) the Vedas, who are dear to parents and teachers and never abuse sacred scriptures, possess discriminating knowledge of absolute and conditional (reality), who are reverent believers and graced by Lakṣmī and Lakṣmī's husband, who understand the divisions of ritual performances and sacrifices, who are familiar with the injunctions of other Tantras and know the process of yoga and its subordinate rites, who know the real nature of things (as expounded) in all sacred scriptures, who know the Vedas and Vedāṅgas as well as the doctrine of Paśupati, who are capable of thinking logically and know all that comes under the discussion of logic and other means of knowledge and who have knowledge of all spiritual sciences, are worthy of receiving this instruction.

oṃ. Adoration to Vāsudeva, whose beloved is Śrī. *oṃ*. Adoration to the wife of Viṣṇu, whose beloved is Nārāyaṇa. Adoration to eternally pure knowledge, the (supreme) cause of creation, the completely tranquil knowledge, that is identical with the (state of) Lakṣmī and Nārāyaṇa.

INDEX OF NAMES AND TECHNICAL TERMS

VEDIC MANTRAS

OTHER MANTRAS

Vaiṣṇava-mantras or vyāpakamantras: p. 134, chs. XXIV and XXXVI
oṃ (praṇava-mantra)
oṃ namo viṣṇave (the six-lettered mantra)
oṃ namo nārāyaṇāya (the eight-lettered mantra)
oṃ namo bhagavate vāsudevāya (the twelve-lettered mantra)
oṃ jitaṃ te puṇḍarīkākṣa namas te viśvabhāvana namas te 'stu hṛṣīkeśa mahāpuruṣa pūrvaja (these last four are pada-mantras of oṃ)

Prāsāda-mantra: ch. XVIII, p. 102
oṃ hauṃ

Haṃsa-mantra: ch. XXIV
oṃ namo haṃsāya svāhā vauṣaḍ huṃ phaṭ

Nārāyaṇa mūrti-mantra: ch. XXI, p. 116
oṃ kṣiṃ kṣiḥ namaḥ nārāyaṇāya viśvātmane hrīṃ svāhā

Viṣṇugāyatrī:
oṃ nārāyaṇāya vidmahe vāsudevāya dhīmahi tan no viṣṇuḥ pracodayāt

Ajapā-mantra: ch. XXX
So 'ham

Sudarśana-mantra group: chs. XXIX, XXX and XXXI
sahasrāra īṃ (sudarśanabīja-mantra)
sahasrāra (sudarśanapiṇḍa-mantra)
oṃ sahasrāra hūṃ phaṭ (the six-lettered sudarśana-mantra)
oṃ saṃ haṃ srāṃ raṃ hūṃ phaṭ (sudarśanasaṃjñā-mantra)
oṃ jraḥ kraḥ phaṭ hūṃ phaṭ phaṭ phaṭ kālacakrāya svāhā (sudarśanapada-mantra)
oṃ ryuṃ (pravartakāgnipiṇḍa-mantra)
oṃ vruṃ (nivartakāgnipiṇḍa-mantra)
namaś cakrāya vidmahe sahasrajvālāya dhīmahi tan no cakraḥ pracodayāt (sudarśanagāyatrī-mantra)
oṃ praṃ mahāsudarśana cakrarāja mahādhvaga astagatasarvaduṣṭabhayaṅkara chindhi chindhi bhindhi bhindhi vidāraya vidāraya paramantrān grasa grasa bhakṣaya bhakṣaya bhūtāni trāsaya trāsaya hūṃ phaṭ svāhā (śaktigrāsa-mantra)

The six basic bīja-mantras besides praṇava: ch. XXVI, XXVII
hrīṃ (Tārā)
śrīṃ (Anutārā)
aiṃ (vāgbhava)
klīṃ (kāma)
auḥ (Sarasvatī)
kṣmrīṃ (Mahālakṣmī)

Mantras belonging to Tārā-mantra, used in daily worship of the Goddess Lakṣmī and Nārāyaṇa: chs. XXXIII and XXXVIII

Tārā's aṅga-mantras:
oṃ hrāṃ jñānāya hṛdayāya namaḥ (hṛnmantra)
oṃ hrīṃ aiśvaryāya śirase svāhā (śiraḥmantra)
oṃ hrūṃ śaktaye śikhāyai vauṣaṭ (śikhā-mantra)
oṃ hraiṃ balāya kavacāya huṃ (kavaca-mantra)
oṃ hrauṃ tejase netrābhyāṃ vauṣaṭ (netra-mantra)
oṃ hraḥ vīryāya astrāya phaṭ (astra-mantra)

Tārā's upāṅga-mantra, see p. 185

(Aṅga and upāṅga mantras are used for nyāsa rites which precede all tantric rituals)

Mantras of ornaments and weapons used by the Goddess: see p. 185 (these also are used for nyāsa rites)

Mantras of the containers (ādhāra), see p. 185

Mantras of the lords of the containers (ādhāreśa), see p. 185

Mantras of avyaktapadma, sūryamaṇḍala, indumaṇḍala, agnimaṇḍala and cidbhāsana, see pp. 185-186

(These last three groups of mantras are used in the preliminary rites, when the adept envisages the entire cosmic structure with the Goddess at the top of it. The adept meditates on the Goddess as she is represented in her cosmic role. He envisages the entire cosmos first within himself and identifies himself with her and then on the maṇḍala and on the seat of the image that he is going to worship. These mantras are represented in the nava-nābha maṇḍala. See diagram V).

Mantras of the parivāra devatā (i.e. deities belonging to Tārā's entourage)

Mantras of kṣetrapāla and dvāradevatās viz., Śrī, Caṇḍa, Pracaṇḍa, Jaya, Vijaya, Gaṅgā, Yamunā, Śaṅkhanidhi and Padmanidhi, see p. 186

Gaṇeśa-mantra, see p. 186

Gaṇeśa's aṅga-mantra, see p. 186

Vāgīsvarī-mantra, see p. 186

Vāgīsvarī's aṇga-mantra, see p. 186

Mantras of guru, paramaguru, parameṣṭhin, pitaras and ādisiddha, see p. 186

Mantras of the lords of the directions (lokeśa), see p. 186

Mantras of the weapons belonging to the lords of the directions, see p. 187

Viṣvaksena-mantra, see p. 187

Viṣvaksena's aṅga-mantra, see p. 187

Garuḍa-mantra,
oṃ khaṃ khagānanāya namaḥ, (this is used when the adept meditates on Viṣṇu's seat);

Mantras used for the worship of mantra-mātṛkā on the mātṛkāpīṭha: ch. XXIII
oṃ hrīṃ namaḥ (this is used for preparing the ground, where mātṛkāpīṭha is to be drawn)
oṃ hrīṃ bhūḥ (this is used while scented clay is being spread on the ground)
oṃ kaṃ namaḥ, oṃ khaṃ namaḥ etc. (thus a mantra is formed with each letter excepting the vowels and these mantras are used to worship the letters inside the mātṛkā-yantra)

Mantra-mātṛkā's upācāra-mantra
om namo mantra-mātṛke idam arghyaṃ gṛhāṇa, (likewise, other mantras of the upācāras, offered to mantra-mātṛkā, should be constructed)

Praṇāma-mantra of mantra-mātṛkā:
oṃ padmasthe padmanilaye padme padmākṣavallabhe sarvatattvakṛtādhāre mantrāṇāṃ janani īśvari vyākuru tvaṃ paraṃ divyaṃ rūpaṃ lakṣmīmayaṃ mama

Mantras used during the performance of the adept's daily religious duties and of the daily worship: chs. XXVIII and XXX

astra-mantra for general protective purposes:
oṃ hrīṃ astrāya phaṭ
lāṅgalāstra-mantra: -
oṃ hrīṃ halāya astrāya hūṃ phaṭ

Mantras belonging to the rite of bhūtaśuddhi: - ch. XXXV, 209
daśaprakṛti-mantras
oṃ hrīṃ pṛthivyai huṃ phaṭ
oṃ hrīṃ adbhyaḥ huṃ phaṭ
oṃ hrīṃ tejase huṃ phaṭ
oṃ hrīm vāyave huṃ phaṭ
oṃ hrīṃ ākāśāya huṃ phaṭ
oṃ hrīṃ manase huṃ phaṭ
oṃ hrīṃ ahaṃkārāya huṃ phaṭ
oṃ hrīṃ buddhaye huṃ phaṭ
oṃ hrīṃ mahate huṃ phaṭ
oṃ hrīṃ traiguṇyāyai huṃ phaṭ
oṃ hrīṃ huṃ māṃsamedarasebhyaḥ ṭhaṃ ṭhaḥ

Mantras of the ten śaktis of the subtle prakṛtis:
oṃ nivṛttaye īṃ
oṃ pratiṣṭhāyai īṃ
oṃ vidyāyai īṃ
oṃ sāntaye īṃ

oṃ śāntyātītāyai īṃ
oṃ abhimānāyai īṃ
oṃ prāṇāyai īṃ
oṃ guṇavatyai īṃ
oṃ guṇasūkṣmāyai īṃ
oṃ nirguṇāyai īṃ

Mantras of the ten tutelary deities of these śaktis:
oṃ īṃ gandhaśriyai rīṃ
oṃ īṃ rasaśriaiyai rīṃ
oṃ īṃ rūpaśriyai rīṃ
oṃ īṃ sparśaśriyai rīṃ
oṃ īṃ śabdaśriyai rīṃ
oṃ īṃ abhimānaśriyai rīṃ
oṃ īṃ guṇaśriyai rīṃ
oṃ īṃ prāṇaśriyai rīṃ
oṃ īṃ guṇasūkṣmaśriyai rīṃ
oṃ īṃ māyāśriyai rīṃ

dāhaka-mantra:
oṃ hrīṃ rthuṃ namaḥ

plāvaka-mantra:
oṃ hrīṃ ṭyaṃ namaḥ
oṃ hrīṃ rtsaṃ ātmane namaḥ (jīva-mantra)

hastanyāsa-mantras:
oṃ hrīṃ aṅguṣṭhābhyāṃ namaḥ
oṃ hrīṃ lakṣmyai tarjanībhyāṃ namaḥ
oṃ hrīṃ kīrtyai madhyamābhyāṃ namaḥ
oṃ-hrīṃ jayāyai anāmikābhyāṃ namaḥ
oṃ hrīṃ māyāyai kaniṣṭhābhyāṃ namaḥ

āvāhana-mantra: chs. XXXIII, XXXVII and XXXVIII, see p. 187

prasādana-mantra, chs. XXXIII, XXXVII and XXXVIII, see p. 187

visarjana-mantra, chs. XXXIII, XXXVII and XXXVIII, see p. 187

arghya-mantra, chs. XXXIII, XXXVII and XXXVIII, see p. 187

(Other upacāras are also offered with similar mantras changing only the name of the relevant upacāra and the gender of the pronoun)

Nārāyaṇa's āvāhana-mantra: ch. XXXVI
oṃ śrīṃ (5) vyāpaka-mantras, the first ṛc of the Puruṣa-sūkta *āvāhayāmi lakṣmīśam paramātmānam avyayam ātiṣṭhatām imām mūrtiṃ madanugraha-kāmyayā śriyā sārdhaṃ jagannātho divyo nārāyaṇaḥ pumān*

Nārāyaṇa's other upacāra-mantras: ch. XXXVI
ṛc (from the Puruṣa-sūkta) *oṃ oṃ bhagavān idam idam idam pādyaṃ priyatāṃ bhagavān vāsudeva*

(Mantras of other upacāras follow the same pattern): p. 221-222

ātmanivedana-mantra: *dāso 'ham te jagannātha saputrādiparigrahaḥ, preṣyaṃ praśādhi kartavye māṃ niyuṅkṣva hite sadā*

snānāsana-mantra
sphuṭīkṛtaṃ mayā deva te idam snānapare tvayi, sapādapīṭhaṃ paramaṃ śubhaṃ snānāsanaṃ mahat, āsādayāsu snānārthaṃ madanugrahakāmyayā;

Surabhi-mantra; ch. XXXVII; see p. 187

Viṣvaksena's visarjana-mantra: ch. XL
oṃ huṃ vauṃ viṣvaksenāya vauṣaṭ oṃ suraśreṣṭha kṣamasva

pañcopaniṣad-mantras: ch. XVII
oṃ ṣāṃ namaḥ parāya parameṣṭhyātmane namaḥ
oṃ yāṃ namaḥ parāya puruṣātmane namaḥ
oṃ rāṃ namaḥ parāya viśvātmane namaḥ
oṃ vāṃ namaḥ parāya nityātmane namaḥ
oṃ lāṃ namaḥ parāya sarvātmane namaḥ

(These mantras are used in connection with the introductory fire sacrifice performed during the pratiṣṭhā ceremony);

Gāyatrī śiraḥ mantra: ch. XXIX.
om āpo jyotī raso 'mṛtam brahma bhūḥ bhuvaḥ suvar om

Bodhana-mantra: ch. XL
oṃ hrīṃ bodhaya oṃ hrīm bodhaya

Tārikā group of mantras for the meditation of Tārikā-vidyā

a particular Tārikā mūrti-mantra:
oṃ hrīṃ subhage svāhā

Tarā's pada-mantra:
oṃ(3) hrīṃ(3) śrīṃ(3) oṃ aṃ(3) hauṃ(3) haṃsaḥ(3) oṃ hrīṃ śrīṃ namo viṣṇave, oṃ hrīṃ śrīṃ namo nārāyaṇāya, om hrīṃ śrīṃ namo bhagavate vāsudevāya oṃ hrīṃ ṣrīṃ, jitam te ..... pūrvaja, oṃ hrīṃ ṣrīṃ bhagavān viṣṇo nārāyaṇa jaganmadhya jagannidhana śrīnivāsa bhagavantam abhigacchāmi bhagavantaṃ prapadye bhagavantaṃ gato 'smi bhagavantam abhyarthaye bhagavantam anudhyāto 'ham bhagavatparikarabhūto 'ham bhagavadanujñāto 'ham bhagavati sṛṣṭo 'ham bhagavatprasādāt bhagavanmayīṃ bhagavatīṃ tārikāmayīṃ lakṣmīṃ padair āvartayiṣyāmi, tad yathā: oṃ śrīṃ hrīṃ gurubhyo gurupatnībhyaḥ oṃ śrīṃ hrīṃ paramagurubhyo paramagurupatnībhyaḥ oṃ hrīṃ śrīṃ parameṣṭhine parameṣṭhinyai oṃ hrīṃ śrīṃ pūrvasiddhebhyo pūrvasiddhābhyaḥ oṃ hrīṃ śrīṃ lakṣmīyogibhyo lakṣmiyoginībhyo namo namaḥ, oṃ hrīṃ śrīṃ īṃ namaḥ saṃsiddhisamṛddhyādipradāyai paramaikarasyāyai paramahaṃsi samastajanavāṅmānasasvātmātivartinyai nirārambhastimitanirañjanaparamānandasaṃdohamahārṇavasvarūpe paraparāyai viṣṇuviṣṇupatnyai viviṣnu īṃ svāhā, oṃ hrīṃ śrīṃ īṃ namo nirantaraprathamānaprathamasāmarasyāyai svasvātantryasamunmiṣitanimiṣonmeṣaparaṃparārambhe svacchandaspandamānavijñānavāridhaye parasūkṣmāyai viṣṇupatnyai māyāyai īṃ svāhā, oṃ śrīṃ hrīṃ śrīṃ īṃ namo svasaṃkalpabalasamunmīlitabhagavatvyāptibhāvasvabhāve svecchāveśavijṛmbhamāṇasattāvibhūtimūrtikāracaturaguṇagrāmayugatrikamahormijā-

lāyai viṣṇupatnyai pañcabindave īṃ svāhā, oṃ hrīṃ śrīṃ hiṃ (3) namo nityoditamahānandaparamasundara bhagavadvigrahaprakāśe vividhasiddhāñjanāspade ṣāḍguṇyaprasaramayaparamasattvarūpaparamavyomaprabhāve vicitrānandanirmalasundarabhogajālaprakāraparināmapravinasvabhāvāyai paramasūkṣmasthūlarūpasūkṣmāyai viṣṇupatnyai pāñcabindave hiṃ(3) svāhā, oṃ hrīṃ śrīṃ aṃ hrīṃ(3) namaḥ svasaṃkalpasamīraṇasamīryamāṇabahuvidhajīvakośadṛṣatpuñjāyai kalitakālakālyavikalpabhedaphenapiṇḍanivahāyai vilāsanidarśitabhoktṛbhogyabhogopakaraṇabhogasampadekamahāsindhave paramasūkṣmasthūlarūpasthūlāyai viṣṇupatnyai pañcabindave hrīm(3) svāhā, oṃ hrīṃ śrīṃ namaḥ samastajagadupakārasvīkṛtabuddhimano 'ṅgapratyaṅgasundarāyai vidhācatuṣṭayasamunmeṣitasamastajanalakṣmīkīrtijayāmāyāprabhāvātmasamastasampadekanidhaye samastaśakticakrasūtradhārāyai samastajanabhogasaubhāgyadāyini vividhaviṣayopaplavapraśamani nārāyaṇāṅkasthitāyai oṃ hrīṃ śrīṃ namo nārāyaṇāya lakṣmīnārāyaṇābhyāṃ svāhā śrīṃ hrīṃ oṃ

Tārikā's aṅga-mantra, see p. 298

Tārikā's parivāra-mantras, see pp. 298-299

Mahālakṣmī-mantra, see p. 300 notes

Lakṣmī's mūrti-mantra:
oṃ hrīṃ laksmyai namaḥ paramalakṣmāvasthitāyai hrīṃ śrīṃ hrīṃ svāhā

Lakṣmī's aṅga-mantras, see p. 304

Lakṣmī's sakhī-mantras, see p. 304

Lakṣmī's anucara-mantras, see p. 304 and notes thereon

Kīrti's mūrti-mantra:
oṃ hrīṃ krīṃ traiṃ kīrtyai namaḥ sadoditānandavigrahāya hrīṃ krīṃ svāhā

Kīrti's aṅga-mantras:
oṃ krām ṭaṃ . . . . (the rest is like Lakṣmī's aṅga-mantra)
oṃ krīm ṭaṃ . . . .
oṃ krūm ṭaṃ . . . .
oṃ kṛṃ ṭaṃ . . . . .
oṃ kraiṃ ṭaṃ . . . .
oṃ krauṃ ṭaṃ . . . . .

Kīrti's sakhī-mantras:
oṃ mrīṃ ṭaṃ dyūtyai svāhā
oṃ śrīṃ ṭaṃ sarasvatyai svāhā
oṃ mrīṃ ṭaṃ medhāyai svāhā
oṃ śrīṃ ṭaṃ śrutyai svāhā

Kīrti's anucara-mantras:
om vāṃ ṭaṃ vāgīśāya namaḥ
oṃ aṃ ṭaṃ jayadevāya namaḥ
oṃ prāṃ ṭaṃ prasādāya namaḥ
oṃ trām ṭaṃ trāṇāya namaḥ

Jayā's mūrti-mantra:
oṃ hrīṃ jayāyai oṃ (na)maḥ ajitadhāmāvasthitāyai hrīṃ jrīṃ svāhā

Jayā's aṅga-mantra:
oṃ jraṃ ṭaṃ (the rest is like Lakṣmī's aṅga-mantra)
oṃ jriṃ ṭaṃ .....
oṃ jruṃ ṭaṃ ....
oṃ jrḷṃ ṭaṃ ....
oṃ jreṃ ṭaṃ .....
oṃ jroṃ ṭaṃ ....

Jayā's sakhī-mantras:
oṃ jiṃ jayantyai svāhā
oṃ viṃ vijayāyai svāhā
oṃ aṃ aparājitāyai svāhā
oṃ siṃ siddhyai svāhā

Jayā's anucara-mantras:
oṃ praṃ ṭaṃ pratāpinyai namaḥ
oṃ jraṃ ṭaṃ jayabhadrāya namaḥ
oṃ mraṃ ṭaṃ mahābalāya namaḥ
oṃ uṃ ṭaṃ utsāhāya namaḥ

Māyā's mūrti mantra:
oṃ hrīṃ māyāyai namaḥ mohātītanāmāśritāyai hrīṃ mrīṃ svāhā

Māyā's aṅga-mantras:
oṃ mrāṃ ṭaṃ (the rest is like Lakṣmī's aṅga-mantra)
oṃ mrīṃ ṭaṃ ....
oṃ mrūṃ ṭaṃ .....
oṃ mrḹm ṭaṃ ....
oṃ mraiṃ ṭaṃ ....
oṃ mrauṃ ṭaṃ ....

Māyā's sakhī-mantras, see p. 307

Māyā's anucara-mantras, see p. 307

(These last five sets of mantras belonging to Tārikā and her four emanations viz. Lakṣmī, Kīrti, Jayā and Māyā are meant for special worship and intensive meditation on them).

Śrī-sūkta-group of mantras belonging to Goddess Lakṣmī: ch. L; see pp. 338-353